Lecture Notes in Computer Science   14708

Founding Editors

Gerhard Goos
Juris Hartmanis

The series Lecture Notes in Computer Science (LNCS), including its subseries Lecture Notes in Artificial Intelligence (LNAI) and Lecture Notes in Bioinformatics (LNBI), has established itself as a medium for the publication of new developments in computer science and information technology research, teaching, and education.

LNCS enjoys close cooperation with the computer science R & D community, the series counts many renowned academics among its volume editors and paper authors, and collaborates with prestigious societies. Its mission is to serve this international community by providing an invaluable service, mainly focused on the publication of conference and workshop proceedings and postproceedings. LNCS commenced publication in 1973.

Jessie Y. C. Chen · Gino Fragomeni
Editors

Virtual, Augmented and Mixed Reality

16th International Conference, VAMR 2024
Held as Part of the 26th HCI International Conference, HCII 2024
Washington, DC, USA, June 29 – July 4, 2024
Proceedings, Part III

 Springer

Editors
Jessie Y. C. Chen
U.S. Army Research Laboratory
Adelphi, MD, USA

Gino Fragomeni
U.S. Army Combat Capabilities
Development Command Soldier Center
Orlando, FL, USA

ISSN 0302-9743   ISSN 1611-3349 (electronic)
Lecture Notes in Computer Science
ISBN 978-3-031-61046-2   ISBN 978-3-031-61047-9 (eBook)
https://doi.org/10.1007/978-3-031-61047-9

This Springer imprint is published by the registered company Springer Nature Switzerland AG
The registered company address is: Gewerbestrasse 11, 6330 Cham, Switzerland

If disposing of this product, please recycle the paper.

Foreword

This year we celebrate 40 years since the establishment of the HCI International (HCII) Conference, which has been a hub for presenting groundbreaking research and novel ideas and collaboration for people from all over the world.

The HCII conference was founded in 1984 by Prof. Gavriel Salvendy (Purdue University, USA, Tsinghua University, P.R. China, and University of Central Florida, USA) and the first event of the series, "1st USA-Japan Conference on Human-Computer Interaction", was held in Honolulu, Hawaii, USA, 18–20 August. Since then, HCI International is held jointly with several Thematic Areas and Affiliated Conferences, with each one under the auspices of a distinguished international Program Board and under one management and one registration. Twenty-six HCI International Conferences have been organized so far (every two years until 2013, and annually thereafter).

Over the years, this conference has served as a platform for scholars, researchers, industry experts and students to exchange ideas, connect, and address challenges in the ever-evolving HCI field. Throughout these 40 years, the conference has evolved itself, adapting to new technologies and emerging trends, while staying committed to its core mission of advancing knowledge and driving change.

As we celebrate this milestone anniversary, we reflect on the contributions of its founding members and appreciate the commitment of its current and past Affiliated Conference Program Board Chairs and members. We are also thankful to all past conference attendees who have shaped this community into what it is today.

The 26th International Conference on Human-Computer Interaction, HCI International 2024 (HCII 2024), was held as a 'hybrid' event at the Washington Hilton Hotel, Washington, DC, USA, during 29 June – 4 July 2024. It incorporated the 21 thematic areas and affiliated conferences listed below.

A total of 5108 individuals from academia, research institutes, industry, and government agencies from 85 countries submitted contributions, and 1271 papers and 309 posters were included in the volumes of the proceedings that were published just before the start of the conference, these are listed below. The contributions thoroughly cover the entire field of human-computer interaction, addressing major advances in knowledge and effective use of computers in a variety of application areas. These papers provide academics, researchers, engineers, scientists, practitioners and students with state-of-the-art information on the most recent advances in HCI.

The HCI International (HCII) conference also offers the option of presenting 'Late Breaking Work', and this applies both for papers and posters, with corresponding volumes of proceedings that will be published after the conference. Full papers will be included in the 'HCII 2024 - Late Breaking Papers' volumes of the proceedings to be published in the Springer LNCS series, while 'Poster Extended Abstracts' will be included as short research papers in the 'HCII 2024 - Late Breaking Posters' volumes to be published in the Springer CCIS series.

I would like to thank the Program Board Chairs and the members of the Program Boards of all thematic areas and affiliated conferences for their contribution towards the high scientific quality and overall success of the HCI International 2024 conference. Their manifold support in terms of paper reviewing (single-blind review process, with a minimum of two reviews per submission), session organization and their willingness to act as goodwill ambassadors for the conference is most highly appreciated.

This conference would not have been possible without the continuous and unwavering support and advice of Gavriel Salvendy, founder, General Chair Emeritus, and Scientific Advisor. For his outstanding efforts, I would like to express my sincere appreciation to Abbas Moallem, Communications Chair and Editor of HCI International News.

July 2024   Constantine Stephanidis

HCI International 2024 Thematic Areas and Affiliated Conferences

- HCI: Human-Computer Interaction Thematic Area
- HIMI: Human Interface and the Management of Information Thematic Area
- EPCE: 21st International Conference on Engineering Psychology and Cognitive Ergonomics
- AC: 18th International Conference on Augmented Cognition
- UAHCI: 18th International Conference on Universal Access in Human-Computer Interaction
- CCD: 16th International Conference on Cross-Cultural Design
- SCSM: 16th International Conference on Social Computing and Social Media
- VAMR: 16th International Conference on Virtual, Augmented and Mixed Reality
- DHM: 15th International Conference on Digital Human Modeling & Applications in Health, Safety, Ergonomics & Risk Management
- DUXU: 13th International Conference on Design, User Experience and Usability
- C&C: 12th International Conference on Culture and Computing
- DAPI: 12th International Conference on Distributed, Ambient and Pervasive Interactions
- HCIBGO: 11th International Conference on HCI in Business, Government and Organizations
- LCT: 11th International Conference on Learning and Collaboration Technologies
- ITAP: 10th International Conference on Human Aspects of IT for the Aged Population
- AIS: 6th International Conference on Adaptive Instructional Systems
- HCI-CPT: 6th International Conference on HCI for Cybersecurity, Privacy and Trust
- HCI-Games: 6th International Conference on HCI in Games
- MobiTAS: 6th International Conference on HCI in Mobility, Transport and Automotive Systems
- AI-HCI: 5th International Conference on Artificial Intelligence in HCI
- MOBILE: 5th International Conference on Human-Centered Design, Operation and Evaluation of Mobile Communications

List of Conference Proceedings Volumes Appearing
Before the Conference

1. LNCS 14684, Human-Computer Interaction: Part I, edited by Masaaki Kurosu and Ayako Hashizume
2. LNCS 14685, Human-Computer Interaction: Part II, edited by Masaaki Kurosu and Ayako Hashizume
3. LNCS 14686, Human-Computer Interaction: Part III, edited by Masaaki Kurosu and Ayako Hashizume
4. LNCS 14687, Human-Computer Interaction: Part IV, edited by Masaaki Kurosu and Ayako Hashizume
5. LNCS 14688, Human-Computer Interaction: Part V, edited by Masaaki Kurosu and Ayako Hashizume
6. LNCS 14689, Human Interface and the Management of Information: Part I, edited by Hirohiko Mori and Yumi Asahi
7. LNCS 14690, Human Interface and the Management of Information: Part II, edited by Hirohiko Mori and Yumi Asahi
8. LNCS 14691, Human Interface and the Management of Information: Part III, edited by Hirohiko Mori and Yumi Asahi
9. LNAI 14692, Engineering Psychology and Cognitive Ergonomics: Part I, edited by Don Harris and Wen-Chin Li
10. LNAI 14693, Engineering Psychology and Cognitive Ergonomics: Part II, edited by Don Harris and Wen-Chin Li
11. LNAI 14694, Augmented Cognition, Part I, edited by Dylan D. Schmorrow and Cali M. Fidopiastis
12. LNAI 14695, Augmented Cognition, Part II, edited by Dylan D. Schmorrow and Cali M. Fidopiastis
13. LNCS 14696, Universal Access in Human-Computer Interaction: Part I, edited by Margherita Antona and Constantine Stephanidis
14. LNCS 14697, Universal Access in Human-Computer Interaction: Part II, edited by Margherita Antona and Constantine Stephanidis
15. LNCS 14698, Universal Access in Human-Computer Interaction: Part III, edited by Margherita Antona and Constantine Stephanidis
16. LNCS 14699, Cross-Cultural Design: Part I, edited by Pei-Luen Patrick Rau
17. LNCS 14700, Cross-Cultural Design: Part II, edited by Pei-Luen Patrick Rau
18. LNCS 14701, Cross-Cultural Design: Part III, edited by Pei-Luen Patrick Rau
19. LNCS 14702, Cross-Cultural Design: Part IV, edited by Pei-Luen Patrick Rau
20. LNCS 14703, Social Computing and Social Media: Part I, edited by Adela Coman and Simona Vasilache
21. LNCS 14704, Social Computing and Social Media: Part II, edited by Adela Coman and Simona Vasilache
22. LNCS 14705, Social Computing and Social Media: Part III, edited by Adela Coman and Simona Vasilache

https://2024.hci.international/proceedings

Preface

With the recent emergence of a new generation of displays, smart devices, and wearables, the field of virtual, augmented, and mixed reality (VAMR) is rapidly expanding, transforming, and moving towards the mainstream market. At the same time, VAMR applications in a variety of domains are also reaching maturity and practical usage. From the point of view of the user experience, VAMR promises possibilities to reduce interaction efforts and cognitive load, while also offering contextualized information, by combining different sources and reducing attention shifts, and opening the 3D space. Such scenarios offer exciting challenges associated with underlying and supporting technologies, interaction, and navigation in virtual and augmented environments, and design and development. VAMR themes encompass a wide range of areas such as education, aviation, social, emotional, psychological, and persuasive applications.

The 16th International Conference on Virtual, Augmented, and Mixed Reality (VAMR 2024), an affiliated conference of the HCI International Conference, provided a forum for researchers and practitioners to disseminate and exchange scientific and technical information on VAMR-related topics in various applications. A considerable number of papers have explored user experience topics including avatar design, walking and moving in VR environments, scene design and complexity, 360o immersive environments and the design of 3D elements, cybersickness, and multisensory feedback. Moreover, submissions offered a comprehensive examination of perception aspects, including our understanding of body image, self-presentation, visual realism, and awareness. A key topic that emerged was interaction in immersive environments such as haptic interaction, tangible VR, and gestures. Furthermore, emphasis was given to the application domains of VAMR including collaboration, cultural heritage, education and learning, health and well-being, but also software programming, crime data analysis, terrain exploration, and astronomical visualization. We are thrilled to present this compilation of VAMR submissions encompassing a wide range of topics and exploring the current state of the art, while also highlighting future avenues in the design and development of immersive experiences.

Three volumes of the HCII 2024 proceedings are dedicated to this year's edition of the VAMR conference. The first focuses on topics related to Perception, Interaction and Design, and User Experience and Evaluation. The second focuses on topics related to Immersive Collaboration and Environment Design, and Sensory, Tangible, and Embodied Interaction in VAMR, while the third focuses on topics related to Immersive Education and Learning, and VAMR Applications and Development.

The papers in these volumes were accepted for publication after a minimum of two single-blind reviews from the members of the VAMR Program Board or, in some cases, from members of the Program Boards of other affiliated conferences. We would like to thank all of them for their invaluable contribution, support, and efforts.

July 2024   Jessie Y. C. Chen
                                                                              Gino Fragomeni

16th International Conference on Virtual, Augmented and Mixed Reality (VAMR 2024)

Program Board Chairs: **Jessie Y. C. Chen,** *U.S. Army Research Laboratory, USA,* and **Gino Fragomeni,** *U.S. Army Combat Capabilities Development Command Soldier Center, USA*

- J. Cecil, *Oklahoma State University, USA*
- Shih-Yi Chien, *National Chengchi University, Taiwan*
- Avinash Gupta, *University of Illinois Urbana-Champaign, USA*
- Sue Kase, *U.S. Army Research Laboratory, USA*
- Daniela Kratchounova, *Federal Aviation Administration (FAA), USA*
- Fotis Liarokapis, *CYENS - Centre of Excellence, Cyprus*
- Jaehyun Park, *Incheon National University (INU), Korea*
- Chao Peng, *Rochester Institute of Technology, USA*
- Jose San Martin, *Universidad Rey Juan Carlos, Spain*
- Andreas Schreiber, *German Aerospace Center (DLR), Germany*
- Sharad Sharma, *University of North Texas, USA*
- Simon Su, *National Institute of Standards and Technology (NIST), USA*
- Denny Yu, *Purdue University, USA*

The full list with the Program Board Chairs and the members of the Program Boards of all thematic areas and affiliated conferences of HCII 2024 is available online at:

http://www.hci.international/board-members-2024.php

HCI International 2025 Conference

The 27th International Conference on Human-Computer Interaction, HCI International 2025, will be held jointly with the affiliated conferences at the Swedish Exhibition & Congress Centre and Gothia Towers Hotel, Gothenburg, Sweden, June 22–27, 2025. It will cover a broad spectrum of themes related to Human-Computer Interaction, including theoretical issues, methods, tools, processes, and case studies in HCI design, as well as novel interaction techniques, interfaces, and applications. The proceedings will be published by Springer. More information will become available on the conference website: https://2025.hci.international/.

General Chair
Prof. Constantine Stephanidis
University of Crete and ICS-FORTH
Heraklion, Crete, Greece
Email: general_chair@2025.hci.international

https://2025.hci.international/

Contents – Part III

VAMR Applications and Development

Immersive Education and Learning

Enhancing Ancient Architecture Virtual Learning Tour Through Virtual Embodiment: Impact on Immersion, Engagement, and Learning Outcomes

Yuetong Chen, Shuhan Shen, and Min Hua(⊠)

Shanghai Jiao Tong University, Shanghai 200240, China
{yuetong_chen,shuhanshen,huamin}@sjtu.edu.cn

Abstract. The integration of digital learning and ICT in architectural design education, particularly in studying ancient architecture, has been transformative. This study focuses on how virtual embodiment in VR affects learning experiences, engagement, and outcomes in ancient Chinese architecture education. A digital landscape of Nanchan Temple was created on VRchat for this purpose, involving 22 architecture students divided into two groups: one with a virtual body (VB group) and the other using only controllers (NB group). The study assessed a sense of embodiment, simulator sickness (SS), virtual tour experience, and a grasp of spatial information through questionnaires and task performance metrics. The VB group reported a stronger sense of embodiment in the virtual environment, indicating that a virtual body enhances engagement, contributes to a deeper understanding of architectural concepts, and improves learning quality in the educational experience. They also showed a higher sense of presence and were more efficient in completing interactive tasks, supporting the idea that virtual bodies improve spatial perception. However, the VB group experienced higher levels of SS, suggesting a challenge in aligning virtual and physical sensations. In conclusion, the presence of a virtual body in VR significantly improves immersion, engagement, and learning outcomes in architectural education, particularly in the context of ancient Chinese architecture. The study highlights the potential of virtual embodiment in educational scenarios and suggests the need for further technological improvements to mitigate simulator sickness.

Keywords: Virtual Reality (VR) · Architectural Education · Virtual Embodiment · Ancient Chinese Architecture

1 Introduction

The advent of digital learning and the seamless integration of Information and Communications Technology (ICT) into educational paradigms have ushered in a new era of pedagogical methodologies [1]. This transformation is particularly pronounced in the realm of architectural design education, where the traditional boundaries of learning are being expanded through innovative technological interventions [2]. The study of

© The Author(s), under exclusive license to Springer Nature Switzerland AG 2024
J. Y. C. Chen and G. Fragomeni (Eds.): HCII 2024, LNCS 14708, pp. 3–18, 2024.
https://doi.org/10.1007/978-3-031-61047-9_1

architecture, with its intricate blend of art, science, and history, presents unique challenges and opportunities for digital learning platforms. Among these, the study of ancient architecture occupies a special place, offering students not only historical insights and a connection to the past but also serving as a rich source of inspiration for innovative design concepts [3, 4]. The exploration of ancient structures and urban designs through digital means promotes a broader awareness and appreciation for monument learning and cultural heritage conservation [2].

The integration of ICT in architectural education has been instrumental in overcoming some of the physical and logistical limitations associated with studying ancient architecture, employing 3D digital models to satiate their scholarly curiosity and nurturing their design sensibilities [5]. Traditional methods of studying these historical structures often require extensive travel, access to restricted sites, and the ability to visualize and understand spaces that may no longer exist in their original form [6]. Personal computer (PC) screens constitute the most common potent means of transporting students to digital realms [7]. However, the advent of virtual reality (VR) technology has revolutionized this aspect of architectural education. VR offers an immersive experience that transcends spatial and temporal boundaries, allowing students to explore and interact with ancient architectural sites in a virtual environment [7]. This not only enhances accessibility but also significantly enriches the learning experience by providing a sense of scale, context, and detail that is difficult to achieve through conventional means [8].

Virtual reality's capacity for creating immersive educational experiences is further augmented by the concept of virtual embodiment [9]. Virtual embodiment refers to the representation of an individual within a digital environment in such a way that the user perceives a virtual body as their own. This phenomenon extends beyond the visual representation of oneself in a virtual space [10, 11]. It encompasses the psychological and physiological integration of the user with the virtual avatar, thereby enabling users to interact with the digital world in a manner that mimics real-life experiences [10]. In the context of architectural education, this means that students can not only view but also interact with ancient structures as if they were physically present within the space [12]. This level of interaction promises a deeper engagement with the material, potentially leading to better understanding and retention of knowledge [13].

Despite the promising advantages of VR and virtual embodiment in educational settings, research on their specific impact on the study of ancient architecture remains limited. The existing literature provides valuable insights into the general benefits of VR embodiment in education. Studies demonstrate VR embodiment's effectiveness in fostering climate change awareness [14], improving spatial learning in geospatial education [15], enhancing medical students' empathy and understanding of dementia [16], and facilitating multimodal meaning-making in elementary education [17]. There is a notable gap in studies focusing on ancient Chinese architectural education, and more rigorous and expansive research is needed to understand VR embodiment's educational value fully. Ancient Chinese architecture boasts a rich history and unique design principles that differ significantly from Western architectural traditions [18].

Given this background, the research question that guides this study is: How does virtual embodiment affect the educational experience, engagement, and learning outcomes in the context of learning ancient Chinese architecture through VR? This question seeks to explore the specific impacts of virtual embodiment on students' ability to engage with, understand, and retain knowledge about ancient Chinese architectural principles and designs. By creating a digital landscape of the Nanchan Temple within the VRchat platform and analyzing the experiences of Bachelor of Architecture candidates, this study aims to shed light on the potential of virtual embodiment to enhance the learning of ancient architecture. Through a comprehensive examination of participants' experiences, engagement levels, and learning outcomes, this research endeavors to contribute to the broader discourse on the integration of VR technologies in architectural education, with a particular focus on the study of ancient structures.

2   Literature Review

2.1   Digital Learning in Architectural Education

The evolution of digital learning within architectural education marks a significant shift from traditional pedagogical methods towards more interactive and immersive learning experiences [19, 20]. This transition has been facilitated by rapid advancements in digital technologies and the increasing integration of ICT in educational settings. Architectural education, characterized by its reliance on spatial understanding, visual analysis, and creative design, has particularly benefited from digital learning platforms and tools [21]. Studies have highlighted the transformative potential of digital technologies in architectural education, enabling students to visualize complex structures and engage with architectural designs in a more interactive manner [21, 22].

The advent of digital tools such as Computer-Aided Design (CAD) software, Building Information Modeling (BIM), and digital fabrication technologies has revolutionized the way architectural concepts are taught, learned, and applied [23, 24]. These tools not only facilitate a deeper understanding of architectural principles but also encourage innovation and creativity in design processes [23]. Furthermore, the integration of virtual reality (VR) and augmented reality (AR) technologies has opened new avenues for immersive learning experiences. VR, in particular, allows students to explore and interact with architectural spaces in a simulated environment, offering a level of immersion and interactivity that traditional classroom settings cannot provide [19, 25]. The research underscores the effectiveness of VR in enhancing spatial understanding and design skills, suggesting that immersive technologies can significantly enrich architectural education [26]. Angulo and de Velasco [27] also explored immersive simulations of architectural spatial experiences, emphasizing the affective appraisal of space.

2.2   Virtual Reality and Embodiment in Learning

Virtual Reality (VR) is a revolutionary shift in human-computer interaction, creating immersive 3D environments through sensor technologies [28]. Through a plethora of sensors encompassing visual, auditory, and tactile stimuli, users find themselves ensconced within a virtual realm, where real-world experiences transpire, and interaction with the digital milieu takes on multifaceted dimensions [29]. VR stands out from traditional desktop interactions by combining high immersion and interactivity [30]. A previous study compared three different investigating modes for place-based STEM, highlighting that immersive virtual reality is more effective than the desktop mode in knowledge acquisition [31]. Embodiment in VR further improves immersive and is achieved through the use of avatars or virtual bodies, which serve as proxies for the user within the virtual space [11]. This sense of being physically present and able to act within a virtual environment is referred to as "presence," a key factor in the effectiveness of VR as an educational tool [32, 33].

Embodiment in VR has been the subject of extensive research, particularly in the context of its psychological and educational effects. Studies by Slater and Sanchez-Vives [34] have demonstrated that a strong sense of embodiment can lead to more impactful learning experiences and improve understanding as users feel more connected to the virtual environment and its content. The sense of presence and embodiment has been shown to enhance cognitive outcomes, including memory retention, spatial awareness, and understanding of complex concepts [10, 34]. In the realm of architectural education, the embodiment allows students to experience architectural spaces and structures firsthand, providing a unique perspective that can deepen their understanding of design principles and historical contexts. Hong, Park, and Cho's research [35] indicates that the use of avatars in digital modeling notably aids in the functional aspects of design, thereby promoting exploratory creativity. This finding aligns with the concept of perception-action coupling and para-perception. Shealy's study [36] highlights that embodied and self-reflected VR experiences, particularly through avatars like birds or humans, significantly expand engineering students' design cognition and their perception of nature-relatedness.

The educational benefits of embodiment in VR are further supported by research on its impact on motivation and engagement. According to the study [37], students who experience a high degree of embodiment in VR environments report greater interest and motivation in the subject matter, leading to improved learning outcomes. These findings suggest that the immersive and interactive nature of embodied VR experiences can significantly enhance the educational process, making it a valuable tool for architectural education.

2.3   VR Technology's Role in Architectural History Research

The literature on the role of Virtual Reality (VR) technology in ancient architectural research highlights its transformative impact on both education and preservation. Previous studies have explored immersive VR technology in architectural history education. For example, Chan, Bogdanovic, and Kalivarapu [38] investigated its use in remote architectural history teaching by simulating the Pantheon historical structures, providing students with a unique experiential engagement with architectural heritage. Eray Şahbaz's research [39] further enriches the literature by focusing on a specific historical Greek bathhouse. This study developed an interactive VR program and tested it with architecture students, finding that VR was an efficient tool for learning architectural details and experiencing the spatial effects of historic structures. Studies currently mainly focus on Western architectural masterpieces. Yanru Ge's research [40] emphasizes VR's potential to teach systematic architectural history more engagingly and interactively. This approach addresses the subject's reliance on textbooks, which causes low student engagement and the complexity of conveying vast historical content. It significantly boosts students' enthusiasm and comprehension.

Preservation and restoration are other aspects mentioned by the literature on VR technology's role in ancient architectural research. Several articles highlight VR in digitally preserving ancient buildings and sites in the context of museums and the audience's reaction [41, 42]. They emphasize the impact of VR in creating interactive, realistic simulations of cultural sites, particularly demonstrated through the digital application of a specific historic monument. A study on the Zhanghua Tower emphasizes VR's utility in reconstructing and optimizing virtual models of traditional Chinese buildings, employing tools like 3ds max, Unity3D, and Virtools [43]. Furthermore, a paper showcases VR's application in the ancient city of Polonnaruwa, a Sri Lankan heritage preservation site. Their VR model of Polonnaruwa offers a realistic, immersive experience, allowing for a virtual exploration of historical sites, which is crucial for both educational purposes and the preservation of cultural heritage [44].

In conclusion, the literature review reveals that VR's role in architectural education is multifaceted, offering immersive experiences that improve spatial understanding, design skills, and cognitive outcomes such as memory retention and spatial awareness. The sense of embodiment in VR, achieved through avatars and virtual environments, has been shown to deepen students' connection to the content, thereby enhancing learning experiences and motivation. Additionally, VR's application in architectural history research demonstrates its effectiveness in providing experiential engagement with architectural heritage, aiding in the preservation and restoration of ancient structures. However, the literature review identifies a gap in the exploration of non-Western architectural masterpieces in VR-based education and the impacts of VR embodiment on space learning interaction flexibility. Research could focus on expanding the scope of VR applications in architectural education to include a broader range of cultural contexts and investigating the sustainable integration of VR in educational settings.

3 Methods

3.1 Study Design

This study employed a between-group design comprising two conditions in which participants were randomly assigned to explore the effects of virtual embodiment within the VR environment. The first group, referred to as the Virtual Body (VB) group, consisted of 11 students who navigated the virtual environment with a fully embodied virtual avatar. The second group, the Non-Virtual Body (NB) group, also comprised 11 students but navigated the environment using standard VR controllers without the representation of a virtual body. Apart from the choice of assuming avatars, the tasks and questionnaires were consistent across both conditions.

3.2 Experimental Setup

The virtual environment was a digital recreation of the Nanchan Temple in Shanxi, a significant historical site known for its ancient Chinese architectural construction.

Architectural models were generated using modelling software, regarding architectural plans, interiors, and section drawings. These models were further refined in Autodesk Maya and subsequently integrated into Unity scenes. The design of the virtual Nanchan Temple landscape was based on extensive research and collaboration with historians and architects to ensure accuracy in architectural details and historical context [45].

In the Nanchan Temple unity project with a VR SDK, we integrate a 3D character model with an Animator for Inverse Kinematics (IK). We use empty GameObjects as IK targets for body parts and VR controllers to mirror real-world movements in the virtual environment. C# scripts control the IK, aligning it with VR controller data. Then, VR testing is crucial for achieving natural movement, requiring potential adjustments in IK and animation blending. Implementing full-body tracking and collision detection further enhances realism.

Interactive tasks were developed to engage participants with key components of ancient Chinese architecture, such as understanding the significance of structural elements, architectural symmetry, and traditional decorative motifs. These tasks were designed to be completed within the VR environment, requiring participants to explore, analyze, and interact with the virtual space. Examples of tasks included identifying specific architectural features, reconstructing a part of the components using virtual tools, and navigating the environment to discover information about the temple's history and construction techniques (see Fig. 1).

Fig. 1. Virtual Environments Setting

3.3 Procedure

The study involved Bachelor of Architecture (B.Arch) candidates with an average age of 21.7 years (SD = 3.1). All participants reported no known mental or physical impairments and possessed normal or corrected-to-normal vision. The selection criteria included students who were in their third year of study to ensure a uniform level of academic exposure and proficiency in architectural concepts.

After providing informed consent, participants completed a pre-questionnaire with demographic data and the Simulator Sickness part. They familiarized themselves with the VR interface, received background information on Nanchan Temple, and then engaged in a 10-min virtual tour to complete Interactive tasks. Following the tour, participants assessed simulator sickness and completed additional questionnaires.

3.4 Measures

Sense of Embodiment Part. The first section explored the sense of Embodiment in virtual environments. This tool incorporates key parameters such as ownership of the virtual body, the ability to act within the virtual environment (agency), and self-location [46]. Virtual body ownership explores the extent to which users perceive a virtual body as their own, focusing on the integration of the virtual body with their physical self. Agency delves into the user's perceived control over the virtual body, assessing their sense of command over its movements and actions within the virtual environment. Change in perceived body schema evaluates how virtual embodiment affects the user's perception of their physical body, including changes in perceived capabilities, shape, or size [46].

The inclusion of these specific aspects was pivotal in assessing how the presence or absence of a virtual body influenced participants' connection to the virtual environment and their overall learning experience. By integrating these elements, the questionnaire provided a comprehensive framework for understanding the multifaceted nature of virtual embodiment and its impact on user experience in digital settings.

Simulator Sickness Part (SS). The second section of the questionnaire addressed Simulator Sickness (SS), with items designed to measure subjective and objective symptoms of SS, such as nausea, dizziness, and eye strain. This part was crucial for understanding the physical comfort levels of participants while navigating the VR environment, as SS can significantly impact the usability and educational effectiveness of VR technologies.

The Simulator Sickness Questionnaire (SSQ) was developed by Kennedy et al. [47]. Participants completed pre- and post-SSQs to measure SS changes (ΔSSQ = post-SSQ - pre-SSQ) before and after engaging with the virtual environment.

Virtual Tour Experience Part. Sutcliffe and Gault [48] devised a heuristic evaluation scale tailored to VR, including naturalness and compatibility. Building upon this foundation, Kabassi et al. [49] applied the updated scale to virtual tours, condensing these factors into four overarching dimensions: VR experience, perception of presence, navigation, and learning. Our study extended the learning support dimension to emphasize educational enhancement.

Task Performance Metrics. In addition to the questionnaire, performance metrics were collected to evaluate the efficiency of participants in completing the interactive tasks.

These metrics included task completion time and accuracy. The combination of subjective feedback from the questionnaire and objective data from performance metrics provided a comprehensive overview of the impact of virtual embodiment on learning outcomes in the context of ancient Chinese architecture education.

Demographic Part. The demographic part collected basic personal details and inquired about prior VR experience and familiarity with Chinese architecture.

4 Results

4.1 Sense of Embodiment Part Score

Independent two-sample t-tests were conducted to compare the sense of embodiment scores between VB and NB groups. Prior to the tests, the criteria of normality and homogeneity of variance were verified and met. Despite the fact that all VB participants use the same set of virtual bodies with no obvious personal characteristics, the VB group reported a higher sense of embodiment compared to the NB group (M $\pm$ SD; NB: 2.9 $\pm$ 0.7; VB: 4.5 $\pm$ 0.6; t(20) = 6.78, p < 0.001) (see Fig. 2).

4.2 Simulator Sickness Part (SS) Score

We conducted independent two-sample t-tests to compare the SS scores between the Virtual Body (VB) group and the Non-Virtual Body (NB) group, with the prerequisites of normality and homogeneity of variance met. The VB group exhibited higher levels of simulator sickness compared to the NB group (M $\pm$ SD; NB: 32.6 $\pm$ 5.9; VB: 37.0 $\pm$ 4.4; t (20) = –1.20, p = 0.059) (see Fig. 2).

4.3 Virtual Tour Experience Part Score

Independent two-sample t-tests were executed to compare the experience scores between the VB and NB groups, with the criteria of normality and homogeneity of variance fulfilled. Participants in the VB group achieved higher scores, although the difference was not statistically significant (M $\pm$ SD; NB: 23.5 $\pm$ 3.9; VB: 25.1 $\pm$ 6.1; t(20) = –0.75, p = 0.464) (see Fig. 2).

After comparison, we found that, except for the perception of presence score, both groups performed similarly in other aspects. So, we conducted a segmented analysis employing a two-sample t-test on the perception of presence between two groups. Adhering to normality and variance assumptions, the results showed a clear pattern: the VB group assigned significantly higher scores (M $\pm$ SD; NB: 4.5 $\pm$ 1.9; VB: 8.6 $\pm$ 1.7; t(20) = 5.79, p < 0.001).

4.4 Task Performance Efficiency

Task performance efficiency, measured in terms of task completion time, as there was little difference in task completion accuracy between the groups, was compared using independent two-sample t-tests. Ensuring normality and homogeneity of variance. The VB group completed tasks more efficiently than the NB group, but the difference was not statistically significant (M ± SD; NB: 8 ± 2.1 min; VB: 6 ± 1.5 min; t(20) = −3.07, p = 0.005) (see Fig. 2).

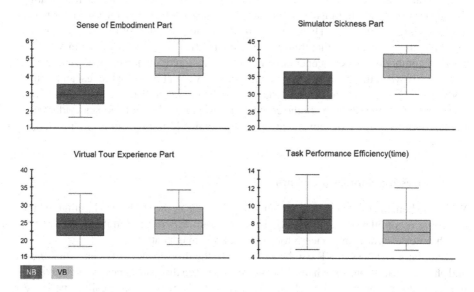

Fig. 2. Results

5 Discussion

5.1 Impact of Virtual Embodiment

The study's results highlight the impact of virtual embodiment on the learning experience in the context of ancient Chinese architecture through VR. The performance of the VB group in the embodiment measurements demonstrates enhanced Immersion. It suggests that the presence of a virtual body in VR can lead to a more profound sense of being 'inside' the virtual environment [50]. The user's acceptance of the virtual body as their own, in conjunction with the multisensory stimulation in the VR environment, these immersive environments often incorporate realistic graphics, spatial audio, and 3D spatial tracking to create a holistic sensory milieu, providing users with a comprehensive experience beyond visuals and motion tracking [51]. This heightened immersion is crucial in architectural education, where there is a need to fully understand the spaciousness and contextual aspects of structures [52]. The immersive experience provided by VR allows students to perceive and interact with architectural elements in ways that are not possible with traditional two-dimensional images or even physical models [53].

Multifaceted factors, including sensorimotor synchronization, realistic visual feedback, first-person perspective, and haptic feedback, support the captivating illusion of body ownership within the immersive realm of VR [54–56]. These elements interact to generate a profound sense of embodiment and also play a role in our study, especially sensorimotor synchronization. To our surprise, our study illuminates no significant differences in the illusion of ownership for the same virtual body, although participants differed in appearance, gender, and age. This outcome aligns with earlier research, demonstrating the capacity to generate illusions across a spectrum of body forms, encompassing very small and large bodies [54]. Therefore, the results underscore the ability to craft convincing illusions of ownership that transcend the boundaries of age or physique in VR. The result of "embodiment" can generate a subjective illusion of ownership with respect to a virtual body when there is real-time synchronous movement between the real and virtual body [54, 57]. The illusion is extinguished when the virtual body moves asynchronously compared with the real body. In the context of this exploration, it becomes evident that the temporal congruity of movement plays a pivotal role in cultivating the illusion of ownership over avatars.

5.2 Addressing Simulator Sickness

While the benefits of virtual embodiment in VR are clear, the study also highlighted the challenge of simulator sickness (SS). The VB group experienced higher levels of SS, which poses a significant concern for the use of VR in education.

Simulator sickness in VR can be attributed to the discrepancy between visual input and physical sensation, known as sensory conflict. When the visual cues in a VR environment suggest movement or spatial changes that the body does not physically experience, it can lead to symptoms like nausea, dizziness, and disorientation [58, 59]. The VB group is more likely to experience the conflict of inconsistency between the virtual body and the actual movement during the virtual journey because the avatar sometimes fails to accurately capture and process complete real-time data of real body rotation and movement.

To mitigate SS, several strategies can be employed. Firstly, improving the technical aspects of VR, such as increasing frame rates and reducing latency, can provide a smoother and more stable visual experience, reducing the likelihood of SS [60]. Secondly, incorporating gradual exposure to VR environments can help users acclimatize to the VR experience, potentially reducing SS symptoms over time [60, 61]. Additionally, designing VR experiences with fewer abrupt movements and providing users with control over their movements can also help minimize SS [62].

In educational settings, it's crucial to balance the immersive experience with the comfort of the learners. This could involve shorter VR sessions, regular breaks, and the option for students to switch to less immersive modes if they experience discomfort.

5.3 Virtual Tour Experience

The study also found that the VB group felt a stronger sense of presence within the VR environment, indicating increased engagement. This engagement is likely due to the embodied interaction that VR facilitates, allowing students to explore and interact with the virtual environment in a more intuitive and natural manner [51]. Such engagement is vital in educational settings, as it can lead to deeper learning and better retention of information.

The VB group's better performance in interactive tasks suggests that virtual embodiment can enhance spatial learning outcomes. The ability to interact with the virtual environment in a more embodied manner may have helped the students in the VB group to better understand and retain the architectural scales being taught. This improved task performance can be explained by previous research suggesting that virtual body representation plays a pivotal role in spatial perception [63, 64]. The virtual body serves as a familiar reference point to improve the judgment of egocentric distances and object dimensions, thereby facilitating streamlining the completion of interactive tasks. This finding is particularly relevant for the study of ancient architecture, where understanding the nuances of design, construction, and historical context is crucial.

6 Conclusion

The key findings of this research underscore the transformative potential of VR, particularly when augmented by the concept of virtual embodiment. The integration of virtual bodies into digital learning environments, particularly in the study of ancient Chinese architecture, has been shown to significantly enhance the educational experience. The research centred around the virtual tour of Nanchan Temple provides compelling evidence that the presence of a virtual body in VR can dramatically improve learners' perception of immersion within an architectural context.

Participants in the Virtual Body (VB) group experienced a heightened sense of immersion and engagement. This increased immersion and engagement are crucial in a field like architecture, where there is a need to understand the spatial, aesthetic, and contextual aspects of structures. The study thus highlights the effectiveness of VR embodiment in bridging the gap between theoretical knowledge and practical, experiential learning, especially in the context of ancient architecture, which often relies heavily on the imagination and interpretation of historical contexts.

However, the study also brings to light the challenge of simulator sickness, a notable concern in the deployment of VR technologies in educational settings. The higher levels of discomfort experienced by some participants indicate a need for further research and development in the technical aspects of VR. Addressing issues such as optimizing frame rates and refining locomotion techniques could enhance user comfort and reduce adverse effects, making VR a more viable tool for education. This aspect of VR development is crucial for ensuring that the educational benefits of virtual embodiment can be fully realized without compromising the comfort and well-being of learners.

Further research in VR embodiment for ancient Chinese architectural education can focus on supplementing and addressing long-term impacts. Longitudinal studies to assess the long-term effect of VR-based learning on knowledge retention, skill development, and academic performance would provide deeper insights into the efficacy of this technology in education. There's also a crucial need for continuous improvement in VR technologies, focusing on hardware and software optimization to address challenges like simulator sickness, thereby enhancing VR's educational effectiveness.

This study represents a stride in understanding the potential of VR and virtual embodiment in enhancing educational experiences, particularly in the field of architectural education. While challenges such as simulator sickness need to be addressed, the benefits observed in terms of engagement, immersion, and learning outcomes highlight the transformative potential of VR in education. As technology continues to evolve, the opportunities to enrich and diversify learning experiences will expand, paving the way for innovative and effective educational methodologies. The implications of this research may extend beyond architecture, suggesting a broader impact on educational practices and the potential for VR to revolutionize how complex subjects are taught and learned.

Acknowledgments. This study was generously supported by a grant from the Shanghai Jiao Tong University's USC-SJTU Institute of Cultural and Creative Industry (ICCI). The authors extend their gratitude to ICCI for their support and belief in the potential of this research. Special thanks are also to the faculty and students of the Department of Architecture at Huaqiao University for their participation and insightful feedback. The authors acknowledge the contributions of all who have supported and facilitated this research, directly or indirectly, in making this study possible.

The authors have no competing interests to declare that are relevant to the content of this article.

References

1. Sayaf, A.M., Alamri, M.M., Alqahtani, M.A., Al-Rahmi, W.M.: Information and communications technology used in higher education: an empirical study on digital learning as sustainability. Sustainability. **13**, 7074 (2021). https://doi.org/10.3390/su13137074
2. Ummihusna, A., Zairul, M.: Investigating immersive learning technology intervention in architecture education: a systematic literature review. JARHE. **14**, 264–281 (2022). https://doi.org/10.1108/jarhe-08-2020-0279
3. Del, M.S.T.T., Tabrizi, S.K.: A methodological assessment of the importance of physical values in architectural conservation using Shannon entropy method. J. Cult. Herit. **44**, 135–151 (2020). https://doi.org/10.1016/j.culher.2019.12.012
4. Clarke, N., Kuipers, M., Stroux, S.: Embedding built heritage values in architectural design education. Int. J. Technol. Des. Educ. **30**, 867–883 (2020). https://doi.org/10.1007/s10798-019-09534-4
5. Banfi, F., Brumana, R., Stanga, C.: Extended reality and informative models for the architectural heritage: from scan-to-BIM process to virtual and augmented reality. Virtual archaeol. rev. **10**, 14 (2019). https://doi.org/10.4995/var.2019.11923
6. Grace Cheng, W.Y., Lo, S.M., Fang, Z., Cheng, C.X.: A view on the means of fire prevention of ancient Chinese buildings – from religious belief to practice. Struct. Surv. **22**(4), 201–209 (2004). https://doi.org/10.1108/02630800410563741
7. Abdel-Moneim Gaffar, A.: Using metaverse to rebuild non-reachable or ruined heritage buildings. Int. J. Archit. Arts Appl. **7**(4), 119 (2021). https://doi.org/10.11648/j.ijaaa.202 10704.13
8. Bevilacqua, M.G., Russo, M., Giordano, A., Spallone, R.: 3D reconstruction, digital twinning, and virtual reality: Architectural Heritage Applications. 2022 IEEE Conference on Virtual Reality and 3D User Interfaces Abstracts and Workshops (VRW). (2022). https://doi.org/10.1109/vrw55335.2022.00031
9. Lindgren, R., Johnson-Glenberg, M.: Emboldened by embodiment. Educ. Res. **42**, 445–452 (2013). https://doi.org/10.3102/0013189x13511661

10. Kilteni, K., Groten, R., Slater, M.: The sense of embodiment in virtual reality. Presence: Teleoperators Virtual Environ. **21**(4), 373–387 (2012). https://doi.org/10.1162/PRES_a_00124
11. Schultze, U.: Embodiment and presence in virtual worlds: a review. J. Inf. Technol. **25**, 434–449 (2010). https://doi.org/10.1057/jit.2010.25
12. Vecchiato, G., Tieri, G., Jelic, A., De Matteis, F., Maglione, A.G., Babiloni, F.: Electroen-cephalographic Correlates of Sensorimotor Integration and Embodiment during the Appre-ciation of Virtual Architectural Environments. Front. Psychol. 6, (2015).https://doi.org/10.1007/s10339-015-0725-6
13. Iranmanesh, A., Onur, Z.: Mandatory virtual design studio for all: exploring the transforma-tions of architectural education amidst the global pandemic. Int J Art Des. Ed. **40**, 251–267 (2021). https://doi.org/10.1111/jade.12350
14. Kreimeier, J., Theelke, L., Denzler, J., Enders, F., Kumar, S., Roth, D.: Towards eco-embodiment: virtual reality for building climate change awareness within education for sustainable development.In: 2023 IEEE International Symposium on Mixed and Aug-mented Reality Adjunct (ISMAR-Adjunct). (2023). https://doi.org/10.1109/ismar-adjunct60411.2023.00130
15. Bagher, M.M., Sajjadi, P., Wallgrün, J.O., LaFemina, P., Klippel, A.: Virtual reality for geospa-tial education: immersive technologies enhance sense of embodiment. Cartography Geogr. Inf. Sci. **50**(3), 233–248 (2023). https://doi.org/10.1080/15230406.2022.2122569
16. Bard, J.T., Chung, H.K., Shaia, J.K., Wellman, L.L., Elzie, C.A.: Increased medical student understanding of dementia through virtual embodiment. Gerontol. Geriatr. Educ. **44**, 211–222 (2023). https://doi.org/10.1080/02701960.2022.2067850
17. Mills, K.A., Scholes, L., Brown, A.: Virtual Reality and Embodiment in Multimodal Meaning Making. Writ. Commun. **39**, 335–369 (2022). https://doi.org/10.1177/07410883221083517
18. Steinhardt, N.: Chinese Architecture: A History. Princeton University Press (2019). https://doi.org/10.1515/9780691191973
19. Maghool, S.A.H., Moeini, S.H. (Iradj), Arefazar, Y.: An educational application based on virtual reality technology for learning architectural details: challenges and benefits. ArchNet-IJAR. 12, 246 (2018). https://doi.org/10.26687/archnet-ijar.v12i3.1719
20. Megahed, N., Hassan, A.: A blended learning strategy: reimagining the post-Covid-19 architectural education. ARCH. **16**, 184–202 (2022). https://doi.org/10.1108/arch-04-2021-0081
21. Salama, A.M.: Transformative Pedagogy in Architecture and Urbanism. Routledge (2021). https://doi.org/10.4324/9781003140047
22. Sepasgozar, S.M.E.: Digital twin and web-based virtual gaming technologies for online edu-cation: a case of construction management and engineering. Appl. Sci. **10**, 4678 (2020). https://doi.org/10.3390/app10134678
23. Holzer, D.: BIM and parametric design in academia and practice: the changing context of knowledge acquisition and application in the digital age. Int. J. Archit. Comput. **13**, 65–82 (2015). https://doi.org/10.1260/1478-0771.13.1.65
24. Mulyadi, M.: Buku Ajar CAD/CAM (Computer Aided Design / Computer Aided Manufac-turing). Umsida Press (2018). https://doi.org/10.21070/2018/978-602-5914-10-2
25. Ibrahim, A., Al-Rababah, A.I., Bani Baker, Q.: Integrating virtual reality technology into architecture education: the case of architectural history courses. OHI. **46**, 498–509 (2021). https://doi.org/10.1108/ohi-12-2020-0190
26. Sopher, H., Kalay, Y.E., Fisher-Gewirtzman, D.: Why Immersive? - Using an immersive virtual environment in architectural education. In: Proceedings of the 35th International Conference on Education and Research in Computer Aided Architectural Design in Europe (eCAADe). Vol 1, pp. 313–322 (2017). https://doi.org/10.52842/conf.ecaade.2017.1.313

27. Ângulo, A., Velasco, G.V. de: Immersive Simulation of Architectural Spatial Experiences. Proceedings of the XVII Conference of the Iberoamerican Society of Digital Graphics - SIGraDi: Knowledge-based Design. (2013).https://doi.org/10.5151/despro-sigradi2013-0095

28. Anthes, C., Garcia-Hernandez, R.J., Wiedemann, M., Kranzlmuller, D.: State of the art of virtual reality technology. In: 2016 IEEE Aerospace Conference. (2016). https://doi.org/10.1109/aero.2016.7500674

29. Brooks, F.P.: What's Real About Virtual Reality? Proceedings IEEE Virtual Reality (Cat. No. 99CB36316). https://doi.org/10.1109/vr.1999.756916

30. Pallavicini, F., Pepe, A., Minissi, M.E.: Gaming in Virtual Reality: What Changes in Terms of Usability, Emotional Response and Sense of Presence Compared to Non-Immersive Video Games? Simul. Gaming **50**, 136–159 (2019). https://doi.org/10.1177/1046878119831420

31. Zhao, J., LaFemina, P., Carr, J., Sajjadi, P., Wallgrun, J.O., Klippel, A.: Learning in the Field: Comparison of Desktop, Immersive Virtual Reality, and Actual Field Trips for Place-Based STEM Education. 2020 IEEE Conference on Virtual Reality and 3D User Interfaces (VR). (2020). https://doi.org/10.1109/vr46266.2020.1581091793502

32. Shin, D.: Empathy and embodied experience in virtual environment: To what extent can virtual reality stimulate empathy and embodied experience? Comput. Hum. Behav. **78**, 64–73 (2018). https://doi.org/10.1016/j.chb.2017.09.012

33. Barfield, W., Zeltzer, D.: Presence and performance within virtual environments. Virtual Environ. And. Adv. Interface Des. (1995). https://doi.org/10.1093/oso/9780195075557.003.0023

34. Slater, M., Sanchez-Vives, M.V.: Enhancing our lives with immersive virtual reality. Frontiers in Robot AI **3**, 74 (2016). https://doi.org/10.3389/frobt.2016.00074

35. Hong, S.W., Park, J., Cho, M.: Virtual vs. actual body: applicability of anthropomorphic avatars to enhance exploratory creativity in architectural design education. Architect. Sci. Rev. **62**(6), 520–527 (2019). https://doi.org/10.1080/00038628.2019.1669526

36. Trump, J., Shealy, T.: Effects of embodied and self-reflected virtual reality on engineering students' design cognition about nature. Proc. Des. Soc. **3**, 1575–1584 (2023). https://doi.org/10.1017/pds.2023.158

37. Lindgren, R., Tscholl, M., Wang, S., Johnson, E.: Enhancing learning and engagement through embodied interaction within a mixed reality simulation. Comput. Educ. **95**, 174–187 (2016). https://doi.org/10.1016/j.compedu.2016.01.001

38. Chan, C.-S., Bogdanovic, J., Kalivarapu, V.: Applying immersive virtual reality for remote teaching architectural history. Educ. Inf. Technol. **27**, 4365–4397 (2022). https://doi.org/10.1007/s10639-021-10786-8

39. Şahbaz, E.: VR-based interactive learning in architectural education: a case on safranbolu historical bathhouse. Iconarp Int. J. Archit. Planning **8**(1), 342–356 (2020). https://doi.org/10.15320/ICONARP.2020.116

40. Ge, Y.: Teaching research on "experience" architecture history with VR technology. Frontier High. Educ. **1**(1), 5–9 (2019). https://doi.org/10.36012/fhe.v1i1.569

41. Huang, J., Gao, H.: Performance and application of virtual reality technology (VR) in digital protection of buildings. IOP Conf. Ser.: Earth Environ. Sci. **508**(1), 012170 (2020). https://doi.org/10.1088/1755-1315/508/1/012170

42. Kwon, H., et al.: Understanding audiences for immersive and interactive museum and gallery experiences and cultural exchanges. Proc. Des. Soc. **3**, 3691–3700 (2023). https://doi.org/10.1017/pds.2023.370

43. He, F.: Restoration design of chu architecture: zhanghua tower based on VR technology. Comput. Intell. Neurosci. **2022**, 1–8 (2022). https://doi.org/10.1155/2022/1310462

44. Thiwanka, M.D., Senanayake, W.S.V., Ranasinghe, R.H.A.C.N., Supeshala, P.K.C., Jayaweera, Y.D.: Purawalokanaya - the virtual tour to ancient city of polonnaruwa - Sri Lanka. Int. J. Comput. Appl. **179**(12), 14–19 (2018). https://doi.org/10.5120/ijca2018916130

45. Steinhardt, N.S.: The tang architectural icon and the politics of Chinese architectural history. Art Bull. **86**, 228 (2004). https://doi.org/10.2307/3177416
46. Roth, D., Latoschik, M.E.: Construction of the virtual embodiment questionnaire (VEQ). IEEE Trans. Vis. Comput. Graph. **26**, 3546–3556 (2020). https://doi.org/10.1109/tvcg.2020.3023603
47. Kennedy, R.S., Lane, N.E., Berbaum, K.S., Lilienthal, M.G.: Simulator sickness questionnaire: an enhanced method for quantifying simulator sickness. Int. J. Aviat. Psychol. **3**, 203–220 (1993). https://doi.org/10.1207/s15327108ijap0303_3
48. Sutcliffe, A., Gault, B.: Heuristic evaluation of virtual reality applications. Interact. Comput. **16**, 831–849 (2004). https://doi.org/10.1016/j.intcom.2004.05.001
49. Kabassi, K., Amelio, A., Komianos, V., Oikonomou, K.: Evaluating museum virtual tours: the case study of Italy. Information **10**, 351 (2019). https://doi.org/10.3390/info10110351
50. Slater, M.: Inducing illusory ownership of a virtual body. Front. Neurosci. **3**, 214–220 (2009). https://doi.org/10.3389/neuro.01.029.2009
51. Slater, M., Spanlang, B., Sanchez-Vives, M.V., Blanke, O.: First person experience of body transfer in virtual reality. PLoS ONE **5**, e10564 (2010). https://doi.org/10.1371/journal.pone.0010564
52. Cho, J.Y., Suh, J.: Spatial ability performance in interior design and architecture: comparison of static and virtual reality modes. Buildings **13**, 3128 (2023). https://doi.org/10.3390/buildings13123128
53. Horvat, N., Martinec, T., Lukačević, F., Perišić, M.M., Škec, S.: The potential of immersive virtual reality for representations in design education. Virtual Reality **26**, 1227–1244 (2022). https://doi.org/10.1007/s10055-022-00630-w
54. Berger, C.C., Lin, B., Lenggenhager, B., Lanier, J., Gonzalez-Franco, M.: Follow your nose: extended arm reach after pinocchio illusion in virtual reality. Frontiers Virtual Reality **3**, 712375 (2022). https://doi.org/10.3389/frvir.2022.712375
55. Saunders, J.A., Knill, D.C.: Visual feedback control of hand movements. J. Neurosci. **24**, 3223–3234 (2004). https://doi.org/10.1523/jneurosci.4319-03.2004
56. Vogeley, K., May, M., Ritzl, A., Falkai, P., Zilles, K., Fink, G.R.: Neural Correlates of First-Person Perspective as One Constituent of Human Self-Consciousness. **16**, 817–827 (2004). https://doi.org/10.1162/089892904970799
57. Lugrin, J.-L., Latt, J., Latoschik, M.E.: Avatar anthropomorphism and illusion of body ownership in VR. 2015 IEEE Virtual Reality (VR). (2015). https://doi.org/10.1109/vr.2015.7223379
58. Kim, J., Kim, W., Ahn, S., Kim, J., Lee, S.: Virtual reality sickness predictor: analysis of visual-vestibular conflict and VR contents. In: 2018 Tenth International Conference on Quality of Multimedia Experience (QoMEX). (2018). https://doi.org/10.1109/qomex.2018.8463413
59. Chang, E., Kim, H.T., Yoo, B.: Virtual Reality sickness: a review of causes and measurements. Int. J. Hum-Comput. Int. **36**, 1658–1682 (2020). https://doi.org/10.1080/10447318.2020.1778351
60. Conner, N.O., et al.: Virtual reality induced symptoms and effects: concerns, causes. Assess. Mitig. Virtual Worlds. **1**, 130–146 (2022). https://doi.org/10.3390/virtualworlds1020008
61. Jasper, A., Cone, N., Meusel, C., Curtis, M., Dorneich, M.C., Gilbert, B.: Visually induced motion sickness susceptibility and recovery based on four mitigation techniques. Frontiers in Virtual Reality **1**, 582108 (2020). https://doi.org/10.3389/frvir.2020.582108
62. Shi, R., Liang, H.-N., Wu, Y., Yu, D., Xu, W.: Virtual reality sickness mitigation methods. Proc. ACM Comput. Graph. Interact. Tech. **4**, 1–16 (2021). https://doi.org/10.1145/3451255

63. Mohler, B.J., Creem-Regehr, S.H., Thompson, W.B., Bülthoff, H.H.: The effect of viewing a self-avatar on distance judgments in an HMD-based virtual environment. Presence: Teleoperators Virtual Environ. **19**(3), 230–242 (2010). https://doi.org/10.1162/pres.19.3.230
64. van der Hoort, B., Ehrsson, H.H.: Body ownership affects visual perception of object size by rescaling the visual representation of external space. Atten. Percept. Psychophys. **76**, 1414–1428 (2014). https://doi.org/10.3758/s13414-014-0664-9

Breaking Barriers for Classical Chinese: Tang Poetry in Virtual Reality

Carrie Ching(✉) (iD)

Rhine-Waal University of Applied Sciences, Kamp-Lintfort, Germany
`kar-wai-carrie.ching@hsrw.org`

Abstract. In this study, five barriers are identified for comprehension of *Classical Chinese* poems in modern times, namely linguistics, literacy, culture, time and geography. Chinese languages are considered hard to learn for foreign communities due to their completely different scripting systems, sound systems and culture. Classical Chinese, as an ancient language with the grammar aiming for extreme conciseness, is even harder to comprehend. Currently, it is no longer as actively in use as in the old days by the Chinese communities although a huge number of important original texts have been passed on. Poems alone are also generally regarded as difficult to consume due to their abstractness. Meanwhile, reading poems in virtual reality (VR) was underexplored although there is a potential in improving comprehension through embodied reading experience [1]. VR experience for a *Tang poem* was created to formulate a methodology that can reduce the quintuple complexities in comprehending and resonating with Classical Chinese poems through reading in VR. As it is *research through design* and design decisions vary with designers, considerations in the VR design process are elucidated in this paper with a *semi-autoethnographical* approach. After pilot test of the design, a VR design methodology is derived for enabling reader to grasp the poem's essence, thus enhancing their comprehension of the text and the language. The methodology is deducibly applicable for any forms of poems in any languages. Fostered understanding of Classical Chinese poems may in return revitalize the ancient language.

Keywords: Reading in virtual reality · Poem comprehension · Digital humanities

1 Introduction

When we communicate with foreigners, due to variations in culture and history, we often find phrases in one language cannot be simply translated to another language without some supplementary explanation of the background even when the two languages belong to the same family of languages. With unique script systems and sound system[1] as well

---

[1] Chinese has a logographic scripting system [2] with 6 ways of character formation from *strokes* and *radicals* [3] and each Chinese character is "an independent symbol that expresses a meaning" [3]. While "each character is pronounced in one syllable", its pronunciation is complicated by *tones* [3].

© The Author(s), under exclusive license to Springer Nature Switzerland AG 2024
J. Y. C. Chen and G. Fragomeni (Eds.): HCII 2024, LNCS 14708, pp. 19–43, 2024.
https://doi.org/10.1007/978-3-031-61047-9_2

as extensive existence of heteronyms [3], Chinese languages have been considered very hard to learn [4], if not completely illegible, for most people from foreign communities, including Koreans [5] although they are also classified as East Asians. Expats from Chinese communities therefore often find it difficult to share their thoughts and emotions with new friends whom they make in the new places. Furthermore, during the long history of Chinese civilization, a lot of classical texts, encompassing literature, philosophical thoughts, scientific/technological findings and historical records, were written in *Classical Chinese*, a language that was used by Chinese educated and upper classes actively and almost exclusively before AD 1368 [5] but now used only limitedly and partially in some occasions [5]. With its grammar aiming for extreme conciseness to minimize the use of the precious recording media (e.g. animal bones, tortoise shells, bronze articles, bamboo strips, silk and papers) [3], Classical Chinese texts are often ambiguous and very often hard to comprehend for the Chinese communities [6], not to mention the foreign communities. New texts are rare and their dissemination is limited.

Against this background, a virtual reality (VR) developer who possessed an architectural design education background, Classical Chinese literacy as well as experience in writing fictions and poems picked a *Tang poem* for creation of VR experience mainly to enable foreigners to grab the essence of the poem without knowledge of the Chinese languages beforehand. Among the three major modes of design research that Christopher Frayling distinguished, *research through design* is "project-based and includes materials research and development" [7]. This approach hence allows the researcher to take the opportunity of a course project to conduct the research. By adopting this approach, focus was given to the design process and thus "the understanding and knowledge gained" rather than the final artefact [8], a methodology was formulated for reducing the quintuple complexities in comprehending and resonating with Classical Chinese poems through reading in VR for foreign communities. To account for the background of the designer, which embodies a paramount set of factors in every design decision during the design process but cannot be exhaustively listed and is practically not reproducible because human individuals are unique and the mind may change over time even for the same designer, this paper is written with a *semi-autoethnographical* approach to comprehensively elucidate the VR design process: in contrast to conventional autoethnography [9], this paper is still written in third-person perspective and the first section of this paper is written as objectively as possible as in a classic research paper in order to provide an overview of the contexts to the designer prior to the commencement of the design process,[2] while the remaining sections will include personal experience and reflections of the researcher so as to clearly explain why certain factors were considered and decisions were made in such ways. In this way, while other designers may make different design decisions, they can take into account the factors considered as well as the knowledge and skills utilized in this VR design.

---

[2] As part of the designer's personal approach to avoid unconsciously constrained imagination, only limited literature regarding reading in VR (as shown in the first section of this paper) was examined before commencement of the design process on 30th October 2022, and no more during the design process.

1.1 Tang Poems, Classical Chinese and Cantonese

Poem can be defined as "work of *poetry*", where poetry is "fiction in verse" [10]. Among a diversity of text genres, poems are most likely equated to "difficulty" [11] and have been challenging to understand for the majority, and even more challenging when it was written in a foreign language or an ancient language and with a background that the readers have never personally experienced [11]. Classical Chinese, the written Chinese language used in ancient time [5], is known to be graceful, rhythmic and condense yet obscure to understand for even average Chinese speakers in the ancient time [5], and worse nowadays due to temporal and cultural barriers. Besides, Mandarin, the currently most widely used Chinese language, has only four *tones* in three *tonal categories*. It has not preserved all the four tonal categories of Classical Chinese [2, 12] and consists of very different vocabulary, which can only be traced back to Song dynasty (AD 960– 1279) [13]. *Cantonese* or *Yue*, the third popular Chinese language [14], has nine tones in four tonal categories, aligning with the tonal categories of Classical Chinese [12, 15, 16]. Dated back to Qin dynasty (221–206 BC) [14], Cantonese in daily life often uses vocabulary still with the same meaning and grammar as Classical Chinese [2]. Although Cantonese is widely acknowledged as a better Chinese language for reading Classical Chinese texts, it is de facto gradually marginalized [2], inducing further decline in comprehension of Classical Chinese in the younger generations [6].[3]

For foreign communities, modernized Chinese languages have already been considered hard to learn due to their completely different scripting systems, pronunciation systems and culture. Nowadays, Chinese learners from foreign communities often prefer Mandarin to Cantonese owing to Mandarin's wider coverage in the Chinese population (and dominance in mainland China), easier and cheaper access to its learning materials and a simpler tone system. The obstacle for understanding Classical Chinese text has thus become so monstrous to foreign communities that it is an impossible mission to many.

However, there are a lot of prominent works written in Classical Chinese, including various forms of literature, philosophical works, accounts of history, scientific research as well as traditional Chinese medical books and records. Although translations and interpretations are sometimes available, there is inevitable loss of information or misinterpretation, intentionally or unintentionally, as studied in hermeneutics [18]. People who cannot understand Classical Chinese without aid therefore miss a lot of wisdom and knowledge in original Classical Chinese texts. This is particularly undesirable since mutual understanding is essential for avoidance of conflicts when inter-cultural contacts and communication have multiplied in recent decades.

---

[3] Therefore, in this paper, Chinese texts are transliterated according to the International Phonetic Alphabet-based transcription system of 黃錫凌式音標 *Wong4Sek3Ling4Sik1Jam1Biu1* [*S. L. Wong Romanization system for Cantonese*] [17]. Except for names, they are accompanied by English translations.

Among all Classical Chinese texts from the ancient time, Tang poems,[4] commonly known as the golden age of Chinese poetry [19], may be the most worthwhile to learn for ordinary people and the easiest to comprehend for beginners. With rigorous format (either 5 or 7 characters per sentence, and either 4 or 8 sentences per poem as in 絕句 *zyut3geoi3* [*minimal form of poetry, with four lines to a stanza, also called "quatrain"*] and 律詩 *leot6si1* [*regulated form of poetry*] respectively) except for those following the format of 古詩 *gu2si1* [*"ancient poem" not so prescribed*] or 樂府 *ngok6fu2* [*ancient songs for court entertainment*] [19, 20], Tang poetry had character limits, ranging from 20 characters (as in *Snow on the River*) to 56 characters. The highly constrained numbers of characters made the poems relatively simple and easy for readers to consume, but also pushed the Tang's poets to refine every character in their poems to maximize the poems' breadth, depth and complexity, leading to extreme conciseness of Tang poems. Ambiguities were common, and sometimes intentional in Tang poems to allow multiple interpretations and rooms for imagination. On top of the character limits, every two lines of a Tang poem should form a 詩聯 *si1lyun4* [*couplet*] [21, 22]. Couplets usually enhance understanding of both sentences when they are analysed in pair. But couplets sometimes also create obstacles due to unprecedented usage of some characters for compliance with the rules.

Apart from structure, rhythm and melody of 絕句 zyut3geoi3 and 律詩 leot6si1 are also restricted [22, 23]. Beginners in Tang poems may ignore such restrictions, as demonstrated in the Tang poetry teaching plan of Clementi Secondary School Chinese Language Education Study Group from Hong Kong [24]. But being able to read Tang poems in the correct tones may help readers grasping the emotions that the poets intended to express. In a certain sense, Tang poems can be easier to comprehend than a prose with clear reasoning logic simply because humans naturally have the ability to empathize, or better, resonate with shared emotions, while Tang poems were written principally to express emotions inspired by scenes or incidents [25] and often formed some 意境 *ji3ging2* [*artistic conception*] [25].

Furthermore, Tang poems were either descriptive or narrative, or hybrid [20, 25]. Most of their contents no longer exist in reality today after dramatic changes in socio-cultural and geographical landscapes across more than 1110 years. However, when a reader knows the meaning of all the characters in a Tang poem, it is still possible to comprehend the poem to a certain extent. Due to this nature, when a designer is able to understand a Tang poem, it is mostly feasible for the designer to visualize it according to the characters' meaning on the surface despite the poem's actual abstractness and complexity.

1.2 Augmentation of Poem Reading

In the past, various forms of analog augmentation have been made for literature, including Tang poems to enhance readers' motivation and comprehension, or to present the

---

[4] Many of the preserved Tang poems are found in the collection *Three Hundred Tang Poems*, a book that was compiled by 蘅塘退士 Hang4Tong4Teoi3Si6 during Qing dynasty. The book has become universally known in the Chinese communities. Tang poems discussed in this paper refer to those poems, which are considered as classic.

artists' interpretations. Calligraphy was perhaps the ordinary form in the ancient times, and many of them could be passed on by engraving and printing. Similarly, some paintings (usually with calligraphy) and their prints have also been passed on, e.g. Wong [26] collected paintings that illustrated Tang poems to compile 8 types of albums and printed them with wood-engraving. Apart from visual augmentation, audio augmentation have also been common, e.g. in the form of reading out the texts and/or playing background music matching the mood of the Tang poems as well as composing a tailor-made music with/without singing out the texts, as shown in the collection of multimedia by National Taiwan University [27]. Besides, performances and animations, which integrated visual and audio augmentation, are not rare. The story of 楊貴妃 Joeng4 gwai3fei1 [Imperial Concubine Joeng4] narrated in 長恨歌 *Coeng4Han6Go1* [A *Song of Everlasting Regrets*], for example, was adapted in a television drama *The Legend of Lady Yang* produced by Television Broadcasts Limited of Hong Kong in 2000.

With the increasing popularity of digital technology, analog augmentation are often also digitalized, or directly implemented with digital means. A design space for digital augmentation of reading in general has been constructed in recent study, which revealed that within the dimension *reality configuration*, the sub-dimension VR was underexplored [1] although VR technologies have gained significant progress in recent years and the industry has invested a lot in constructing a metaverse. Thanks to the benefits of its "three pillars", namely immersion, presence and interactivity [28], VR has great potential in innovatively enhancing reading comprehension through embodied reading experience [1]. Adapting a Tang poem into a story to be presented in VR may thus be a good approach for enhancing foreigners' comprehension of the poems.

1.3 Movies in VR

Movies, as a popular form of storytelling in modern time, have been produced for VR although their classification in VR is still unclear as seen in the study of VR genres in Sorensen's study [29]. In VR, freedom of head movement allows 360° view for audience, disallowing framing of scenes, transition of scenes as well as camera setting and movement in traditional movies by director; freedom of foot movement allows spatial exploration by audience, disallowing duration control by director. Similar to cinematography, *transition* and *duration* are aspects that should be configured in the temporal dimension of a design space for digitally enriched storytelling [30].

In August 2022, Maher [31] described *Gloomy Eyes* from AtlasV [32] as "one of the most well-reviewed VR movies across headsets". It utilized VR to realize 360° storytelling in six degrees of freedom (6DoF) and 3D real time [33]. However, audience in general had to follow the movement of the leading roles along a specific path to watch the story even if it is presented with a third-person perspective. This comment was subsequently shared by Pérez Valero's study [34], stating that the experience is still "inherently linear", similar to a *walking simulator*. The theoretically infinite space of VR was therefore not sufficiently utilized. The application of existing cinematographic techniques, which may improve the quality of a movie, was sometimes dissatisfactory. Transition between scenes was quite well handled within each episode, but transition from one "episode" (essentially just another scene) to another disrupted the flow and thus the feeling of immersion. As it is not intended for reading some existing text, display of text was minimal (texts were found only in "menu" for selecting episodes, the title in the beginning and credits at the end).

While VR was still a "new medium" in cinematography and under exploration an year prior to this study [35], presenting a poem via storytelling in VR with the aid of cinematography was expected to be more challenging.

1.4 Spatial Experience Design in Architecture and in VR

When infinitely large space is theoretically possible in VR, VR experience design is in large *spatial experience* design, a subject already deeply explored in the disciplines of architecture, interior design and urban design.

Although the application of VR in those design disciplines is not new, transfer of the mature spatial experience design skills from those design disciplines into VR experience creation in other disciplines is unexplored.

For architecture, there is indeed no consensus for the definition of spatial experience and *spatial sense*, which is believed to be a sense beyond the known six senses.[5] The ideas are too abstract and perhaps touching the metaphysics dimensions in the current scientific progress. In architectural education, the ideas and the corresponding design skills have only been passed on to students through in-person spatial experience, drawing, photos and practicing design. The same teaching approach was adopted by Angulo although it was implemented via VR since architectural spatial experience design had been lacking without sufficient access to decent simulation tools for representing space in elapse of time [37]. Some scholars examined the idea of spatial experience via study of how a person may "construct unique spatial experiences through direct perception and its amalgamation with memory" [38]. A number of diagrams were created to illustrate "the interaction between users and space" as a way of simulating and thus predicting users' spatial experiences although this is still "almost an impossible task for those who don't have enough experience" [39]. The user-space interaction is however only one aspect of spatial experience. Angulo [37] suggested that spatial experience "can be [..] the ego-centric perception of the individual and his/her interpretation of the phenomenological characteristics of the space" and for description of a space, characterizing spatial experiences is more important than portraying the *space defining objects*. *Spatial perception*, a term in the field of cognitive science, is defined from the perspective of the relationship between *self* and the environment [40] and relevant research is rich. Although the term sounds similar to spatial sense, spatial sense actually involves far more than such relationship.

Despite unclear definitions spatial experience and spatial sense, techniques for sculpting spatial experience have been well developed in architecture and should be transferrable to VR experience creation by people who have sufficient architectural training.

---

[5] In existing scientific research, six senses have been defined, including the five well-known "Aristotelian" senses (namely, visual, auditory, haptic, gustatory, and olfactory) and the sense of *interoception*, which is "the perception of sensations from inside the body, both physical such as hunger and pain, and emotional, such as joy" [36].

1.5   Conflicts and Collaboration Between Designers and Developers

When a designer develops and implements a design, use of technology is always involved. Many designers have grasped a set of technical skills for design, but when it comes to the state-of-the-art digital technologies, they very often lack a comprehensive set of fundamental skills and an engineering mindset. That means they often need to collaborate with developers who have the technical skills and knowledge. Conflicts then arise, partly due to differences between the logics of design and computation [41], and partly due to knowledge gaps and distinct foci. Complement of strengths and weaknesses is the rationale for collaboration between designers and developers, but is also a ubiquitous root of miscommunication and conflicts. Owing to unclear definitions, transfer of the idea of spatial experience from an architectural designer to a VR developer will further widen the communication gap. Bridging the gap is thus critical for a good and successful final artefact.

Though a good architectural designer can in their mind simulate and predict the user's spatial experience, how can they express it and convince someone who only believes in scientific research? In practice, architects tackle this issue by leading the projects (which is a tradition), by various forms of visualization and/or by relying on the long history of collaboration between architects and various types of engineers. Yet, the difficult situation in VR design and development was still an unexplored issue. It is foreseeably very hard when VR originated from computer science research and VR developers would therefore naturally feel they are more authoritative in this realm. While there may exist many solutions to experiment, a direct and doubtlessly effective solution is overlapping the roles of VR design and VR development in one person.

In the subsections above, the cultural context of Tang poems, Classical Chinese and Cantonese has been set out, showing linguistic, literate, cultural, temporal and geographical barriers nowadays in learning Classical Chinese for Chinese communities, and such obstacles are multiplied for non-Chinese. As for the technical context, both analog and digital (in particular VR) augmentation of poem reading in some existing studies and artefacts have been reviewed, spawning the idea of adapting a Tang poem into a story. Movies in VR for storytelling was found immature while discussion of spatial experience design in VR was lacking. With such knowledge in mind, it became evident that expressing a Tang poem in VR by storytelling with spatial experience has the potential to remove the quintuple barriers for readers in understanding Classical Chinese poems. Nonetheless, the organizational context of VR design and development poses non-trivial challenge among the opportunity.

Under such contexts, the research through design of a VR reading room for a Tang poem started to explore a way of reducing the quintuple complexities in comprehending and resonating with Classical Chinese poems for foreigners. Design process, including the apparatus involved, are illustrated in the next section. The subsequent section provides the results (including the resulting spatial experience in the VR, pilot test results and the design methodology thereby formulated) and the corresponding discussion. Overall discussion and outlook of this research conclude this paper.

2 The Design Process

There was one co-developer in addition to the researcher since it was required to be a group project in a course. The researcher played multiple roles, i.e. writer, designer, developer and project manager. The co-developer participated in design when suitable free VR assets could not be found and new assets had to be developed.

At the beginning of the design process, the researcher established a central idea that the design intention should be expressing the ambience of the Tang poem, which is silence and solitude, with a meticulous and holistic design of spatial experience. Although the course required creation of a "reading room", she decided to challenge the common conception that it should be a room bounded by walls, floor and ceiling in order to fully utilize the spatial potential of VR. Although multiple *scenes* are possible in Unity, only one scene was built so that time and efforts can be focused on the single scene for possible perfection. Scripts in Unity are written in C#, as default.

Prior to sketching a storyboard, the researcher intended to create personas for the project but managed to interview only 3 people within the project schedule. All of the interviewees were asked the same set of basic questions, plus ad-hoc additional questions when the researcher found some answers were interesting. The basic question set were formulated on the basis of a commonly used Persona template, and contained additional questions to examine aspects related to VR, reading, movies and gaming.

Although creation of persona was not feasible with the small number of interviewees, the researcher was inspired by the answers collected: a respondent liked hiking but had not done it since the pandemic of COVID-19 started. The regrets that the respondent expressed gave the researcher the idea of making the VR user climb mountains step by step to closely experience hiking, instead of "quick and dirty" teleports from one spot to another distant spot in the VR. Technical equipment and design considerations of creating each of the main components in the Unity Project are described in the following subsections.

2.1 Technical Equipment

The hardware includes an HTC Vive headset with two controllers which allow users to teleport across the VR environment and interact with the game objects. The industry-standard software Unity (ver. 2012.3.12f1) was used to create the virtual environment. In addition to importing some free assets from the Unity Asset Store, objects and materials were also built to adapt to the design needs of this project.

2.2 Text in Books

The chosen Tang poem 江雪 *Gong1Syut3 [Snow on the River]* (Fig. 1) described an outdoor natural scene in winter, which composed of both typical and atypical elements. The researcher determined that all those elements were feasible to create with a satisfactory quality in VR within two months since the poem does not involve characters (human or animal) who have facial expressions. Moreover, the poem expressed the poet's exceptional resilience among the life difficulties that he had faced, which the researcher could resonate. As a five-character quatrain, the poem perfectly reflects the condense nature of Classical Chinese. While English translation of *Three Hundred Tang Poems* was not readily accessible in Germany, a English translation online [42] was taken as a reference.

江雪 *Gong1Syut3* [*Snow on the River*] (written by 柳宗元 *Lau5Zung1Jyun4*)				
千	山	鳥	飛	絕
cin1	*saan1*	*niu5*	*fei1*	*zyut3*
thousand	mountain	bird	fly	extinct
'Not a bird in a thousand hills.'				
萬	徑	人	蹤	滅
maan6	*ging3*	*jan4*	*zung1*	*mit6*
ten thousand	trail	human	trace	obliterate
'Not a soul on ten thousand trails.'				
孤	舟	簑	笠	翁
gu1	*zau1*	*so1*	*lap1*	*jung1*
lone	rowboat	raincoat	bamboo hat	old man
'An old man on a raft in straw quilts'				
獨	釣	寒	江	雪
duk6	*diu3*	*hon4*	*gong1*	*syut3*
alone	fish	cold	river	snow
'Fishes alone with snowy chills.'				

Fig. 1. The original Classical Chinese of the Tang poem chosen for the VR experience design text, with transliteration, interlinear word-by-word glosses [43] and its English translation [42] below each line

To help facilitate comprehension of the poem, the researcher derived a story from the poem from the first-person perspective of hiker. Storyboard, including scenes in designed spatial sequence, camera positions and movements, lighting, audio, allowed duration as well as transitions and the conditions to trigger those transitions, was then sketched according to traditional cinematography. She further broke the text of the story down into smaller parts (see Appendix) to fit into the size of the books in VR, while ensuring the font size is good for reading in VR. The corresponding original Classical Chinese sentence is also displayed in the book, considering that users may have knowledge of Chinese or may be interested in learning (Classical) Chinese. Otherwise, the Chinese characters serve as nice graphics. Besides, the background of the poem and this project were briefly described in the first book, and concise instructions for the VR experience were also given in two books at the first scene of the VR. Details of the text in the resulting books in the VR can be found in Appendix, which includes a sample display of a book cover and a test display of an internal page (Fig. 5). Every book consists of a cover and one page. The size of the book was adjusted such that it is close to a real book and can be read easily in VR while it is held in hand. Book cover with plain brown colour was chosen for its historic feeling and to ensure some contrast with the surroundings such that users can spot the books easily. A *Canva* with *Button* with *TextMeshPro* was used to display texts in the books. After experimenting 10 font types, *DFKai-SB* was found to be able to display Chinese characters properly and the English characters clearly plus readable. Blurring texts in the edge of the VR view was however inevitable due to technical constraints of hardware. A configured *Attach* object makes the user grab the book on the left edge (the hinge of the book) in a slightly inclined way in VR so that the user will feel it natural. Grabbing with the left controller is hence recommended to avoid awkward twist of user's right wrist. Such control may be not intuitive for right-hand users. Nonetheless, a natural experience with books was prioritized.

The positions of the books were averagely distributed throughout the designed route. Together with the locations and teleport network of Teleport Spheres, the user will be led along a route that they could multi-sensory experience the meaning of the poem and strengthen their understanding of the text. Numbering on the book covers may help user orientate themselves in indistinguishable surroundings and make sure they did not miss any parts of the poem or its derivative story.

On flatlands, books are initially laid on the ground. On the mountains, as steps on the hiking trails are mostly not deep enough to properly place the books, stone platforms were constructed aside the hiking trails for books to lie on to avoid their falls from the planned locations before the user reaches them. Those platforms are simple *Cube* to reduce computational load. The material is the colour of snow in the mountains (as those stones are expected to be covered by snow) and half embedded into the mountains so that they appear to be a natural and integrated part of the mountains instead of man-built structure. Users will discover that if they do not put a book back into the platform carefully after reading, the book will fall into the mountain's snow, then they cannot revisit the text in such book whenever they wish. With the need of placing the book back to the corresponding stone platform, user may form a feeling that the books should be cherished and they should try to remember the contents of the book.

2.3 Snow

Obviously from the title of the poem, snow and river are key components of the poem although the corresponding Chinese character 雪 *syut3* was mentioned only once in the last sentence. This is a typical literature writing technique in Classical Chinese poems, so-called "painting the eyes of the dragon" (which always come last in Chinese tradition).

The *particle system* in Unity was found well-developed and allowing configuration of a wide range of parameters. A suitable snowflake.PNG image was sourced from the Internet. In the process, too delicate details of.PNG image were found to be unnoticeable in the VR headset and would only lower the performance of the VR.

Although the effect of the particle system was almost perfect (Fig. 2), it is so delicate that when the complexity of the particle system was increased above a certain threshold (e.g. maximum number of "particles" in the system was increased, coverage of the system was expanded, rate of emission of particles was increased), the performance of the "Game" would be severely hampered, sometimes leading to *Blue Screen of Death* of the Windows operating system. The parameters could not be further reduced as both the second mountain in the route and both sides of riverbanks had to be covered so as to visualize the scene described by the poem. Since the snow is an essential component that cannot be removed, script was applied to limit the activation of the snow particle system by user's collision with a specific teleport sphere, which teleports the user to the middle of a mountain and thus marks the beginning of the VR reading of the contents of the poem and its derivative story. The snowfall is designed to become heavier and heavier as time elapses to accentuate the ambience of coldness and solitude.

Fig. 2. Falling snowflakes in the project

2.4 River

The corresponding Chinese character 江 gong1 of "river" was the second last character in the poem and is almost equally important as "snow" in the poem. The shape of the technically stationary river roughly followed the shape of 柳江 Lau5Gong1 (a river's name) (Fig. 3) in an ancient survey map of 桂林 Gwai3Lam4 in the now Guangxi Province [44], which shares karst topography with 永州 Wing5Zau1, the city where poet was exiled to and wrote the classic poem after exploring the nature.

2.5 Mountains, Trails and Locomotion

Approximately 60 instances from an asset *Free Snow Mountain* [45] were placed along the two sides of the river, with varied scales, orientation and vertical positions (*y-position*) to realistically visualize "countless hills" in the poem. This highly increased the computational complexity of the project as each mountain consist of a lot of polygons. Conflicts thereby arose between the researcher and the co-developer about the priority between the (a) strength of expression of the poem and aesthetics and (b) development effort and technical practicality. The co-developer naturally opted to reducing the number of mountains, while the researcher found the simplification unacceptable after review. In the end, the researcher re-added some mountains and spent efforts to reduce the computational complexity of the snow particle system for the overall technical practicality. Similar to the river, the heights of the mountains and layout also roughly follows the same ancient survey map to realize the scenery that the poet visited when he created the poem, but no longer exists for readers to see today. The actual heights of mountains in the VR scene range from 10 m to 1200 m, and the two mountains that have teleportable hiking trails are 100 m high. With mountains enclosing the scene all taller than those two mountains and mountains of vary heights in between the two groups in all directions, the user will always feel surrounded by mountains (Fig. 3).

Fig. 3. Layout of "countless" mountains and a river

From experiments, teleporting to and fro oblique planes at different heights was found impossible in Unity due to occlusion and the angle of raycast. To allow user to hike in the mountains in order to align with the perspective of the derivative story, trails with steps on two of the mountains were built and configured to be teleportable. The trails consist of small sections to fit into the varying slopes of the mountains and to avoid a straight artificial stair that would be impossible in Tang Dynasty, matching the cultural background of the poem. Again, the same material as the mountain was applied to ensure the steps integrate well into the mountains (Fig. 4).

User can teleport across designated parts of the scene according to the designed route to experience different parts of the poem in the actual order of the sentences in the original poem. A standing position is recommended by the researcher both for logistic reasons and for aligned perception as sitting is not expected in the VR. To allow locomotion of the user within the VR environment without walking in the reality, three ways of teleport were offered. Teleport in the reverse direction is possible to provide flexibility and encourage re-reading of some text in case the user has not fully understood it previously.

Fig. 4. The hiking trails in the mountains

2.6 An Old Man in Quilt Fishing on a Raft

As the only sign of life and relatively dynamic element in the poem, the raft together with the old man was scripted to move between one point to another, where the speed was adjusted such that the movement would not end before a user commonly finishes the designed route including some free wandering.

2.7 Sky, Lighting, Colour Tone and Audio

Well-designed lighting is essential for good rendering in computer graphics. To align with the dull ambience of the poem, a grey-blue sky was created by adjusting the default skybox (*GreySkyProcedural*), a part of the *lighting configuration*. 3D angles of *Directional Light* were configured such that the mountains would not be completely in shade and the textures would be recognizable in VR, but not too bright to avoid an lively ambience.

Similarly, although in general sound effect may enhance user's experience, only sound of wind was added to *XR Origin object*, meaning the wind sound will always follow the user. The wind sound was selected from an asset from lumino [46]. Augmentation with Cantonese pronunciation of the original poem may possibly help learning the language of Classical Chinese and enhance understanding of the poem's rhythm and thus the emotions expressed, but it was ruled out to avoid contradiction with the special ambience of this poem.

3 Results and Analysis

The first result is the final artefact. The expected spatial experience in the VR thereof derived is described in the coming subsection. Then three users were invited for a pilot test for evaluating the design, and success of the design was confirmed, as explained in the second subsection. The key result of this study is a design methodology in the third subsection, which is formulated from the VR design process and analysis of the pilot test result.

3.1 Spatial Experience in the VR

4 different types of spatial experience were designed for single user, corresponding to the 4 sentences of the original poem: (1) climbing up Mountain 1 until the top, (2) going down Mountain 2 (snow falling on the way, user getting closer and closer to the river), (3) seeing the river and the raft, and (4) arriving at a flatland and walking along the riverbanks.

Upon inception into the VR environment, the user[6] will find themselves on a small piece of snow-white flatland circled by tall snowy and stony mountains. They can freely wander around and will soon discover three books, which include the background of the poems and instructions. The books lead the user to a translucent sphere for teleport. Without much to explore there, the user will not hesitate much to enter the teleport sphere.

After the first teleport to the middle of a mountain and facing a trail leading upwards, the actual poem reading journey in VR begins, marked by start of snowfall which is not yet noticeable. The user then naturally try to hike the mountain along the trail, and pick up the eye-catching brown-covered books aside the trail for reading. They most likely do not understand the original Classical Chinese text of the poem, but can understand the simple English of the derivative story. As hinted by the texts, they look around and find themselves in an endless mountain range. They also look up to the sky, and notice the lack of birds and clouds in a dull grey-blue sky. Difficulty in pointing on the steps and repeatedly hitting the VR controller button for teleport makes them tired, resembling the tiredness and occasional boredom in hiking. When they finally reach the top of the mountain, they feel relieved and happily enter a teleport sphere, and thus immediately relocate to another mountain top.

In the other mountain, the user finally sees the falling snowflakes and try to catch some. They look around and confirm there is no other person in the vast nature, same as the description in the book. Amid the lack of vivid or warm colours, and accompanied by the sound of strong and chilly wind, they feel so lonely and cold. They will try to climb down the mountain as fast as possible so as to reach the ground.

On the way of descending, sooner or later than reading a specific book, they spot a river and a raft, naturally believing that someone is over there on the raft. Although the raft is so distant and the man is completely covered by straw quilt that he is barely distinguishable, the user will still feel excited.

The user continues with descending the mountain, with a lighter heart. After the middle of the mountain, they enter a teleport sphere and get directly teleported to the foot of the mountain, which leads them to a flatland. They can freely wander around the terrain, but they have a strong urge to reach the riverbank to get closer to the old man

---

[6] For simplicity, neutral pronoun "they" is used in this subsection to refer to the single user. Actual gender of user was not expected to vary the experience and was not a factor in design consideration.

on the raft even though he did not notice the little user in a thousand mountains. They discover new books on the ground as they spot the old man again. They wave and say "hello" to the old man, but the old man does not respond. As indicated by the book, they are still too far apart from each other.

The user can only enter the teleport sphere right next to a book, and get relocated to the other side of the river. There, the user may or may not see the old man again. Whichever way, waving or shouting cannot get a response. With some exploration around the other riverbank, the user will find the last book. They are told by the book that they can "only continue to hike alone" while the old man goes on "fishing on his own". Yet, the user does not feel frustrated since the old man fishing in chilly snow equates to a refreshing sign of life and resilience, thus passing strength to the user. They resonate with the last line of the book: "We were alone, and we were chilling". They enter the other teleport sphere on this riverbank, which leads the user back to the starting point of this VR. As we all know, "start" and "end" are dual concept.

Now, the user may want to re-experience the VR just for the ambience, for re-reading some books to strengthen understanding of the poem, or find out some books that they missed during the journey. Otherwise, the re-entry to the starting zone marks the end of this VR experience.

3.2 Pilot Test

The pilot test of this VR is similar to the beta testing stage of software engineering, involving testing and bug-fixing/finetuning. Beta testing is more an integrated and on-going part of software design and development than scientific research of users' feedback, but can still effectively serve as evaluation of the design. The three beta testers are external parties with a background in computer science and rich experience in VR. They are all native Germans, have very good knowledge of English but had no prior knowledge of Chinese languages or Tang poems. Prior to entry into VR, they were only told to read some text in the VR. The researcher closely observed each tester' reaction when they were in the VR and asked them for feedback after they quit the VR. The project was then refined (where feasible within limited time) after each tester gave their feedback so that the next tester could possibly have a relatively optimized experience and provide feedback for further improvements.

Two of the three beta testers were very positive towards the VR experience. Initially there was some glitch with the snow particle system and therefore the first tester could not see the snow, but he could accurately give the keywords of the ambience of the poem, which is expression of silence and solitude. He was very immersed and waved to the old man on the raft before he would be hinted by a specific book "Sentence 4.1" (see Appendix). He was also positive regarding the overall VR design, locomotion and interactions. The second tester unfortunately faced an unexpected glitch of the system, where frames per second (FPS) was abnormally low, causing great discomfort. He also expressed dissatisfaction regarding the performance and the weight of the headset. Although he quit the VR early, he could tell that the VR experience was designed to let the users "observe the natural environment" and compared it to an existing VR creation approach "walking simulator". The third user was highly satisfied with the overall experience and explicitly commented that the VR experience could well achieve the project goal. Overall, the first and the last testers were satisfied with the sound effect and the "very nice scenery". The falling snowflakes were described as "astonishing". The positive feedback confirmed success of the design. The first and the last testers each in only around 15 min could accurately grasp the poem's essence, which is exactly the design intention. The design was therefore determined to be successful.

It Is noteworthy that the second tester quit the VR early, partially due to discomfort and partially due to boredom. In contrast to common standard, such early quit is not a sign of failure of the design. Firstly, boredom is an expected feeling of user in this VR. Secondly, the ambience of poems, by its nature, are not expected to be resonated and appreciated by every reader. It is fine if a reader opts to put down a poem that is unpleasant to them. The same principle applies for a VR that presents a poem.

Some may be reserved about the validity of the first tester due to the system glitch. However, the reason that test subjects are usually invalidated upon presence of systems glitches is because glitches are expected to hamper an experience. While the first tester could still accurately and quickly grasp the poem's essence, it is unreasonable to classify the test with the first tester as a failure. Instead, it means that falling snowflakes is not a necessary condition for the first tester to feel the coldness and solitude in the VR.

3.3   The Design Methodology

The methodology formulated is expressing a Tang poem via storytelling in English and designing spatial experience in VR, but one may reasonably deduce that it is transferrable to poems of any languages and formats, plus potentially to other genres of literature.

Same as every design, first and most important of all, design intention of the VR must be established and its top priority be declared to all participating designers and developers (the team). The design intention of the VR in this study, i.e. expressing the ambience of the poem, is expected to be feasible and applicable for presenting any Tang poem in VR. Considering its importance for enhancing reader's comprehension of the whole poem, it is recommended to be the central design intention. Other design intentions, e.g. expression of the precise meaning of every character (or word in non-Chinese languages), assisting learning of Cantonese or Classical Chinese (or other languages in case of non-Chinese poems), etc., can also be feasible and desirable, in parallel or not with the first intention. Whichever case, the leading designer should determine the priorities between potentially conflicting design intentions early to minimize internal disputes and/or waste of development efforts.

Then, adapting the poem into a derivative story is a key step to overcome the linguistic and literary barriers of a poem. Writing the story in a relatively universal language like English (or the native language of a target user group) is also crucial when the users may not be proficient in the original language of the poem. Identification of the ambience as well as the key components of the poem and their relationships with the central emotion (or idea) of the poem is a pre-requisite. Setting the point of view to a role that the users had some experience in reality helps them immersed into the plot better and therefore follow and comprehend the plot easier. Good and mixed use of storytelling techniques in narrative writing, which have been studied extensively across various culture, is definitely beneficial. A well narrated story will positively influence the quality of the spatial experience in the VR, which is based on the story.

As stated in Subsect. 2.7, although augmentation with Cantonese pronunciation of the original poem was not included in this VR for alignment with the poem's ambience, it has the potential to enhance comprehension of a Tang poem's rhythm and emotions. In future designs of VR for a poem, the designer may verify this recommendation by including pronunciation of the original language of the poem that is synchronized with the display of the corresponding text.

The theoretically infinite space of VR allows realization of any scenes in the past and/or in another geographical location, where users may feel immersed and present in the poem/story. Suitably placed and expressive components as well as meticulously designed interactions (or no interaction) enhance the user's perception of immersion and presence. Together they help users overcome the cultural, temporal and geographical barriers of a poem. Having that said, conscious consideration of the three pillars of VR is not necessary in the design process. They come more naturally when the designer is capable of creating a holistic design, meaning all scales and all aspects of the VR must be considered thoroughly for making every design decision, same as a good practice in architectural design. If one takes the VR design as scientific research and insists to focus on one or a few specific parameters, a good design will not be formed.

Spatial experience is a "language" more universal than spoken/written language although the experience may vary with individuals' personalities and backgrounds. The architecture in our reality shows that well-designed spatial experience has a stronger retaining effect than simply reading text, listening to the pronunciation or music, or watching a performance. Inclusion of a good spatial designer, preferably as the leading designer, is thus critical for a successful spatial experience design for the VR. As shown by this project, it is unrealistic to expect designers without sufficient relevant experience or developers to fully understand what spatial experience is and have sufficient spatial sense to design a spatial experience holistically. Contrary to architectural design traditions, it is unnecessary to consciously take aesthetics into account in the VR design. Actually, aesthetics should give way in case it conflicts with the design intention(s).

Although most traditional cinematographic skills are not directly applicable in VR, mastery of those skills indirectly facilitates design of VR for storytelling due to a good awareness of the relevant parameters. Implicit control of transition and duration of the experience should be adopted, e.g. by deliberately making a certain part so dull that it expels user away, by creating suspense to induce user forward, by placing appealing/interactive objects to direct user, etc. Limiting locomotable zones is necessary to reduce unexpected user actions (as user's interests can go beyond designer's prediction and no human can finish design for an unbounded space).

Classic designer-developer conflicts can be effectively solved when designers possess the technical skills for development. The efforts for communication, which is potentially fruitless, can then be used more efficiently for development, ultimately improving the design. Designers insist in prioritizing design intentions will no longer be annoying to developers as developers know designers fully share their concerns. Similarly, communication barrier between writers (specialist in texts) and designers (specialist in visuals) is dissolved when one person can perform both roles. In any case, technical constraints of the accessible hardware and the existing VR technology cannot be disregarded as they may render a non-functioning VR.

While the pilot test showed that presenting a Tang poem via storytelling in English with spatial experience in VR can break barriers in linguistics, literacy, culture, time and geography for comprehension of the Tang poem *Snow on the River*, an experiment of a larger scale is planned to further evaluate and investigate the VR's effectiveness and usability. However, number of important parameters in the design is too high for a comprehensive A/B testing for user experience research. Eye-tracking in VR is expected to be more efficient in finding out weaknesses of the design, if any.

It is visioned that promotion of the formulated design methodology and dissemination of the VR thereof produced on various VR application stores will foster understanding of Classical Chinese poems among the global population, thus revitalizing the ancient language and its texts, contributing to preservation of cultural heritage.

Some may suggest creation of a serious VR game for reading a Classical Chinese poem. This approach sounds appealing but is likely to destroy the ambience of a poem, unless the poem is a playful one or its contents is related to some games. Decision should be made carefully depending on the target users' primary goal of reading the poem. A serious game can be helpful in "learning" a poem, but learning is not always the major goal of reading. There is a common misconception that all VR are games, especially when VR are usually developed by existing "game engines" and distributed by game platforms. However, poetry and reading in VR do not necessarily involve a set of rules to follow and target(s) to meet, while gaming does. If the designers and developers hold the misconception, they can easily deviate from a proper track for design and development of VR for poetry and reading.

Most of the factors to be dealt with in VR design are not parameters with only a few possible values. This contributes to a widely-spread saying in design disciplines: "the work is never finished". Designers may be tempted to make slight adjustments here and there, but a schedule for different design stages should be defined early and be stuck with to ensure sufficient time for debugging and finetuning after user testing. This sounds like common sense, but VR is multimodal, making its development more complicated than other types of software development and a slight change in one parameter can produce a chain effect. More time should therefore be scheduled for every stage of VR development.

4   Conclusion, Limitations and Outlook

A holistic design of VR was created by integrating storytelling skills in novels and cinematography as well as spatial design skills in architecture to enhance reader's comprehension of the Tang poem *Snow on the River* through spatial experience in the VR. A reproducible methodology was deduced to outline how designers and developers may produce a VR for presentation of a Tang poem via storytelling in English with spatial experience. While the pilot test showed that this VR can break linguistic, literate, cultural, temporal and geographical barriers for comprehension for Germans, a larger scale experiment is under planning to quantitatively evaluate the VR's effectiveness and usability. Although quantitative evaluation is considered essential by many scientists, its necessity actually depends on individual research. For design through research, the deduced methodology stands with a successful artefact. Verification of applicability of the methodology will be convincing only if some other VR designers/developers follow it to create VR experience, regardless for the same poem, other Tang poems, other types of poems in Classical Chinese, poems in other languages, or even other forms of literature. In addition, as literature review prior to the design process were deliberately limited, a more extensive literature review for comparison of the existing studies with the findings of this research will be helpful in evaluating the design process. Both directions may contribute to improvement of the formulated methodology.

The formulated methodology is of course not perfect. Theoretically, enabling readers to grasp a literary work's essence should enhance their comprehension of the original text and the language. Literally, all ideas can be expressed through storytelling. But for some poem that is dedicated to record abstract thoughts, we can imagine that deriving a story will be highly challenging. Moreover, the methodology requires formation of a team of writer and spatial designer with Classical Chinese literacy, as well as VR developer. While acquisition of talent for any one of these three positions is not easy in today's labour market, it is still possible. However, the feasibility of finding a single person who can perform multiple roles may be low.

The major obstacle of the research on this topic is availability of resources. Finding researchers interested in this uncommon topic for collaboration is not yet successful. Hopefully publication of this paper will help. Recruiting a sufficient number of experiment participants who are Chinese speakers, especially Cantonese speakers, in Germany as a control group or target group is not less challenging. Since VR equipment and the computer system are influential to the performance of VR, it is not easy to hold experiments with equal conditions in different cities to adapt to subjects.

It is worth noting that after the pilot test of this VR experience was conducted, a richly augmented reading room was seen in a literary exhibition *13 Morgen* [47], which involved reading of some stories and poems in a designed space. The exhibition offered more modalities of sensory experience, e.g. texture from fabric and temperature from materials, than VR technologies that are currently readily accessible for the public. Nevertheless, compared with a VR application, the reach of such type of in-person exhibitions is relatively limited since digital dissemination is impossible without sacrificing some modalities, and their reproduction in another venue is much more costly in terms of both time and resources.

More recently, remarkable progress for VR topics related to this research has been noticed. VR was proved useful in enhancement of learning by reading, e.g. *I-Ulysses* [48] and preservation of cultural heritage, e.g. *Mingshan Temple: A Digital Tour* [49]. On the topic of poetry in VR, there are fewer research and artefacts, but not rare, e.g. *A Virtual Poem* [50], performance by hip-hop poets [51],[7] a video authoring tool for poetry appreciation [52], poetry writing via VR game [53] and methods for expression of ancient Chinese poems in VR proposed by Li & Hao [54]. It is expected that a more extensive literature review with a comparison against the results and findings of this study may show research directions for the topic of poem reading in VR.

---

[7] Whether songs can be classified as poems is still controversial. If this is acceptable, classification will be confusing for many other genres of texts, including prose, which can sometimes also be poetic.

VR is, as mentioned, an emerging technology and is considered disruptive [55]. With the recent rapid and revolutionary development of technologies related to large language models (LLM), it is predictable that the role of artificial intelligence (AI), in particular natural language processing (NLP), will be vital in keeping the metaverse dynamic and absorbing. However, we cannot have a clear direction for NLP application development for reading/presenting poems or Classical Chinese in VR unless we know what constitutes a good design of these types of VR. Although this paper is far from a comprehensive study on this research topic, it contributes by suggesting a feasible design methodology via integration of cross disciplinary knowledge and skills.

As depicted in the first section, Tang poetry has its unique features. Traditional researcher or fans of Chinese poetry may find it unacceptable that those linguistic and artistic aspects are discarded for consumption of the poem *Snow of the River* in VR. However, one should be aware that languages, first and foremost, are tools of communication. Poems, or any other forms of literature, are still a subset of those tools regardless of their linguistic and artistic values. From the perspective of a writer, effective communication of the central idea to the reader is more important than any other goals. A piece of text has meaning only when some starts to read it and try to understand it. Besides, as good designers and artists know, a design or an artwork has to be selective in its focus. We can hardly present all the characteristics of Tang poetry in one work. This project therefore distinctively held on the central goal of language and put emphasis on presenting the common central message of typical Tang poems: the emotions that the poets intended to express. A Tang poet's emotion(s) are commonly entangled with the scene description in and the ambience of the poem.

Despite the researcher's choice in this study, there is no absolute "right"/"good" or "wrong"/"bad" regarding the selection of design focus. Design by nature should be versatile. Proposal of the design methodology in this paper does not imply that any single design methodology for a certain application can override all the other possibilities. After all, possibilities in design are infinite. Even a small variation in an apparently trivial parameter may give everyone a surprise. Future designers and researchers may consider exploring for feasible and innovative ways of presenting Tang poems in VR by utilizing those characteristics such that it will be more effective than pure text and other existing methods of augmentation. For example, to address ambiguity of meaning of a poem, a designer can create multiple versions of VR experiences for the same poem by offering options in some menu, by means of interactivity in the VR, or by randomization of parameter values in the VR.

Last but not least, this VR design has explored an underexplored sub-dimension revealed by the design space for digital augmentation of reading and is therefore considered "innovative" [1]. A deeper study of this VR with respect to the design space is planned to help fill in some current voids of the design space, including but not limited to specifying the sub-dimension of VR. Hopefully the new findings can then be generalized for some other dimensions.

Acknowledgments. Gratitude to the study programme Infotronic Systems Engineering of Rhine-Waal University of Applied Sciences (HSRW) for offering the course, the Intelligent Assistive Systems Research Group of HSRW for hardware support, Duc Huy Quang Nguyen for co-development of the VR project. Additional thanks to the voluntary interviewees and pilot test subjects. The author's response to reviews from three reviewers of LREC-COLING 2024 is incorporated into this paper. Publication and presentation of this paper are funded by the Faculty of Communication and Environment of HSRW.

Disclosure of Interests.   The author has no competing interests to declare that are relevant to the content of this article.

Appendix: Texts in the Books in the VR

Background

"Snow on the River" (江雪)is a classical Tang poem written by Liu Zhong Yuan (柳宗元)(773–819 AD, China).

In this VR experience, you can read its derivative story (from a hiker's perspective) in English, and feel its meaning and ambience from the VR environment.

Instruction 1 for New User

To read the poem, find and pick up books with your left controller.

To experience the poem, roam around via teleporting.

Instruction 2 for New User

When you enter the white "text-sphere",

you will be relocated to another environment to expand your experience of the poem.

Sentence 1.1

千山鳥飛絕，

In a freezing winter, I went exploring a mountain range on my own.

Sentence 1.2

千山鳥飛絕，

I climbed countless hills,

but have not seen any birds.

Sentence 2.1

萬徑人蹤滅。

I walked past many more trails,

but have not met any people.

Sentence 2.2

萬徑人蹤滅。

Among the falling snowflakes and chilly winds, everything was covered by monotonously white snow.

I felt so cold, tired, hungry and lonely.

I walked slower and slower…

Sentence 3.1

孤舟簑笠翁，

Somehow, I found I could overlook a running river.

I stopped to rest a little bit and enjoy the breath-taking scenery.

Sentence 3.2

孤舟簑笠翁，

All of a sudden, I spotted a lonely raft on the river.
There was an old man in straw quilts sitting on the raft.

Sentence 4.1

獨釣寒江雪。

He was alone fishing the snowflakes in the chilly wind.
I felt I am no longer alone and waved to him.

Sentence 4.2

獨釣寒江雪。

But we were too distant from each other.
He could not notice me at all.

Sentence 4.3

獨釣寒江雪。

I could only continue to hike alone,
and he went on fishing on his own.
We were alone, and we were chilling.

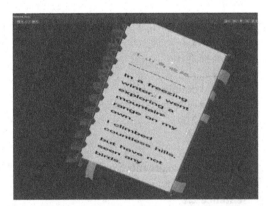

Fig. 5. Screenshots from Unity showing the cover of the first book "Background" (left) and testing of display of Sentence 1 of the original poem in Classical Chinese (in Traditional Chinese characters and font type *DFKai-SB*) together with the derivative story in English (right) in the VR. In the final design, Sentence 1 was split into Sentence 1.1 and Sentence 1.2, which are displayed separately in two successive books.

References

1. Ribeiro, P., Müller, W., Iurgel, I., Ressel, C., Ching, C.: A design space for digital augmentation of reading. In: Stephanidis, C., Antona, M., Ntoa, S., Salvendy, G. (eds.) HCII 2023. CCIS, vol. 1957, pp. 200–208. Springer, Cham (2024). https://doi.org/10.1007/978-3-031-49212-9_27

2. Cheng, S.-P., Tang, S.-W.: Cantonese. In: The Routledge Encyclopedia of the Chinese Language, pp. 18–34. Routledge, London (2016)

3. Yin, J.J.: Chinese characters. In: The Routledge Encyclopedia of the Chinese Language, pp. 51–63. Routledge, London (2016)

4. Xing, J.Z.: Teaching and Learning Chinese as a Foreign Language: A Pedagogical Grammar. Hong Kong University Press, Hong Kong (2006)

5. Li, C.W.: Classical Chinese. In: The Routledge Encyclopedia of the Chinese Language, pp. 408–419. Routledge, London (2016)

6. Feng, S.: Modern Chinese: written Chinese. In: The Routledge Encyclopedia of the Chinese Language, pp. 645–663. Routledge, London (2016)

7. Preface: The Design Cluster. MIT Press, Cambridge (2003)

8. Bin Shamsul Amri, I.: Probing burn-out while burned-out: An exploration into combining autoethnography and prototyping design probes as a burned-out designer (2022). https://aaltodoc.aalto.fi:443/handle/123456789/119261

9. Doloriert, C., Sambrook, S.: Ethical confessions of the "I" of autoethnography: the student's dilemma. Qual. Res. Organ. Manag. Int. J. **4**, 27–45 (2009). https://doi.org/10.1108/17465640910951435

10. van Dijk, T.A.: Discourse and Literature: New Approaches to the Analysis of Literary Genres. John Benjamins Publishing Company, Amsterdam (1985)

11. Yaron, I.: What is a "difficult poem"? towards a definition. J. Lit. Semant. **37**, 129–150 (2008). https://doi.org/10.1515/jlse.2008.008

12. Peyraube, A.: Ancient Chinese. In: The Routledge Encyclopedia of the Chinese Language, pp. 1–17. Routledge, London (2016)

13. Dong, H.: A History of the Chinese Language. Routledge, London (2020)

14. Chappell, H., Lan, L.: Mandarin and other Sinitic languages. In: The Routledge Encyclopedia of the Chinese Language, pp. 605–628. Routledge, London (2016)

15. Cheng, S.-P., Tang, S.-W.: Cantonese romanization. In: The Routledge Encyclopedia of the Chinese Language, pp. 35–50. Routledge, London (2016)

16. Wang, W.S.-Y.: Chinese linguistics. In: The Routledge Encyclopedia of the Chinese Language, pp. 152–183. Routledge, London (2016)

17. Wong4 黃, Sek3Ling4 錫凌: [A Chinese syllabary pronounced according to the dialect of Canton] 粵音韻彙: 廣州標準音之研究Jyut6Jam1Wan6Wui6 : Gwong2Zau1Biu1Zeon2Jam1Zi1Yin4Gau3. Chung Hwa Book Co. (H.K.) Ltd.中華書局香港有限公司, Hong Kong (1941)

18. Shane, J.W.: Hermeneutics and the meaning of understanding. In: Theoretical Frameworks for Research in Chemistry/Science Education, pp. 108–121 (2007)

19. Sou1 蘇, Syut3Lam4 雪林: [Conspectus of Tang Poetry] 唐詩概論 Tong4Si1Koi3Leon6. The Commercial Press, Shanghai (1933)

20. Zoeng1 章, Sip3 燮: [Comments on Three Hundred Tang Poems] 唐詩三百首注疏 Tong4Si1Saam1Baak3Sau2Zyu3So1. Sou3Jip6Saan1Fong4 掃葉山房, Shanghai (1913)

21. Song, Y.: Chinese couplet generation with syntactic information. In: Proceedings of the 29th International Conference on Computational Linguistics, pp. 6436–6446. International Committee on Computational Linguistics, Gyeongju (2022)

22. Lu, J.: Stylistic-Register Grammar and Register Contrasts among Old-style Poetry and the Regulated of Tang 語體語法與唐代古、律詩體的語體對立 (2021). https://repository.lib. cuhk.edu.hk/en/item/cuhk-3121911

23. Feng, S.: Poetic prosody. In: The Routledge Encyclopedia of the Chinese Language, pp. 664– 684. Routledge, London (2016)

24. Clementi Secondary School Chinese Language Education Study Group 金文泰中學中 文科教學研究小組: [A Brief Discussion on the Teaching of Tang Poetry] 淺談唐詩教 學Cin2Taam4Tong4Si1Gaau3Hok6. [Chinese Communications] 中文通訊 (1981)

25. Gam1 金, Daat6Hoi2 達凱: [Ideology and Artistry in Tang Poetry] 唐詩的思想性與藝術 性 Tong4Si1Koi3Leon6. [Democratic Commentary] 民主評論 Man4Zyu2Ping4Leon6. 8, 11–14 (1957)

26. Wong4 黃, Fung6Ci4 鳳池: [Eight Types of Painting Albums for Tang Poems] 唐詩畫譜 : 八種Tong4Si1Waa2Pou2 : Baat3Zung2. Zaap6Ngaa5Zaai1 : Cing1Kui2Zaai1 集雅齋 : 清 繪齋, China (1620)

27. National Taiwan University 國立臺灣大學: [Full Text of Three Hundred Tang Poems] 唐 詩三百首全文 Tong4Si1Saam1Baak3Sau2Cyun4Man4. http://cls.lib.ntu.edu.tw/300/ALL/ ALLFRAME.htm

28. Mütterlein, J.: The three pillars of virtual reality? Investigating the roles of immersion, presence, and interactivity (2018)

29. Sorensen, M.S.: Active virtual reality gaming: a content analysis and case study (2023). https://scholarworks.calstate.edu/downloads/9g54xq84c

30. Ribeiro, P., Sylla, C., Iurgel, I., Müller, W., Ressel, C.: STREEN – designing smart environments for story reading with children (2017)

31. Maher, M.: The Best VR Movies (So Far) Ranked (2022). https://www.premiumbeat.com/ blog/the-best-vr-movies/

32. Gloomy Eyes - AtlasV award winning VR experience, narrated by Colin Farrell. 3DAR, Atlas V (2020)

33. Atlas V: Gloomy Eyes - Atlas V. https://atlasv.io/projects/gloomy-eyes/

34. Pérez Valero, V.J. (ed.): "Meanwhile…" multiplicity of plots in VR experiences. In: Unusual Shapes, Fantasy & Horror, pp. 123–135. Ediciones Universidad de Salamanca (2023). https:// doi.org/10.14201/0AQ0352

35. Marañes, C., Gutierrez, D., Serrano, A.: Towards assisting the decision-making process for content creators in cinematic virtual reality through the analysis of movie cuts and their influence on viewers' behavior. Int. Trans. Oper. Res. **30**, 1245–1262 (2023). https://doi.org/ 10.1111/itor.13106

36. Khalid, O., Srinivasan, P.: Smells like teen spirit: an exploration of sensorial style in literary genres. In: Proceedings of the 29th International Conference on Computational Linguistics, pp. 55–64. International Committee on Computational Linguistics, Gyeongju (2022)

37. Angulo, A.: Rediscovering virtual reality in the education of architectural design: the immersive simulation of spatial experiences. Ambiances. Environnement sensible, architecture et espace urbain. (2015). https://doi.org/10.4000/ambiances.594

38. Schwarzer, M.: The Extremes of Spatial Experience. AA Files. 67–73 (2008)

39. Mei, X., Pang, L.: Diagrams of spatial experience based on mathematical models. Nexus Netw. J. **25**, 407–414 (2023). https://doi.org/10.1007/s00004-023-00675-7

40. Dolins, F.L., Mitchell, R.W. eds: Spatial cognition, spatial perception: mapping the self and space. Cambridge University Press, Cambridge, UK ; New York (2010)

41. Tien, Y.-C., Chang, T.-W., Tsai, S.-T.: Automated tools recommendation system for computing workshops. In: HCI International 2023 Posters, pp. 154–161. Springer, Cham (2023)

42. Sun, Y.: Tang Poems - English Translation. https://musicated.com/syh/TangPoems.htm#Liu Zongyuan01

43. Comrie, B., Haspelmath, M., Bick, B.: The Leipzig Glossing Rules: conventions for interlinear morpheme-by-morpheme glosses (2015). https://www.eva.mpg.de/lingua/pdf/Glossing-Rules.pdf

44. The Max Planck Institute for the History of Science: CHMap. https://chmap.mpiwg-berlin.mpg.de/lgtu-new/map.html

45. ProAssets: Free Snow Mountain | 3D Landscapes | Unity Asset Store (2016). https://assetstore.unity.com/packages/3d/environments/landscapes/free-snow-mountain-63002

46. lumino: Nature Sound FX | Audio Sound FX | Unity Asset Store (2021). https://assetstore.unity.com/packages/audio/sound-fx/nature-sound-fx-180413

47. Buch, J., Mantwill, T.: 13 Morgen 13 Mornings (2023)

48. Colreavy-Donnelly, S., O'Connor, S., Homapour, E.: I-Ulysses: a technical report. Entertain. Comput. 32, 100321 (2019). https://doi.org/10.1016/j.entcom.2019.100321

49. Chen, W.W.: Virtual platforms for the Asian religious deities in the era of pandemic. In: Mori, H., Asahi, Y., Coman, A., Vasilache, S., Rauterberg, M. (eds.) HCII 2023. LNCS, vol. 14056, pp. 239–253. Springer, Cham (2023). https://doi.org/10.1007/978-3-031-48044-7_18

50. Hartman, D.E., Brock, T.: Extracts from a virtual poem: extending classroom reality? SIGGRAPH Comput. Graph. 31, 75–77 (1997). https://doi.org/10.1145/262171.262269

51. Benford, S., Reynard, G., Greenhalgh, C., Snowdon, D., Bullock, A.: A poetry performance in a collaborative virtual environment. IEEE Comput. Graphics Appl. 20, 66–75 (2000). https://doi.org/10.1109/38.844374

52. Zhao, Z., Ma, X.: ShadowPlay2.5D: a 360-degree video authoring tool for immersive appreciation of Classical Chinese poetry. J. Comput. Cult. Herit. 13, 5:1–5:20 (2020). https://doi.org/10.1145/3352590

53. Choi, J.F.: The effects of immersive learning for poetry writing via a VR GAME for generation Z students' creativity: focusing on "Forum VR: artist of Oz." Rob. AI Ethics 6, 33–44 (2021)

54. Li, K., Hao, W.: Poetic expression by virtual reality technology. Adv. Eng. Technol. Res. 7, 7–13 (2023). https://doi.org/10.56028/aetr.7.1.7.2023

55. Rosedale, P.: Virtual reality: the next disruptor: a new kind of worldwide communication. IEEE Consum. Electron. Maga. 6, 48–50 (2017). https://doi.org/10.1109/MCE.2016.2614416

Conceptualizing Collaborative Team Learning in XR for Medical Education and Training

Chris Hartman[1], Inki Kim[2(✉)], and Jeeheon Ryu[3]

[1] GigXR, Inc., Los Angeles, CA 90405, USA
chris.hartman@gigxr.com
[2] University of Illinois Urbana-Champaign, Champaign, IL 61801, USA
inkikim@illinois.edu
[3] Chonnam National University, Gwangju 61186, South Korea

Abstract. Rapid advancement of extended reality (XR) poses new challenges in the design and implementation of technologies, methods, and curriculums for medical training and education. Particularly, a paucity of research lies in XR-based learning approach to a group of learners: How can we ensure that collaborative team experiences in simulation will transfer to actual patient care? In this regard, we aim to conceptualize new challenges of team learning in XR for next-generation medical education. Contrary to part-task simulation, teamwork involves complex group dynamics for aggregated performance and thus a referent world-model essential for building simulation is not simple to derive. Imagine, for example, the many possible ways that a group of physicians and nurses may collaborate to treat a severely asthmatic patient in diverse clinical settings. To this end, we adopted the abstraction hierarchy to conceptualize an array of issues related to complex team interactions in XR-based professional education and training. As results of this representation, we identified the complex means-end relationships and couplings that exist among goals, functional interactions, and technological elements that altogether allow for team collaboration in XR. Discussions focused on key challenges and frictions within this web of interdependence.

Keywords: XR simulation · team-based collaborative learning · medical training · work domain analysis · abstraction hierarchy

1 Introduction

1.1 XR in Professional Training

The ability to create immersive professional education and on-the-job training has substantially advanced through the adaption of virtual reality (VR), augmented reality (AR), and mixed reality (MR), or extended reality (XR) as an all-encompassing technology, in various learning contexts. XR-based learning applications may potentially enhance diverse competencies, including *cognitive* skills such as memory, reasoning, and spatial abilities, *physical* skills such as psychomotor, motor, and sensorimotor skills, or *team-based* skills such as communication and coordination. In practice though, those skills

© The Author(s), under exclusive license to Springer Nature Switzerland AG 2024
J. Y. C. Chen and G. Fragomeni (Eds.): HCII 2024, LNCS 14708, pp. 44–63, 2024.
https://doi.org/10.1007/978-3-031-61047-9_3

are not consistently defined, taught, assessed, or followed up on to check if they are transferred to real-world competencies [1]. An extensive, domain-wide review of VR-based professional training [2] shows highly disproportionate and unbalanced placement of learning goals; predominantly focusing on cognitive skills including procedural and spatial knowledge acquisition, over physical skills. On this comparative scale, the instances of training for team-based skills are even fewer.

In our domain of medical education and training, this lack of balance in learning goals, as well as limited scope in learning priorities, persist. The review on medical VR training [2] identifies that clinical competencies in surgical skills (e.g., [3]) or nursing care [4] (e.g., [5]), professional knowledge of surgical procedures, safety awareness, and compliance (e.g., [6]) are the most common priorities. The review of medical AR/MR training [7] also identifies that most applications focus on improving surgical skills, and knowledge of anatomy or anesthetic procedures, with limited emphases on team-based skills.

In this paper, we differentiate between VR, AR and MR based on the differences in user experience and their relationship to learning goals and priorities, not in relation to the technical capabilities of the utilized hardware. As such we consider a VR experience to be one where the users' entire field of view is occupied by a virtual environment, thus occluding the physical world, an AR experience to be where virtual objects are placed in front of the users view of the physical world, and MR experience where virtual experiences are integrated into the physical world. Specifically in relation to MR based immersion for multi-user experiences that are co-located, participants would view and interact with virtual objects in the same real-world location, thus supporting a fully integrated virtual and physical environment, allowing for a shared "sense of presence" despite differences in physical space.

1.2 Collaborative Team-Based Learning

One grand challenge in XR-based professional training is, particularly, to actualize the concept of *collaborative* team activities and learning into justifiable, reproducible, and transferrable outcomes in clinical settings. Compared to single-user training scenarios, collaborative concepts introduce substantial degrees of complexity, and thus open new challenges and opportunities [8]. Recently, multi-user collaboration has been implemented in a growing number of XR applications in medicine, engineering, and education [9]. The volume of new applications inspired by rapidly emerging XR technologies, however, is not sufficiently backed up by solid theoretical foundations, nor best-practice evidence.

In fact, the consequences of XR-based training for *collaborative learning* are not fully understood, because the quality of group interactions and communication is subject to the choice of technology and XR design elements. The nature of the collaborative task (for example, do all team members perform their own tasks under (de)centralized control, and collaboration takes place at a single location in a time-synchronized manner, or otherwise?) also affects the outcome of learning gains. As such, the outcomes may have limited generalization once the collaborative task is modified under a slightly different learning context. In other words, changes in the roles or dynamics of the team will not guarantee the equivalent learning outcomes as before. Besides, learning gains in VR cannot easily translate to the equivalent outcomes in AR or MR, because VR applications replace the team's reality with a complete virtual environment (constituting a "fully immersive" technology [10]), whereas AR or MR applications must devise their own way to overlay virtual objects and integrate multi-user interactions in a shared space context [9]. For a team of remote learners in AR-based collaboration, for example, how virtual objects and remote interactions are presented may depend on the individual users' own space, and thus the level of immersion may vary substantially. Immersive collaboration in VR, on the other hand, is relatively less affected by whether the learners are co-located or remote.

Therefore, for comprehensive examination of XR-based team collaboration in the context of professional education and training, it is necessary to holistically investigate [11], 1) learning context, materials, assessment, and curriculum building, 2) XR User Interface elements, use-case scenarios, and hardware (such as head-mounted display [HMD] including AR/VR headsets and smart glasses [12], mobile device, display monitor, whole-body projection), 3) the XR application domains and domain-specific requirements, and 4) underlying learning theories. Encompassing those four areas, the current work aims to provide a comprehensive map of issues, challenges, and key frictions in XR-based collaborative team learning. Key frictions within this web of interdependence particularly focused on appropriate management of shared scenarios/devices/apps, and objective methods to track, measure, and infer learning gains at both individual and team levels. The proposed representation outcomes and discussions will contribute to sustainable education in XR.

2 Related Works

2.1 VR and Team-Based Learning

Current VR technologies used for team-based learning do not necessarily support all instructional activities and teaching needs. An interview/workshop of nine instructors and nine students who currently use VR in higher education across sixteen different colleges revealed that no one-size-fits-all technology can possibly satisfy a large breadth of stakeholders and fulfill their specific goals throughout XR systems design, contents creation, course development, delivery, and management, and learning assessment [13].

Immediate issues while adopting VR for training, either for an individual or for a team, may arise due to the limitations of technology, such as battery life, image resolution, and tracking issues. Predominantly, technology and cost are the two inter-related constraining factors [14]. Most consumer-grade VR hardware (particularly HMDs) is designed for gaming and entertainment, and thus application to professional training forces substantial modification to the learning program. For example, current manufacturers recommend frequent breaks while using HMDs to avoid discomfort, which keeps from the implementation of long, non-interrupted scenarios [2]. Besides, incompatibilities among different VR hardware and software components make it more difficult to provide uniform learning experiences to the students.

Further, the empirical study of VR use in higher education identified *equity* concerns as a fundamental barrier to its broader adoption [13]. Inequity in VR use potentially originates from the set of demographic characteristics, including gender [15], personal ability, economic status, age, and ethnicity [16]. For example, students who are physically disabled, feel uncomfortable with VR HMDs due to severe cybersickness [17], or those who cannot afford the potential cost of HMDs, are less likely to experience the benefits of XR education.

To address inequality, enhancing accessibility is desired across all aspects of learning. *Inclusive design* principles for equity are crucial here; XR technologies must consider the possible diversity of user characteristics, including students having physical/cognitive disabilities or other general accessibility issues; and learning programs must carefully design the educational contexts that mitigate potential discomfort of students [13].

Collaborative team-based learning in VR brings a new layer of challenges to professional education and training. Students could work individually in their own headsets, but it is hard to facilitate collaboration that promotes "meaningful" learning in the context of team performance [13]. Social Presence Theory [18] defines *social presence*, a special form of presence in virtual environments [19], as "the extent to which other beings also exist in the virtual environment". This sense of social presence explains how meaningful social experiences can be implemented in VR [20]. The processes through which social presence is activated, strengthened, and transformed into social experiences, may vary by different learning contexts. In general, the fidelity of other beings (e.g., avatar) [21] and the environment, as well as the authenticity of how the user interacts with those other beings and environment, are known determinants of social presence. In addition, diverse teaching strategies for instructors, such as switching between the omniscient perspective and a shared first-person view [22], and using collaborative scaffolding tools (e.g., sketching, presentation, object manipulation) [23], could facilitate effective collaboration.

Production of VR simulations is still expensive, although the rapid advancement of the hardware has made it relatively cheaper and easier to create flexible simulations [2]. Creation of learning contents and development of them into VR scenarios takes substantial cost, time, and commitment of an interdisciplinary team. For example, content creators who lack a technical background often have unrealistic assumptions and expectations about what VR can provide [20].

For broader adoption and integration of VR into traditional learning settings, it is important to create the inclusive, closed-loop processes that link content creation, deployment, and management [13]. Contrary to collaboration among students, this challenge necessitates back-end coordination among end-user developers, content creators, instructors, technicians, and technology managers. Common language, shared concepts, and tools to support mutual communication are useful to promote this back-end coordination [20].

2.2 AR/MR and Team-Based Learning

Earlier, augmented reality (AR) or mixed reality (MR) has demonstrated potential for hands-on learning thanks to its ability to stimulate *engagement* [24] and the sense of *immersion* [25] in a specific learning environment. For collaborative learning, evidence has further uncovered the benefits of using AR/MR over traditional methods. In the experimental study of 200 students enrolled in the course of climate change and energy use [26], those who used AR/MR technology for team-based learning expressed the benefits of understanding difficult concepts and facilitating a discussion. Besides, it is expected that AR/MR-based learning is beneficial to memory, conceptual understanding, reasoning, and critical thinking, and user satisfaction [24, 27], but evidence is still sparse.

On the downside, similar to VR, significant challenges in team-based learning arise with effectively forming a team [28], in which individual commitment to a collaborative effort is fully activated and workload is equitably distributed across all team members without having indifference or mediocrity shown by some. Two contradictory cultures, [26] between the one that values individual efforts and competitions, and the other that promotes collaboration and combining forces at an organizational level, fundamentally interferes with multidisciplinary team formation. Another impediment to effective teamwork is the vulnerability of team communication and interaction, of which the process could be easily influenced, deteriorated, or failed by any member of the team, technology, and contexts. An adoption of AR/MR technology in group behaviors were observed to bring substantial changes in the frequency, quantity, and quality of communication [29], which may, in turn, affect teamwork.

Evaluating the dynamics and performance of teamwork is another issue that lacks common consensus in terms of conceptual grounds, methods, and tools. A viable approach in practice [26] is to apply self-evaluation and co-evaluation schemes among the team members, along with objective criteria that are translated into observable team behaviors in the multiple aspects of participation, communication, and team-dynamic regulation. Evaluation by humans (self, peers, or instructor) is simpler and intuitive, yet may not scale to a larger team size, more complex chains of interactions and communications, as well as asynchronized or remote collaboration contexts. Evaluation by machine, on the other hand, would require not only tracking/inference of individual learning activities and team-level dynamics, but the choice of scheme in learning contents design. More on this will be discussed in Sects. 4.4 and 5.1.

In addition, technological constraints and issues were observed in the use of AR/MR for collaborative learning. For instance, the empirical study [26] identified the need of students to spend more time using AR technology in order for their activities to mature into meaningful learning outcomes, but the actual duration of user activities within AR is significantly constrained by the capacities of hardware [7] (e.g., battery life, reliable sensing without drift, limited computing power, occlusion of the user's visual field of view, and poor ergonomics). Further, AR/MR technology could be detrimental to learning outcomes if team activities involve open-ended inquiry to examine information sources both from the real and virtual world, because visually-stimulating graphical information in AR/MR predominates visual attention of the individuals [30], and information from the real world could be relatively, glossed over [24].

Finally, the form factor of existing AR/MR HMD, including headsets and smart glasses, that partly occludes the other user's eyes and faces could possibly interfere with making eye contact or nonverbal gestures, limiting communication. Thanks to the rapid advancement in hardware technology, the form factor is growing smaller and lighter weight [12]. Regardless of this trend, the study of communication among mobile-based AR-user teams observed substantial reduction in the quantity of verbal communication, and concluded that it is (not the form factor but) the visual nature of AR itself that eliminated the need to use verbal communication to carry out team activities [29].

Research is needed to fully understand the negative and positive effects of AR/MR on team communication.

2.3 Groundworks on Collaborative Learning

Team-based learning (TBL) is a pedagogical paradigm intended to stimulate learning experiences through interactions among small groups of students. At the core of the TBL is collaborative learning (CL), for which "the work must not be done individually or divided among the group members to become merely the sum of isolated individual pieces that produce a very complex final product" [26]. Essential elements that accompany CL are cooperation, responsibility, communication, self-assessment, and teamwork. To put it differently, students solve complex problems together in teams that are formed and maintained through leadership, responsibility, trust, and communication. This teamwork provides opportunities for the team members to learn from each other, form shared understanding, and resolve conflicts.

In the context of XR-based learning, collaborative learning environment (CLE) refers to a virtual environment that stimulates students' engagement in a common task where each individual is accountable to each other [9]. From an interaction perspective, CLE is characterized by multi-user interactions in a single "shared" space context [31]. Multi-user interactions here serve to promote the sense of social presence [18] through the use of highly intuitive verbal and/or gesture interactions. Simultaneously, individual users in CLE are authorized to have independent control over their own viewpoint and interaction without necessarily engaging others in the same environment. Finally, the notion of shared context can be crystallized by using collaborative interface [32] that enables all individuals within CLE to observe the same virtual content in a consistent manner. In this regard, adapted from [33], CLE technology must support the implementation of social presence, independent control, and shared visibility, respectively.

3 Problem Mapping

Methodologically, the object of our discussion, i.e., collaborative team-based learning in XR, is itself a complex system, in the sense that technology, human resources, or knowledge alone cannot solve all the problems involved, necessitating the use of systems approach to represent and analyze related problems. To this end, we adopted the abstraction-decomposition mapping (or, the abstraction hierarchy) to describe complex team interactions for learning in an XR system [34]; its representation particularly helps analyze the hierarchical structure of cognitive work. One method generally practiced during the early phases of cognitive work analysis is the work domain analysis (WDA). WDA analyzes literature, design specifications, and interviews with subject matter experts to identify the purpose of a work domain, the values and priorities held by entities within the domain, the type of work being completed in the domain, and the technical functions fulfilled by the physical resources to satisfy the purpose of the domain [35]. As a part of WDA, the abstraction-decomposition space serves to provide a context-independent representation of the work domain to help evaluate how information from the physical resources of a domain achieves the goal of that domain [36]. This representation of the context-free, functional structure of a system provides a unique look into the range of possible activity within the system.

In our case, higher levels of abstraction will represent the domain-specific team-based learning in XR in terms of purposes and generalized functions, whereas lower levels represent the XR systems in terms of physical implementation. The level-wide conceptual items and functions were derived from the literature, as well as from subject matter experts in XR design and educational research in the author's team. Table 1 places general elements related to team-based learning onto the hierarchy.

Table 1. Elements of the abstraction hierarchy for team-based learning in medicine.

Domain Purpose	- Team-based skills - Physical skills, including psychomotor, motor, and sensorimotor skills - Cognitive skills, including clinical reasoning, memory, and spatial abilities	
Domain Values	*<Pursuit of Personal Excellence>* - Professional knowledge (e.g., of procedures and anatomy) - Clinical Competency - Conceptual Understanding - Critical Thinking	*<Pursuit of Organizational Excellence>* - Awareness of Organizational Initiatives (on safety, quality, and other organizational agenda) - Behavioral compliance - Teamwork (consisting of leadership, responsibility, trust, and conflicts resolution
	<Social Values of Learning> - Personalized learning - Collaborative learning - Generalizable learning outcomes - Sustainable education program - Equitable learning opportunities	*<Socio-Technical Constraints>* - Cost (of simulation development, deployment, and maintenance) - Access (to simulation tools and resources) - Tool-Specific Constraints (on people's behaviors, such as battery life)
Generalized (Work) Functions	*<User Perception/Experiences>* - Comfort/ Perceived Ease-of-Use - User Acceptance - Broader Adoption (across different user populations) - Flexible Simulation Experiences - User Engagement - User Satisfaction	*<Simulation-Building Functions>* - Using Standardized Terminology - Understanding XR Technology - Building XR Simulation/System - Resolving Compatibility Issues (in multi-device platform) - Building Collaborative Learning Environment (CLE) - Building Observable Performance Metrics (both for individuals and team)

(continued)

Table 1. (*continued*)

	<<Simulation Functions>> - Fidelity/Authenticity - Immersion - Presence - Social Presence (= shared sense of presence)	*<<Pedagogical Functions>>* - Learning Content Creation - Course Design/Delivery/Management - Coordination (among program providers, including content creators, XR developers, instructors, technicians, and technology managers)
	<<Team-Building Functions>> - Team Formation (including workload distribution, pairing team members with tools, commitment to team) - Information Gathering (from dispersed sources in virtual/physical environment) - Group Interaction/Communication (could differ by environment, device platforms, geographical location, and timing) - Teamwork Assessment (evaluation by instructor, self, peer group, or system) - Debriefing (for discussion and improvement)	
Technical Functions	- User Identification (such as registration, logging in, personal check-in,) - Displaying Virtual Objects - Interacting with Virtual Objects - Tracking User Interactions (such as visual gazes, hand gestures) - Composing Virtual Environment - Integrating Virtual and Physical Environments - Authorizing User Control (for customized view/interaction/CLE) - Accommodating Multi-User Interactions in a Shared Space - Accommodating Multi-User Communication (textual/verbal/gesture) - Providing a Shared Viewpoint as Collaborative Interface - Supporting Viewpoint Changes - Using Collaborative Scaffolding Tools (including sketching, presentation, object manipulation) - Using Virtual Guidance to Facilitate Teamwork - Building Personalized Learning Profile	
Resources	- XR Hardware (such as HMD, mobile device, display monitor) - Learning infrastructure (including XR systems) - Use-Case Scenarios - XR User-Interface Elements - Virtual Assets (including 3D objects and avatars) - Best Practices/ Clinical Standards	

For the abstraction-decomposition mapping, logical relationships should be identified, to link horizontally among the same-level items (i.e., couplings), as well as vertically through the abstraction hierarchy (i.e., means-end relationships). Figure 1 illustrates hierarchical relationships between purpose, value, and generalized functions, that were identified from the literature and case reports on team-based learning. For brevity, the concepts and functions that were not related to team-based skills, were not listed in the mapping. Note also that the connections between generalized functions and technical functions were not depicted for simplicity.

As results of this representation, we illustrated the complex means-end relationships and couplings that exist among goals, functional interactions, and technological elements that altogether allow for team collaboration in XR. Guided by this map, the next section elaborates on some of the key issues and friction points.

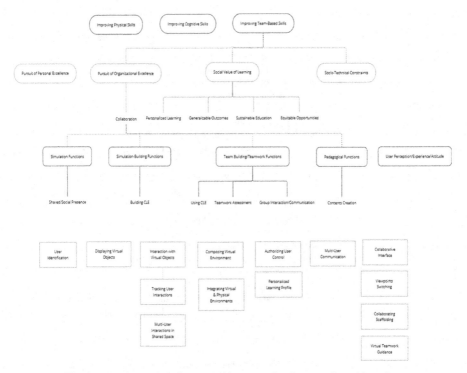

Fig. 1. The abstraction-decomposition mapping for team-based learning.

4   Key Issues and Friction Points

4.1   Multi-user XR Training in Medicine: Trends and Issues

As it was noted in Sect. 1, the great majority of XR training in medicine is concentrated on improving surgical skills and procedures [2, 7]. Successful surgical outcomes require not only technical skills of an individual surgeon, but coordinated teamwork of the surgeons, anesthesiologist, nurses, hospital staff, and clinical information systems. One area of recent attention for the related XR training is to improve as a team, "the cognitive skills to integrate and apply different types of knowledge, weigh evidence critically and reflect upon the process used to arrive at a diagnosis are central to clinical reasoning" [37].

Surveys report that the competencies of effective teamwork are often lacking in operation rooms (ORs) [38], and discrepancy exists in OR team members' views on appropriate team structure and importance of effective communication [39]. Effective XR simulation of multidisciplinary surgical teams can help training, as well as the identification of factors essential for overall team performance. Such simulations often require standardized scenarios, simulated equipment, a human actor or manikin for standardized patient, and a surgical team. The high cost of assembling such multi-factor simulations has resulted in a relatively lower number of successful training cases. For this reason, XR based medical simulation offers an opportunity to increase the adoption of similar training programs for healthcare training where cognitive skills, teamwork and communication are key learning goals.

The integrated clinical environment (ICE) in VR developed by Lockheed Martin Corporation (Oswego, NY) [40] was one such approach. The application of the ICE to the "loss of laparoscopic visualization" scenario, despite confirmed face validity, revealed the key problems, including limited simulation scope, too short duration, and less-than-usual workload of simulation session, which were altogether insufficient to yield meaningful learning outcomes. Those problems, again, attest to the need for a holistic view of XR application encompassing learning contexts and domain-specific requirements.

Clinical Skills Training at Scale. While multi-user experiences may be supported, a primary focus is preparing individuals for complex procedures in a safe space prior to practicing on equipment, or human subjects [41]. Developing physical and cognitive skills in XR is not separable from multi-user experiences. In a broader sense, multi-user experiences incorporate a collection of individual task skills, as well as their synergistic combinations. Current alternatives to using XR for clinical skills training, includes part-task training manikins, cadavers, or other physical equipment, which can be costly to purchase and maintain. For fidelity, XR simulation for individual skills requires high-precision reproduction of task and task environment including medical devices and equipment, as well as realistic patient conditions and the patient's behavioral and physiological reactions to the treatment; see Fig. 2 for a part-task XR scenario created by GigXR, Inc. In addition, administering these training scenarios in XR at scale, with a standardized method of assessment that does not rely on an instructor being present is an issue.

It has been generally agreed that contemporary nursing students and professionals at early stages of nursing careers lack sufficient opportunities to experience clinical procedures before they encounter actual patient cases [42]. Although there are limited applications, the use of XR to train with interactive and authentic learning contexts is well accepted among the nursing education community. A recent training application [43] further advocated the XR designs to be based on situational learning [44], which presumes professional skill learning is highly dependent on the specific contexts that the learner is situated in. Learning based on realistic situations is a plausible approach, but the learning effects are not guaranteed to be reproduced in different contexts, nor scaled up to broader situations; see Fig. 3 for an example created by GigXR, Inc.

Large Multi-user Emergency Training. A growing application area for XR concerns the improvement of safety awareness and emergency preparedness across diverse aspects

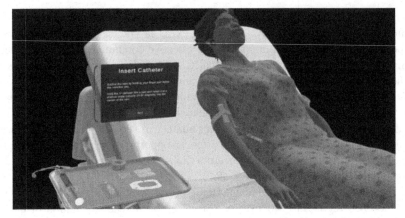

Fig. 2. A peripheral intravenous training simulation as an example of part-task training (Created by GigXR, Inc.)

Fig. 3. Multiple users attending to a virtual asthmatic patient in a mixed-reality simulation (Created by GigXR. Inc.)

of healthcare systems, first responders, government organizations and civil defense. Simulation scenarios are often characterized by a large number of stakeholders involved in the management of adverse events or crisis, which creates operational complexity in the chains of command and the coordination of activities (for example, see for [45] related projects). Many of these simulations occur outdoors, involve mass-casualty events, and require intensive use of physical simulation equipment. For these reasons, such simulations are well suited for the use of AR and MR technologies as participants may be moving physically over large areas, and may encounter multiple teams within the same simulation. Such simulations are highly dependent on advanced networks, including 5G/6G. The growth of this area of simulation has been hampered by the durability of headsets, constraints on network capacity and development of simulation software that can handle these elaborate and highly complex scenarios [46].

Furthermore, these simulations strain the already discussed issues inherent in multi-user clinical reasoning scenarios. XR-based multi-professional training for emergency management warrants a more complex and sophisticated theoretical framework that can help effectively decompose the overall activity of the team into a number of typical actions, operations, tools used, and feedback on own actions [47]. In general, the fidelity of actors, object, tools, community, roles, and outcomes are key to successful simulation development. The next subsection details out the key criteria useful to identify the learning context for simulation development.

4.2 Identification of Learning Context

One challenge in supporting collaborative learning in XR is to first identify the learning contexts and then determine the most appropriate design options that yield desirable learning outcomes specific to the context. The major criteria extracted from the literature, that can be used to identify learning contexts include:

Environment. Does the learning involve interaction with the user's own physical space (i.e., MR) or can the material be learned in a fully immersive virtual world? Alternatively, the asymmetric setting [48], where interaction and visualization are distinct for each user (i.e., one user interacts in VR and the other interacts in AR), can achieve better performance than the symmetric settings (i.e., AR or VR only), depending on the task characteristics. This asymmetric setting has technological considerations in common with the multi-device platform below.

Multi-device Platform. Is every member of the team equipped with a device with the same capabilities, or are the capabilities dissimilar on purpose? For example, some participants are using MR enabled HMDs while others are viewing the experience via a mobile device where interaction is more limited. It may be that collaborative team activities necessitate the use of different device platforms (e.g., HMD, mobile, desktop) and/or device specs (e.g., hand tracking vs. hand controller) to fulfill complementary teamwork [11]. In practice, the former question is often related to issues of inequality/accessibility, where the number of available headsets could limit the number of students who are able to join the team at the same time [49]. The latter use of multi-device platform could incur additional issues of resolving technical compatibility in device-to-device signal exchanges, as well as ensuring consistent presentation of learning contents.

Location. Are multi-users co-located, or remotely distributed across different geographical locations? The choice of interaction and communication methods may differ by team location, and thus affects performance [50].

Timing. Are collaboration activities fully synchronized to all participants, or is the collaboration asynchronous among teams working across different time-zones or working hours? The XR design to support asynchronous collaboration is an active research area [51]. The key design challenge for both synchronous and asynchronous interaction/communication in XR is ensuring a shared space where the interactions of each participant are visible to one another and understood consistently as a team. For example, if one's task performance is visually obstructed by some of the other team members, it could generate a perceptual discrepancy and affect team cognition.

Instructor vs. Virtual Guidance. Will the collaboration activities be facilitated by a trained instructor who serves as a guide and conducts assessment based on observation, or will the software provide the guidance and features necessary to ensure that the activities run smoothly, and support learning objectives. Some examples of virtual guidance include step by step guides; redirections if incorrect interventions occur; changes to the immersive content based on participant behavior; and assessment.

4.3 Connection to Personalized Learning

As indicated as the domain values in the abstraction hierarchy (Sect. 3), some aspects of collaborative team-based learning are linked to personalized learning. The enhanced capabilities of XR offer opportunities to flexibly present multisensory materials that consider individual differences in terms of personality types, learning preferences, and attitudes toward learning. Theoretically, more than 70 learning style models have been identified [52], including the Kolb's model, [53] which is well suited for describing experiential learning in teams. However, there is yet little evidence that links different learning styles to XR education [54]. The lack of evidence supporting personalized learning experience causes the design issues in collaborative XR.

To actualize personalized learning in the context of collaborative learning in XR, systems must be able to identify each individual user's role and contribution under teamwork flow. The systems can build a profile of collaborators' behaviors across learning activities and provide a mechanism for learners to present situated instructional feedback for each member's role. XR systems prompt individually customized feedback in terms of teamwork to embrace the collaborative learning environment (CLE). The learners in CLE can engage in the collaborative process by providing personalized feedback for their role. Further, the learners may choose to engage with the learning materials in the manner that interests them the most [54].

For implementation of personalized CLE, several design strategies can be used including personal check-in as part of the registration, as well as a personalized learning space (presented on a shared dashboard) that enables learners to manage their own learning progress. XR simulation creates learning progressions for both in terms of collaboration and personal contributions with considerations of how the person fits well to the collaborative work. In addition, online tracking of user interactions, such as eyes and hand gestures, may help determine the individual's primary information gathering preference, as a preliminary step to personalization. This tracking of an individual user's interactions also supports another value of collaborative learning via the generalized function of team assessment.

4.4 Strategies for Team Building and Performance Assessment

Within medicine and beyond, collaborative team-based learning (TBL) bears significance in education, business, and society. Building and maintaining team competencies is key to sustaining organizational success [55], and training for team competencies is a critical mission of higher education [56]. Even beyond the context of XR-based learning, pedagogical programs designed for team competencies in higher-educational settings, generally share the problem that participation in group activities is not alone sufficient to produce meaningful learning experiences. Free riders in the team could frustrate other team members, and thus undermine the team morale and performance. Conversely, the learners who were not fairly recognized for their contribution could be discouraged and lose motivation. TBL defined in the context of business performance, refers to the iterative process of reflection and action, strengthened by communication among team members, feedback, experimenting, and reflecting on errors [57]. For TBL in business context, the concepts of cooperative learning, social learning within groups, shared knowledge, and collaboration are considered essential elements [58].

However, translating the conceptual elements of TBL into specific metrics in XR simulation is not straightforward. The literature is inconsistent about the core elements of effective team learning. Furthermore, the lack of accountable mechanisms that can precisely relate TBL-related dimensions and metrics to team competencies, is a fundamental problem. This problem further aggravates in training for multidisciplinary teams and inter-professional communication. Inconsistencies between each member's perceptions of a situation could affect problem-solving, and lead to conflict [59].

In medicine, assessment of improvement in clinical reasoning in the multi-user training context is particularly challenging. Learning in this context may include a wide range of possible team-member contributions, that may result in successful outcomes even if the path of achieving success is inconsistent. Properly defining a measure of successful collaboration is a critical component when the learning content is being created, especially given the broad range of possible human interactions that could be considered.

For example, consider measuring the success of a team of learners in MR correctly diagnosing and treating a virtual patient with severe asthma exacerbation; see Fig. 3. Would the team be measured on their ability to complete a series of specific tasks? Would the simulation be considered successful if the tasks were all completed by the same team member, or would the tasks need to be distributed across all members equally? In either case, the patient may have had a successful outcome, but were the learning outcomes met? How can the assessment consider the possible challenges that may have occurred during the simulation that would have caused the team to decide how tasks would be distributed to maximum efficiency? Furthermore, how can we prevent the potential for team members from gaming the system, such that they try to maximize their contributions during the simulation to benefit a score, rather than to contribute to team goals. In simple terms, the idea of "the team worked well together" is difficult to define and apply across learning contexts.

Even more challenging is mapping assessments to individual learners where contributions are asymmetrical and distributed. In multi-user simulations, learners are often provided with specific roles, which define what is expected of them to contribute, and what they may be assessed on. However, technology needs to consider variable team sizes, and the possibility that the instructor may not use the technology with optimal team size it was designed for. Consider a simulation of a ventricular fibrillation arrest, where learners may be assigned the roles of leader, compressions, respirations, drug administrations, and timing. If success is related to each learner performing their defined role, but the number of learners is only three, then the assessments would need to take this variable into account. This poses a design challenge given the large variability not only in learning contexts, but also the necessity for medical accuracy across a large library of scenarios.

4.5 Instructor, Monitoring, and Innovation

The role of instructor who is ultimately responsible for teaching collaborative benefits to a group of learners, can be designed into XR platform as instructor-in-the-loop (IITL; see an example in safety training [60]). IITL may help bring individual learners to the team to stimulate team formation, customize the learning content on-the-fly to support personalized learning, or monitor teamwork for qualitative assessment. However, the wide range of activities served by human instructors within IITL does not necessarily indicate its superiority over alternatives. To our knowledge, few applications and research attend to alternative options beyond IITL. In nursing, where the number of students is outpacing the availability of instructors [61], and where the cost of instructors is high, replacing IITL with virtual or self-led instruction is an area of strong interest.

To develop alternatives to IITL, a close comparison of IITL to no-instructor scenarios in XR would be informative. In fact, having an instructor present during a multi-user simulation is common practice in non-XR simulations. The presence of a human being to guide a scenario, observe learner activity, and conduct debriefing to discuss areas of success and improvement is a key part of the current use of simulation in healthcare. With XR simulations, many institutions are looking to produce efficiency by reducing the number of instructors needed per student cohort. This creates challenges as technology is expected to replace this IITL dynamic even when learning outcomes are related to issues of collaboration.

Even if a scenario is based on a defined algorithm, the precise following of that algorithm by learners may not indicate a successful learning outcome, as much of the value of simulation is the opportunity to discuss why certain decisions were made, what the learners were thinking in the moment, and how they may apply that experience to realistic circumstances. The risks of replacing instructors with more quantitative measures of success in clinical reasoning simulations include learners "playing the game", as they will know that every action they take is being counted, the difficulty in defining success across multiple factors (e.g., communication, collaboration, clinical accuracy, patient outcome), and the various definitions of learning objectives and outcomes that may exist across instructors and institutions.

5 Discussions

This section further discusses an array of multifactorial issues and frictions in the context of medical inter-professional team-based learning, that may possibly arise at the early phase of learning-contents design and XR simulation development, followed by the later phase of course delivery, learning, and outcome assessment.

5.1 Frictions at the Early Phase of Design and Development

Designing contents to teach standardized responses, versus non-standardized responses that include trials and errors under a "fail-safe" scheme, is a key decision to make for content creators. The fail-safe scheme, where learners are presented with a broader range of possible options and are then allowed to make incorrect choices and take different paths to success, is often at odds with the requirement to present every learner the same set of response options that must be completed in a precise order. Implementing this fail-safe, sandbox-type mechanism where learners are allowed to make mistakes (such as administering the wrong medications, performing interactions out of order, or otherwise not following the standard procedure precisely) could be much less costly to produce if an instructor is known to be present, i.e., IITL for corrective comments.

With the scheme of standardized responses, on the other hand, content designers are required to ensure that clinically correct causal relationships are implemented between each set of responses and the subsequent patient outcomes in the simulation. The risk here is to present an incorrect intervention that may not accurately demonstrate the possibility of patient harm such as overdosing a patient, yet the patient does not deteriorate nor demonstrate the likely response to such a gross error. Coding scenarios to handle every possible intervention the learner may take are significantly more complex from both a design and development perspective, even with the advancement of physiological engines. Despite that complexity, instructors often prefer to standardize the learning content so that they can more efficiently run large groups of learners through the identical simulations and provide quantitative pass/fail scores with limited instructor involvement. An example is in nursing programs, where the shortage of instructors is leading to growing interest in simulation training that can be conducted without an instructor present.

Friction at design and development stages arises due to the real-world differences in "best practices" across healthcare institutions on a global scale. Learning content is often created within a multidisciplinary team of subject matter experts, technologists, and artists. To provide a realistic learning environment, the content may be based on a specific market need, such that the medical algorithms tend to follow a specific standard, and the immersive environment may reflect that of a specific hospital, medical group or governing body. Often the design and interface of medical equipment may resemble what is "most popular" in the market to appeal to the broadest audience. For these reasons, creating XR learning content that meets the individual needs of instructors and institutions, across differences of language, geography, and institutional, regional and national policy, is challenging. Some common challenges include:

- Brand names versus generic drug names.
- Preferred forms, dosages, and routes of administration. These differences may be the result of access to medications, cost, and regional or environmental factors.
- Preference of make/model/interface of medical equipment.
- Familiarity with specific EHR systems, and processes for ordering medications and procedures.
- Variation in medical algorithms designed for the same clinical case.

5.2 Frictions of Learners in Simulation-Based Learning

Reiterating our research theme of transferring collaborative team experiences in XR to actual patient care, several issues linger, particularly in establishing shared understanding and awareness among the group of learners. Successful outcomes would include inter-professional communication in a multi-disciplinary team, as well as pedagogical communication between the team and instructor, as described in Sect. 4.

Friction also exists between learners and the methods employed by software to understand user intent in ways that support methods of communication that learners use in practice. For example, in an emergency simulation, proper closed loop communication may be a key learning objective. In a non-XR simulation in the physical world, a doctor may instruct a nurse to administer a certain drug and dose, the nurse may then verbally confirm their understanding of the instruction, go to a drawer, get the drug and administer it, confirm to the team that is has been completed, and document that action using a scanner. A challenge here is that the doctor's spoken intent must be a viable option in the learning content, otherwise the nurse will not be able to administer it using virtual objects. This challenge is currently solved using technical implementation methods such as: offering a menu system that mimics a virtual Electronic Health Records (EHRs) that learners can use to place orders; or a selection of "pre-determined" interventions that the learner can select from. The former providing a much broader range of options that may require more critical thinking, whereas the latter may reduce user friction, but greatly reduces the realism that a provider may encounter in the real world. Using either of these solutions, the doctor may not be aware of the exact options the content would accept before directing their team, which may cause friction during the simulation if those options are not available exactly as expected, perhaps due to subtle variations in drug names (e.g., generic vs. brand names), dose, or route. The use of AI to bridge this gap shows promise for machine-learned intent detection and response generation [62], but despite its rapid growth, is still nascent in its application for medical training and further research is warranted.

Disclosure of Interests.   The authors have no competing interests to declare that are relevant to the content of this article.

References

1. Abildgren, et al.: The effectiveness of improving healthcare teams' human factor skills using simulation-based training: a systematic review. Adv. Simul. **7**(1), 12 (2022)
2. Renganayagalu, S.K., Mallam, S.C., Nazir, S.: Effectiveness of VR head mounted displays in professional training: a systematic review. Technol. Knowl. Learn. **26**(4), 999–1041 (2021). https://doi.org/10.1007/s10758-020-09489-9
3. Yoganathan, S., Finch, D.A., Parkin, E., Pollard, J.: 360 virtual reality video for the acquisition of knot tying skills: a randomised controlled trial. Int. J. Surg. **54**, 24–27 (2018)
4. Nabizadeh-Gharghozar, Z., Alavi, N.M., Ajorpaz, N.M.: Clinical competence in nursing: a hybrid concept analysis. Nurse Educ. Today **97**, 104728 (2021). https://doi.org/10.1016/j.nedt.2020.104728
5. Dang, B.K., Palicte, J.S., Valdez, A., O'Leary-Kelley, C.: Assessing simulation, virtual reality, and television modalities in clinical training. Clin. Simul. Nurs. **19**, 30–37 (2018)
6. Sankaranarayanan, G., et al.: Immersive virtual reality-based training improves response in a simulated operating room fire scenario. Surg. Endosc. Other Interv. Tech. **32**(8), 3439–3449 (2018). https://doi.org/10.1007/s00464-018-6063-x
7. Gerup, J., Soerensen, C.B., Dieckmann, P.: Augmented reality and mixed reality for healthcare education beyond surgery: an integrative review. Int. J. Med. Educ. **11**, 1 (2020)

8. Robinson, M.: Design for unanticipated use..... In: de Michelis, G., Simone, C., Schmidt, K. (eds.) ECSCW 1993, pp. 187–202. Springer, Dordrecht (1993). https://doi.org/10.1007/978-94-011-2094-4_13

9. Wanis, I.A.: A review on collaborative learning environment across virtual and augmented reality technology. In: IOP Conference Series: Materials Science and Engineering, IOP Publishing, p. 12050 (2019)

10. Berg, L.P., Vance, J.M.: Industry use of virtual reality in product design and manufacturing: a survey. Virtual Real. **21**, 1–17 (2017)

11. Radianti, J., Majchrzak, T.A., Fromm, J., Wohlgenannt, I.: A systematic review of immersive virtual reality applications for higher education: design elements, lessons learned, and research agenda. Comput. Educ. **147**, 103778 (2020)

12. Draper, S.: Smartglasses in comparison to VR/AR Headsets. Wearable Technologies. https://wearable-technologies.com/news/whats-the-difference-between-smartglasses-and-vr-ar-headsets#:~:text=Compared to VR%2FAR headsets, and have less processing capacity

13. Jin, Q., Liu, Y., Yarosh, S., Han, B., Qian, F., ACM: How Will VR enter university classrooms? Multi-stakeholders investigation of VR in higher education. In: Proceedings of the CHI Conference on Human Factors in Computing Systems (CHI' 22) (2022). https://doi.org/10.1145/3491102.3517542

14. Neubauer, C., Khooshabeh, P., Campbell, J.: When less is more: studying the role of functional fidelity in a low fidelity mixed-reality tank simulator. In: Cassenti, D. (ed.) AHFE 2017. LNCS, vol. 591, pp. 220–229. Springer, Cham (2018). https://doi.org/10.1007/978-3-319-60591-3_20

15. MacArthur, C., Grinberg, A., Harley, D., Hancock, M.: You're making me sick: a systematic review of how virtual reality research considers gender & cybersickness. In: Proceedings of the 2021 CHI Conference on Human Factors in Computing Systems, pp. 1–15 (2021)

16. Jensen, L., Konradsen, F.: A review of the use of virtual reality head-mounted displays in education and training. Educ. Inf. Technol. **23**, 1515–1529 (2018)

17. Shafer, D.M., Carbonara, C.P., Korpi, M.F.: Modern virtual reality technology: cybersickness, sense of presence, and gender. Media Psychol. Rev. **11**(2), 1 (2017)

18. Gunawardena, C.N.: Social presence theory and implications for interaction and collaborative learning in computer conferences. Int. J. Educ. Telecommun. **1**(2), 147–166 (1995)

19. Witmer, B.G., Singer, M.J.: Measuring presence in virtual environments: a presence questionnaire. Presence **7**(3), 225–240 (1998)

20. Krauß, V., Boden, A., Oppermann, L., Reiners, R.: Current practices, challenges, and design implications for collaborative AR/VR application development. In: Proceedings of the 2021 CHI Conference on Human Factors in Computing Systems, pp. 1–15 (2021)

21. Petersen, G.B., Mottelson, A., Makransky, G.: Pedagogical agents in educational VR: an in the wild study. In: Proceedings of the 2021 CHI Conference on Human Factors in Computing Systems, pp. 1–12 (2021)

22. Teo, T., Lawrence, L., Lee, G.A., Billinghurst, M., Adcock, M.: Mixed reality remote collaboration combining 360 video and 3D reconstruction. In: Proceedings of the 2019 CHI Conference on Human Factors in Computing Systems, pp. 1–14 (2019)

23. He, Z., Du, R., Perlin, K.: CollaboVR: a reconfigurable framework for creative collaboration in virtual reality. In: IEEE International Symposium on Mixed and Augmented Reality (ISMAR), pp. 542–554. IEEE (2020)

24. Radu, I., Schneider, B., Machinery, A.C.: What can we learn from augmented reality (AR)? Benefits and drawbacks of AR for inquiry-based learning of physics. In: Proceedings of the 2019 CHI Conference on Human Factors in Computing Systems (CHI) (2019). https://doi.org/10.1145/3290605.3300774

25. Akçayır, M., Akçayır, G., Pektaş, H.M., Ocak, M.A.: Augmented reality in science laboratories: the effects of augmented reality on university students' laboratory skills and attitudes toward science laboratories. Comput. Human Behav. **57**, 334–342 (2016)
26. E.G. Toriz García, A.D. García García, and M. Aparicio Ponce: Augmented reality in collaborative learning. In: Hosseini, S., Peluffo, D.H., Nganji, J., Arrona-Palacios, A. (eds) CIIE 2020. TCSN, pp. 305–315. Springer, Singapore (2022). https://doi.org/10.1007/978-981-19-3383-7_24
27. Baranyi, P., Csapo, A., Sallai, G.: Cognitive Infocommunications (Coginfocom). Springer, Cham (2015). https://doi.org/10.1007/978-3-319-19608-4
28. Riebe, L., Girardi, A., Whitsed, C.: Teaching teamwork in Australian university business disciplines: evidence from a systematic literature review. Issues Educ. Res. **27**(1), 134–150 (2017)
29. Schiffeler, N., Stehling, V., Hees, F., Isenhardt, I.: Effects of collaborative augmented reality on communication and interaction in learning contexts–results of a qualitative pre-study. In: 2019 ASEE Annual Conference and Exposition (2019)
30. Deshpande, A., Kim, I.: Effectiveness of augmented reality in improving spatial ability and mental representations in ready-to-assembly (RTA) furniture. Adv. Eng. Inform. In Review (2018)
31. Boonbrahm, P., Kaewrat, C., Boonbrahm, S.: Interactive augmented reality: a new approach for collaborative learning. In: Zaphiris, P., Ioannou, A. (eds.) LCT 2016. LNCS, vol. 9753, pp. 115–124. Springer, Cham (2016). https://doi.org/10.1007/978-3-319-39483-1_11
32. Grandi, J.G., Debarba, H.G., Nedel, L., Maciel, A.: Design and evaluation of a handheld-based 3D user interface for collaborative object manipulation. In: Proceedings of the 2017 CHI Conference on Human Factors in Computing Systems, pp. 5881–5891 (2017)
33. Ismail, A.W., Sunar, M.S.: Survey on collaborative AR for multi-user in urban studies and planning. In: Learning By Playing: Game-Based Education System Design and Development, 4rd International Conference on E-Learning and Games (Edutainment 2009), vol. 5670, pp. 444–455 (2009). https://doi.org/10.1007/978-3-642-03364-3_53
34. Bisantz, A.M., Vicente, K.J.: Making the abstraction hierarchy concrete. Int. J. Hum. Comput. Stud. **40**(1), 83–117 (1994)
35. Lintern, G.: Work-focused analysis and design. Cogn. Technol. Work **14**(1), 71–81 (2012)
36. Vicente, M.K.J.: Work domain analysis and task analysis: a difference that matters. In: Cognitive Task Analysis, pp. 115–132. Psychology Press, London (2000)
37. Modi, J.N., Anshu, P.G., Singh, T.: Teaching and assessing clinical reasoning skills. Indian Pediatr. **52**, 787–794 (2015)
38. Sexton, J.B., Thomas, E.J., Helmreich, R.L.: Error, stress, and teamwork in medicine and aviation: cross sectional surveys. BMJ **320**(7237), 745–749 (2000)
39. Flin, R., Yule, S., McKenzie, L., Paterson-Brown, S., Maran, N.: Attitudes to teamwork and safety in the operating theatre. Surgeon **4**(3), 145–151 (2006). https://doi.org/10.1016/S1479-666X(06)80084-3
40. Abelson, J.S., Silverman, E., Banfelder, J., Naides, A., Costa, R., Dakin, G.: Virtual operating room for team training in surgery. Am. J. Surg. **210**(3), 585–590 (2015). https://doi.org/10.1016/j.amjsurg.2015.01.024
41. Al-Elq, A.H.: Simulation-based medical teaching and learning. J. Fam. Community Med. **17**(1), 35 (2010)
42. Keshk, L.I., Qalawa, S.A.A., Ibrahim, N.A.: Effectiveness of an educational program regarding nursing process on acquiring advanced skills among internship nursing students. Int. J. Nurs. **5**(2), 32–44 (2018)
43. Chang, C.Y., Panjaburee, P., Chang, S.C.: Effects of integrating maternity VR-based situated learning into professional training on students' learning performances. Interact. Learn. Environ. (2022). https://doi.org/10.1080/10494820.2022.2141263

44. Billett, S.: Situated learning: bridging sociocultural and cognitive theorising. Learn. Instr. **6**(3), 263–280 (1996)
45. National Institute of Standards and Technology: Extended Reality at NIST. NIST XR Community. https://www.nist.gov/information-technology/extended-reality
46. Brown, N., Margus, C., Hart, A., Sarin, R., Hertelendy, A., Ciottone, G.: Virtual reality training in disaster medicine: a systematic review of the literature. Simul. Healthc. **18**(4), 255–261 (2023)
47. Prasolova-Forland, E., Molka-Danielsen, J., Fominykh, M., Lamb, K., IEEE: Active learning modules for multi-professional emergency management training in virtual reality. In: Proceedings of 2017 IEEE 6th International Conference on Teaching, Assessment, and Learning for Engineering (TALE), pp. 461–468 (2017)
48. Grandi, J.G., Debarba, H.G., Maciel, A.: Characterizing asymmetric collaborative interactions in virtual and augmented realities. In: 2019 IEEE Conference on Virtual Reality and 3D User Interfaces (VR), pp. 127–135. IEEE (2019)
49. Forland, E.P., McCallum, S., Estrada, J.G.: Collaborative learning in VR for cross-disciplinary distributed student teams. In: 2021 28th IEEE Conference on Virtual Reality and 3D User Interfaces Abstracts and Workshops (VRW 2021), (IEEE VR), pp. 320–325 (2021). https://doi.org/10.1109/VRW52623.2021.00064
50. Hatzipanayioti, A., et al.: Collaborative problem solving in local and remote VR situations. In: 2019 IEEE Conference on Virtual Reality and 3D User Interfaces (VR), pp. 964–965. IEEE (2019)
51. Chow, K., Coyiuto, C., Nguyen, C., Yoon, D.: Challenges and design considerations for multimodal asynchronous collaboration in VR. Proc. ACM Hum.-Comput. Interact. **3**(CSCW), 1–24 (2019)
52. Coffield, F., Ecclestone, K., Hall, E., Moseley, D.: Learning styles and pedagogy in post-16 learning: a systematic and critical review (2004)
53. Kayes, A.B., Kayes, D.C., Kolb, D.A.: Experiential learning in teams. Simul. Gaming **36**(3), 330–354 (2005)
54. Horváth, I.: An analysis of personalized learning opportunities in 3D VR. Front. Comput. Sci. **3** (2021). https://doi.org/10.3389/fcomp.2021.673826
55. Duhigg, C.: What Google learned from its quest to build the perfect team. N. Y. Times Mag. **26**(2016), 2016 (2016)
56. Johnson, D.W., Johnson, R.T., Stanne, M.B.: Cooperative learning methods: a meta-analysis (2000)
57. Edmondson, A.: Psychological safety and learning behavior in work teams. Adm. Sci. Q. **44**(2), 350–383 (1999)
58. Katzenbach, J.R., Smith, D.K.: The Wisdom of Teams: Creating the High-Performance Organization. Harvard Business Review Press, Brighton (2015)
59. Kay, M.J., Kay, S.A., Tuininga, A.R.: Green teams: a collaborative training model. J. Clean. Prod. **176**, 909–919 (2018). https://doi.org/10.1016/j.jclepro.2017.12.032
60. Roofigari-Esfahan, N., et al.: Group-based VR training to improve hazard recognition, evaluation, and control for highway construction workers. In: 2022 IEEE Conference on Virtual Reality and 3D User Interfaces Abstracts and Workshops (VRW 2022), (IEEE VR)., pp. 504–507 (2022). https://doi.org/10.1109/VRW55335.2022.00114
61. Rosseter, R.: Fact Sheet: Nursing Shortage (2022)
62. Chuang, H.-M., Cheng, D.-W.: Conversational AI over military scenarios using intent detection and response generation. Appl. Sci. **12**(5), 2494 (2022)

Enhancing Cognitive Rehabilitation with Augmented Reality: The Role of Virtual Characters in Attention Restoration

Hanfu He[1,2], Wei Cui[1], and Yu Wang[1,3]($\boxtimes$)

[1] College of Design and Innovation, Tongji University, Shanghai, China
asterwangyu@126.com
[2] School of Humanities, Data Finance Journalism Teaching and Research Center,
Shanghai University of Finance and Economics, Shanghai, China
[3] Shanghai Institute of Visual Arts, Shanghai, China

Abstract. This study investigates the efficacy of Augmented Reality (AR) in enhancing attention restoration, leveraging the conceptual framework of Attention Restoration Theory (ART) within a digitally crafted narrative space centered around a bonfire scene. Through the innovative application of AR technology, using Unity software, the research explores the addition of virtual characters to this narrative space and its impact on improving attention recovery. Employing a controlled experimental design, participants were divided into two groups to assess the restorative effect facilitated by the presence or absence of virtual characters within the AR environment. The Perceived Restorativeness Scale (PRS) was utilized to quantify attention restoration levels, offering empirical evidence to test the hypothesis that virtual characters significantly enhance the restorative experience. The findings contribute to the interdisciplinary fields of cognitive rehabilitation and digital therapeutics, underscoring the potential of AR as a powerful tool in creating immersive, therapeutic environments that support mental well-being. This research not only expands our understanding of AR's application in psychological restoration but also delineates a novel approach to integrating digital narrative spaces with therapeutic objectives, paving the way for future innovations in mental health interventions.

Keywords: Augmented Reality (AR) · Attention Restoration Theory (ART) · Virtual Characters · Cognitive Rehabilitation-Interaction

1 Introduction

In the realm of therapeutic interventions, Augmented Reality (AR) has emerged as a promising tool for enhancing mental well-being. This study explores the potential of AR in facilitating attention restoration, employing a narrative space design embedded within a virtual bonfire scene—a concept resonant with Attention Restoration Theory (ART). The integration of virtual characters within this AR environment posits a novel approach to cognitive rehabilitation, aiming to augment the attention recovery process beyond traditional methods.

H. He and W. Cui—co-first authors and contributed equally.

© The Author(s), under exclusive license to Springer Nature Switzerland AG 2024
J. Y. C. Chen and G. Fragomeni (Eds.): HCII 2024, LNCS 14708, pp. 64–83, 2024.
https://doi.org/10.1007/978-3-031-61047-9_4

The significance of this research lies in its exploration of AR's capacity to create immersive, restorative experiences that can be tailored to individual therapeutic needs. By harnessing the principles of ART within a digital context, this study seeks to bridge the gap between virtual and physical therapeutic landscapes, offering a new dimension to attention restoration practices.

Our hypothesis suggests that the inclusion of virtual characters in the AR bonfire scene will enhance the restorative effect, facilitating greater attention recovery compared to scenarios devoid of such characters. To test this hypothesis, we employed the Perceived Restorativeness Scale (PRS) in a controlled experimental design, analyzing the impact of virtual characters on participants' attention restoration levels.

Utilizing Unity software, we crafted an AR scene that embodies the tranquility and restorative potential of a bonfire, augmented with virtual characters to enrich the narrative space. The experimental design involved two groups: one experiencing the AR scene with virtual characters and the other without. Through quantitative analysis of PRS data, we aimed to validate the hypothesized benefits of our AR design on attention restoration.

This investigation not only contributes to the burgeoning field of AR in therapeutic settings but also offers insights into the design of digital environments that support cognitive health and well-being, marking a significant step forward in the application of AR technologies for psychological restoration.

2 Background and Related Work

2.1 Overview of Augmented Reality Technology

The evolution of Augmented Reality (AR) technology, tracing its roots back to the 1960s, marks a significant journey from an experimental concept to a transformative tool across various domains. Ronald T. Azuma, in his pivotal 1997 work "A Survey of Augmented Reality," offered an expansive view of AR's early development, defining it as an integration of real and virtual environments, characterized by real-time interactivity and three-dimensional registration. This comprehensive definition has been instrumental in shaping the trajectory of AR technology [1].

The genesis of AR can be attributed to Ivan Sutherland's early head-mounted display system, a rudimentary yet groundbreaking step in the 1960s. The 1980s witnessed substantial progress, culminating in Tom Caudell coining the term "Augmented Reality" in the early 1990s. This period was marked by rapid advancements, notably in hardware, facilitating AR's application in military training and aviation. The advent of smartphones and mobile computing heralded a new era for AR, transitioning from specialized to widespread commercial and consumer use. Recent developments in display technology, tracking systems, and user experience design have expanded AR's applicability into healthcare, education, and entertainment, demonstrating its versatility and potential [2].

2.2 Defining Narrative Spaces in AR

In the realm of AR, the conceptualization of narrative spaces signifies a transformative shift in storytelling and interactive media. Richard Rouse's 2005 exploration in "Game

Design: Theory & Practice" delves into AR's capability to craft immersive story experiences, surpassing conventional narrative limits [3]. AR's unique ability to amalgamate digital augmentations with the physical world invites users into an interactive narrative, transitioning them from passive observers to active participants. This dynamic interaction not only personalizes the storytelling experience but also enhances immersion by contextually aligning digital narratives with the user's surroundings.

Furthermore, AR redefines traditional narrative structures, enabling stories to unfold in a multidimensional space. This paradigm shift, as illustrated in Carmigniani and Furht's "Augmented Reality: An Overview" (2011), showcases AR's successful integration into storytelling. For instance, museums utilize AR to create engaging and educational exhibits by augmenting historical narratives with interactive digital content. Similarly, the gaming industry, exemplified by titles like "Pokemon GO," has pioneered AR storytelling, merging virtual elements with the real-world environment, thereby captivating a diverse audience and setting a benchmark for future applications in AR-based entertainment [4].

The effectiveness of this AR scene in facilitating attention recovery was attributed to several factors grounded in spatial narratology:

- Immersive Storytelling: The bonfire scene creates an immersive narrative experience.
- Emotional Engagement: The narrative of finding hope and opportunity in the bonfire resonates on an emotional level.
- Sensory Stimulation: The stimulation is known to enhance cognitive processing and memory retention, aiding in attention recovery.
- Spatial Interaction: Researchers in these fields have explored how spatial narratives in virtual environments can impact user experience and cognitive processes.

The integration of narrative theories in AR is a critical aspect of creating compelling experiences.

In the field of digital storytelling, particularly within the context of Augmented Reality (AR), Marie-Laure Ryan's work stands as a cornerstone. Her book "Narrative as Virtual Reality: Immersion and Interactivity in Literature and Electronic Media" (2001) offers an in-depth analysis of how narrative theories are intricately woven into the fabric of AR experiences [5]. Ryan's exploration centers on the concepts of "immersion" and "interactivity," essential components deeply embedded in the AR narrative experience.

Ryan posits that the immersive aspect of AR fundamentally alters the storytelling process, allowing users to literally 'step into' a story. This immersion effectively blurs the boundaries between narrative and reality, creating a seamless continuum where the physical and the virtual coalesce. Such an environment not only captivates the user's senses but also their cognitive faculties, leading to a more profound engagement with the narrative content.

Further, Ryan emphasizes the role of interactivity in these immersive AR narratives. Unlike traditional storytelling mediums where the audience remains passive, AR empowers users to become active participants. Their actions and decisions within the AR environment can influence the narrative's trajectory, leading to a dynamic and responsive storytelling experience. This interactive feature is not merely a technological gimmick but a fundamental shift in how stories are told and experienced, aligning with contemporary trends in interactive design and user engagement [6].

The synthesis of immersion and interactivity in AR, as elucidated by Ryan, heralds a new era of storytelling—a medium that is not static but alive, responding to and evolving with the user's involvement. This novel approach to narrative construction and delivery in AR environments opens up unprecedented possibilities in storytelling, offering a more personalized and impactful narrative experience.

2.3 Attention Restoration Theory

The "Attention Restoration Theory" (ART), initially conceptualized by psychologist Stephen Kaplan, refers to environments that can potentially replenish, restore, or reju-venate depleted psychological resources. Specifically, it addresses the need for restora-tive environments in urban settings where mental and physical resources are continu-ally taxed. ART, rooted in cognitive psychology, posits that directed attention serves as a medium for environmental cognition; excessive consumption of this attention leads to mental fatigue, which can be effectively mitigated in natural settings, thereby replenishing cognitive resources.

In the context of examining restorative experiences within augmented reality (AR) environments, it is essential to consider foundational work in environmental psychology. Kaplan and Kaplan's experimental research identified four key elements that contribute to a restorative experience in natural settings: 'Being Away,' which signifies a sense of mental detachment from routine or stress; 'Extent,' indicating the depth or richness of the environment that engages the individual; 'Fascination,' representing an effortless attention or interest triggered by the environment; and 'Compatibility,' which refers to the congruence between user intentions and environmental support [7].

Building upon these elements, the Attention Restoration Theory (ART) was pro-posed, providing a theoretical framework for understanding how natural environments can contribute to cognitive restoration, with significant implications for evaluating health benefits. Subsequently, Hartig et al. developed the Perceived Restorativeness Scale (PRS) in 1996, designed to quantitatively assess the quality of restorative environments based on these four ART attributes. The scale employs a series of declarative statements rated on a seven-point scale, allowing for nuanced measurement of restorative qualities [8].

In 1997, Hartig et al. refined the PRS, further exploring its factor structure and model, enhancing its applicability in diverse environmental contexts. The revised PRS has since been widely employed to evaluate restorative potential in various settings, including buildings, urban landscapes, indoor spaces, and natural environments [9].

In the current study, we extend the application of the PRS to AR environments, par-ticularly focusing on narrative space design that aims to restore attention by merging elements of virtuality and reality. This innovative approach involves assessing the restora-tive impact of different design elements within AR scenes, guided by the foundational principles of ART and the validated methodology of the PRS.

Based on this theory, Hartig et al. developed the Perceived Restorativeness Scale (PRS) to gauge individuals' subjective restorative experiences. This scale measures people's perceived restorative benefits, reflecting their sense of recovery [10] (Fig. 1).

ART suggests that restorative environments can revive previously depleted cogni-tive resources, particularly directed attention, thereby promoting health. Such restorative experiences should encompass four characteristics: being away, fascination, extent, and

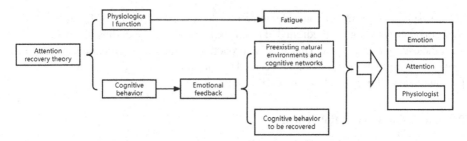

Fig. 1. "Attention recovery theory" affects the mechanism (by author)

compatibility. 'Being away' implies psychological and geographical distance from usual environments causing stress and fatigue, thereby reducing the demand for directed attention and offering relaxation opportunities. 'Fascination' indicates that when an environment is sufficiently engaging, it can invoke involuntary attention, alleviating fatigue and releasing stress [11]. 'Extent' refers to the environment's scope and coherence, providing enough space and content for exploration and discovery, aiding in overcoming negative states and facilitating recovery. Compatibility' means that the activities supported by the environment align with individual goals and preferences. An environment's restorative effect is diminished if its activities do not match personal preferences and motivations [12].

3   Theoretical Framework and Application

3.1   ARs 'Sense of Presence' Improve the Effect of Attention Recovery

The effect of the natural environment on reducing human attention [13], cognition and stress is significant [14]. Natural immersion through virtual reality technology can also effectively alleviate negative emotions [15]. The study found that before and after virtual natural immersion, Self-reported anxiety levels of participants [16]. Compared to virtual urban environments, Virtual natural environment can significantly relieve confusion, fatigue, anger, hostility, tension, depression And other negative emotions [17]. Compared to the real natural environment [18], Virtual nature is not inferior to the expression of negative emotions [19] (Fig. 2).

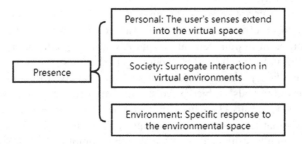

Fig. 2. Specific expression of "Sense of Presence" (by author)

AR technology has been shown to elicit greater improvements in positive emotions, mediated by a stronger sense of presence and natural interaction [20]. "Presence," also referred to as "being there," is the sensation of existing within a mediated environment, a psychological state of existence [21]; that is, the individual's psychological experience of being in a virtual environment created by a computer display [22]. This concept is categorized into three domains: personal, social, and environmental presence. Personal presence refers to extending the sensation and emotional feelings into the virtual environment, thereby creating an immersive experience and a sense of psychological involvement. Social presence indicates the degree to which it coexists and interacts with other entities within the virtual environment, while environmental presence pertains to the level of response to the environment [23]. Self-efficacy is seen as a mediator between social and cognitive presence [24]. Researchers suggest that it is necessary to further explore the differences in virtual reality technology under different environments and the impact of these differences on individual self-efficacy [25].

Factors influencing presence include time [26], content [27], user characteristics [28], attention resources [29] and engagement, immersion, and interactivity [30]. Its measurement methods comprise objective measurements and subjective reports. Observing the amplitude of postural responses, measuring heart rate and skin conductance [31], observing social behaviors such as facial expressions, gestures, head movements, eye contact, and tone of voice can all reflect the sense of presence [32].

Studies have found that emotions in virtual environments are related to presence, which also explains the interplay between presence and emotions.

Exploring the connections between environmental settings, behaviors, and psychological experiences, this research investigates the differences in healing and experiences evoked by different scenarios, as well as the impact of restorative environments in AR scenes, which combine virtuality and reality, on the degree of attention restoration.

3.2   The Performance of AR in the Process of Attention Recovery

The scene of virtual reality technology is better on the media, such as immersion, authenticity, 3d, depth, and even comfort [33]. This technique allows people to realize the possibility of achieving goals by "hiding" in front of the "hidden" opposite nature.

The Advantages of AR Technology in Healing. AR's potential in healthcare, particularly in attention recovery, is significant. For instance, an AR-based Joint Attention Training Platform for Autistic Children demonstrates AR's ability to engage users in interactive exercises that improve attention and communication skills [34].This indicates that AR's interactive and engaging nature can be beneficial in attention recovery processes, offering a novel approach to heal interventions. Compared with the traditional psychological intervention methods, the scene-real combination design has significant advantages [35] (Table 1).

Comparison of AR and VR Experience in the Field of "Presence". In AR, users remain in their physical environment while digital elements are superimposed onto it. This blending of real and virtual worlds allows for a continuation of natural, physical interactions with the environment. Embodied cognition emphasizes the role of sensory feedback and physical interaction in shaping cognitive experiences [39]. Users can see

Table 1. The Advantages of AR in Attention Recovery (by author)

Advantage	Description
Enhanced Engagement and Motivation	• AR's interactive nature significantly increases user engagement and motivation. This is particularly beneficial in attention recovery, where sustained engagement is crucial • For instance, the Augmented Class application, used in educational settings, demonstrates how AR can stimulate interest and creativity, essential for cognitive development and attention recovery [36]
Personalized and Adaptive	• Personalized and flexible educational experiences are made possible with AR. This is particularly advantageous in attention recovery, as each individual's needs and progress rates can vary significantly • These environments can cater to the specific needs of individuals, allowing for a more tailored approach to attention recovery, thereby enhancing the effectiveness of the healing process [37]
Multisensory stimulation	• AR's ability to provide multisensory stimulation is another significant advantage. This stimulation can help with attention recovery by engaging multiple senses, thereby enhancing cognitive processing and memory retention [38]

their own bodies and interact with real-world objects, which are crucial sensory inputs for reinforcing the feeling of presence – the psychological state of "being there" in a particular environment. This is less pronounced in VR, where users are fully immersed in a digitally created environment, often losing sight of their actual physical surroundings and experiencing a disconnect with their real-world bodily context.

In AR scenarios, the cognitive processing benefits from the user's familiarity with their physical surroundings. This familiarity aids in faster comprehension and interaction with augmented elements, as the cognitive load is reduced due to the real-world context [40]. The brain seamlessly integrates sensory input from both the real and virtual components of the experience, enhancing the overall cognitive engagement and presence.

Conversely, in VR, the brain needs to process an entirely new environment, often requiring a period of adaptation. This adjustment can be cognitively demanding and may lead to a sense of disorientation or a lack of presence, especially if the virtual environment lacks cues that the brain expects based on real-world experiences.

Emotional engagement in AR is often more immediate and intense compared to VR. This is due to the direct overlay of digital content onto the real world, which can evoke stronger emotional responses. For instance, seeing a virtual historical figure appear in one's living room can be more impactful than encountering the same figure in a purely virtual environment. This heightened emotional engagement contributes to the sense of presence, making the experience more memorable and impactful [41].

3.3 The Impact of AR's "Presence" Experience on the Degree of User Attention Recovery

AR has emerged as a transformative technology in various fields, including therapeutic interventions for attention restoration. The integration of AR into therapeutic practice offers several advantages over traditional approaches, mainly due to its ability to provide multisensory stimulation, personalized experiences, and real-time feedback.

AR's ability to provide multisensory stimuli has significant advantages in capturing and maintaining user attention over traditional methods. Digital content is overlaid on the real world and captures the immediate context of the user, making therapeutic activities more relevant and engaging [42]. This correlation is essential for attentional restoration, as it encourages sustained focus and engagement in the therapeutic task. Studies have shown that augmented reality interfaces, such as omnidirectional attention funnel, can effectively guide users' attention, improve search speed by more than 50%, and reduce perceived cognitive load by 18% [43].

Augmented reality allows personalization and adaptation in therapy and is essential for keeping users interested and engaged [44]. By tailoring the AR experience to individual needs and preferences, users are more likely to remain focused and attentive during the treatment. Educational technology research has demonstrated that augmented reality can significantly improve student attention when interacting with augmented reality applications compared to traditional interfaces.

The interactivity provided by augmented reality plays an important role in maintaining attention. Interactive tasks in augmented reality require active participation so as to cultivate a high state of vigilance and concentration [45]. Furthermore, AR's ability to provide real-time feedback is a powerful tool for attention restoration. This feedback ensures that users are continuously engaged and can immediately see the results of their actions, reinforcing the learning and recovery process [46] (Fig. 3).

In addition, there are many performances of AR to improve the level of user attention recovery. For example, augmented reality provides information in a more understandable and interactive form, which can effectively manage cognitive load, which is crucial for attention restoration [47].

Improving emotional balance: Augmented reality can be used to control emotional balance, which is essential in therapeutic Settings, especially for users with attention deficits [48].

The immersion of augmented reality increases user engagement and motivation, which is a key factor in maintaining attention and promoting recovery [49]. Augmented reality allows the creation of customized environments that can be tailored to each user's specific needs, enhancing the effectiveness of attention restoration therapy [50].

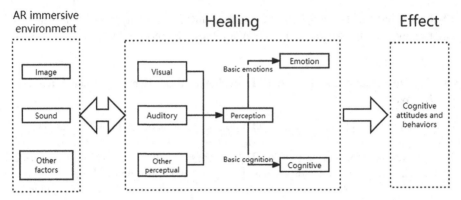

Fig. 3. The Influence Mechanism of "Sense of Presence" feature of AR on attention Recovery (by author)

4   Experimental Design

4.1   The Scene Design Based on AR Technology Meets the Requirements of Attention Recovery

According to Lynn. C (2014) et al., the choice of a "campfire" as the central element in designing an AR scene for attention recovery is rooted in its psychological and cultural significance [51]. Campfires have historically been symbols of community, safety, and storytelling, offering a natural focal point for human attention and interaction. This intrinsic allure is leveraged in the AR context to create a calming, engaging environment conducive to cognitive restoration [52]. The familiar and comforting imagery of a campfire in AR scenes taps into deep-seated human instincts, fostering a sense of relaxation and focus, thereby enhancing the attention recovery process. This design choice reflects a nuanced understanding of the interplay between environmental cues and cognitive function [53].

To this end, the team used the Unity platform to design and create an AR scene incorporating campfire and narrative elements. We put a "campfire" in the first set of scenes and designed the campfire to burn. At the same time, put the following in the background: "I hope to find warmth and hope through this campfire. Every day a firewood is an opportunity, an unknown possibility. I don't know how long the fire will burn, but I can clearly feel the rising flame and the energy of the freshness. Do you get what you want at that moment?" This is an original piece of content by the author, which uses "narratology" to help users improve the effect of attention restoration. The application of spatial narratology theory to augmented reality (AR) spaces, particularly in the context of a bonfire scene, provides a compelling explanation for the attention recovery effect experienced by users. Spatial narratology, which explores the narrative structure within a spatial context, offers insights into how the arrangement and interaction of elements in a virtual space can influence cognitive and emotional responses. In the AR scenario described, the bonfire serves as a central narrative element, symbolizing warmth and hope. Each log, representing an opportunity or possibility, adds to the narrative depth, creating a story that unfolds within the user's interactive space. The rising flame and the energy of freshness contribute to a dynamic environment that engages the user's senses and attention.

The spatial arrangement of the bonfire and its symbolic elements (logs, flames) within the AR environment captivates the user's attention, drawing them into the narrative.

Meanwhile, this emotional engagement is crucial for attention recovery, as it fosters a deeper connection with the content. The dynamic nature of the bonfire, with its rising flames and the implied sensory experience of warmth, provides multisensory stimulation. The user's ability to interact with the bonfire scene in the AR space, such as adding logs or observing the changing flames, enhances the sense of presence and involvement, further aiding in attention recovery. The design and creation of the above AR narrative space conforms to the four design strategies of "immersive narrative", "emotional engagement", "sensory stimulation" and "spatial interaction" discussed in the second part (Fig. 4).

Fig. 4. Campfire with "changing" fire in the first set of AR images (by author)

To test the research hypothesis, the research team conducted a controlled experiment in which we used Unity software to add characters to the original "campfire" AR space narrative scene (Fig. 5).

Fig. 5. Add virtual characters based on the first group of influences (by author)

Through character design, the research team changed the "narrative content" from "voiceover" to spoken by virtual characters, giving users a feeling of "communicating with people" (Fig. 6).

Fig. 6. AR image after adding virtual character (by author)

In the second set of AR scene images, the virtual characters we selected were the images of "tourists in the wilderness". The avatars serve as active narrative agents that can create a more engaging story environment. Traditional narrative theory emphasizes the role of characters in driving a story forward and engaging the audience [54]. In an AR setting, avatars can assume this role, making the narrative more dynamic and relatable. The presence of a character with whom the user can interact introduces a level of personalization and emotional engagement that is less achievable through voiceover narration alone [55].

This emotional engagement is crucial for attention recovery, as it fosters a deeper connection with the content. The user is no longer a passive recipient of information but an active participant in a narrative unfolding in their immediate environment. This active participation can enhance cognitive processing and memory retention, aiding in attention recovery [56].

4.2 Experimental Method

In this experimental study, we sought to validate a research hypothesis through a comparative analysis of two design approaches in Augmented Reality (AR) scenarios: the hypothesis posits that the incorporation of virtual character elements in AR scenes significantly enhances attention restoration in individuals.

The experiment engaged 20 undergraduate and master's students, aged between 18 to 24 years, maintaining an equal gender ratio. All participants were subjected to stress tests of uniform difficulty.

Conducted in an indoor setting, the experiment comprised two segments, each consisting of phases of stress induction and stress alleviation. For the "stress induction" phase, established methodologies included having participants imagine mentally exhausting scenarios, watch accident educational videos, or complete tasks such as driving to a test location, undergoing a psychological test, or experiencing an examination setting. Preliminary experiments evaluated these methods and, through discussions with early participants, deduced that imagining mentally exhausting scenarios was relatively challenging; the impact of watching accident educational videos varied greatly among individuals [57] and was influenced by their usual viewing habits. Moreover, participants expressed that such videos induced a blend of emotions [58], including fear and sadness, which did not entirely align with the objectives of this study [59]. Consequently, an English oral examination was selected as the medium for stress induction. This choice was driven by two factors: firstly, all participants, being university students, were familiar with and typically stressed by examination settings, allowing for the natural induction of mild stress; secondly, preliminary physiological measurements, such as skin conductance, electromyography, and heart rate, demonstrated significant variations during the oral examination, confirming its effectiveness in inducing a certain level of stress.

This research aims to explore the influence of AR scene design, particularly the role of virtual character elements, on the extent of attention restoration, thus providing empirical evidence for the application of AR in psychological healing fields.

Perceptual Recovery Scale used in this experiment [60], the specific contents are as follows (Table 2):

Table 2. Perception Recovery Scale

	Content		Content
Being Away	1. Here I just came to relief		12. It's charming here
	2. This is where I get some rest		13. Nothing to see here(x)
	3. This place gives me a break from stress	Extent	14. There are too many things here(x)
	4. I can relax here		15. I'm confused here(x)

(*continued*)

Table 2. (*continued*)

	Content		Content
	5. I can reduce unnecessary attention		16. There are too many things here to distract me(x)
Fascination	6. I find this scene attractive		17. It's chaotic here.(x)
	7. My attention is drawn to many interesting things	Compatibility	18. This is the place for me
	8. I want to know more about this place		19. I can do what I want here
	9. There is so much to explore and discover here		20. Here I just feel like I belong
	10. I wish I could spend more time looking around		21. I can enjoy happiness here
	11. It's boring here. (x)		22. I feel so connected to the scene

5 Analysis and Discussion

5.1 Data Analysis

To facilitate observation, the research team juxtaposed the data from the four dimensions of the Perceived Restorativeness Scale (PRS) measured without virtual characters with the data obtained after incorporating virtual characters. The same four dimensions in the PRS were encoded and labeled as "Fifth Dimension," "Sixth Dimension," "Seventh Dimension," and "Eighth Dimension."

The team employed Intraclass Correlations Coefficient (ICC) to calculate inter-rater reliability, Cronbach's α to determine internal consistency reliability, and Pearson correlation coefficient to assess the correlation between individual item scores and the total score. Investigative factor analysis was used to assess the scale's structure reliability. Univariate analysis of variance was conducted on the perceived restorativeness scale scores, and Tukey's post-hoc test was used to investigate differences across various scenarios. Data was analyzed using statistics software from IBM SPSS 19.

This approach allowed for a comprehensive evaluation of the impact of virtual character elements on perceived restorativeness in AR environments. The analytical methodology provided robust insights into the variations in restorative experiences between scenarios with and without virtual characters, contributing to the understanding of AR's efficacy in attention restoration. In the realm of AR, the integration of human images within virtual scenes represents a pivotal aspect of user experience, potentially influencing cognitive processes such as attention recovery. This research aims to meticulously examine the effects of incorporating human images in AR environments on the efficacy of attention recovery. The premise of this investigation is anchored in the hypothesis that human images, as familiar and relatable elements, might significantly enhance the attention restoration process compared to AR scenes devoid of such elements.

The study employs a methodical approach, leveraging quantitative measures to assess attention recovery. The Attention Recovery Scale serves as the primary tool for evaluating the participants' attention levels post-exposure to these scenarios. This research not only seeks to contribute to the existing body of knowledge in AR technology but also aims to provide practical insights for the design of AR applications.

For ultimate precision and dependability, this study's data was analyzed utilizing robust statistical approaches. The Attention Recovery Scale scores, collected from participants after experiencing AR scenarios, were analyzed using comparative statistics, including t-tests and correlation. These methods facilitated a comprehensive evaluation of the differential impact of human images in AR on attention recovery.

The authors conducted an analysis of means and correlations of the data collected. Utilizing SPSS software for analysis, it was revealed that the data obtained from the Perceived Restorativeness Scale (PRS) in AR scenes without virtual characters, as recorded by the 30 participants, showed that the average values for the first to fourth dimensions had an overall mean of approximately 2.91. In contrast, when virtual characters were introduced into the designed AR scenes, the overall average value of the PRS as reported by the participants increased to approximately 3.18. Notably, the statistical significance of this difference was confirmed with a p-value of 0.0051 ($p < 0.05$), indicating a significant variation in the data before and after the introduction of virtual character elements.

To effectively communicate these findings, the authors created bar graphs for a visual representation of the data. This visualization underscored the impact of integrating virtual characters into AR environments on the perceived restorativeness, as measured by the PRS. The graphical representation provided a clear and concise way to observe the significant enhancement in the restorative experience of participants interacting with AR scenes featuring virtual characters (Fig. 7).

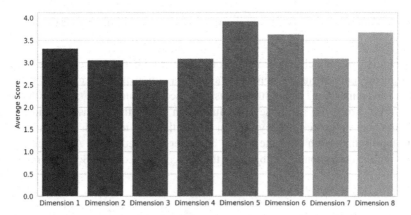

Fig. 7. Comparison of the average values of each dimension (by author)

The box plot analysis of the Attention Recovery Scale responses revealed a diverse distribution of data, encapsulating the variability and range of participant reactions to AR scenes with human images. The interquartile range highlighted the central tendency of responses, while the whiskers extended to capture the full spectrum of participant experiences. Notably, a few outliers suggested atypical responses, potentially indicating unique individual interactions with the AR environment. The distribution pattern underscored a correlation between the presence of human images and enhanced attention recovery, with the majority of responses clustering towards higher attention scores, suggesting the effectiveness of human imagery in facilitating cognitive engagement in AR scenarios [61] (Fig. 8).

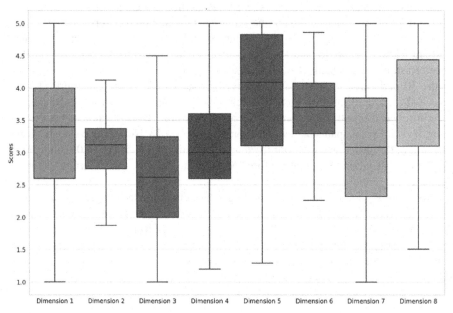

Fig. 8. Correlation analysis between attention restoration of AR image users (by author)

In addition, we can clearly see the strong correlation between these dimensions by comparing the four dimensions before and after the addition of virtual characters (Fig. 9).

The "first dimension" and "fifth dimension", "second dimension" and "sixth dimension", "third dimension" and "seventh dimension", "fourth dimension" and "eighth dimension" are compared one by one, in which the fifth to eighth dimension is the first to fourth dimension after the virtual character is added to the AR scene and the attention of the corresponding subjects in the "Perceptual recovery Scale" is improved.

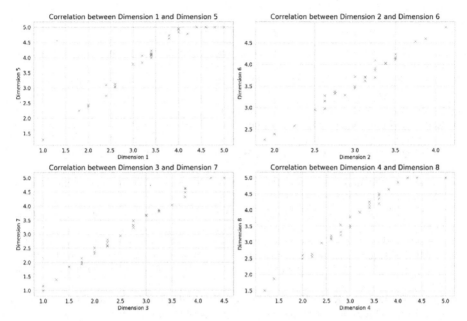

Fig. 9. Correlation analysis of dimensions before and after adding virtual characters (by author)

5.2 Discussion

This study has meticulously demonstrated that augmented reality (AR), particularly through the inclusion of virtual characters, significantly amplifies the sense of presence and immersion, crucial factors in the realm of cognitive rehabilitation and attention recovery therapies. The interactive dynamics enabled by virtual avatars not only deepen the engagement of users but also foster an enriched sense of 'being there,' a pivotal aspect for engendering a restorative experience. Our findings reveal that such immersive environments, facilitated by AR, are instrumental in enhancing focus and attention—key elements underpinning successful therapeutic outcomes.

The empirical evidence garnered from the controlled experiments underscores the efficacy of AR in transcending traditional therapeutic modalities, offering a more engaging and potentially more effective avenue for attention restoration. The interaction with avatars within these digitally crafted narrative spaces not only serves to captivate the users' attention but also significantly contributes to their cognitive restoration process.

In conclusion, the application of AR in therapeutic settings, as substantiated by our research, marks a promising frontier in cognitive rehabilitation. It beckons a future where digital and virtual interventions could become commonplace in addressing attention-related disorders, advocating for a broader integration of immersive technologies in therapeutic practices. This study lays the groundwork for subsequent research to explore diverse applications of AR in mental health, promising a new trajectory for enhancing therapeutic efficacy and patient engagement in cognitive rehabilitation.

References

1. Azuma, R.T.: A survey of augmented reality. Presence Teleoper. Virt. Environ. **6**(4), 355–385 (1997)
2. Caudell, T., Mizell, D.: Augmented reality: an application of heads-up display technology to manual manufacturing processes. In: Proceedings of the Twenty-Fifth Hawaii International Conference on System Sciences, pp. 659–669 (1992)
3. Rouse, R.: Game Design: Theory & Practice, 2nd edn. Wordware Publishing, Inc. (2005)
4. Carmigniani, J., Furht, B.: Augmented reality: an overview. In: Furht, B. (ed.) Handbook of Augmented Reality, pp. 3–46. Springer, Heidelberg (2011). https://doi.org/10.1007/978-1-4614-0064-6_1
5. Ryan, M.L.: Narrative as Virtual Reality: Immersion and Interactivity in Literature and Electronic Media. Johns Hopkins University Press (2001)
6. Murray, J.H.: Hamlet on the Holodeck: The Future of Narrative in Cyberspace. MIT Press (1997)
7. Kaplan, S., Talbot, J.F.: Psychological benefits of a wilderness experience. In: Altman, I., Wohlwill, J.F. (eds.) Behavior and the Natural Environment. Human Behavior and Environment, vol. 6, pp. 163–203. Springer, Boston (1983). https://doi.org/10.1007/978-1-4613-353 9-9_6
8. Hartig, T., Korpela, K.M., Evans, G.W., et al.: Validation of a measure of perceived environmenta l restorativeness. Göteborg Psychological Reports (1996)
9. Hartig, T., et al.: A measure of restorative quality in environments. Scand. J. Psychol. **38**(4), 315–328 (1997)
10. Hartig, T., et al.: The perceived restorativeness of environments: its utility for planning health promotion and disease prevention programs. Annu. Rev. Public Health **17**, 455–469 (1996)
11. von Lindern, E., Lymeus, F., Hartig, T.: The restorative environment: a complementary concept for salutogenesis studies. In: Mittelmark, M.B., et al. (eds.) The Handbook of Salutogenesis, pp. 181–195. Springer, Cham (2017). https://doi.org/10.1007/978-3-319-04600-6_19
12. Stevenson, M.P., et al.: Attention restoration theory II: a systematic review to clarify attention processes affected by exposure to natural environments. J. Toxicol. Environ. Health Part B **21**(4), 227–268 (2018)
13. Mattila, O., Korhonen, A., Pöyry, E., Hauru, K., Holopainen, J., Parvinen, P.: Restoration in a virtual reality forest environment. Comput. Hum. Behav. **107**, 106295 (2020)
14. Herman, L.M., Sherman, J.: Virtual nature: a psychologically beneficial experience. In: Chen, J., Fragomeni, G. (eds.) Virtual, Augmented and Mixed Reality. Multimodal Interaction, HCII 2019. LN CS, vol. 11574, pp. 441–449. Springer, Cham (2019). https://doi.org/10.1007/978-3-030-21607-8_34
15. Valtchanov, D., Barton, K.R., Ellard, C.: Restorative effects of virtual nature settings. Cyberpsychol. Behav. Soc. Netw. **13**(5), 503–512 (2010)
16. Yu, C.P., Lee, H.-Y., Luo, X.-Y.: The effect of virtual reality forest and urban environments on physiological and psychological responses. Urban Forest. Urban Greening **35**, 106–114 (2018)
17. Browning, M.H.E.M., Mimnaugh, K.J., van Riper, C.J., Laurent, H.K., LaValle, S.M.: Can simulated nature support mental health? Comparing short, single-doses of 360-degree nature videos in virtual reality with the outdoors. Front. Psychol. **10**, 2667 (2020). https://doi.org/10.3389/fpsyg.2019.02667
18. Chirico, A., et al.: Virtual reality and music therapy as distraction interventions to alleviate anxiety and improve mood states in breast cancer patients during chemotherapy. J. Cell. Physiol. **235**, 5353–5362 (2019)

19. Lindner, P., Hamilton, W., Miloff, A., Carlbring, P.: How to treat depression with low-intensity virtual reality interventions: perspectives on translating cognitive behavioral techniques into the virtual reality modality and how to make anti-depressive use of virtual reality-unique experience. Front. Psychiatry **10**, 792 (2019)

20. Yeo, N., et al.: What is the best way of delivering virtual nature for improving mood? An experimental comparison of high definition TV, 360° video, and computer generated virtual reality. J. Environ. Psychol. **72**, 101500 (2020)

21. Ijsselsteijn, W., Ridder, H., Freeman, J., Have, S.: Presence: concept, determinants and measurement. In: Proceedings of the SPIE—Human Vision and Electronic Imaging V, San Jose, CA, USA, 22–28 January 2000, vol. 3959, pp. 520–529 (2000)

22. Triberti, S., Villani, D., Riva, G.: Unconscious goal pursuit primes attitudes towards technology usage: a virtual reality experiment. Comput. Hum. Behav. **64**, 163–172 (2016)

23. Heater, C.: Being there: the subjective experience of presence. Presence **1**, 262–271 (1992)

24. Lin, C.J., Woldegiorgis, B.H.: Interaction and visual performance in stereoscopic displays: a review. J. Soc. Inf. Disp. **23**, 319–332 (2015)

25. Shu, Y., Huang, Y., Chang, S., Chen, M.: Do virtual reality head-mounted displays make a difference? A comparison of presence and self-efficacy between head-mounted displays and desktop computer-facilitated virtual environments. Virtual Real. **23**, 437–446 (2019)

26. Yildirim, I.G.: Time pressure as video game design element and basic need satisfaction. In: Proceedings of the 2016 CHI Conference Extended Abstracts, San Jose, CA, USA, May 2016 (2016)

27. Slater, M., Udoh, M.: Presence in immersive virtual environments. In: Proceedings of the IEEE Virtual Reality Annual International Symposium, Seattle, WA, USA, 18–22 September 1993 (1993)

28. Huang, M.P., Alessi, N.E.: Presence as an emotional experience. Stud. Health Technol. Inform. **62**, 148–153 (1999)

29. Draper, J.V., Kaber, D.B., Usher, J.M.: Telepresence. Hum. Fact. **40**, 354–375 (1998)

30. Barfield, W., Weghorst, S.: The sense of presence within virtual environments: a conceptual framework. In: Proceedings of the International Conference on Human-Computer Interaction: Software & Hardware Interfaces, Orlando, FL, USA, 8–13 August 1993 (1993)

31. Palanca, A., Lyons, A., Cooper, M., Lee, A., Moat, Y.: A comparison of nature and urban environments on creative thinking across different levels of reality. J. Environ. Psychol. **63**, 44–51 (2019)

32. Riva, G., Waterworth, J.A., Waterworth, E.L.: The layers of presence: a bio-cultural approach to understanding presence in natural and mediated environments. Cyberpsychol. Behav. **7**, 402–416 (2004)

33. Cheng, Y., Cui, Z.: An experimental methodology study on healthy lighting for the elderly with ad based on VR technology. In: 9th CJK Lighting Conference (2022)

34. Samantaray, A., Majumder, C., Kaur, T., Gulati, S., Gandhi, T.: Development of an augmented reality based joint attention training platform for autistic children. In: 2023 14th International Conference on Computing Communication and Networking Technologies (ICCCNT), July 2023 (2023)

35. Kazdin, A.E., Kendall, P.C.: Current progress and future plans for developing effective treatments: comments and perspectives. J. Clin. Child Psychol. **27**(2), 217–226 (1998)

36. Poliakov, S., Hrytsenko, L.: The usage of augmented class application for graphic competence development of students of the 5th–7th grades in the process of creating augmented reality projects. In: Problems, Achievements and Prospects of Vocational Education at Home and Abroad, October 2023 (2023)

37. Amelina, S., Tarasenko, R., Semerikov, S., Shen, L.: Using mobile applications with augmented reality elements in the self-study process of prospective translators. In: 14th International Conference on Computing Communication and Networking Technologies (ICCCNT), July 2023 (2023)
38. de Villers-Sidani, É., Mishra, J., Zhou, X., Voss, P.: Neuroplastic mechanisms underlying perceptual and cognitive enhancement. Neural Plast. **2016**, 6238571 (2016)
39. Dourish, P.: Where the Action Is: The Foundations of Embodied Interaction. MIT Press (2001)
40. Milgram, P., Kishino, F.: A taxonomy of mixed reality visual displays. IEICE Trans. Inf. Syst. **E77-D**(12), 1321–1329 (1994)
41. Biocca, F.: The Cyborg's Dilemma: progressive embodiment in virtual environments. J. Comput. Mediat. Commun. **3**(2), JCMC324 (1997)
42. Milgram, P., Kishino, F.: A taxonomy of mixed reality visual displays. IEICE Trans. Inf. Syst. **E77-D**(12), 1321–1329 (1994)
43. Biocca, F., Owen, C., Tang, A., Bohil, C.: Attention issues in spatial information systems: directing mobile users' visual attention using augmented reality. J. Manag. Inf. Syst. **23**(4), 163–184 (2007)
44. Slater, M., Wilbur, S.: A framework for immersive virtual environments (FIVE): speculations on the role of presence in virtual environments. Presence Teleoper. Virt. Environ. **6**(6), 603–616 (1997)
45. Zhou, F., Duh, H.B., Billinghurst, M.: Trends in augmented reality tracking, interaction and display: a review of ten years of ISMAR. In: Proceedings of the 7th IEEE/ACM International Symposium on Mixed and Augmented Reality, pp. 193–202 (2008)
46. Witmer, B.G., Singer, M.J.: Measuring presence in virtual environments: a presence questionnaire. Presence Teleoper. Virt. Environ. **7**(3), 225–240 (1998)
47. Jacko, J.: HCI Intelligent Multimodal Interaction Environments (2006)
48. Hookk, D.: Loop control of emotional balance in a museum reality-virtualization continuum problem definition and proposed approach (2006)
49. Veas, E., Méndez, E., Feiner, S.K., Schmalstieg, D.: Directing attention and influencing memory with visual saliency modulation. In: Proceedings of the SIGCHI Conference on Human Factors in Computing Systems (2011)
50. Volmer, B., et al.: A comparison of predictive spatial augmented reality cues for procedural tasks. IEEE Trans. Vis. Comput. Graph. **24**(10), 2846–2856 (2018)
51. Lynn, C.: Hearth and campfire influences on arterial blood pressure: defraying the costs of the social brain through fireside relaxation. Evol. Psychol. Int. J. Evol. Approach. Psychol. Behav. **12**(5), 983–1003 (2014)
52. Dunbar, R.I.M.: How conversations around campfires came to be. Proc. Natl. Acad. Sci. **111**, 14013–14014 (2014)
53. Aldeias, V.: Experimental approaches to archaeological fire features and their behavioral relevance. Curr. Anthropol. **58**, S191–S205 (2017)
54. Bal, M.: Narratology: Introduction to the Theory of Narrative. University of Toronto Press (1997)
55. Ryan, M.L.: Avatars of Story. University of Minnesota Press (2006)
56. Green, M.C., Brock, T.C.: The role of transportation in the persuasiveness of public narratives. J. Pers. Soc. Psychol. **79**(5), 701–721 (2000)
57. Hartig, T., Staats, H.: Linking preference for environments with their restorative quality. In: Tress, B., Tres, G., Fry, G., et al. (eds.) From Landscape Research to Landscape Planning: Aspects of Integration, Education and Application. Springer, Dordrecht (2005)
58. Ulrich, R.S., Simons, R.F., Losito, B.D., et al.: Stress recovery during exposure to natural and urban environments. J. Environ. Psychol. **11**(3), 201–230 (1991)

59. Karmanov, D., Hamel, R.: Assessing the restorative potential of contemporary urban environment(s): beyond the nature versus urban dichotomy. Landsc. Urban Plan. **86**(2), 115–125 (2008)
60. Wang, X., Rodiek, S., Wu, C., et al.: Stress recovery and restorative effects of viewing different urban park scenes in Shanghai, China. Urban Forest. Urban Green. **15**, 112–122 (2016)
61. Pramono, A., Wardhana, M., Rahayuningtyas, W., Iriaji, I., Hidajat, R., Puspasari, B.D.: Markerless mobile augmented reality (MAR) development of Wayang Krucil figures as an effort to increase knowledge and character learning (2021)

Design and Implementation of a Virtual Reality Tennis Serve Practice System for Creative Tennis Serve Practice

Yuichiro Hiramoto[1]([✉]), Mohammed Al-Sada[2], and Tatsuo Nakajima[1]

[1] Department of Computer Science and Engineering, Waseda University, Tokyo, Japan
{hira2023,tatsuo}@dcl.cs.waseda.ac.jp
[2] Department of Computer Science and Engineering, KINDI Center for Computing Research, Qatar University, Doha, Qatar
mohammed.alsada@qu.edu.qa

Abstract. We propose a Virtual Reality Tennis Serve Practice (VRTSP) system that utilizes 3D skeletal estimation from videos. VRTSP system employs a 3D skeletal estimation model with video shot from a single viewpoint as input to extract the movements of the professional athlete who serve as coaches. The user's movements are captured using motion capture sensors, allowing them to compare their own movements with those of the athlete in the VR space. This approach enables users to freely observe the athlete's movements from multiple angles, which, compared to the traditional practice method of watching videos on a screen, makes learning the tennis serve more enjoyable and expands the range of practice, contributing to creative tennis serve training. Furthermore, VRTSP system is not limited to tennis and has the potential to be applied to other sports as well.

Keywords: Artificial intelligence/machine learning · Entertainment and gaming · Tracking technologies · Training education and tutoring

1 Introduction

One method of improving sports performance is to observe and imitate the performance of highly skilled athletes [1–5]. For example, beginners can observe and practice how a professional tennis player serves or how a basketball player dribbles. However, in such scenarios, imitation is primarily based on visually observing professional athletes, and compared to practicing with a coach who can provide direct and detailed performance feedback, it can take a considerable amount of time to achieve the desired performance. Therefore, providing the ability to capture professional player's motions and systematically translating them to training procedures with real-time performance feedback is a critical aspect for successful training.

Accordingly, we introduce the design of a Virtual Reality Tennis Serve Practice (VRTSP) system using 3D skeletal estimation that is extracted from a single-viewpoint video. To capture the athlete's motion from the video, a pre-trained machine learning

© The Author(s), under exclusive license to Springer Nature Switzerland AG 2024
J. Y. C. Chen and G. Fragomeni (Eds.): HCII 2024, LNCS 14708, pp. 84–102, 2024.
https://doi.org/10.1007/978-3-031-61047-9_5

model is used to estimate the athlete's 3D motion from tennis serve videos shot taken from a single viewpoint. Then, the estimated 3D motion is projected onto a 3D model avatar in the VR space. Within the VR environment, users can practice serving while watching the 3D model's avatar, which is used to reproduce and display various movements of a professional athletes. In order to provide feedback, our system captures the user's movements using motion capture sensors and provides performance feedback to improve performance using the base motions of the professional athlete.

Our proposed approach has two main advantages. First, it enables capturing the movements of professional athletes from single-viewpoint video, which is easier than methods that require motion capture sensors or multiple-viewpoint video. Such capability enables users to virtually import and use any athlete's motion that are captured from a single video. Second, it enables users to observe and inspect tennis serves motions from multiple angles on the avatar in VR. By providing the ability to view the avatar's motion from multiple angles and to compare user's performance with captured the avatar's motions, users can adjust their body in real time and accurately learn how to imitate professional athletes body motion.

We conducted an evaluation of our system that focused on investigating our system's effectiveness in enabling casual users to learn professional athlete's serve motions. Overall, the results are positive and indicates that VRTSP system can lead to creative practice in tennis serve training where the user is free to customize the skill acquisition practice and find it enjoyable. Furthermore, the system showed potential for use in other training routines and other sports. In light of our results, we discuss future work direction and provide our conclusion.

2   Related Work

2.1   Skill Training Systems

Training systems for efficient acquisition of sports skills have been examined by various studies. Chan et al. proposed a system to support the acquisition of dance skills, where both the coach and the user wear motion capture sensors, and the discrepancy in the movement of each joint is fed back to the user in real time [6]. Kamel et al. proposed a motion practice system for practicing Tai Chi [7]. The movements of the user and the coach are captured with an RGB camera equipped with a depth sensor, and a machine learning model predicts the 3D skeleton. The user is provided with feedback on the coach's movements and correction points for each joint. OptiMotion is a golf training system that estimates the 3D skeleton from images of the user's front and side taken with two calibrated cameras and provides guidance on swing form [8].

Tennis, which involves complex movements of the limbs and joints, has been studied for practice systems using IT technology, just like other sports. Jiang et al. proposed a VR system for practicing tennis volleys [9]. In this system, no motion data of the coach is provided, and the user practices by hitting the ball with a racket towards a target point on the court in the VR space. At the beginning of the practice, the ball moves in slow motion, but as the user continues to hit the ball with the center of the racket, the speed of the ball approaches that of actual play. By adjusting the speed of the ball according to the user's skill level, the user can experience training that is different from that of real space practice. Moreover, compared to previous studies, this system combines 3D skeletal estimation from video with motion capture sensors to obtain real-time feedback from the movements of professional tennis players more easily.

2.2 Pose Estimation

Pose estimation is the task of predicting the positions of human body joints from images or sequences of images. With the advancement of deep learning technology, the accuracy of skeletal estimation from video has improved rapidly [10]. There are two types of pose estimation: two-dimensional skeletal estimation and 3D skeletal estimation.

Many highly accurate algorithms have been proposed for two-dimensional skeletal estimation. In particular, OpenPose is widely used as a two-dimensional pose estimation library [11].

For 3D skeletal estimation, there are methods that use single-viewpoint video as input and methods that use synchronized video from multiple viewpoints as input. 3D skeletal estimation from single-viewpoint video is convenient, but it is a difficult task because it requires predicting depth information to estimate the 3D skeleton from two-dimensional video. Skeletal estimation from single-viewpoint video is further divided into predictions for Single-person and Multi-person. For Single-person skeletal estimation, there are multiple approaches, including heatmap-based methods, methods that lift two-dimensional skeletons, and approaches that attempt to resolve data scarcity and ambiguity. Among these approaches, the two-stage pipeline approach, which predicts a two-dimensional skeleton from images and then estimates a 3D skeleton from a sequence of two-dimensional skeletons, has high skeletal estimation accuracy because it utilizes existing high-precision two-dimensional skeletal estimation models. Methods that predict a 3D skeleton from a sequence of two-dimensional skeletons include those using multilayer perceptrons [12], LSTM [13], and convolutional neural networks (CNN) [14]. There is also a model called Strided Transformer [15], which applies the Transformer [16], developed in the field of natural language processing and capable of extracting long-term features in time series data, to predict 3D skeletons from a sequence of two-dimensional skeletons. In this study, we use the Strided Transformer to obtain 3D skeletal information of an athlete's tennis serve from videos of the serve.

3 Design and Implementation of a Virtual Reality Tennis Serve Practice System

3.1 Requirements

We set the following requirements for the tennis serve practice system. VRTSP system was designed to meet these requirements during the development:

- A 3D serve-motion dataset of an athlete should be constructed from only the information in a single viewpoint video.
- The system should support the use of serve motions from multiple athletes.
- The system should enable user's to inspect and view an athlete's motion in VR from multiple directions.

- The system should allow user's to play, pause and replay motions at any speed, enabling users to inspect motion.
- The system should enable user's to compare their motion to the motions produced by professional athletes, providing users' with feedback about their performance.

By meeting these requirements, VRTSP system can effectively construct data on the athlete's serve motion. Furthermore, users can freely use viewpoint changes, playback speed adjustments, and pause functions to review and analyze the athlete's movements. Real-time comparison and feedback with the athlete lead to more creative tennis serve practice compared to practicing by watching videos.

3.2 Overview of the Design and Implementation

VRTSP system consists of the following two subsystems, as shown in Fig. 1:

1. An athlete motion prediction system that captures the movements of the athlete acting as a coach.
2. A VR tennis serve practice application where the user wears a VR headset and receives feedback.

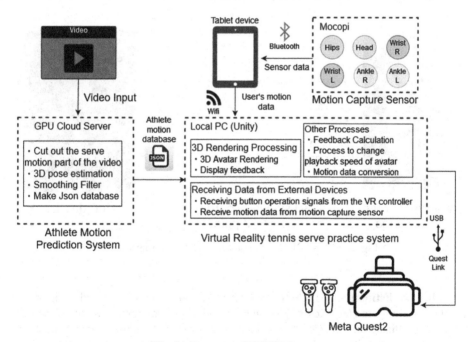

Fig. 1. Structure of VRTSP System

The training feedback information is visualized in three steps based on the captured and processed motion data. First, the athlete motion prediction system operates on a GPU cloud server [17]. This system takes single-viewpoint video (e.g., tennis match footage) as input, and a machine learning model predicts the athlete's movements. The predicted motion data is smoothed and filtered to remove noise, then downloaded from the server to the local environment for use in the subsequent VR tennis serve practice application (Fig. 1).

Next, the application is implemented as a Unity3D application on a PC, comparing the captured athlete's tennis serve motion data with the user's serve motion captured by motion sensors (mocopi [18]) in real-time (Fig. 1). Finally, the differences between the detected user's motion and the professional athlete's motion data are visualized on the Meta Quest2. This visual feedback helps detect discrepancies between the athlete's movements and the user's body movements.

3.3 Athlete Motion Prediction System

The athlete motion prediction system consists of a 3D skeletal estimation machine learning model [15] and a smoothing filter [19]. The input data is video shot from a single viewpoint, and the output data is a Json file containing frame numbers and coordinates for each skeletal joint. As shown in Fig. 2, the system pipeline predicts 17 points of skeletal coordinate information from the input athlete's video, which is then smoothed and output as a Json format database that can be downloaded.

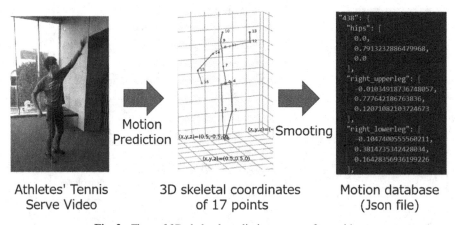

Athletes' Tennis   3D skeletal coordinates   Motion database
Serve Video   of 17 points   (Json file)

Fig. 2. Flow of 3D skeletal prediction process from video

3D Skeletal Estimation Machine Learning Model. The 3D skeletal estimation machine learning model takes single-viewpoint video as input and outputs 17 points of joint coordinate information. The Strided Transformer [15] is used for skeletal estimation from video. The model treats video as time-series data, so the input video is not processed frame by frame, but rather in batches of a few seconds. While skeletal estimation accuracy may decrease compared to methods using calibrated video shot from multiple viewpoints, there is the advantage of more easily capturing the athlete's movements.

The 17 joint coordinate names are "hips", "right-upperleg", "right-lowerleg", "right-foot", "left-upperleg", "left-lowerleg", "left-foot", "spine", "neck", "head1", "head2", "left-upperarm", "left-lowerarm", "left-hand", "right-upperarm", "right-lowerarm" and "right-hand."

Smoothing Filter. Since the 3D skeletal data obtained from the 3D skeletal estimation machine learning model contains noise, it is necessary to smooth the motion data. The Savitzky-Golay Filter [19] was adopted as the smoothing method. This filter performs a least-squares approximation of an n-th degree polynomial using data within a specified window size and smooths the data using the midpoint within the window of the approximated n-th degree polynomial. In this system, the motion data is smoothed using a least-squares approximation with a second-order polynomial by setting window_size = 50 and n = 2. This reduces the impact of noise and provides smooth motion data.

Json Database. The obtained 3D skeletal data can be downloaded as a Json format file, as shown in Fig. 3, for use in the VR tennis serve practice application. This Json file database records the xyz coordinates in 3D space for each of the 17 joints, allowing the predicted 3D skeleton of the athlete to be treated as 3D motion data. The Json file format is designed to include the skeletal coordinates of 17 joints for each frame. Each frame is indicated by keys such as "0", "1", "2", and each key stores the joint coordinate data. Furthermore, each joint is represented by a list containing three values (x coordinate, y coordinate, z coordinate) with the joint name (e.g., "hips", "right-upperleg") as the key. For example, the value of the "hips" key in the Json file in Fig. 3 is [0.0, 0.86, 0.0], representing the x, y, and z coordinates of the hips. This format allows the motion data to be structured and used as 3D motion data of an athlete in a VR tennis serve practice application.

```
 1   {
 2       "0": {
 3           "hips": [
 4               0.0,
 5               0.8647274597791526,
 6               0.0
 7           ],
 8           "right_upperleg": [
 9               0.10341249987280747,
10               0.8646388223160445,
11               0.0026149485027628233
12           ],
```

Fig. 3. Athlete Motion Json File

3.4 VR Tennis Serve Practice Application

The VR tennis serve practice application consists of the following three subsystems:

1. Unity application
2. Motion capture sensor
3. VR head-mounted display (Meta Quest2)

Figure 4 shows the relationship between these subsystems. The athlete motion database stores the athlete's motion data (Json file describing joint coordinates) obtained from the athlete motion prediction system described in Sect. 3.3. The user's motion data is acquired from the motion capture sensor and compared to the motion data of the athlete's motion. The comparison results and movements of the user and athlete are displayed through 3D rendering processing.

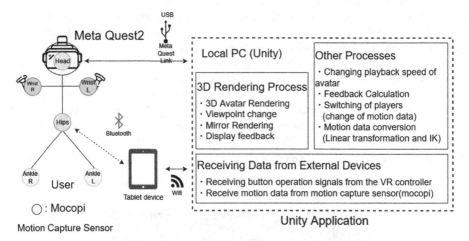

Fig. 4. VR Tennis Serve Practice Application

Unity Application. The design and implementation of the Unity application is as follows:

Receiving Data from External Devices. As shown in Fig. 4, the Unity application communicates with two external devices, the motion capture sensor and Meta Quest2, for data transmission and reception.

For communication between the Unity application and the motion capture sensor (mocopi), the mocopi Receiver Plugin for Unity, a Unity-oriented API library, is used to receive motion data. This library enables real-time and stable reception of motion data through UDP communication over Wifi between the PC and the mocopi application (tablet device).

Next, for communication between the Unity application and Meta Quest2, Meta Quest Link is used to transmit video data and receive input data from the Quest2 controllers. The Unity application detects button press signals from the controllers by polling the state of the buttons via Quest Link, enabling user application operations (selecting athletes, adjusting avatar playback speed/pausing, changing viewpoints).

Rendering Athlete 3D Motion Data. The rendering process for the athlete's 3D motion data involves three steps: 1) linear transformation of motion data, 2) calculation of rotation angles for each joint through IK, and 3) projection onto a 3D avatar.

First, a linear transformation of the motion data is performed to apply the athlete's 3D motion data to a 3D avatar. A linear transformation is performed to match the athlete's 3D motion data obtained from the athlete motion prediction system in Sect. 3.3 to the joint lengths of the 3D model avatar. Skeletal unit vectors between joints such as arms and legs are calculated from the athlete's motion data, and by multiplying these unit vectors by the lengths of the 3D model avatar's skeleton, coordinate data is adjusted to fit the size of the 3D avatar.

Next, in the calculation of rotation angles for each joint through IK, the motion data after linear transformation is applied to the athlete's 3D model by converting the coordinate values for each joint into angles. BioIK [20], which provides the functionality to calculate the rotation angles for all joints of the body, is adopted to calculate the rotation angles for each joint.

Finally, in the projection onto the 3D avatar, the angles for each joint calculated by BioIK [20] are projected onto the Unity Chan 3D avatar[1]. This renders the athlete's motion as a 3D avatar, providing users with intuitive visual feedback.

Rendering User 3D Motion Data. In the Unity application, the 3D motion data received from the mocopi Receiver Plugin for Unity is applied to the Unity Chan 3D avatar, allowing the user to see their own movements in the VR environment.

Real-Time Feedback Processing. In real-time feedback calculation, the movements of the athlete projected onto the 3D avatar and the user's movements captured from mocopi are compared for each joint by projecting them onto the 3D avatar. The Euclidean distance between the coordinates of the athlete's 3D avatar and the user's 3D avatar is calculated for each joint every 0.1 s.

This Euclidean distance value is used as an indicator of joints with significant discrepancies. A larger Euclidean distance value indicates a greater difference between the movements of the athlete and the user, making it clear which joints have particularly large discrepancies. The calculated Euclidean distances are sorted in descending order for each joint, and the top five joints with the largest discrepancies are displayed in the VR space. This allows the user to understand in real-time which parts of their body have significant differences from the athlete's movements and receive effective feedback.

Mirror and Feedback Rendering. In the Unity application, as shown in Fig. 5, the discrepancies between the motions of the athlete and the user can be checked through a mirror and real-time feedback. Regarding the mirror, the front and side views of the user's and athlete's 3D avatars are projected, and they can be observed from a rear perspective. The real-time feedback displays the top five joints with the largest errors in red when observed from a rear perspective.

---

[1] © Unity Technologies Japan/UCL.

Other Processes. This paragraph explains the user operation processes in the Unity application for changing viewpoints, adjusting the playback speed and pausing the athlete's motion, and changing athletes. For viewpoint change operations, pressing the A button on the right controller of Meta Quest2 allows the user to change the viewpoint from which the athlete's motion is observed to four different perspectives: front, front-right diagonal, front-left diagonal, and rear. Regarding athlete motion playback, pressing the X button on the left controller of Meta Quest2 allows for playback and pausing. The playback speed can be adjusted from 0.5x to 1x speed using the "Speed" scrollbar displayed at the top right of the screen in Fig. 5, using the trigger buttons on the left and right controllers of Meta Quest2. The motion of one athlete can be changed to that of another by using the trigger buttons on the left and right controllers of Quest2 from the "Athlete" drop-down list displayed on the top left of the screen in Fig. 5.

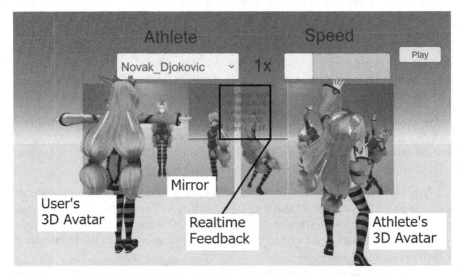

Fig. 5. A Screenshot of VR Tennis Serve Practice Application

Motion Capture Sensor. The mocopi motion capture sensor is used to capture the user's movements. Mocopi, as shown in Fig. 6, uses data from sensors attached to six locations on the head, waist, both hands, and both feet to estimate the position and posture of the user's body joints. The acceleration and angular velocity data obtained from the sensors are transmitted via Bluetooth to the mocopi application (running on a tablet terminal), which makes the estimation of the 3D skeleton posture. The mocopi application also estimates the positions of joints not equipped with sensors using a machine learning model, enabling full-body motion capture. The full-body joint data predicted by the mocopi application are transmitted to the Unity application on the PC via UDP communication over Wifi. This allows for the real-time acquisition of the user's motion data and the reproduction of movements in the Unity application.

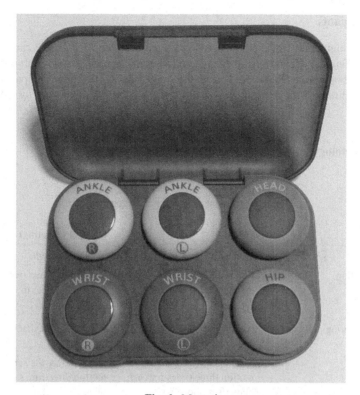

Fig. 6. Mocopi

VR Head-Mounted Display. We adopt Meta Quest2 as a VR head-mounted display. Through Meta Quest Link, the screen of the Unity application on the PC is projected onto the Meta Quest2 via USB3. The application itself operates on the PC, not on the Quest2.

4 Evaluation

We designed our experiment to investigate whether or our system is effective in enabling user's to successfully learn professional athletes tennis motion. Therefore, we designed the evaluation to compare the VRTSP system with a video viewing tennis serve practice system (VVTSP), which uses a screen to view tennis motion. We accordingly captured and compared the motion data of both systems, and also compared them qualitatively based on a questionnaire and the System Usability Scale (SUS) [21].

4.1 Participants

We hired 12 university and graduate students aged between 21 and 27 years, with 11 males and 1 female. All participants were tennis beginners, and did not report significant eye-sight or body issues that would effect the study. We divided the participants evenly on each condition of the experiment, six used the VRTSP and the other used VVTSP (baseline).

4.2 Methodology

Table 1. Content of the control experiment

	Group 1	Group 2 (baseline)
System	VRTSP System	VVTSP System
Type of motion	Randomly select two of three different athlete motions	Randomly select two of three different athlete motions
Practice time	10 min	10 min
operations during practice	Adjustable playback speed and pause	Adjustable playback speed and pause
Motion test	Demonstrate the serving motion three times for each player's motion	Demonstrate the serving motion three times for each player's motion
Equipment during practice and testing	Quest2 Controller, Quest2, mocopi	Quest2 Controller, Quest2, mocopi
System Usability Evaluation from Subjects	Questionnaire, SUS score	Questionnaire, SUS score
Serve Motion Evaluation Method	Expert Evaluation, Quantitative Comparison of Motion Data	Expert Evaluation, Quantitative Comparison of Motion Data

The flow of our experiment is shown in Table 1. VRTSP system allowed participants to practice serves by watching and confirming the athlete's 3D model avatar in the VR space. In addition, VRTSP system allowed for playback speed adjustment (0.5 to 1 times, continuously variable), pausing, viewpoint changing, and changing the observed player using the Meta Quest2 controller (Table 1). On the other hand, VVTSP system allowed participants to practice serves by watching and confirming the athlete's serve motion on a screen. VVTSP system also allowed for playback speed adjustment (0.25, 0.5, and 1 times), loop playback, and pausing and changing the observed player using mouse operations.

Participants practiced two randomly assigned serve motions out of three types of serve motions performed by the following professional tennis players: Grigor Dimitrov, Daniil Medvedev, and Novak Djokovic in ATP2020 matches. Participants in each group used their corresponding system to practice for 10 min. Participants in the VRTSP system group could adjust the playback speed and pause the 3D avatar acting as the teacher. Participants in the VVTSP system group could adjust the playback speed and pause the athlete's video.

At the test time, both groups performed three tests for each of the two types of athlete serve motions they had learned during practice. During both practice and testing, participants wore Meta Quest2 controllers and mocopi motion capture sensors. In addition, participants in the VRTSP system group wore the Meta Quest2 head-mounted display. The participant's serve motions were evaluated by a tennis expert (with 8 years of experience). Furthermore, a quantitative evaluation comparing the participant's motion data with the athlete's motion data were conducted. Lastly, participants also took a usability questionnaire and SUS questionnaire.

4.3 Experiment Procedure

The procedure of this experiment is as follows:

First, a researcher randomly assigned each participant to either VRTSP or VVTSP, and briefed each participant about the flow of the experiment, the content of the tasks, and how to operate each system. Participants in both groups were then asked to wear a motion capture sensor (Mocopi) and hold a Meta Quest2 controller in their hands. Participants in the VRTSP group additionally wore a Meta Quest2 head-mounted display.

Next, each participant was given about 3 min to get accustomed to using the system. During the familiarization stage, the functions of the system were explained verbally the researcher, and participants were required to try each system function at least once. Once the usability of the system was confirmed by participants, a 10-min practice task was started. A researcher informed participants when there was 5 min and 1 min remaining to finish the practice stage. After the practice stage, the motion test was conducted. Participants were tested immediately after a signal from the researcher, performing each of the two types of athlete serve motions they had practiced three times, for a total of six times. During the test, participants were asked to perform the serve motions at the same speed as during practice. After the test, participants answered a questionnaire on a PC, and the experiment was concluded. To ensure accurate motion data acquisition, we recalibrated mocopi sensors approx. every 5 min throughout the experiment. Overall, each trial took approx. 20 min to finish.

4.4 Evaluation Design

We used both quantitative and qualitative evaluations. First, for the quantitative evaluation, we conducted an expert evaluation, motion data comparison evaluation, and SUS score evaluation. The expert evaluation included a tennis specialist who evaluated the participants' serve motions and giving them a score on a scale from 0 to 100 points to the following movement-segment: movements of both arms, legs, and the torso. The average of the three segments' scores was calculated as the overall score for one serve motion. The detailed evaluation criteria are shown in Table 2.

Table 2. Expert Evaluation Items and Criteria

Evaluation item	Evaluation criteria
Arm movement	Position of hands and elbows, Whether the elbows are extended in a straight line or not
Foot movement	Position of feet and knees, Whether there is foot elasticity or not
Movement of the torso	Body orientation, warp

Next, in the motion data comparison, the similarity between the participants' motion data obtained during the tennis serve test and the athlete's motion data was evaluated. The participants' motion data captured from the sensors were recorded every 0.1 s. To measure the similarity between the participants' and athletes' motion data, the Dynamic Time Warping (DTW) distance [22] was calculated. DTW distance is a method that finds the optimal alignment between two time-dependent arrays and nonlinearly warps the arrays to match each other. DTW distance is suitable for comparing time-series data with different speeds between participants, such as serve motion data, because it can automatically deal with time deformations and different speeds related to time-dependent data. A t-test was conducted to investigate whether there was a significant difference between the groups using VRTSP system and VVTSP system based on this DTW distance. Finally, the SUS score was evaluated using the SUS score obtained from the questionnaire conducted on the PC after the test to investigate the difference in SUS scores between VRTSP system and VVTSP system. A t-test was conducted. Subsequently, for qualitative evaluation, a questionnaire was conducted on the PC after the tennis serve test to investigate the usability of each system. The content of the questionnaire conducted after the tennis serve test is listed in Table 3. Q1, Q2, Q3, and Q4 were rated on a 5-point Likert scale from 1 to 5, and Q5 was an open-ended response.

Table 3. Questionnaire Questions

No.	Question	Answer Style
1	Have you found the system useful in practicing your tennis serve?	5-point Likert scale (1: Strongly Disagree -5: Strongly Agree)
2	Do you think it would be interesting to use this system for tennis practice lessons?	5-point Likert scale (1: Strongly Disagree -5: Strongly Agree)
3	Did you find it easy to practice your tennis serve?	5-point Likert scale (1: Strongly Disagree -5: Strongly Agree)
4	How likely would you be to recommend practicing tennis serves with this system to a friend?	5-point Likert scale (1: Strongly Disagree -5: Strongly Agree)
5	What are your impressions of the training system?	Open-ended

4.5 Results

Figure 7 below shows the results of the questionnaire (Q1, Q2, Q3, Q4) for the practice group on VVTSP system and the practice group on VRTSP system.

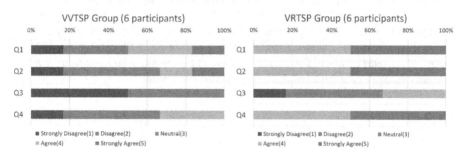

Fig. 7. Questionnaire results (5-point Likert scale) for VVTSP system group and VRTSP system group

Table 4. Average score and standard deviation of 5-point Likert scale questions

	Q1		Q2		Q3		Q3	
	Mean	SD	Mean	SD	Mean	SD	Mean	SD
VVTSP	3.00	1.55	3.00	1.41	1.50	0.55	2.50	1.22
VRTSP	4.50	0.55	4.50	0.55	2.83	1.17	4.50	0.55

Table 4 shows the mean and standard deviation of the 5-point Likert scale scores in the questionnaire results for the groups practiced with the VVTSP and VRTSP systems. Unpaired two-tailed t-tests were conducted to examine whether the scores in each question were significantly different between the two groups. The results were $t(10) = -2.24, p = 0.049$ for Q1, $t(10) = -2.42, p = 0.036$ for Q2, $t(10) = -2.53, p = 0.030$ for Q3, and $t(10) = -3.65, p = 0.004$ for Q4. The results of the t-test show that $p < 0.05$ for all cases of Q1, Q2, Q3, and Q4, which indicates a significant difference.

Impressions of Using the System. Regarding the questionnaire results for Q5 on impressions of using the system, the following comments were obtained from the group practicing with VVTSP system:

"It is helpful to refer to the movements of a professional, but it is difficult to know how well I am imitating the professional's movements.", "It was hard to understand how to move my body just from two-dimensional footage.", "Without using a racket or ball, it is difficult to check progress or feel improvement.", "By adjusting the speed of the video and comparing my movements, I was able to practice tennis serves and felt that I had improved compared to before using the system."

On the other hand, the following comments were obtained from the group practicing with VRTSP system:

"I thought it was good to be able to see myself in the third person in VR. It would be nice to have a feature to memorize and review movements,", "I could check the professional's motions from multiple angles, and the differences from my own motions were numerically represented, so I felt it was easy to learn the correct form on my own.", "Looking in the mirror in the VR space, I noticed differences from the professional's motions, and the mirror also helped with corrections.", "I thought it would be useful for people with tennis experience who want to refer to professionals.", "It seemed difficult for beginners to master."

SUS Score

Table 5. The results of SUS score

Type of system	Average of SUS score	Standard deviation of SUS score
VVTSP System	73.33	17.37
VRTSP System	75.00	17.75

The following Table 5 shows the average values and unbiased standard deviations of the SUS scores for the group that used VVTSP system and the group that used VRTSP system. In addition, an independent two-tailed t-test was conducted to evaluate the significant difference in SUS scores between the two groups. The degrees of freedom were 10, the p-value was 0.873, and the t-value was -0.164. Since $p > 0.05$, there is no significant difference in scores between the participants who used VVTSP and VRTSP system.

Expert Evaluation. The following Table 6 shows the results of the Expert Evaluation for the group that used VVTSP system and the group that used proposed VRTSP system. In addition, an independent two-tailed t-test was conducted to evaluate the change in Expert Evaluation scores between the two groups. The degrees of freedom were 10, the p-value was 0.136, and the t-value was -1.620. Since $p > 0.05$, therefore, there is no significant difference in scores between the participants who used VVTSP and VRTSP system.

Table 6. The results of Expert Evaluation

Type of system	Average of Expert Evaluation	Standard deviation of Expert Evaluation
VVTSP System	68.61	9.96
VRTSP System	76.39	6.26

Motion Data Similarity Comparison. Table 7 shows the average values and unbiased standard deviations of the DTW distances between the participants' and athletes' serve motion data for the group that used VVTSP system and the group that used VRTSP system. The smaller DTW distance indicates that the participant's and athlete's motions are more similar. In addition, an independent two-tailed t-test was conducted to evaluate the significant difference in DTW distances between the two groups. The degrees of freedom were 10, the p-value was 0.52, and the t-value was 0.639. Since $p > 0.05$, there is no significant difference.

Table 7. The results of Motion Data Similarity Comparison

Type of system	Average of DTW distance	Standard deviation of DTW distance
VVTSP System	5.35	1.63
VRTSP System	5.06	2.20

4.6 Discussion

System Usability. The questionnaire results shown in Fig. 7 and Table 4 indicate that participants found practicing the VRTSP system more effective, interesting, and easier to practice than practicing the VVTSP system. The t-test results for all 5-point Likert scale scores for Q1, Q2, Q3, and Q4 confirmed significant differences, with the VRTSP system scores higher than those of the VVTSP system. These results indicate that the VRTSP system contributes to creative tennis serve practice that makes practice feel easy and fun.

The results of the Q5 questionnaire showed that the participants felt that it was easier to check the players' movements and correct their own movements when practicing with the VRTSP system than when practicing with the VVTSP system, due to the multiple angles of observation, mirrors, and feedback functions in the VR space.

SUS Score. From the results in Table 5 and the t-test, we can't see there is a significant difference in SUS scores between VVTSP system and VRTSP system. This may be due to the fact that many participants are accustomed to the usual operation of video viewing, while some are unfamiliar with the operation of VR use.

Expert Evaluation. From the results in Table 6 and the t-test, we can't see a significant difference in the results of the Expert Evaluation between VVTSP system and VRTSP system. This may be due to the short practice time in the experiment and the differences in the basic physical abilities of the participants affecting the scores. In addition, in the group practicing with VRTSP system, a few participants were not fully able to utilize the viewpoint changing and slow-motion playback features during practice, which may not have effectively translated into skill improvement. In particular, the practice time during the experiment was 10 min, and a longer practice time is needed to master the features. On the other hand, the video operations were more familiar to many participants, unlike VR, and they may have been able to use them effectively for skill improvement.

Quantitative Comparison of Motion Data. From the results in Table 7 and the t-test, we can't see a significant difference in the DTW distances between the participants' and athletes' motion data between the VVTSP system group and the VRTSP system group. This may be due to the same reasons as the Expert Evaluation, such as the short practice time in the experiment, differences in the participants' physical abilities, and unfamiliarity with VRTSP system's operations. Additionally, the large measurement errors of the mocopi motion capture sensors may have had a significant impact on the DTW distances.

5   Conclusion

In this study, we aimed to provide a creative method for practicing tennis serves and developed a VR tennis serve practice system using 3D skeletal estimation from videos. The results of our evaluations showed that practicing serves with VRTSP system was perceived by participants as more interesting and useful compared to practicing with the baseline video viewing system. In the usability study of VRTSP system, the ability to observe athletes' movements from multiple angles and to check the discrepancy between athletes' and their own movements through mirrors and feedback were found to be effective for tennis serve practice. These results indicate that VRTSP system is effective as a creative method for practicing tennis serves.

The results of the expert evaluation and the quantitative comparison of motion data did not show a significant difference in tennis serve skills acquisition between VRTSP system and VVTSP system. This may be due to the low accuracy of motion capture and 3D skeletal estimation. Furthermore, the experiment allowed only 10 min of practice time, which may not have been sufficient for participants to fully utilize the features of VRTSP system and translate them into skill improvement. The SUS evaluation did not show significant improvement in VRTSP system compared to the video viewing system.

This may be due to the fact that many participants were already accustomed to using the video viewing system and the visual feedback in VRTSP system may have been difficult to understand.

As future work, improving the system's usability is a challenge. Methods for improving usability include enhancing the accuracy of motion capture and 3D skeletal estimation from videos, improving the accuracy of IK processing when projecting the estimated skeletal coordinate data onto a 3D avatar, introducing visual feedback, and introducing objects such as rackets and balls for a more realistic serve practice method. Additionally, to measure the effectiveness of practice with the system more accurately, it is necessary to allow for longer practice times than 10 min. Another challenge is to verify the effectiveness of this system for skill acquisition in sports fields other than tennis.

References

1. Ste-Marie, D.M., Law, B., Rymal, A.M., Jenny, O., Hall, C., McCullagh, P.: Observation interventions for motor skill learning and performance: an applied model for the use of observation. Int. Rev. Sport Exerc. Psychol. 5(2), 145–176 (2012)
2. Al-Abood, S.A., Davids, K., Bennett, S.J.: Specificity of task constraints and effects of visual demonstrations and verbal instructions in directing learners' search during skill acquisition. J. Mot. Behav. 33(3), 295–305 (2001)
3. McCullagh, P., Weiss, M.R., Ross, D.: Modeling considerations in motor skill acquisition and performance: an integrated, approach. Exerc. Sport Sci. Rev. 17(1), 475–514 (1989)
4. Heyes, C.M., Foster, C.L.: Motor learning by observation: evidence from a serial reaction time task. Q. J. Exp. Psychol. Sect. A 55(2), 593–607 (2002)
5. Martens, R., Burwitz, L., Zuckerman, J.: Modeling effects on motor performance. Res. Q. Am. Alliance Health Phys. Educ. Recreation 47(2), 277–291 (1976)
6. Chan, J.C., Leung, H., Tang, J.K., Komura, T.: A virtual reality dance training system using motion capture technology. IEEE Trans. Learn. Technol. 4(2), 187–195 (2010)
7. Kamel, A., Liu, B., Li, P., Sheng, B.: An investigation of 3D human pose estimation for learning Tai Chi: a human factor perspective. Int. J. Hum.-Comput. Interact. 35(4–5), 427–439 (2019)
8. OptiMotion GOLFTEC. https://www.golftec.com/optimotion. Accessed 9 Jan 2024
9. Jiang, S., Rekimoto, J.: Mediated-timescale learning: manipulating timescales in virtual reality to improve real-world tennis forehand volley. In: Proceedings of the 26th ACM Symposium on Virtual Reality Software and Technology, pp. 1–2 (2020)
10. Liu, W., Bao, Q., Sun, Y., Mei, T.: Recent advances of monocular 2D and 3D human pose estimation: a deep learning perspective. ACM Comput. Surv. 55(4), 1–41 (2022)
11. Cao, Z., Simon, T., Wei, S.E., Sheikh, Y.: Realtime multi-person 2D pose estimation using part affinity fields. In: Proceedings of the IEEE Conference on Computer Vision and Pattern Recognition, pp. 7291–7299 (2017)
12. Martinez, J., Hossain, R., Romero, J., Little, J.J.: A simple yet effective baseline for 3D human pose estimation. In: Proceedings of the IEEE International Conference on Computer Vision, pp. 2640–2649 (2017)
13. Hossain, M.R.I., Little, J.J.: Exploiting temporal information for 3D human pose estimation. In: Ferrari, V., Hebert, M., Sminchisescu, C., Weiss, Y. (eds.) Proceedings of the European Conference on Computer Vision (ECCV), pp. 68–84. Springer, Cham (2018). https://doi.org/10.1007/978-3-030-01249-6_5
14. Pavllo, D., Feichtenhofer, C., Grangier, D., Auli, M.: 3D human pose estimation in video with temporal convolutions and semi-supervised training. In: Proceedings of the IEEE/CVF Conference on Computer Vision and Pattern Recognition, pp. 7753–7762 (2019)

15. Li, W., Liu, H., Ding, R., Liu, M., Wang, P., Yang, W.: Exploiting temporal contexts with strided transformer for 3D human pose estimation. IEEE Trans. Multimedia **25**, 1282–1293 (2022)
16. Vaswani, A., et al.: Attention is all you need. In: Advances in Neural Information Processing Systems, vol. 30 (2017)
17. Welcome To Colaboratory. https://colab.research.google.com/. Accessed 1 Feb 2024
18. Sony Corporation-mocopi. https://www.sony.net/Products/mocopi-dev/en/. Accessed 18 Jan 2024
19. Schafer, R.W.: What is a Savitzky-Golay filter? (lecture notes). IEEE Signal Process. Mag. **28**(4), 111–117 (2011)
20. Starke, S.: Bio IK: a memetic evolutionary algorithm for generic multi-objective inverse kinematics. Doctoral dissertation, Staats-und Universitätsbibliothek Hamburg Carl von Ossietzky (2020)
21. Brooke, J.: SUS: a 'quick and dirty' usability. Usability Eval. Ind. **189**(3), 189–194 (1996)
22. Senin, P.: Dynamic time warping algorithm review. Inf. Comput. Sci. Dept. Univ. Hawaii Manoa Honolulu **855**(1–23), 40 (2008)

Designing Immersive Music Visualization Experience for Preschoolers Based on MR

Xin Hu[✉]

City University of Macau, SAR 82000, Macau, China
xinhu@cityu.edu.mo

Abstract. The traditional 'teacher-centered' indoctrination model of music education reduces children's enjoyment of learning music. Preschool children are naturally curious, energetic, and have short attention spans, making it difficult to explore traditional music. This teaching model is increasingly unsuitable for the needs of contemporary enlightenment education. This study is based on the actual implementation of the "MR Music Classroom" project, using mixed reality (MR) technology to draw inspiration from traditional Chinese children's stories and transform them into Visually rich content. Virtual teaching content and real space are superimposed on children for learning and interaction. The modular 25-min music teaching process is both educational and entertaining, providing preschool children with an overall experience in visual, tactile, and interactive dimensions. In the context of integrating MR into introductory music education, the project feasibility assessment included evaluating typical examples of complex MR system environments and measuring the popularity of the Music Magic Classroom. This move is intended to demonstrate the feasibility of the project. The results of this research have certain reference value for the application of MR teaching model and user interface interaction in educational environments. Words.

Keywords: MR · Preschoolers · Music Classroom · Experience design

1 Introduction

Preschoolers' music education is an important part of pre-school education. With the help of scientific and systematic preschool children music education, teachers and parents can better stimulate children's creativity, aesthetic ability, and expressive ability, and promote the healthy development of children's physiology and psychology [1]. According to Paul Milgram and Fumio Kishino's classification of MR [2], applications of MR include (1) environment understanding: spatial mapping and localization of points; (2) human understanding: manual tracking, visual tracking, and voice input; (3) spatial sound effects; (4) location and localization in both physical and virtual spaces; (5) 3D asset collaboration in MR spaces. Asset Collaboration. MR is becoming mainstream among consumers and businesses, providing instinctive interactions with inhabited spatial data and buddies, freeing us from screen-bound experiences.

J. Y. C. Chen and G. Fragomeni (Eds.): HCII 2024, LNCS 14708, pp. 103–111, 2024.
https://doi.org/10.1007/978-3-031-61047-9_6

MR is a combination of technologies that provide not only new ways of viewing, but also new ways of inputting, and it is a further development of virtual reality (VR) technology, which enhances the immersion of the user's experience by presenting virtual scene information in the real scene and building an interactive feedback information loop between the real world, the virtual world, and the user. This study focuses on MR narratives and user interactions in conjunction with preschool children, which is a specific subset of VR that involves interactions between computers, humans, and environments in the convergence of the real and virtual worlds. The combination of these three fundamental elements lays the foundation for creating a true "MR Music Classroom" mixed reality experience, including cloud-powered computer processing, advanced input methods, and environmental awareness. As preschoolers move through the physical world, their activities are reflected in the digital reality. Physical boundaries affect mixed reality experiences such as story interactions or task-based guidance during interactions. With environmental input and perception, experiences begin to merge between physical and digital reality.

MR blends the physical and digital worlds. These two realities define the two extremes of a range called the "virtual continuum". We refer to this range of realities as the " MR Range", where one end is the physical reality where human beings are located, and the other end is the corresponding digital reality (see Fig. 1). This study focuses on three aspects of the MR music teaching characteristics, Preschoolers ' perception of rhythm measurement and the design of MR music classroom interaction: (1) Analyzing and comparing the current state of research and demand characteristics of traditional music teaching at home and abroad. (2) To propose a child-centered hybrid music teaching model based on the assessment of children's visual, auditory, and tactile abilities and the connection between basic music theory and students' visual, auditory, and behavioral factors. (3) Preliminary evaluation of the MR music classroom teaching model .

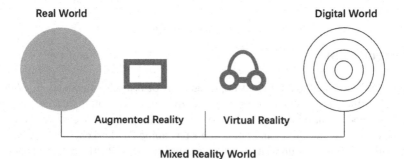

Fig. 1. Schematic of MR in relation to VR and AR.

2 Current Situation of Music Enlightenment Teaching

2.1 Pre-school Practice Stage

Currently, preschool music education research in foreign countries has reached a high level of maturity, resulting in the development of well-established methods. For instance, the Orff teaching method primarily emphasizes fostering children's enthusiasm and initiative towards music learning, effectively stimulating their passion for musical exploration. The Kodaly teaching method focuses on enhancing overall musical comprehension and establishing a solid foundation for comprehensive music learning. Dalcroze body rhythm addresses the coordination of physical expression during Preschoolers' engagement with music [3].

2.2 Creative Practice Stage

The implementation of preschool music education is demonstrated through the utilization of musical instruments. Due to children's incomplete knowledge structure, their ability to develop creative thinking in music is currently unattainable. The progression from memory to creation in human thinking requires a lengthy accumulation of knowledge systems (see Fig. 2), Bloom's taxonomy serves as the backbone of many teaching philosophies, in particular, those that lean more towards skills rather than content. Presently, many Chinese parents opt for professional instrument teachers and mobile courses to provide their children with music education; however, mobile devices lack environmental awareness and fail to integrate physical and digital realities.

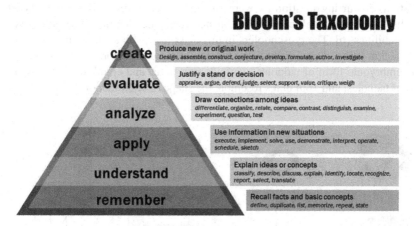

Fig. 2. Bloom's taxonomy [5].

2.3 Student-Centered Teaching Strategies

According to the practical teaching experience of music education in China, diversification is considered one of the crucial directions for music education in China. Preschool music education for children should also incorporate a diversified development strategy and establish a comprehensive preschool music education system. In music teaching activities, it is essential to adopt a student-centered approach that encourages students' initiative and enthusiasm. Utilizing MR Technology to create a situational atmosphere becomes highly significant by extracting story construction elements from real cultural backgrounds and integrating them with musical content. This enables students to seamlessly integrate their learning into real-life scenarios, imbuing new structured knowledge with meaning and fostering an environment where they can apply what they have learned. Such an approach proves beneficial for consolidating knowledge and enhancing learning outcomes.

3   Music Class for Preschoolers

3.1   The Selection of Instructional Materials in the Class

In terms of content and application, China's traditional culture is extensive and profound. This course specifically selects "Little Tadpoles Looking for their mother" as the basis for designing teaching materials, with a focus on staff music learning. The developmental journey of tadpoles' bears striking resemblance to the syllables represented by musical notes on the staff. Preschool children find it relatively simple to associate tadpole shapes with musical notes through visual thinking, making it easily comprehensible for them to grasp this concept (see Fig. 3), Additionally, children are inclined towards repetition and interaction; therefore, it is essential to incorporate elements in the curriculum that facilitate easy memorization and active participation. This can be achieved through the utilization of recurring question-answer structures or action-oriented instructions, which not only enhance children's engagement but also foster their learning interest and expressive capabilities [6]. The preschoolers in this class primarily acquire an understanding of musical notation. They observe that whole notes and half notes bear a resemblance to the embryonic form of tadpoles, while quarter notes and eighth notes resemble the shape of tadpoles, and 16th notes resemble the shape of adult tadpoles.

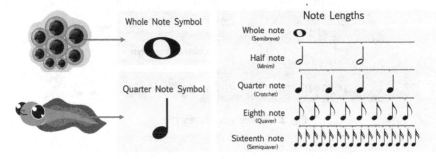

Fig. 3. The development stages of tadpoles align with musical notes.

3.2 Modular Music Instruction Design

Preschoolers possess a limited comprehension and grasp of rhythm, as their musical sense and coordination are still in the developmental stage. They may not have fully mastered the intricate rhythm and beat of music. Employing modular storytelling with concise narratives that align with the rhythm can effectively cater to their short attention span while sustaining their interest and focus. This approach facilitates progress in music learning, fostering an enduring passion for music and bolstering confidence [7].

3.3 The Design of Interactive Behavior in Preschool Children

The interactive design of this project primarily focuses on enhancing music learning by transitioning from simple auditory perception to a comprehensive perception that incorporates visual, tactile, and interactive elements. The design of interactive behavior is based on the behavioral characteristics and cognitive model specific to preschool children. The primary objective of this project's interactive design is to enhance music learning by facilitating a transition from basic auditory perception to a more holistic perception that integrates visual, tactile, and interactive components. The integration of "real" and "virtual" elements in 3D simulation learning environments created within digital classrooms can be effectively achieved, teachers and students can interact in MR Classrooms (see Fig. 4). The design of interactive behavior is informed by the unique behavioral characteristics and cognitive model associated with preschool-aged children.

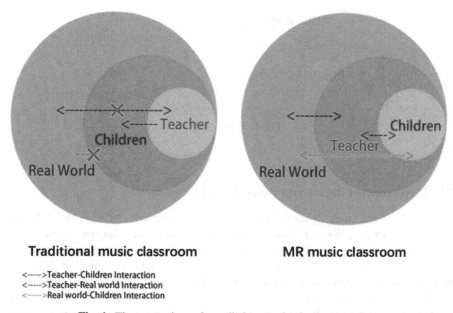

Traditional music classroom   MR music classroom

<----->Teacher-Children Interaction
<----->Teacher-Real world Interaction
<----->Real world-Children Interaction

Fig. 4. The comparison of two distinct music classroom models.

4 MR Music Course Project Implementation

4.1 The User Needs Analysis is Conducted Through Expert Interviews

Based on market research and in-depth interviews with 14 experts, the requirements of the MR Classroom environment were integrated, including interactive contact points combining reality and virtual reality, as well as hardware and software integration configuration. Regarding indoor environment design requirements: Firstly, it is essential to address teaching needs by incorporating sound, photoelectric technology, and other relevant technologies. By considering children's psychology, a concept of an MR Music classroom atmosphere should be created to captivate students upon entering the classroom and stimulate their strong interest in activities and learning [8]. Secondly, a combination of reality decoration and virtual reality technology should be employed to meet the demands of interactive teaching. This can be achieved by "landscaping" the top surface of the classroom, walls, and floor to establish an immersive environmental atmosphere. The hardware comprises a drum with a 360° arc screen, a circular dome screen, floor and projection equipment, a non-wearable student simultaneous interactive device, a wearable teacher motion capture device, a non-wearable student expression capture interactive device, and a pressure-sensitive floor mat. The software includes holograms, software programming, and computer configuration requirements (see Fig. 5).

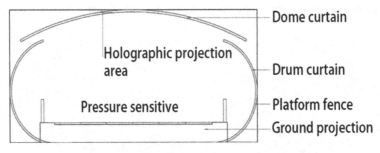

Fig. 5. Profile map.

4.2 The Content of the Interest Points Based on Preschoolers

The story "Tadpoles looking for their mother" is a narrative that captivates the childlike curiosity. It portrays a group of innocent and vibrant tadpoles embarking on a quest to find their mother, unknowingly undergoing metamorphosis into small frogs while assisting their mother in pest control. This engaging story immerses children in the situation while presenting scientific knowledge about frog growth through the medium of fairy tales, conveying the truth that young ones can live independently and actively explore. In a pond resides a cluster of tadpoles with prominent heads, black and gray bodies, and long tails swaying as they joyfully swim around [9].

4.3 The Establishment of an MR System Environment

The term MR refers to the integration of VR and AR technologies. AR involves overlaying graphics, video streams, or holograms onto the physical world, while VR provides a fully immersive digital experience by blocking the view. MR combines these two experiences seamlessly, allowing digital objects like holograms to appear as if they were real in the physical world and enabling individuals to collaborate asynchronously with others through their digital avatars. As depicted in the illustration, when preschoolers engage in virtual reality, they are digitally presented with physical obstacles such as walls and children's furniture during their immersive experience, resulting in collisions with these obstacles. The image demonstrates that subjects enter through the entrance after donning wearables, select their respective roles, and commence their MR Music class encounter (see Fig. 6). There are two primary device types: (1) Holographic devices possess the capability to render digital objects so realistically that they appear to exist within the real world; (2) Immersive VR devices offer a fully immersive digital experience by concealing the physical environment and generating a profound "sense of presence." Considering the physiological and psychological characteristics of preschool children mentioned earlier, this MR System environment adopts the former form. The actual classroom usage area is determined based on practical requirements ranging from approximately 100–150 m^2; however, it should not exceed 150 m^2. Additionally, adhering to hardware equipment installation specifications, the ceiling height is maintained between 3.5–4 m. The classroom can accommodate up to 25 preschoolers along with 2–3 teachers or teaching assistants.

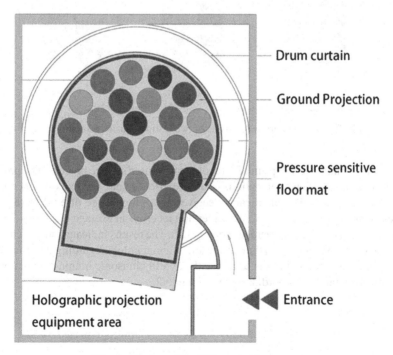

Drum curtain

Ground Projection

Pressure sensitive
floor mat

Holographic projection
equipment area

Entrance

Fig. 6. Display of the MR music classroom.

4.4   Testing Result of the MR System Environment

The VR/AR/MR Learning Systems and Environmental Quality assessment framework aims to evaluate the quality of VR/AR/MR platforms/environments using [10]. VR/AR/MR learning systems and environmental quality assessment require a personalized framework for both expert-centric (top-down) and user-centric optimal performance. Quality assessment of these platforms/environments should incorporate (bottom-up) assessment methods [8]. Comparing traditional music classrooms with MR music classrooms was conducted the evaluation study involved 36 novices and four on 26 subjects, including four specialists and specialists, comparing the performance of a hybrid simulator with 22 preschoolers who completed a 5-point Likert scale questionnaire. Usability testing considered ethical design questions such as the young age of preschoolers and parental assistance in interpreting results (see Fig. 7).

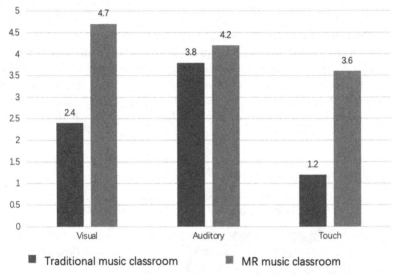

Fig. 7. The comparative analysis of two distinct music class formats.

The questionnaire design primarily focuses on the user's usage process. The problem setting encompasses scene perception, visual experience, and tactile experience in the MR Music classroom. The practicality receives an average score of 5.00, ease of use receives an average score of 4.25, 3D perception receives an average score of 4.75, and Phantom realism receives an average score of 3.25. The results indicate that preschoolers in the MR Class express astonishment towards vibrant colors regarding environmental perception, while finding it easier to utilize the hybrid ultrasonic training simulator as a highly effective hand-eye coordination teaching tool.

5 Conclusion

This research has the potential to enhance children's interest in music education, while offering beginners a more accessible and efficient approach to getting started. The combined augmented reality and virtual reality experiences of this MR System represent only a fraction of the vast possibilities within MR. The "MR Music Classroom" has been designed with scalability in mind, allowing for future integration of digital representations of children, locations, and objects in the real world. Mixed reality experiences are made possible by advancements in technology. The Music Magic Classroom project serves as a comprehensive mixed reality platform for device manufacturers and developers alike. Currently available devices can support specific segments within the mixed reality spectrum; however, it is anticipated that future devices will offer broader support: holographic devices will provide even more immersive experiences, while immersive devices will incorporate greater holographic elements.

Limitation and Future Work. Due to technical and site issues, this research project has not been fully demonstrated in real-life scenarios, and the evaluation method provided by the project scheme is limited. The sample size for measurements is small, leaving ample room for improvement in interaction design. MR technology can be regarded as a fusion of technologies that not only offer novel viewing methods but also provide innovative input approaches. The synergy between techniques and devices can drive the development and innovation of the music education industry. In terms of integrating VR and AR applications with MR system platform design to create immersive experiences in an MR music classroom, further experimental designs are required to enhance practical application.

References

1. Wang, C., Lu, Y.: Selection of music education methods for preschool children--a review of music education for preschool children. Res. Preschool Educ. **11**(2), 99–110 (2023)
2. Milgram, P., Kishino, F.: A taxonomy of mixed reality visual displays. IEICE Trans. Inf. Syst. **E77-D**(12), 1321–1329 (1994)
3. Peng, S.: Out of the misunderstanding of preschool music education. Music Educ. China **09**, 7–9 (2013)
4. Rathwohl, D.R.: A revision of Bloom's taxonomy: an overview. Theory Pract. **41**(4), 212–218 (2002)
5. Bloom's taxonomy. https://en.wikipedia.org/wiki/Bloom%27s_taxonomy. Accessed 3 Feb 2024
6. Gao, Y.: Setting curriculum objectives for music education in preschools in the context of "learner-centeredness"-an example of singing activities in preschool children's music education. House Drama **32**, 181–183 (2023)
7. Eccles, J.S.: The development of children ages 6 to 14. The future of children, 30–44(1999)
8. Kurilovas, E., Kubilinskiene, S., Dagiene, V.: Web 3.0–based personalisation of learning objects in virtual learning environments. Comp. Hum. Behav. **30**, 654–662 (2014)
9. Tadpoles looking for their mother. https://baike.baidu.com/item/小蝌蚪找妈妈/4820144?fr=ge_ala. Accessed 3 Feb 2024
10. Hih, J.L., Jheng, S.C., Tseng, J.J.: A simulated learning environment of history games for enhancing players' cultural awareness. Interact. Learn. Environ. **23**(2), 191–211 (2015)

Enhancing Spatial Design Pedagogy: An Empirical Investigation of VR Technology in Environmental Design Education

Jie Ling[1] , Li Ou Yang[2]([envelope]) , Weilin Su[1] , and Dan Li[1]

[1] Zhongkai University of Agriculture and Engineering, Guangzhou 510220, Guangdong, China
[2] The Guangzhou Academy of Fine Arts, Guangzhou 510261, Guangdong, China
oylee@163.com

Abstract. The foundational course "Design Composition" is integral for freshmen in the Environmental Design undergraduate program. Given the observed limitations in students' spatial thinking capacities, coupled with challenges in perceiving classical architectural spaces and the real-time presentation of construction materials, the incorporation of VR (Virtual Reality) technology into curriculum reform be-comes paramount. For this empirical study, two academic classes were chosen: one control groups (n = 25) and one experimental groups (n = 25). While adhering to an identical teaching syllabus, the control groups were subjected to conventional pedagogical methods, whereas the experimental groups employed VR technology. Three distinctive tests were devised, targeting spatial cognition, perception of master architectural spaces, and material experimentation. Post-evaluation, a questionnaire assessed students' grasp of key concepts and course satisfaction. Data analysis revealed that students from the experimental groups consistently outperformed those from the control groups across all tests, indicating a pronounced enhancement in learning outcomes. Consequently, this investigation underscores the efficacious role of VR technology in spatial design instruction, advocating its further integration into pedagogical reforms.

Keywords: VR Technolog · Environmental Design · Spatial Cognition · Pedagogical Reform · Architectural Perception

1 Introduction

Environmental design education lays the groundwork for students new to the field, offering a basic understanding of three-dimensional spaces. However, transitioning from 2D images to 3D concepts and grasping the intricate techniques used by master architects in space construction and material handling often pose significant challenges. Traditional teaching methods, reliant on 2D drawings and models, frequently fall short in nurturing an intuitive perception of space among students. The advent of Virtual Reality (VR) technology, known for its immersive and interactive features, is increasingly recognized as a potent solution to these educational hurdles. Yet, the creation of VR content can be complex and time-consuming, making it imperative to find viable VR pathways that align

© The Author(s), under exclusive license to Springer Nature Switzerland AG 2024
J. Y. C. Chen and G. Fragomeni (Eds.): HCII 2024, LNCS 14708, pp. 112–122, 2024.
https://doi.org/10.1007/978-3-031-61047-9_7

with teaching needs. This study delves into the application of VR in environmental design education, evaluating its impact on enhancing students' spatial cognition. Utilizing Mars VR software, it sets up three simulated teaching experiments aimed at addressing the gaps in students' spatial cognition, comprehension of masterpieces, and material perception, while also reflecting on the effectiveness and practical challenges of implementing VR in teaching environments.

2 Literature Review and Related Work

2.1 Current Status and Challenges in Environmental Design Education

The primary challenge in environmental design education lies in the insufficiency of traditional teaching methods to profoundly develop students' understanding of spatial structures and material characteristics. Despite students' proficiency in precise diagramming, transforming these diagrams into practical 3D space designs remains problematic, largely due to a lack of hands-on practice. Theoretical teachings often inadequately convey critical concepts such as spatial sequences, material textures, and lighting effects, largely because two-dimensional representations fail to capture the depth and proportion of real spaces, and static images do not adequately depict material details and lighting effects. While field trips [1] and material experiments [2] offer partial solutions, they are often impractical for most students due to time and cost constraints. Additionally, limitations in teaching resources and time hinder students from engaging deeply in practice and experimentation, affecting the cultivation of spatial perception and practical project application skills.

The integration of new technologies has enhanced teaching efficiency to some extent. However, the challenges of software production learning curves and the high costs of equipment have led to a preference for lightweight VR applications in current teaching practices, such as Google Maps [3], simulated panoramic images, or VR animations [4]. Some educators are also combining software technology with VR in teaching practices, for instance, integrating VR with BIM software for teaching [5], or developing VR courseware using 3DMAX and Unity3D [6]. These practices suggest that while the mode of VR experimentation might not necessarily involve VR equipment, any method that effectively enhances students' spatial cognition can be a valuable educational tool. The direction for future teaching lies in cost-effective and efficient VR experiments, emphasizing the importance of improving teaching results within limited resources.

2.2 The Importance of Spatial Cognition in Environmental Design

Spatial cognition, pivotal for designers, involves the understanding, reasoning, and memory of spatial relationships. In environmental design, it's essential not only for the precise perception of physical space dimensions but also for integrating spatial functions, user experience, and aesthetic values. Designers rely on spatial cognition to transform abstract ideas into concrete designs, impacting the creativity, practicality, and aesthetics of their work. Enhancing spatial cognition directly influences the accuracy and functionality of design solutions, improving efficiency and reducing unnecessary iterations, thereby minimizing resource usage and fostering innovation in design [7]. Educators [1, 2, 8] widely regard augmenting students' spatial cognition as crucial for their skill development in design. Research has validated the utility of VR in improving spatial cognition, especially among students with weaker spatial abilities [9], highlighting its effectiveness in elevating spatial cognition scores [10]. However, opinions vary regarding the necessity of VR equipment for conducting spatial visualization experiments. Some studies [11] have indicated that participants using static modes outperform those using VR modes in spatial visualization tests. Consequently, VR experiments are valuable for enhancing spatial cognition, and their implementation does not necessarily require VR modes. The direction for future educational applications lies in effective, low-cost VR experiments, even if VR equipment is not utilized.

2.3 Overview of VR Technology Application in Education

With technological advancements, Virtual Reality (VR) technology has revolutionized the educational sector, notably in the realm of environmental design. Known for its 3D environmental simulations, interactivity, and immersive experiences, VR is acknowledged as a powerful pedagogical tool, particularly in delivering immersive learning experiences. The 'Double Ten Thousand Plan' initiated by the Chinese Ministry of Education underscores the national emphasis on VR-based courses [12] as top-tier educational programs. Despite the underrepresentation of environment-related VR courses and challenges like low usage rates and the need for enhanced simulation quality, the potential of VR in augmenting educational quality and student learning outcomes is undeniable. Addressing the high costs, entry barriers, and usability of VR experiments is crucial to amplify its adoption in education. Further research and development of VR courses tailored for foundational environmental design education are imperative to realize its full potential.

3 Research Methods

This study involved the development of VR experiments using Mars VR software by educators, taking approximately ten working days, aiming to explore its application in environmental design education and assess its impact on enhancing students' spatial cognition, 3D design comprehension, and material handling skills. The methodological framework includes:

3.1 Research Design

A controlled experimental design was utilized, dividing fifty first-year environmental design students into experimental and control groups, each comprising twenty-five students. The experimental group engaged in VR-based training for spatial cognition, architectural space perception, and material understanding, while the control group received traditional teaching methods.

3.2 Participants

All participants were first-year undergraduate students in environmental design. A comprehensive baseline test was conducted before the study to assess the students' initial capabilities in spatial cognition, perception of classical architectural space, and material understanding.

3.3 Experimental Materials

The VR system utilized by the experimental group encompassed high-quality head-mounted displays, precise motion-tracking devices, and virtual environments specifically tailored for this research. These environments accurately simulated real architectural spaces and material properties, allowing students to design, modify, and experiment within an immersive setting, receiving instant feedback. The VR experiments entailed three main phases: spatial cognition training, a virtual tour of classic architectural spaces, and material selection and experimentation (Fig. 1).

Fig. 1. Spatial Cognition Training.

Spatial Cognition Training involved three primary scenarios focusing on the spatial perception of spheres, cylinders, and cones. The interface comprised two main scenes:

theoretical explanations and real-life simulations. SketchUp models, including Disney's Spaceship Earth, MIT's chapel, and the Melbourne shopping center, served as examples. Theoretical scenes provided geometric explanations and miniature models, while real-life simulations in Mars VR offered a new environment compatible with the simulation models for immersive exploration (Fig. 2).

Fig. 2. Classic Architectural Spaces.

Classic Architectural Spaces featured the German Pavilion from the 1929 Barcelona World Expo and the Rietveld Schröder House from 1924, both epitomizing modern architecture's paradigm shift. These buildings showcased innovative design, spatial layout, material usage, and functionality, representing the essence of 20th-century modernist architecture with their clear structure, open-plan spaces, and minimalist design language. Analyzing these architectural masterpieces enhances students' understanding of design principles and historical context (Fig. 3).

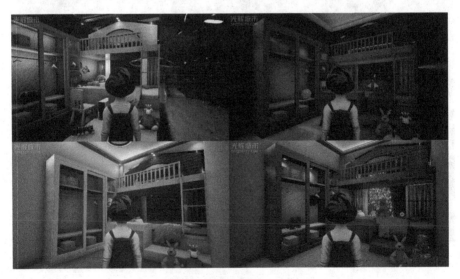

Fig. 3. Material Selection.

Material Selection involved designing four children's rooms with identical layouts but distinct color schemes, materials, and decorative elements. This setup offers students a unique opportunity for hands-on interior design experience, encouraging them to explore various combinations and assess the impact of different textures, hues, and accessories on the room's ambiance and functionality. The exercise aims to develop students' aesthetic sensitivity and understanding of material selection's transformative effect on space.

3.4 Data Collection Methods

Data were collected through pre-experiment and post-experiment questionnaire surveys, comprising six questions aimed at assessing student performance in spatial cognition, architectural space understanding, and material experimentation. The questionnaire design ensured alignment with teaching objectives and quantification of student learning outcomes. Both groups received identical questions to maintain consistency in the assessment. Questionnaires were distributed via the Questionnaire Star website, disseminated through QR codes, and students completed the survey on their mobile devices. This method facilitated efficient data collection and analysis.

3.5 Data Analysis Methods

Data were analyzed using descriptive statistics and single-sample t-tests. Descriptive statistics provided an overview of the sample's basic characteristics, and t-tests compared the performance differences between the experimental and control groups. These methods collectively aimed to comprehensively assess the effectiveness of VR technology in environmental design education.

4 Research Findings

This section of the research aimed to assess the effectiveness of VR technology in environmental design education. A controlled experiment involving 100 first-year environmental design students was conducted, leading to findings in several key areas: baseline test results, spatial cognition, comprehension of three-dimensional space design, material handling skills, and student feedback on the VR experience.

4.1 Baseline Test Results

Descriptive analysis using SPSSAU compared the pre-test scores of both experimental and control groups, focusing on spatial cognition, architectural space understanding, and material recognition. Initial findings indicated similar performance levels between the two groups, suggesting comparable baseline capabilities. The data emphasized the need to concentrate on the impact of VR intervention on these skills, and a similar statistical approach was proposed for post-test analysis to gauge the influence of VR teaching methods on student capabilities (Table 1).

Table 1. Baseline test scores overview.

Test Item	Group	Sample Size	Mean	Standard Deviation	Median
Spatial Cognition	Experimental Group	25	2.600	0.577	3
	Control Group	25	2.520	0.653	3
Architectural Space Understanding	Experimental Group	25	1.840	0.374	2
	Control Group	25	1.880	0.526	2
Material Recognition	Experimental Group	25	1.840	0.374	2
	Control Group	25	1.800	0.5	2

4.2 Post-VR Experimental Test Results

The post-experimental test results demonstrated significant differences between the experimental and control groups. As indicated in Table 2, the experimental group outperformed the control group across critical areas: spatial cognition, architectural space understanding, and material recognition. These findings highlight the substantial impact of VR technology in enhancing student capabilities in these key domains.

Table 2. Post-lab test score comparison.

Test Item	Group	Sample Size	Mean	Standard Deviation	Median
Spatial Cognition	Experimental Group	25	4.040	0.525	4
	Control Group	25	3.120	0.526	3
Architectural Space Understanding	Experimental Group	25	4.060	0.520	4
	Control Group	25	3.160	0.374	3
Material Recognition	Experimental Group	25	4.240	0.436	4
	Control Group	25	2.960	0.351	3

Spatial Cognition Test Results. In the spatial cognition tests, students in the experimental group significantly outperformed the control group. Notably, in tasks involving spatial transformation and understanding spatial relationships, the experimental group scored higher on average, indicating statistically significant differences. This suggests that the immersive and interactive learning environment of VR effectively enhances students' spatial cognition, aiding in their comprehension and manipulation of three-dimensional space.

Perception of Classical Architectural Spaces. Students in the experimental group also achieved higher scores in perceiving classical architectural spaces. Through virtual tours, they gained a deeper understanding of the layout, proportion, and materials of architectural spaces. The results show that the experimental group excelled in identifying architectural styles, understanding spatial fluidity, and evaluating materials and textures, highlighting the potential of VR technology in providing immersive and multisensory learning experiences.

Assessment of Material Handling Capability. In terms of material handling, students in the experimental group demonstrated a profound understanding and application of material properties. They were able to perceive and adjust material attributes in real-time within the virtual environment, showcasing heightened sensitivity and creativity in material selection and application. Compared to the control group, students in the experimental group achieved better results in the complexity and aesthetic quality of material handling.

4.3   Comparison of Performance Between Experimental and Control Groups

Comparative analysis further underscores the impact of VR technology. As shown in Table 3, the improvement levels in all assessment areas (spatial cognition, architectural space understanding, and material recognition) were notably higher in the experimental group than in the control group. The p-values of all test items were 0.000, indicating statistically significant differences between the two groups. The t-test results (see Table 3) confirm these differences are significant, reinforcing the effectiveness of VR technology in enhancing spatial cognition and design skills.

Table 3. Comparison of performance between experimental group and control group.

Test Item	Improvement in Experimental Group	Improvement in Control Group	Significance of Difference (p-value)
Spatial Cognition	1.440	0.620	0.000**
Architectural Space Understanding	2.220	1.280	0.000**
Material Recognition	2.400	1.160	0.000**

* $p < 0.05$ ** $p < 0.01$

Overall, the study underscores the efficacy of VR technology in enhancing spatial cognition, architectural space comprehension, and material experimentation and selection. It confirms VR's value in design education, highlighting its potential in fostering a deeper understanding of 3D space and elevating creative design capabilities. The study also underscores the importance of adopting advanced technologies like VR in teaching innovations, as evidenced by statistical analysis and positive student feedback.

5 Discussion

5.1 Interpretation and Significance of Results

The findings convincingly demonstrate that VR technology, with its immersive and interactive features, significantly enhances environmental design students' spatial cognition, perception of classical architectural spaces, and innovation in material experimentation and selection. These results not only affirm the applicability of VR in environmental design education but also underscore its potential in fostering a profound understanding of 3D spaces and enhancing design creativity. VR technology facilitates an interactive and intuitive learning environment, enabling students to explore and execute innovative designs more freely, thereby broadening the scope of design education. Moreover, Mars VR-produced experiments support teaching, address students' spatial cognition challenges, and alleviate the teachers' lesson preparation burden to some extent. The presentation of experiments can be flexibly adapted to equipment availability, using panoramic images, VR devices, or mobile VR, marking a promising direction for design application. Efficacy of VR in Spatial Design Education:

The study supports VR's effectiveness in spatial design education. VR's immersive experiences and multi-sensory characteristics provide a platform for students to understand the complexity of spaces and materials, thereby enhancing teaching quality and learning outcomes.

5.2 Experimental Limitations and Potential Biases

The study affirms the efficacy of VR technology in spatial design education. Mars VR, with its real-time material, lighting, and climate alterations, allows students to effortlessly engage in immersive learning experiences, closely simulating real-world spatial conditions. The technology enables students to experience and analyze designs in novel ways. Additionally, VR's multisensory and interactive features provide an intuitive platform for understanding the complexities of space and materials, significantly enhancing teaching quality and student learning outcomes.

5.3 Comparative Analysis with International Research

While the outcomes of this study are significant, it's imperative to recognize the limitations inherent in the experimental design and potential biases. The scope of the research could be narrowed by the sample size, suggesting the need for future studies to encompass a more diverse and extensive participant base. Individual variances among students, such as their familiarity with technology and learning styles, could influence learning outcomes and should be carefully considered in data interpretation. Furthermore, the effectiveness of lightweight VR technology for teachers not well-versed in computer skills remains to be further validated.

5.4 Comparative Analysis with Advanced International Research

This study's findings, aligned with global research, affirm the potential of VR technology in enhancing spatial understanding and design capabilities among students. However, discrepancies in technological implementation, educational settings, and cultural backgrounds across different nations might influence the efficacy of VR technology and its acceptance by students. Recognizing these differences is essential before broadening VR's application in varied educational contexts. This research not only highlights VR's potential in spatial design education but also identifies challenges needing further exploration. Integrating insights from advanced international studies, a deeper understanding of these challenges can significantly improve educational practices and student learning outcomes through VR technology.

6 Conclusion

This study aimed to explore and evaluate the application and impact of Virtual Reality (VR) technology in environmental design education. Conducted on 50 freshmen, the controlled experiment revealed that VR significantly enhances spatial cognition, understanding of architectural space, and innovative handling of materials. The immersive and interactive environment of VR proved superior to traditional teaching methods in improving spatial cognition, understanding of architectural layouts, proportions, and material properties, and innovating in material handling. Despite some limitations and biases, such as sample size and technology choice, the research underscores VR's potential in design education and paves the way for future educational practices and research. Integrating global research and practices, VR technology can be leveraged to enhance education and student outcomes, positioning students as future leaders in their fields. This study provides valuable insights and direction for the use of VR technology to enhance educational quality and student learning outcomes in the field of environmental design education.

Acknowledgments. This study was supported by several esteemed institutions and projects: the Guangzhou Academy of Fine Arts for the 2024 first-class course "Design Basics" (6040324137), the 2021 Ideological and Political Demonstration Course "Design Basics (Three-Dimensional Space)" (6040321061), the provincial-level first-class offline course "Design Composition" (KA24YY044), Zhongkai University of Agriculture and Engineering for the virtual simulation course "Design Composition", the virtual research office for the "Design Basics" course (ZG2023011), and the deep integration practice of information technology with "Design Composition" education under the concept of "Tolerant Beauty, Integrated Art Education, and Promoting School Excellence". Their generous support greatly facilitated the research.

References

1. Li, S.: Cognize·space·environment: study on teaching mode of architectural design basics course of qingdao agricultural university. Huazhong Arch. 182–185 (2015). https://doi.org/10.13942/j.cnki.hzjz.2015.04.041
2. Wu, Q., Wang, J., Xiao, F.: Research on teaching reform of "Tectonic Lab" in the course of "Architectural Design Basis": taking the practice of the architecture department of nanchang university as an example. Arch. Cult. 176–178 (2021). https://doi.org/10.19875/j.cnki.jzywh.2021.06.066

3. An, Y., Zhang, H.: Research on hybrid teaching reform of foreign architectural history based on three-dimensional digital technology. Become Talent. 106–107 (2023)

4. Li, H.: An analysis of the role of VR animation in teaching innovation in the digital media environment. China News. Ind. 100–101 (2019). https://doi.org/10.13854/j.cnki.cni.2019.20.052

5. Wu, X., Liu, B., Wang, J.: Teaching reform and practice of "Residential Space Design" in architecture department in the context of "BIM+VR" technology. Urban. Arch. 83–85 (2020). https://doi.org/10.19892/j.cnki.csjz.2020.09.028

6. Wang, W.: Research on methods of making teaching courseware based on VR technology. J. Changchun Univ. 24–27 (2020)

7. Xia, Y.: Virtual reality expression of spatial thinking—reform and innovation of teaching methods for environmental design major based on VR technology application. Art Educ. Res. 138–139 (2018)

8. Li, J., Zhang, J.: Space-concept training in architecture design basics course. J. Arch. Educ. Inst. High. Learn. **18**, 109–111 (2009)

9. Lee, E.A.-L., Wong, K.W.: Learning with desktop virtual reality: low spatial ability learners are more positively affected. Comput. Educ. **79**, 49–58 (2014). https://doi.org/10.1016/j.compedu.2014.07.010

10. Darwish, M., Kamel, S., Assem, A.: Extended reality for enhancing spatial ability in architecture design education. Ain Shams Eng. J. **14**, 102104 (2023). https://doi.org/10.1016/j.asej.2022.102104

11. Cho, J.Y., Suh, J.: Spatial ability performance in interior design and architecture: Comparison of static and virtual reality modes. Buildings **13**, 3128 (2023)

12. Virtual Experiment - National Higher Education Smart Education Platform. https://higher.smartedu.cn/vlab. Accessed 23 Jan 2024

Z3VR - An Interactive VR Learning Environment for One of the First Computers (Konrad Zuse's Z3)

Lukas Moersler, David A. Plecher[✉], Christian Eichhorn, and Gudrun Klinker

Chair for Computer Aided Medical Procedures and Augmented Reality,
The Technical University of Munich, Munich, Germany
{moerslel,plecher,klinker}@in.tum.de, christian.eichhorn@tum.de

Abstract. This paper presents Z3VR, an interactive simulation of Konrad Zuse's Z3 computer in a Virtual Reality (VR) environment, intended to give users the full experience of working with this historically significant machine. The paper explores other Z3 simulations and VR programming environments and draws comparison to Z3VR in terms of their accuracy and interface approach, where applicable. It details the creation of the project in various aspects and lessons learned from implementing and testing the VR user interface. It further evaluates how effective the project is as an educational tool in terms of teaching users about some concepts of low-level programming, and proposes future work to be done on Z3VR for higher usability and potential application in museums.

Keywords: Training education and tutoring · Serious XR · Serious VR · Zuse · Z3

1 Introduction

Virtual Reality (VR) is a technology that excels in creating immersive and engaging experiences, and which lends itself to letting users see and interact with places and objects they would otherwise not be able to. The Z3 computer, initially built by Konrad Zuse in 1941, is a prime candidate for such an environment. Clear historical significance aside, this machine is remarkable in both its accessible user interface and the numerous ways in which it mirrors modern processor and computer design. Among others, these characteristics make it a great example to teach users about the history of computing and low-level programming in a way that the skills learned can be translated into modern machine languages.

It should also be noted that, aside from other existing simulations (see *Related Work*), there is currently no possibility to work with the machine or even see it in person. The only full physical recreation at the *Deutsches Museum* in Munich is inaccessible at this time, as such this project aims to fill this gap by providing an immersive environment in which the Z3 can be seen from all angles and interacted with as if it were a real device. The main target demographic of the project is

J. Y. C. Chen and G. Fragomeni (Eds.): HCII 2024, LNCS 14708, pp. 123–141, 2024.
https://doi.org/10.1007/978-3-031-61047-9_8

people in their late teens and above, with at least marginal interest in computer science. Various interfaces are provided to make programming the machine as accessible as possible while trying to maintain immersion and historical accuracy.

The aim of this paper is to analyze the implemented VR interface in terms of its usability and to evaluate its effectiveness in teaching basic low-level programming concepts by analyzing data from play tests.

2 Related Work

Serious games have shown to be an effective approach to teaching in various fields [4]. By letting users participate in an immersive experience and giving them an active role in interacting with the subject matter, engagement and learning are amplified greatly. VR allows us to push the immersion aspect even further by fully enveloping users in interactive environments.

VR as a medium for serious applications and learning environments is a flourishing area of development [3,6], especially as the drop in cost of the necessary hardware in recent years has made it accessible for general audiences outside of research and military applications [3]. Serious games and applications using VR technology have successfully been used for teaching in a wide selection of disciplines, ranging from areas like public speaking [10,12] to physical assembly tasks [11], physics [26], virtual shopping [5,7,22] and even medical procedures [18]. And while VR is a cost-effective alternative to training in a physical environment, it also presents the unique opportunity to show places and objects which are normally inaccessible, be it because of insurmountable distances like different celestial bodies [1,2] or the content shown is in the past. Various prior works have dealt with the digital reconstruction of historical artefacts, such as underwater archaeological sites [13], reassembled ancient Greek statues [14], or the evolving state of historic buildings through the centuries [8]. In light of these examples, teaching programming, a traditionally text-heavy endeavour, may seem like an unusual application of this technology. However, Z3VR is far from the first project to experiment in this field [9,19–21].

The following will first cover the current extent of simulations of the Z3, followed by an examination of VR applications with similar goals to Z3VR in terms of historical simulations and teaching programming.

2.1 Previous Z3 Simulations

There have been various simulations and emulations of the Z3, with varying degrees of accuracy. How the Z3 operates has been covered in detail by Rojas et al. [17], for this section it's only necessary to know that it was programmed through punched tape, operated on two binary floating point registers, and it both received and displayed numbers through a console unit in a decimal floating point format.

2D and Terminal Simulations. A simulation by Mike Riley, published on their website[1], presents the user with an application window, interactive buttons and display fields mimicking the layout of the machine's console. Different tabs at the top of the window let users write programs, see the state of memory, and view debugging information. Riley's implementation executes faithfully the algorithms used to compute the various operations. The registers are abstracted as unsigned integers, and all the algorithmic steps as described by Rojas et al. [17] are taken to compute the results. The code for this was a valuable resource for checking the correctness of Z3VR's implementation of the arithmetic unit.

A different project named *pipZuseZ3*[2] runs entirely in a terminal and expects the name of a text file containing a Z3 program as an argument on startup. As such there is no option to simulate manual operations through the console. Since the program terminates after the instruction sequence has ended, the simulated machine's memory is not persistent, making programs that operate on the results of prior executions difficult. Furthermore, there is no option to create looping programs (possible on the real machine by sticking both ends of the punched tape program together), and the simulation does not implement the Z3's exception handling.

VRML Simulation. The prior work closest to Z3VR in terms of Z3 simulations is the 3D simulation of the machine available on the *Konrad Zuse Internet Archive* [15,16] (Fig. 1). It was constructed using the *Virtual Reality Modeling Language (VRML)*[3], used for displaying simple interactive 3D scenes embedded in web pages. Within it, users are presented with a scene featuring the Z3 machine and can navigate using the mouse via tank controls, or by switching between preset perspectives. The console can be interacted with by clicking on the buttons, and it mimics the real machine by displaying values and exceptions through illuminating the appropriate fields. Outside of the 3D view, the web page also features a section where users can write a program to be run, though this also does not offer the option of looping programs. Unfortunately, while the console interaction and programming both work as expected, the machine itself behaves in strange ways. Some of the buttons' functions seem to be swapped, and some don't appear to do anything at all. These issues are likely caused by incompatibilities with the software required to run this now unsupported format, and attempts at unpacking the VRML file to try and fix these were unsuccessful.

These three projects are currently the only publicly available simulations of the Z3. Since all of them are either non-functional due to unsupported formats or do not accurately represent the user interface, there is no possibility to accurately experience working with the Z3 (in an immersive way) - something Z3VR aims to change.

---

[1] http://www.historicsimulations.com/ZuseZ3.html, accessed 13.8.2023.

[2] https://sourceforge.net/projects/pipzusez3, accessed 13.8.2023.

[3] https://www.web3d.org/content/vrml97-functional-specification-and-vrml97-external-authoring-interface-eai, accessed 14.8.2023.

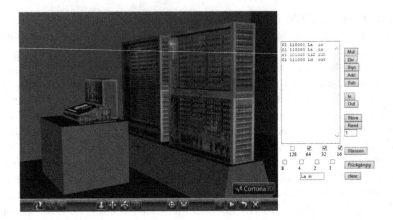

Fig. 1. VRML scene, navigable 3D scene to the left, programming view to the right

2.2 Other VR Simulations and Learning Environments

To put Z3VR into context, it's worth taking a brief look at other VR applications intended to simulate old computers or provide learning environments for programming.

ENIAC-VR. A remarkably similar project, only found after Z3VR's completion, is ENIAC-VR [25], presented at the MuC 2020 (Fig. 2). It had the same goal of providing an immersive virtual environment for users to experience programming one of the first computers, namely the ENIAC. This was extended further by including a guided tour which details the historical context and significance of the machine, as well as a *Maintenance mode*, in which users are instructed on how to spot and fix issues with the machine, which were a frequent occurrence on the real counterpart.

It features an introduction similar to Z3VR, which guides users by explicitly telling them what actions to perform to arrive at their first program, involving plugging in cables and turning knobs to a specific setting. Given the vastly higher number of interactable components, and far more complex programming model, ENIAC-VR makes heavier use of text-based instructions (Fig. 2), though it is difficult to imagine a purely visual or gesture-based tutorial similar to Z3VR's that could convey this level of information density effectively.

Block-Based Programming Environments. A notable commonality between the majority of VR experiences aimed at teaching programming is that the programming itself is usually done through the Block-Based approach popularised through services like *Scratch*[4]. This system has shown to be an effective tool for introducing students to programming while achieving a higher level of

---

[4] https://scratch.mit.edu/, accessed 14.1.2024.

Fig. 2. Screenshot of the introduction to ENIAC-VR, text labels guide the user

engagement than traditional text-based programming [24]. A further common aspect is that the programs are often used to navigate a character through a level in much the same way as *Karel the Robot*[5], another established application for teaching basic programming.

Fig. 3. A program in VR-OCKS, instructions are represented as cubes in a line

In *VR-OCKS* by Segura et al. [19] the code blocks which represent actions of the player character and concepts like loops are represented as literal blocks in the 3D scene which the user can pick up and place in a specific order (Fig. 3) to navigate their character around obstacles throughout a level. An earlier work by Vincur et al. [21], *Cubely*, presents effectively the same concept, but in the style of a popular video game franchise.

---

[5] https://xkarel.sourceforge.net/eng/, accessed 14.1.2024.

Z3VR took a similar approach to programming, as the programs are not written by the user in the traditional way, but are assembled from pre-set parts. However, an obvious difference is that Z3VR's pieces are merely textual entries in a 2D list, as will be detailed in the next section, and due to a lack of conditionals or finite loops in the Z3 instruction set, there are no "meta blocks" which contain a series of other pieces within them.

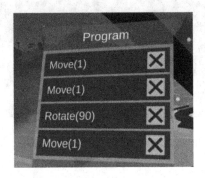

Fig. 4. A Program within Zenva Sky (Screenshots taken from https://www.youtube. com/watch?v=hMqiroApt2I, accessed 5.9.2023)

Zenva Sky also takes a similar approach to the prior two applications, however, in this case the user's programs control a vehicle in which they themselves are sitting [9]. Users have buttons in front of them that correspond to each possible instruction, and when they press them, they are added to an instruction list not unlike the one in Z3VR (Fig. 4). The game consists of a series of levels with increasing difficulty, in which the vehicle is used to reach an exit. Later the game is complicated by introducing locked doors and boolean inputs that the vehicle can activate, in combination with logic gates to open the doors.

In the first levels, the focus is on introducing the various logic gates; in later levels, the movement system is expanded with loops. The connection between the puzzles and their appearance in the code is shown by a screenshot of the corresponding Python[6] code in front of the user after each level.

A drastically different approach to teaching programming is provided by *Thinkercise*, a project by Theethum et al. [20]. The gameplay, seemingly inspired by *Beat Saber*[7], consists of hitting incoming coloured blocks with the correct hand, pictured in Fig. 5. Questions about Python (See Footnote 6) are regularly shown, with an upcoming set of three blocks being labelled with one possible answer each and the user being tasked with punching the correct one.

---

[6] https://www.python.org/, accessed 6.9.2023.
[7] https://www.beatsaber.com/, accessed 14.1.2024.

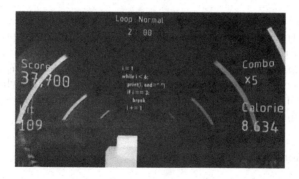

Fig. 5. Thinkercise gameplay, a programming question is presented while colored cubes approach the user (Screenshot from https://youtu.be/RFNkRtcWwas, accessed 14.1.2024)

This application is designed for users with at least rudimentary understanding of Python code, because the questions focus on advanced concepts of programming. Additionally, *Thinkercise* prompts the users to enter their weight to determine approximately how many calories they have burned during their session, adding a secondary motivation for users in addition to the educational aspect.

This project is far more gamified than Z3VR, and the focus of the training is on deepening existing programming knowledge rather than acquiring new skills.

3   Recreating the Z3 in VR

The following provides a quick introduction to the Z3 itself, to give context to all the VR interfaces which had to be implemented for it.

3.1   Z3

The Z3 was a programmable calculating machine operating on binary floating point numbers, completed by the engineer Konrad Zuse in 1941 [17]. Its operational model is effectively *Reverse Polish Notation*[8]: a mathematical operation requires first giving the operands and then the operator. The machine had instructions for receiving a number input through the console, displaying an output, accessing memory, and all four basic mathematical operations plus taking the square root. Calculations could be done in a "manual mode" by inputting numbers and pressing operation buttons. Alternatively, a reading unit could automatically run through a program stored on 35mm film stock with holes punched into it to encode instructions. The memory could only be accessed through such a program.

---

[8] https://en.wikipedia.org/wiki/Reverse_Polish_notation, accessed 1.9.2023.

Interaction with the machine happens almost exclusively through the console unit, which features a keyboard for number inputs and manual operation, and a light matrix for displaying results and exceptions. Fortunately, Zuse specifically set out to design his machines to be as user-friendly as possible [27], and working with the console is a simple process. A short introduction in which users are shown which buttons to press is enough to teach them how everything works within a few minutes.

3.2 Implementation

The project was implemented within the Unity3D game engine[9], which provides an OpenXR[10] API allowing the application to be used with VR hardware. Behaviours of objects within the engine are primarily governed by C# scripts. In Z3VR, each of the machine's separate units and peripherals has one script of that kind attached to emulate its function, with references to others allowing for communication where necessary.

The arithmetic unit is simulated on an algorithmic level, with the sets of relays representing numbers being abstracted as numerical values. The algorithms are executed within C# coroutines, which allows simulating the machine's speed (or lack thereof) by timing out the coroutine for the duration of a real Z3 processor cycle after each simulated one.

Aside from negligible technical details, a potentially inaccurate aspect of the simulated Z3 is its behaviour in various edge cases, which is largely undocumented. Z3VR implements a *watchdog* which monitors the current state of the machine and the upcoming instruction, and throws a generic exception on the machine's console if an invalid program sequence is detected. This system has shown to be a valuable aid for new users, as it prevents them from accidentally putting the machine in an invalid state. Such a system only requires a check of how many registers are currently filled and what the next operation expects, and as such is feasible to have been implemented on the real machine, but confirming this would require an extensive deep dive into its electrical plans.

An extra safeguard that clears both registers if a new program is inserted was certainly not part of the Z3's design, but was also necessary to stop users from putting the machine in an invalid state.

3.3 Interface

Programming in VR is a unique challenge which has been previously tackled through block-based programming for the most part as shown in the related work. Z3VR took a similar approach, but with some alterations. The requirements for creating Z3 programs both simplify and restrict the possibilities for

---

[9] https://unity.com/, accessed 30.8.2023.
[10] https://www.khronos.org/openxr/, accessed 30.8.2023.

the programming interface. On the one hand, as the Z3 had no if-statements or jump instructions, there is no need for complex systems that allow nested or branching scopes. On the other hand, since these programs are not used to, for instance, guide a character to the end of a level, they must be able to get arbitrarily long, so blocks that have to be physically assembled by hand would quickly become very cumbersome. The implemented interface will be detailed in the following.

In the real world, the Z3 was mainly programmed on paper. "Calculating plans" (Rechenpläne) were written by hand, with tables to keep track of which variables and constants are in which memory cell, and annotations describing what number inputs were expected at which time. These plans were then translated to punched film, though notes about the program had to be included to tell the operator how to use it properly. Such notes were especially important if a calculation required the sequenced execution of several programs in a specific order.

Z3VR provides interfaces and interactive elements to emulate this process without forcing the user to write anything by hand, and to and to minimize typing. These systems are introduced step by step to not overwhelm the users. At the beginning, users are placed in a bare scene in which they receive a quick introduction to the movement system and all types of interactions needed.

Interactable objects in Z3VR can be categorized as such:

- **Push buttons** → Physical buttons that gradually retract when the user places their virtual finger on them. As soon as a threshold value is reached, they fully engage and trigger whatever they are linked to. Examples include the console keyboard and the lever buttons of the film puncher.
- **Grabbables** → Objects that can be picked up using the trigger button and carried around. They are unaffected by gravity and can be placed anywhere or put into specialised *deposits*, which can have various functions. Examples include sticky notes and program films.
- **Openables** → Grabbables that can be opened by tilting them such that their spine points downwards. These include an info/trivia book and program folders.
- **2D UI buttons** → Standard Unity UI buttons on world space canvases. A raycast visualised by a laser pointer attached to each hand acts as the user's cursor, with the trigger button acting as the click action. This laser is only visible when aiming at the canvas.

Other interactions produce a small haptic feedback in the respective controller, to further enhance the immersion and responsiveness of the interface. Of note is also that the user's controllers are represented within the application as hands attached to their body with arms using simple inverse kinematics. These hands provide a rudimentary digital twin, and further act as an indicator for the type of interaction. This is currently available when the user's pose is changed next to an interactable object. These poses include a pointing gesture with the index finger extended near push buttons, a further opening of the hand near grabbing objects, and the manifestation of a laser pointer while aiming at a 2D canvas to create an appropriate origin for the displayed laser.

The most common items that users will be interacting with are the program films. They're grabbables that open a 2D UI display of the program held within when approaching them, shown in Fig. 6. This display also features two buttons with which users can toggle to a plain text view (eye icon) and whether the program should loop or not (∞). The plain text view translates the instruction code names given by Zuse to a literal name describing what it does, for instance, *Ls1* becomes *Add*.

The book, referred to as the *Info Book*, provides extra information and trivia about various things, including individual sections of the machine and background info about how and why film strips were used for programming. The text within changes based on which marked section of the machine the user points at while holding the book.

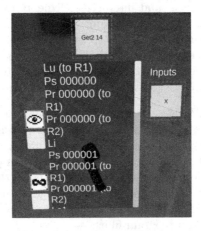

Fig. 6. Instruction list (middle) and sticky notes for name (top) and input (right)

Sticky notes were added as a simple and intuitive way to name programs and metaprograms for saving, and to define the expected inputs of a program. A large typewriter-style keyboard is provided to allow users to write on them. Even if it is not an optimal interface for writing in VR, it was sufficient, as the content of these notes is rarely more than one or two words. The program display that opens when holding a punched film has an outlined box at the top. If a sticky note is placed there, the program is saved under this name. The display also allows users to add comments to input instructions using sticky notes. These comments will appear within the *Info Book* if it is placed on the console while running a program.

The Z3 does not have an instruction for immediate values, so the only way to obtain constants is through user input. In addition, the machine has no way of telling which variables should be entered in which order, which can be arbitrary depending on the program. The sticky notes were implemented to emulate the hand-written notes used back then while being as simple to grasp and use as possible. However, this system is not sufficient to communicate sequences of programs to the operator, so program folders were added.

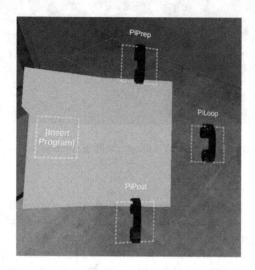

Fig. 7. Program folder containing three programs for approximating Pi

Program folders are used to store program films in a defined sequence. They can be opened the same way as the *Info Book* and offer a clock-like arrangement of boxes where programs can be placed, shown in Fig. 7. The number and positioning of these slots adjust automatically depending on the number of programs included. The folders themselves can be named and saved as well, to make the entries in the list of saved programs more compact.

Once the users has completed the interactive introduction, they are transported to the main scene, in which the Z3 is situated. At this point, the console does not feature any of the operation buttons, and the only option the users have is to start selecting a number by using the mantissa and exponent keys. Once a number has been selected, a small tutorial will start, guiding the user through their first calculation of $A + B$. There is no text telling them what to do, instead translucent hands indicate the action to be performed, in this case mainly pressing the operation buttons (Fig. 8). The next step does not start until the previous one has been performed. The only text added to the console is large numbers which reflect the currently selected number input and output number in the format $+1234 * 10^5$. This was added because some early testers had difficulty recognising the small button labels. These help texts can be disabled through the options menu. An additional aid in this respect is the option to double the size of the keyboard, which users are reminded of by an additional text on the console that disappears after the first number is entered.

Fig. 8. Console introduction. A hand is shown telling the user to press the *Add* button.

This introduction system, internally titled *Step Tutorials*, has been implemented as a finite state machine, in which each state defines which scene objects should be enabled and disabled. Once the simple console introduction has been completed, all the remaining operation buttons appear, and the next scene element is shown to the user. This is indicated by a green arrow pointing to the next tutorial, which only appears when the objectives have been achieved. This indicator should be conspicuous but unobtrusive so as not to push the player to the next station, but to encourage them to experiment with what they have learnt previously.

The programming board (Fig. 9a) is the main utility for writing programs, and implements the aforementioned simplified Block-Based programming. A scroll view in the middle shows the current list of instructions, and the left-hand side features buttons for each of the available operations. Clicking on one of these operations will add it to the instruction list where the cursor is located (indicated by <, can be moved by clicking on list entries). Further buttons allow for toggling a plain text view and program looping, as well as instantiating a punched film object with the current program.

As seen in Fig. 9a, some operations are greyed out. The *watchdog* is also used here to determine which operations are valid. The columns for $R1$ and $R2$ show the user which registers are filled after each instruction. If an invalid sequence is created, whether by inserting or deleting an instruction in the middle of the program, the invalid instruction will be marked red.

A film puncher is also present in the scene and an accurate reproduction of the device used for creating programs for the real machine. It can be used to punch films by hand in Z3VR as well, to get the full experience of programming the Z3. Users press the lever buttons corresponding to the bits of the current instruction code, then click the wheel on the right-hand side to advance to the next instruction (Fig. 9b). A list to the left of the puncher shows what instructions have been punched, so users can see if they've made a mistake right away.

Further interaction stations are placed in the scene to allow the removing, saving or loading of programs.

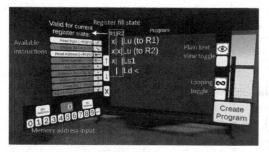
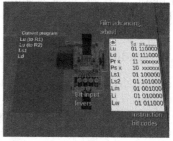

(a) Programming board, featuring the current program (middle) and available instructions (left). Invalid instructions are greyed out.

(b) Manual film puncher (middle) with instruction code reference (right) and currently punched program (left)

Fig. 9. Programming stations

3.4 Visuals

(a) View from one camera, 3D model visible as wireframe overlay, corresponding reference photo underneath

(b) Scene view of the 3D model surrounded by all reference cameras

Fig. 10. 3D recreation process

The Z3 model was recreated by extrapolating the position and orientation of cameras from online photos through *fSpy*[11], and importing these virtual cameras

---
[11] https://fspy.io/, accessed 21.8.2023.

into *Blender*[12]. Archived plans of the machine [28] revealed the height of the two relay cabinets, so an almost complete reconstruction of the machine was possible. (Fig. 10)

A notable detail of Z3VR is that the punched films have procedurally generated textures to reflect the program in them (visible in Fig. 6 behind the program display). Also an offset is applied to the texture for every step by moving the whole film forward by the length of one instruction.

3.5　Audio

Aside from greatly amplifying the immersion [23], audio provides feedback to the user. This ranges from the immediate response of a clicking noise when a button on the console is pressed, to the dozens of relays clacking away while the machine is crunching numbers. A video by the Deutsches Museum[13] was sampled to retrieve audio of the console buttons and the Z3 itself at work, with a short loop of the latter being played while the machine is calculating. To break up this loop and give at least some indication of which instruction is being run, an additional single-shot relay sound is played during memory access operations, implying the activation of the address decoder. When running a program, a loop of the pulse drum spinning is played while the machine waits for an input or is displaying a result, and is stopped when a program ends.

4　Evaluation

Evaluation of the project was done in the form of two testing phases. During these tests, each participant was guided through the application by the built-in introduction guide. They were then given a task in the form of a mathematical problem for which they had to create a Z3 program and were then given a questionnaire. This consisted of the *Standard Usability Scale (SUS)* questions supplemented with a few project-specific ones.

The first round of tests were run during development, just after a first draft of the introduction system had been implemented. At this point, it consisted of a series of text-bubbles, which the user could browse. All stations were present in the scene from the start. Some of testers simply skipped all the bubbles and were then left quite confused as to what to do.

To prevent this, the current version was introduced, which requires almost no text and introduces one thing at a time without distracting the user with unintroduced objects in the scene. The testing of this system was much smoother, the testers could follow the instructions and the necessary intervention of the test leader when the testers got stuck was much less frequent than in version 1.

Although the number of participants in each study was relatively small ($n = 7$, $SD = 19.548$ for version 1 and $n = 15$, $SD = 12.308$ for version 2), a clear

---

[12] https://www.blender.org/, accessed 21.8.2023.
[13] https://www.youtube.com/watch?v=aUXnhVrT4CI, accessed 21.8.2023.

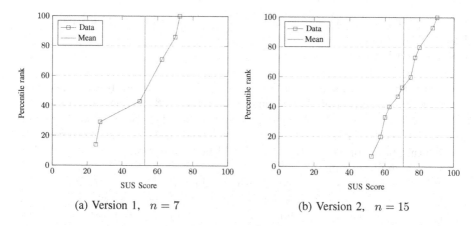

(a) Version 1, $n = 7$ (b) Version 2, $n = 15$

Fig. 11. Percentile distribution of SUS scores across the two introduction versions

improvement in usability is evident looking at Fig. 11, with a shift of the average SUS score from 52.86 to 70.83. A two-sample t-test between the two data-sets confirms a significant difference: $t(20) = 2.64$, $p = 0.015$

During the testing of the second introduction iteration, 80% of participants chose to try and tackle the programming challenge. These were categorised into three levels of difficulty, with most subjects choosing the easiest. Nearly all subjects who took on a challenge completed it successfully, especially those who stated that they had no previous experience with low-level programming, suggesting that the introduction was successful in providing at least the minimum necessary to solve simple equations with hardware-level instructions.

5 Future Work

There is still room for improvement in some parts of the user interface, and with a few adjustments and additions, improving user-friendliness certainly seems possible.

Gamification. While some testers have already found the project entertaining, a separate game mode would be an interesting way to reward users for their learning and give them a sense of fulfilment. One suggestion that came up was a sort of "story mode" where the user is placed in an exaggerated scenario where an electromagnetic pulse has rendered all transistor-based technology inoperable and they must use the Z3 to calculate the trajectory of an incoming meteorite or something similar.

The gamification can of course be much simpler and more reasonable, like an interface in the scene supplying users with tasks (not unlike the challenges testers received) and rewarding users if they complete them, perhaps by unlocking further functionalities. Such a system could also be integrated into the introduction system, giving users very simple tasks at first and then incrementally increasing the difficulty level to gradually imbue them with the mindset necessary to write programs for the machine.

General Improvements. An interesting addition would be a toggle-able abstract representation of the arithmetic unit that reflects the contents of the registers at all times, with the option to watch the algorithms at work in slow motion. Since the Z3's arithmetic unit is virtually identical to that of any current-day floating point processor [17], this would be a tremendous tool for teaching users about modern computers as well.

Only few people enjoyed working with the film puncher. Some testers had difficulty making the logical connection between the instructions, which are coded as bits, and the holes in the film, and of those who made the leap, only a few punched the program on the board in front of them. Obviously some work needs to be done on this interface to make it more accessible. One possibility would be to add a more rigorous version of the console's watchdog. A copy of the program on the programming board could be displayed next to the puncher, with commands that have not yet been punched greyed out and only the bit levers corresponding to the next command could be pressed at all. This would more clearly guide the user to press the correct levers and prevent them from accidentally punching an invalid instruction, which unfortunately often happens with virtual fingers that can easily slide over non-physical levers.

Address selection currently consists of a small text field below the instruction list with a numerical 2D UI keyboard, seen in Fig. 9a. While there are extra buttons for retrieving and setting the address of written memory instructions, this is still a very inconvenient system to use. A board containing sticky note deposits for each of the 32 possible memory cells could be a far better approach, being more accessible, more functional, better suited for VR specifically, and providing yet another use for sticky notes. Users can place notes to label addresses as you would on paper when planning a Z3 program by hand, to avoid keeping in mind which address corresponds to which variable or constant. The board also serves as a 2D UI, where clicking on a cell will transfer the corresponding address to a small text display next to the two memory instructions, and select it for adding either of those instructions to the program. While few testers tried programming with memory accesses, a further trial with this system would still be interesting, as the direct visualisation of the available memory might encourage its use.

Use in Musems. With some modifications Z3VR could be used as part of exhibitions in museums. A cooperation with the *Deutsches Museum* (where the real Z3 used to be on display) would be especially beneficial, as the real machine will not be demonstrated anymore due to fire safety concerns, and a full rewiring to fulfil requirements may not be possible[14].

To facilitate the usage in museums, a separate "guided tour" mode may be interesting. This would merely guide visitors around the different parts of the

---

[14] "Die letzte Rechnung der Zuse Z3" https://youtu.be/TbW-qNxD1lE.

machine with narrated descriptions and run some predetermined programs. The occasional genuinely interested visitor could still have the option to switch to the programming mode.

6 Conclusion

To return to the original research question: The current introduction system and programming interfaces have been shown to be effective, but still offer potential for further improvement. A follow-up study with more participants is needed to further investigate the capabilities of Z3VR for teaching low-level programming concepts. However, the test participants so far successfully applied what they learned in the introduction and in their own experiments when solving the math problems given to them, even those who stated that they had no previous experience with low-level programming.

Acknowledgments. This project would not have been possible without the plentiful resources provided by the *Konrad Zuse Internet Archive* [15], and especially professor Raúl Rojas, whose works on Konrad Zuse's calculating machines are a very good resource for anyone intending to learn about them.

References

1. Caravaca, G., Le Mouélic, S., Mangold, N., L'Haridon, J., Le Deit, L., Massé, M.: 3d digital outcrop model reconstruction of the Kimberley outcrop (gale crater, mars) and its integration into virtual reality for simulated geological analysis. Planet. Space Sci. **182**, 104808 (2020). https://doi.org/10.1016/j.pss.2019.104808
2. Casini, A.E., et al.: Analysis of a moon outpost for mars enabling technologies through a virtual reality environment. Acta Astronaut. **143**, 353–361 (2018). https://doi.org/10.1016/j.actaastro.2017.11.023
3. Checa, D., Bustillo, A.: A review of immersive virtual reality serious games to enhance learning and training. Multimedia Tools Appli. (2020)
4. Connolly, T.M., Boyle, E.A., MacArthur, E., Hainey, T., Boyle, J.M.: A systematic literature review of empirical evidence on computer games and serious games. Comput. Educ. **59**(2), 661–686 (2012). https://doi.org/10.1016/j.compedu.2012.03.004
5. Eichhorn, C., et al.: Inspiring healthy food choices in a virtual reality supermarket by adding a tangible dimension in the form of an augmented virtuality smartphone. In: 2021 IEEE Conference on Virtual Reality and 3D User Interfaces Abstracts and Workshops (VRW), pp. 548–549. IEEE (2021)
6. Eichhorn, C., Plecher, D., Klinker, G.: VR enabling knowledge gain for the user (Venus). Technical report, TUM (2022)
7. Eichhorn, C., et al.: Shopping in between realities-using an augmented virtuality smartphone in a virtual supermarket. In: 2023 IEEE International Symposium on Mixed and Augmented Reality (ISMAR), pp. 1161–1170. IEEE (2023)
8. Kersten, T.P., Tschirschwitz, F., Deggim, S.: Development of a virtual museum including a 4d presentation of building history in virtual reality. Int. Arch. Photogram. Remote Sens. Spatial Inf. Sci. **XLII-2/W3**, 361–367 (2017). https://doi.org/10.5194/isprs-archives-XLII-2-W3-361-2017, https://isprs-archives.copernicus.org/articles/XLII-2-W3/361/2017/

9. Navarro, P.F.: Zenva sky - VR app to learn computer science. Game published on Oculus store (https://devmesh.intel.com/projects/zenva-sky-the-world-s-first-vr-app-to-learn-computer-science) (2019)
10. Palmas, F., Cichor, J., Plecher, D.A., Klinker, G.: Acceptance and effectiveness of a virtual reality public speaking training. In: 2019 IEEE International Symposium on Mixed and Augmented Reality (ISMAR), pp. 363–371. IEEE (2019)
11. Palmas, F., Labode, D., Plecher, D.A., Klinker, G.: Comparison of a gamified and non-gamified virtual reality training assembly task. In: 2019 11th International Conference on Virtual Worlds and Games for Serious Applications (VS-Games), pp. 1–8. IEEE (2019)
12. Palmas, F., Reinelt, R., Cichor, J.E., Plecher, D.A., Klinker, G.: Virtual reality public speaking training: experimental evaluation of direct feedback technology acceptance. In: 2021 IEEE Virtual Reality and 3D User Interfaces (VR), pp. 463–472. IEEE (2021)
13. Plecher, D.A., Keil, L., Kost, G., Fiederling, M., Eichhorn, C., Klinker, G.: Exploring underwater archaeology findings with a diving simulator in virtual reality. Front. Virtual Reality **3**, 901335 (2022)
14. Plecher, D.A., Wandinger, M., Klinker, G.: Mixed reality for cultural heritage. In: 2019 IEEE Conference on Virtual Reality and 3D User Interfaces (VR), pp. 1618–1622. IEEE (2019)
15. Röder, J., Rojas, R., Nguyen, H.: Konrad Zuse internet archive. Website of the ZIB (2013). (http://zuse.zib.de. Accessed 14 Aug 2023
16. Röder, J., Rojas, R., Nguyen, H.: The Konrad Zuse internet archive project. In: Tatnall, A., Blyth, T., Johnson, R. (eds.) HC 2013. IAICT, vol. 416, pp. 89–95. Springer, Heidelberg (2013). https://doi.org/10.1007/978-3-642-41650-7_8
17. Rojas, R.: Die Rechenmaschinen von Konrad Zuse. Springer, Heidelberg (1998). https://doi.org/10.1007/978-3-642-71944-8
18. Ruikar, D.D., Hegadi, R.S., Santosh, K.C.: A systematic review on orthopedic simulators for psycho-motor skill and surgical procedure training. J. Med. Syst. (2018)
19. Segura, R.J., del Pino, F.J., Ogáyar, C.J., Rueda, A.J.: VR-OCKS: a virtual reality game for learning the basic concepts of programming. Comput. Appl. Eng. Educ. **28**(1), 31–41 (2020)
20. Theethum, T., Arpornrat, A., Vittayakorn, S.: Thinkercise: an educational VR game for python programming. In: 2021 18th International Conference on Electrical Engineering/Electronics, Computer, Telecommunications and Information Technology (ECTI-CON), pp. 439–442. IEEE (2021)
21. Vincur, J., Konopka, M., Tvarozek, J., Hoang, M., Navrat, P.: Cubely: virtual reality block-based programming environment. In: Proceedings of the 23rd ACM Symposium on Virtual Reality Software and Technology. VRST '17. Association for Computing Machinery, New York, NY, USA (2017). https://doi.org/10.1145/3139131.3141785
22. Walchshäusl, S., et al.: Generating an environment for socializing between older adults in a VR supermarket. In: INFORMATIK 2023 - Designing Futures: Zukünfte gestalten, pp. 325–337. Gesellschaft für Informatik e.V., Bonn (2023). https://doi.org/10.18420/inf2023_30
23. Warp, R., Zhu, M., Kiprijanovska, I., Wiesler, J., Stafford, S., Mavridou, I.: Validating the effects of immersion and spatial audio using novel continuous biometric sensor measures for virtual reality. In: 2022 IEEE International Symposium on Mixed and Augmented Reality Adjunct (ISMAR-Adjunct), pp. 262–265 (2022). https://doi.org/10.1109/ISMAR-Adjunct57072.2022.00058

24. Weintrop, D., Wilensky, U.: Comparing block-based and text-based programming in high school computer science classrooms. ACM Trans. Comput. Educ. **18**(1) (2017). https://doi.org/10.1145/3089799

25. Yigitbas, E., Tejedor, C.B., Engels, G.: Experiencing and programming the ENIAC in VR. In: Proceedings of Mensch Und Computer 2020. MuC '20, pp. 505–506. Association for Computing Machinery, New York, NY, USA (2020). https://doi.org/10.1145/3404983.3410419

26. Zengerle, T., Plecher, D.A., Flegr, S., Kuhn, J., Fischer, M.R.: Teaching optical principles in XR. In: INFORMATIK 2023 - Designing Futures: Zukünfte gestalten, pp. 313–323. Gesellschaft für Informatik e.V., Bonn (2023). https://doi.org/10.18420/inf2023_29

27. Zuse, H.: Die ergonomischen Erfindungen der Zuse-Maschinen im internationalen Kontext, pp. 95–120 (2008). https://doi.org/10.1515/9783839405642-002

28. Zuse, K.: Electrical plans of the rebuilt z3 (1960). Available on the Konrad Zuse Internet Archive http://zuse.zib.de. Accessed 14 Aug 2023

Stepping into Recovery with an Immersive Virtual Reality Serious Game for Upper Limb Rehabilitation: A Supermarket Experience for Stroke Survivors

Sérgio Oliveira[1], Bernardo Marques[1(✉)], Paula Amorim[2,3], Paulo Dias[1], and Beatriz Sousa Santos[1]

[1] IEETA, DETI, LASI, University of Aveiro, Aveiro, Portugal
bernardo.marques@qa.pt
[2] Rovisco Pais Rehabilitation Center, Tocha, Portugal
[3] FCS, University of Beira Interior, Covilhã, Portugal

Abstract. One of the leading causes of disability and death worldwide is stroke, affecting the arteries leading to and within the brain. To help survivors relearn lost skills, post-stroke rehabilitation becomes a paramount part of their life, focusing on attaining the best possible quality of life. Regardless, one main challenge is maintaining survivors' motivation, which when lost, can lead to social isolation, and possibly depression or anxiety. This work proposes the use of a Virtual Reality (VR) serious game to assist during upper-limb physical rehabilitation. The design and development were based on a Human-Centered Design (HCD) methodology with the healthcare professionals and stroke survivors from a rehabilitation center. The game narrative was carefully designed according to pre-determined gestures that survivors should perform for helping them increase upper-limb movement, based on two modes: 1- static - survivors use any arm to pick products from a supermarket shelf; 2- exploratory - survivors move throughout the supermarket to grab all products. During this, it is also possible to enable the mirror feature, allowing survivors to do these activities while the healthy limb is reflected. The game can also be cast to other devices for understanding and support, i.e., assessment sessions with a therapist team. We report the first impressions from healthcare professionals and stroke survivors, suggesting the VR serious game has the potential to increase survivors' motivation.

Keywords: Stroke · Rehabilitation · Upper Limb · Virtual Reality · Serious Game · Human-Centered Design

1 Introduction

Stroke is one of the leading causes of disability and death affecting the world population. Each year, more than 17 million individuals suffer a stroke [4,8,11].

J. Y. C. Chen and G. Fragomeni (Eds.): HCII 2024, LNCS 14708, pp. 142–153, 2024.
https://doi.org/10.1007/978-3-031-61047-9_9

It can be caused by an interruption of the blood supply to the brain, causing several physical and cognitive impairments. Considering recent healthcare advances, stroke mortality has been decreasing, resulting in a growing number of survivors with psychological, cognitive, social, and motor limitations. Consequently, this affects their daily living and quality of life [4,19]. In particular, survivors face a reduced functional ability, which can lead to loss of independence. For example, upper limb motor abilities often remain affected, becoming a chronic condition [4,17]. In this context and considering the reported increase in stroke survivors' life expectancy, it becomes paramount to allocate resources to handle the challenges survivors need to face [2,11,18].

After suffering from a stroke, survivors have access to rehabilitative care, which can take place at hospitals, clinics, or rehabilitation centers, with the objective of attaining the best possible quality of life for the survivors and their family [10,11]. Rehabilitation becomes than a relevant part of stroke survivors' life. Much of the recovery can be achieved in the acute phase (up to two weeks) and subacute phase (up to six months). As for the chronic phase (more than six months), most techniques focus on maintaining muscle strength and avoiding deterioration and weakness [4,16]. For example, conventional methods for upper-limb rehabilitation require survivors to to practice physical exercises to improve their motor condition [7], as is the case of the Constraint-Induced Movement Therapy (CIMT), which restricts the healthy limb to promote the use of the affected one, or Mirror Therapy (MT), taking advantage of a standard mirror to reflect the healthy limb and hide the affected one, among other possibilities [2,6]. Nevertheless, this traditional rehabilitation process may become annoying and mundane, i.e., due to the repetitive nature of these exercises, maintaining motivation is a challenging effort for survivors. This lack of interest in the rehabilitation process can in turn have some serious consequences for survivors' rehabilitation, e.g., social isolation, depression, or anxiety [11,15,18].

Virtual Reality (VR) technologies may be a solution to overcome these challenges, given their ability to immerse users in engaging multiple stimuli (visual, auditory, haptic, etc.) environments that simulate real-life scenarios. These may overshadow medical facilities and tedious rehabilitation exercises while promoting entertainment and socialization [2,6,9,11,17]. Solutions exploring VR technologies are being regarded as a promising treatment tool, which may be used as a complementary to conventional therapy for stroke rehabilitation, having the potential to be used in real-life settings (e.g., at home) and to increase motivation and engagement for rehabilitation exercises, for example, through the use of serious games, which can be highly personalized to the necessary exercises. Likewise, VR meets the four basic principles of rehabilitation, namely task-oriented training, intensity, motivation, and biofeedback. As such, it appears feasible for survivors to continue their treatment over larger periods of time [1,3,5,12,20].

This work proposes a VR serious game using a supermarket scenario for upper-limb physical rehabilitation. This daily activity is used in therapy and was considered following an analysis of needs and challenges of stroke survivors from a rehabilitation center, based on a Human-Centered Design (HCD) methodology.

Following the list of requirements generated, two modes were designed: static - survivors use any arm to pick products from a single shelf; exploratory - survivors must move throughout the supermarket to grab all products. Both modes also feature the mirror approach, allowing survivors to do these activities while the healthy limb is reflected. In the next section, the methodology used is presented; then, the first impressions gathered from distinct audiences and last final remarks are drawn and further research opportunities are presented.

2   Methodology

To understand the needs and challenges of stroke survivors, aiming to contribute to their quality of life and independence, focusing on upper limb, a HCD methodology (Fig. 1) was conducted with distinct audiences from a rehabilitation center. This process included the following moments: 1- online questionnaire with 20 survivors; 2- focus group with 8 survivors, 1 healthcare professional, and 3 domain experts in Human-Computer Interaction (HCI). 3- requirement elicitation based on the insights gathered during the 2 initial moments; 4- design and development of a VR serious game, having a healthcare professional with vast experience in upper limb rehabilitation constantly available to provide feedback; 5- Initial assessment with distinct audiences.

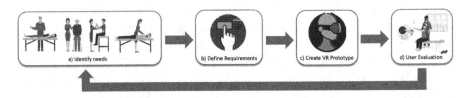

Fig. 1. Methodology adopted to bring stroke survivors and healthcare professionals into the design of a VR-based serious game: a) identify needs of target users; b) definition of requirements; c) creation of a VR-based prototype; d) user evaluation. Adapted from: [14, 16]

Regarding the online questionnaire, it was made available to the survivors of the rehabilitation center, having questions associated with survivors' preferences in leisure and exercising, the amount of time they spend doing such activities, as well as what activities they would like to see recreated. Also, their experience with video games and VR, and their willingness to try such technologies. To provide context and understand what type of experiences survivors prefer, snippets of game-play associated with simulation, action, adventure, and puzzles were displayed. After analyzing the results obtained, it was possible to understand that a trend existed towards two types of experiences, simulation and action games, suggesting that there is potential for using VR for addressing these.

During the focus group, the concept of VR and serious games were introduced, as well as their usage in rehabilitation and potential benefits. This was done with illustrative storyboards designed for the scope being addressed. This participatory process allowed to collected data of survivors' needs, concerns, and opinions, in particular, what motivates them and what limitations should be taken into consideration. For example, providing any type of feedback must be carefully considered. While in other domains, having 'negative' feedback can challenge users to try again, and push themselves further, when handling stroke survivors that is not the case, given that it may be a demotivator, in particular for depressed survivors. Hence, Some type of leniency or positive reinforcement should be considered instead. Another interesting discovery was the fact that survivors in the chronic stage appear more open to engaging with experiences they can easily relate to daily-life real-world activities, e.g., walking, traveling, swimming, playing tabletop games, cooking, or gardening, among others [14,16]. This is quite relevant, given that conventional approaches fail to take this into consideration, leading to a lack of interest over time, as described in the introduction. All in all, focus group participants appeared interested in exploring new VR solutions, as long as they are tailored to their basic needs and limitations.

Afterward, a set of requirements were defined, allowing to guide the design of a framework for enhancing upper limb rehabilitation for stroke survivors. To elaborate, it was emphasized the need to have a game that mapped simple gestures included in Enjalbert's test to conduct upper-limb rehabilitation, a well-known scale used for assessment of the upper limb mobility [7]. In this context, given survivors' constraints, interaction is not advised with the use of controllers. Alternatively, gesture recognition should be prioritized. As stated before, the game needs to explore daily activities, which the survivors can relate to in order to boost motivation. Furthermore, given that each survivor is different, the game should include distinct levels of complexity, allowing adapting the rehabilitation process accordingly. Also relevant, the game should offer the capacity to select, manipulate and navigate throughout the virtual environment. Equally important, was to integrate an approach to the mirror therapy, traditionally used and with proven results. Additionally, there should not be any mention of duration or any type of feedback at the end of the game that could be misunderstood by the survivors. On the other hand, having a simple, easy-to-use interface is mandatory, allowing survivors to be able to use the game by themselves, i.e., having a gentle learning curve.

3   Virtual Reality Serious Game for Upper-Limb Physical Rehabilitation

Next, a first proposal towards supporting upper limb rehabilitation of stroke survivors is described. It offers an overview of the main modules of the proposed framework, designed following the aforementioned requirements. For now, rehabilitation at home is being considered as the ultimate goal. Although this represents an important topic, the authors strongly believe that before we can advance to such settings, first, an effort should be made to validate an initial prototype with target users, and only then, advance to integrate additional features. For example, it may be possible to combine telerehabilitation with VR and serious games. Yet, before moving to more challenging scenarios, it is important to create a strong work base that can be scalable to ensure its use over time.

Figure 2 illustrates the vision of the proposed framework, including the various modules ensuring an engaging and interactive VR serious game narrative for stroke survivors, including VR stimuli, visualization manager, interaction manager, data processing, and data storage. At the core of the framework are the interaction and visualization modules, responsible for managing all changes within the supermarket environment (displayed using the VR stimuli module) based on the survivor's actions. These modules enable them to interact with virtual objects and navigate through the supermarket, promoting upper limb motor rehabilitation and cognitive engagement. Moreover, the data processing module is responsible for monitoring the survivor's progress during the game. It records and analyzes the products selected by the survivor in alignment with the provided shopping list, tracking the time taken and any errors made during the process. This information is stored in a dedicated database, allowing healthcare professionals to review and assess the survivor's performance at the end of the rehabilitation process. Such data-driven insights provide valuable feedback for personalized treatment plans and progress evaluation. Following the requirements, sensitive data or any type of feedback are not presented to the survivors. Only the healthcare team has access to this data and is responsible for adjusting the rehabilitation process and discussing with the survivors what they need to improve if anything. Moreover, the VR environment can be cast onto an external display, such as a computer, smart TV, or projector [13]. This feature enables healthcare professionals to observe and follow the game's progress in real-time. The external display also allows healthcare professionals to provide cues and guidance to the survivor during the rehabilitation session, facilitating a supportive and collaborative therapeutic experience. This feature may also be relevant later on when addressing rehabilitation at home, where the survivor's family members can also be involved.

With the goal of recovering the upper limb motor functions, and fostering cognitive functions (memory and reasoning) of stroke survivors, a VR serious game was created following the requirements established. Regarding the environment, an Activity of Daily Life (ADL) was selected, i.e., finding all the ingredients of a recipe at a supermarket (Fig. 3). Thus, replicating an activity that is used at the Rehabilitation Center by occupational therapists in the scope of cognitive rehabilitation activities. This way, all survivors can relate to this activity, since they need to face it at any given moment of their lives.

Figure 4 - 1 displays an initial concept of the supermarket, used to obtain feedback from the target users during the HCD process. Likewise, Fig. 4 - 2 illustrates an initial prototype used to validate the main principle of the game, as well as the intended gestures, e.g., grabbing the pre-determined products and placing them on the shopping cart. Finally, Fig. 4 - 3 and 4 present the last version of the supermarket environment designed for survivors to face rehabilitation heads-on. The environment has a rectangular shape that the survivors must navigate. Throughout the supermarket, several aisles exist composed of multiple shelves

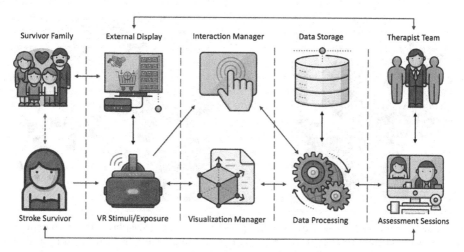

Fig. 2. Framework overview, allowing a stroke survivor to experience an immersive VR serious game. The game narrative and all changes in the supermarket environment are ensured by the interaction and visualization modules. Plus, a data processing module maintains track of the products being picked-up according to the shopping list, as well as the time needed and errors conducted during this process. This information is stored in a dedicated database, allowing it to be consulted during assessment sessions by healthcare professionals at the end of the rehabilitation process. Additionally, the VR environment can be cast to an external display (e.g., computer, smart TV, or projector, etc.), allowing the survivor family or the healthcare professionals to follow up what is happening, as well as provided cues if necessary. Assets from iconfinder.com.

with distinct products. After collecting all the necessary ingredients of the recipe, survivors must move to the end of the supermarket and perform the payment for the products, which implies collecting all products from the shopping cart and placing them in the self-checkout zone.

After being equipped with the VR headset, survivors are confronted with a main menu that will guide them through the rehabilitation experience. First, a tutorial is offered, which guides them through all the basic game mechanisms before advancing to more complex levels while being presented with images, illustrative videos, and audio feedback. When survivors are ready to move on, two modes are offered: 1- static mode - where the survivors face a single shelf and need to select a reduced number of ingredients; 2- exploratory mode - survivor must move throughout the supermarket environment using gesture recognition, in order to grab all products. This implies a larger list of ingredients, being considered a more complex level for later stages of the rehabilitation treatment. During both modes, survivors can enable the mirror feature, which allows for conducting shopping activities while the healthy limb is reflected, following the traditional approach, mentioned at the beginning of this paper. To complement, all levels include audio and visual cues to help survivors have a grasp of what is happening and what they are intended to do.

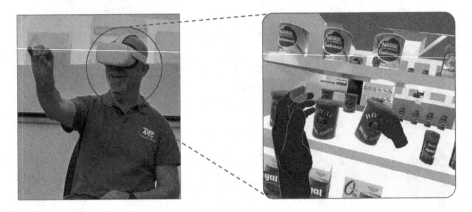

Fig. 3. Example of a stroke survivor using a Head-Mounted Display (HMD) to experience a Virtual Reality (VR) serious game, in particular, using his right arm to grab a set of virtual products from a supermarket shelf. The gestures used during this follow existing patterns, considered as very useful for upper-limb stroke survivors' physical rehabilitation.

Fig. 4. Illustration of the supermarket environment: 1- initial concept modeled in Blender. 2- first prototype created using the Unity game engine. 3 and 4 - VR serious game final version, illustrating the various supermarket aisles, shelves, and products, as well as the user's capacity to move throughout the environment.

Besides this, a locomotion mechanism was also integrated, in which the survivor needs to point to one of the various blue lights available throughout the environment and make a specific gesture to change its location (Fig. 4 - 3 and 4). By using this process, the rehabilitation process can even be conducted by survivors in wheelchairs, making the VR serious game more inclusive to a larger audience. Figure 5 - 1 illustrates a survivor facing a shelve, where it is possible to view the list of ingredients in the left hand. This list can be turned on and off beforehand, allowing to train the survivor's cognitive response, in particular, short-term memory. During the game, all products must be placed inside a shopping cart (see Fig. 5 - 2), which automatically follows the survivor position throughout the environment. By the end of the experience, survivors need to conduct the payment process (see Fig. 5 - 3 and 4), where a virtual wallet with money exists for survivors to grab and use. This was integrated following suggestions by the healthcare professionals, in order to foster the cognitive process of the survivors. It is also important to emphasize that the process of grabbing the products, placing them in the shopping cart, as well as conduct the final payment follows the gestures reported in the literature as some of the ones that should be used for upper limb rehabilitation [7].

Fig. 5. Examples of user interfaces when immersed in the VR serious game environment: 1- grabbing a specific product from the shopping list; 2- placing the selected product in the shopping cart that follows the user throughout the environment; 3 - moving the products from the shopping cart to the payment balance); 4- conducting the payment on the automatic machine of the supermarket. All interaction is done using gesture recognition thanks to the VR headset (Meta Quest 2).

Regarding the tools used, all models for the products and the supermarket itself were modeled and textured in Blender and then exported to the Unity game engine as .fbx file. Known brands were used in the textures of the products, since these would be more familiar to the survivors and would not imply the need to draw abstract textures which could confuse survivors. All menus, navigation, interaction, and manipulation were also developed using the Unity game engine, based on C# scripts. Additionally, the Oculus System Development Kit (SDK) was used to export the environment to the intended headset - Meta Quest 2. This device is a standalone HMD, which means it doesn't need a computer to operate and uses inside-out markerless tracking, which allows it to work without wires, with minimal preparation of the physical space. Additionally, the device is one of the cheapest HMDs on the market and supports hand tracking without the need for supplementary hardware. Casting to a large display can occur using the Meta Quest native support for such a purpose.

4 First Impressions over Various Events with Distinct Audiences

The VR supermarket serious game has been demonstrated to different audiences in distinct events to gather first impressions. In particular, regarding the game narrative, interaction methods, and usability, as well as collecting comments and suggestions to elicit the next steps of our research (Fig. 6). First, a preliminary user study was conducted with 6 participants (none was a survivor) having experience in the design and development of serious games, as well as VR applications. Participants were introduced to the VR game narrative and asked to explore the featured modes. At the end, participants filled out a questionnaire and an interview occurred to collect feedback.

During a scientific event, the VR game was displayed for anyone to experience it. In total, 15 participants with a background in computer science, as well as digital media and game design tried it out, while the experience was being cast to an external display for everyone else to follow up. This allowed to collect direct feedback from participants with the VR headset, as well as the general audience that interacted with the research team promoting the experience.

The VR game was also presented during a stroke survivor follow-up meeting, an event that happens periodically, allowing survivors from distinct places to gather, connect with each other, share their feelings and concerns, as well as discuss their rehabilitation experiences. In this particular event, we were able to describe our approach, explain why the supermarket scenario was chosen, and display some contextual videos that illustrated the game developed. Later, 3 survivors used the game while their experience was shared on a distinct display for the remaining audience to see. At the end, an interview was conducted, including their reaction to the game narrative and how easy it was to complete it. Also, their reaction to the mirror approach, and if they felt any discomfort during and after the game.

Last, we had the opportunity to promote the VR game in the rehabilitation center we had been collaborating with, in this case, having two survivors and two healthcare professionals using the VR supermarket experience, while being cast to an external display, only for the research team to understand what was happening and provide assistance if necessary. None of these had participated in the design and development of the VR game. This was an informal way to gather first impressions, based on interviews at the end of the experience.

Fig. 6. First impressions spawn over different events and with distinct audiences: 1- domain expert in VR and serious games; 2- domain expert in multimodal interaction; 3- stroke survivor; 4- healthcare professional.

All the feedback collected was used to conduct improvements before advancing to next steps. For example, improve an initial approach for navigating through the supermarket aisles. Also, change the color of some virtual objects, to better emphasize selected areas of interest. Plus, we were able to understand that the supermarket game should take into consideration the way survivors sit in the wheelchair, avoiding the need to grab products from the lower shelf or from the floor, if the survivor drops them, given that doing such movements could be a safety hazard, causing them to fall over. This important fact was not possible to uncover otherwise, proving the importance of demonstrating the prototypes created to target users, following the HCD methodology adopted.

Subsequently, the VR serious game is going to be evaluated in a formal user study with stroke survivors and healthcare professionals from a rehabilitation center. Recently, we have obtained ethical approval from the rehabilitation center ethics committee and are finishing the study protocol, having already listed more than 10 participants, willing to try our approach as a complementary approach. With this, we intend to verify if the proposed VR supermarket game meets the established requirements, as well as assess usability, acceptance, and collect comments and suggestions that can improve the quality of what we have developed. Only by collecting this data with target audiences, can we truly understand if survivors are willing to use VR serious games for longer periods and the real impact on motivation and engagement.

As mentioned before, this is an initial step towards the ultimate goal of being able to have VR serious games for rehabilitation exercises at survivors' homes. Notwithstanding, before we can move into these challenging settings where survivors' families can also take part in the rehabilitation process, first, we need to ensure that a solid base is established, starting with the proposal being described in this document.

5 Final Remarks and Future Work

Upper-limb physical rehabilitation caused by stroke presents several challenges, which can vary depending on the severity of the stroke, the individual's overall health, and the resources available for rehabilitation. This work proposed an immersive VR serious game for upper-limb post-stroke physical rehabilitation, developed with healthcare professionals and stroke survivors from a rehabilitation center following a HCD methodology. By focusing on a typical daily activity, supermarket shopping, our proposal can help survivors more easily relate with the game narrative. Likewise, by having distinct modes, with dynamic list of products, the game offers an increasingly manner for survivor's to maintain motivation and attention, as emphasized by them. Overall, the healthcare professionals also believe in the potential of the VR serious game, being satisfied with the integration of the mirror mode feature, an essential method to help with the rehabilitation process, albeit pointing out some ways to improve it. They also highlighted the importance of having a shopping list, allowing survivors to train not only the physical gestures, but also their memory at the same time.

This study is being expanded by designing a platform for data collection and analysis, allowing healthcare professionals to adjust the rehabilitation process according to the results. It is also important to explore game personalization, providing means for individualizing the rehabilitation to the needs of each patient. One possible way is to have game parameters that healthcare professionals can add or change during an assessment session, as well a features directly related with the survivor's life (e.g. photos). Afterward, we also intend to conduct a longitudinal study (at least 3 months) with stroke survivors, aiming to verify the impact of VR serious games on motivation and motor evolution. Thereafter, investigate how social interaction affects survivor's rehabilitation process. This will require that the game supports a multi-player setting, providing a healthy competition approach. Also relevant, integrate the survivor's family in the narrative of the serious game, eliciting the use of rehabilitation at home, a more ecological setting, conducted outside a controlled laboratory environment.

Acknowledgments. To everyone involved in discussion sessions and user studies, thanks for your time and expertise, in particular, the stroke survivors. This research was supported by IEETA, in the context of project [UIDB/00127/2020].

Disclosure of Interests. The authors have no competing interests to declare that are relevant to the content of this article.

References

1. Amorim, P., Santos, B.S., Dias, P., Silva, S., Martins, H.: Serious games for stroke telerehabilitation of upper limb - a review for future research. Int. J. Telerehabil. **12**(2), 65 (2020)
2. Amorim, P., Serra, H., Sousa, B.S., Dias, P., Castelo-Branco, M., Martins, H.: Chronic stroke survivors' perspective on the use of serious games to motivate upper limb rehabilitation–a qualitative study. Health Inform. J. **29**(2) (2023)
3. Andreikanich, A., et al.: An exploratory study on the use of virtual reality in balance rehabilitation. In: International Conference of the IEEE Engineering in Medicine and Biology Society (EMBC), pp. 3416–3419 (2019)
4. Bui, J., Luauté, J., Farnè, A.: Enhancing upper limb rehabilitation of stroke patients with virtual reality: a mini review. Front. Virtual Reality **2** (2021)
5. Cameirão, M.S., Bermúdez i Badia, S., Verschure, P.F.: Virtual reality based upper extremity rehabilitation following stroke: a review. J. CyberTherapy Rehabil. **1**(1), 63–74 (2008)
6. Dias, P., et al.: Using virtual reality to increase motivation in poststroke rehabilitation. IEEE Comput. Graph. Appl. **39**(1), 64–70 (2019)
7. Enjalbert, M., Benaïm, C.: Classification fonctionnelle de la préhension chez l'hémiplégique adulte. In: Annales de readaptation et de medecine physique, vol. 7 (1999)
8. Feigin, V., et al.: Global and regional burden of stroke during 1990–2010: findings from the global burden of disease study. Lancet **383**(9913), 245–255 (2014)
9. Felipe, F.A., et al.: Evaluation instruments for physical therapy using virtual reality in stroke patients: a systematic review. Physiotherapy **106**, 194–210 (2020)
10. Hebert, D., et al.: Canadian stroke best practice recommendations: stroke rehabilitation practice guidelines. Int. J. Stroke **11**(4), 459–484 (2016)
11. Juan, M.C., Elexpuru, J., Dias, P., Santos, B.S., Amorim, P.: Immersive virtual reality for upper limb rehabilitation: comparing hand and controller interaction. Virtual Reality, 1–15 (2022)

12. Kern, F., Winter, C., Gall, D., Käthner, I., Pauli, P., Latoschik, M.E.: Immersive virtual reality and gamification within procedurally generated environments to increase motivation during gait rehabilitation. In: IEEE Conference on Virtual Reality and 3D User Interfaces, pp. 500–509 (2019)

13. Marques, B., et al.: Supporting multi-user co-located training for industrial procedures through immersive virtual reality (VR) and a large-scale display. In: IEEE International Symposium on Mixed and Augmented Reality Adjunct (ISMAR-Adjunct), pp. 749–750 (2022)

14. Marques, B., et al.: Evaluating outside the box: lessons learned on extended reality multi-modal experiments beyond the laboratory. In: Proceedings of the 25th International Conference on Multimodal Interaction, pp. 234–242 (2023)

15. O'Keefe, L., Doran, S., Mwilambwe-Tshilobo, L., Conti, L., Venna, V., McCullough, L.: Social isolation after stroke leads to depressive-like behavior and decreased BDNF levels in mice. Behav. Brain Res. **260**, 162–170 (2014)

16. Paraense, H., Marques, B., Amorim, P., Dias, P., Santos, B.S.: Whac-a-mole: exploring virtual reality (VR) for upper-limb post-stroke physical rehabilitation based on participatory design and serious games. In: 2022 IEEE Conference on Virtual Reality and 3D User Interfaces Abstracts and Workshops (VRW), pp. 716–717 (2022)

17. Patsaki, I., et al.: The effectiveness of immersive virtual reality in physical recovery of stroke patients: a systematic review. Front. Syst. Neurosci. **16** (2022)

18. Postolache, O., Hemanth, D.J., Alexandre, R., Gupta, D., Geman, O., Khanna, A.: Remote monitoring of physical rehabilitation of stroke patients using IoT and virtual reality. IEEE J. Sel. Areas Commun. **39**(2), 562–573 (2020)

19. Towfighi, A., et al.: Poststroke depression: a scientific statement for healthcare professionals from the American Heart Association/American Stroke Association. Int. J. Stroke **48**(2), 30–43 (2017)

20. Weiss, P.L., Keshner, E.A., Levin, M.F.: Virtual Reality for Physical and Motor Rehabilitation. Springer, New York (2014). https://doi.org/10.1007/978-1-4939-0968-1

Design, Development, and Evaluation of a Virtual Reality-Based Distance Learning Application in Manual Medicine and Therapy

Laura Steffny[1]([✉]) [ID], Nils Ove Beese[2] [ID], Kevin Gisa[1] [ID], Nina Christine Peters[1] [ID], Jan Spilski[2] [ID], Thomas Lachmann[2,3,4] [ID], and Dirk Werth[1] [ID]

[1] August-Wilhelm Scheer Institut für Digitale Produkte und Prozesse gGmbH, Uni Campus Nord D 5 1, 66123 Saarbrücken, Germany
laura.steffny@aws-institut.de

[2] Rheinland-Pfälzische Universität Kaiserslautern-Landau – Center for Cognitive Science, Gottlieb-Daimler-Straße, 67663 Kaiserslautern, Germany

[3] Facultad de Lenguas y Educación, Universidad Nebrija – Centro de Investigación Nebrija en Cognición, Madrid, Spain

[4] Katholieke Universiteit Leuven – Brain and Cognition Research Unit, 3000 Leuven, Belgium

Abstract. This study focuses on the design, development, and evaluation of a virtual reality (VR)-based distance learning application for manual medicine and therapy (MM and MT). Traditional medical education, often lecture-based, faces challenges in the acquisition of practical skills. The rise of digital technology, particularly VR, offers a promising solution for modernizing medical education. VR technologies provide immersive, interactive environments, and the incorporation of haptic interaction, such as data gloves with sensors and actuators, enhances the realistic experience. The study addresses the lack of research in applying VR to MT, a field that relies heavily on tactile and proprioceptive stimulation. The objective is to develop and evaluate a prototype VR application for MM and MT, focusing on cervicothoracic junction (CTJ) mobilization. The study explores the potential effects of VR and the use of data gloves for this specific learning scenario. Materials and methods include ethical considerations, hardware and software details, qualitative interviews, and quantitative prototype usability testing (PUT). The PUT includes questionnaires assessing presence, simulator sickness, system usability, and user experience. The analysis of the results shows positive feedback on the usability of the VR application, the overall presence, and the user experience while acknowledging the need for improvement in certain aspects. The study highlights the potential of VR in health education to provide realistic training experiences without compromising patient safety. The detailed design, development process and evaluation results provide valuable insights into the application of VR in the field of MM and MT, addressing the specific needs of professionals in this field.

Keywords: Virtual Reality · VR · Distance Learning · Manual Therapy · Manual Medicine · Haptic Learning · Data Gloves

© The Author(s), under exclusive license to Springer Nature Switzerland AG 2024
J. Y. C. Chen and G. Fragomeni (Eds.): HCII 2024, LNCS 14708, pp. 154–169, 2024.
https://doi.org/10.1007/978-3-031-61047-9_10

1 Introduction

Traditional medical education has long relied on lecture-centered and didactic approaches that emphasize attendance and memorization [1]. While theoretical learning is critical, the limitations of such methods, including monotony and lack of standardization, prevent students from fully mastering practical skills [2]. The advent of digital technology has provided a promising avenue for modernizing medical education and training [3].

Digital media, which includes web-based training, collaborative platforms, mobile applications, and educational videos, has experienced significant growth in various educational contexts over the past decade [4]. Among these, virtual reality (VR)-based technologies have gained traction in various fields, driven by increased commercial availability [5], advances in visualization and interaction, and the immersive experience provided by head-mounted displays (HMD) [6]. VR technologies create immersive, interactive, and imaginative environments [7] and provide dynamic and adaptive learning opportunities in remote learning contexts [7].

While VR systems primarily provide visual and auditory feedback, the incorporation of haptic interaction has been identified as essential to enhance the immersive experience [8, 9]. Haptic technologies, particularly data gloves equipped with sensors and actuators, have emerged as a key component. They enable users to touch or manipulate virtual objects and receive haptic feedback, including vibration and pressure changes [8, 9].

Including more intuitive and direct interaction opportunities, coupled with haptic feedback, allows learners to be immersed in a virtual environment that closely mirrors their real-world practice or exam settings [10, 11]. This proximity to authentic scenarios increases the likelihood that learners will retain actions and knowledge. Previous studies suggest that skill recall is more effective when the learning environment replicates the original context [10, 11]. In the field of health education, digital technologies have become versatile tools capable of meeting a wide range of educational needs of professionals. These needs cover a broad spectrum, including different teaching and training requirements, clinical competencies, and skills such as therapeutic, diagnostic, and communication [12]. Modern technologies provide a realistic training experience without compromising patient safety [12]. Their scalability and repeatability, independent of time and location, establish a standardized quality for medical technical skills, ensuring that proficiency is achieved before practical application [12]. For example, Wan et al. [13] developed an immersive VR training system for orthognathic surgical education to improve technical proficiency, decrease operation time, and increase the attractiveness and degree of participation in surgical training.

The domain of manual medicine (MM) could also benefit of the advantages of VR. MM aims to treat dysfunctions of the musculoskeletal system, relieve pain, and restore mobility and performance based on clinical reasoning [14]. This approach utilizes highly specific treatment approaches, including manual techniques and therapeutic exercises, such as various types of massage and osteopathic manipulative treatment, which focus on the manipulation of tissue [15]. Consequently, MM and manual therapy (MT) fundamentally relies on touch to elicit tactile, proprioceptive, and interoceptive stimulation. Despite the integration of VR in physiotherapy, there is a notable lack of research evaluating its application in MT [14].

Hence, the objective of this study was to develop and evaluate a prototype VR-based distance learning application for MM and MT. Throughout the research, particular attention was given to exploring the potential effects of VR in MM and MT for educational purposes, specifically concentrating on the learning scenario involving the 'mobilization of the cervicothoracic junction (CTJ)'. Additionally, the investigation included the exploration of the application of data gloves for enhancing this scenario.

This article proceeds as follows: First, the applied materials and methods are described, including two design loops to capture the requirements from the perspective of experts, teachers, and students (qualitative interviews) and their assessment of usability (quantitative questionnaires). Subsequently, the results of the two design loops are presented and the VR application designed and developed on this basis is showcased. Finally, the results are critically discussed in the context of potentials and limitations and an outlook on further research steps is given.

2 Material and Methods

2.1 Ethical and Legal Aspects of the Research

The study was approved by the ethics committee of social sciences faculty of the University of Kaiserslautern (Ethics Committee Vote Number 30) without any further requirements or restrictions. Furthermore, the study was also approved by the ethics committee of the Universitätsklinikum Halle. This study is also in compliance with the WMA Declaration of Helsinki (World Medical Association, 2013) and the APA Code of Ethics (American Psychological Association, 2017) including all respective amendments at the time of this study.

2.2 Hardware and Software for the Prototype VR Application

A Meta Quest 2 (Meta Platforms Inc., USA) HMD was used. The Meta Quest 2 has a resolution of 1832 by 1920 pixels per eye and a refresh rate of up to 90 Hz. The data gloves used in this study were the SenseGlove Nova (SenseGlove, Netherlands) (Fig. 1). These haptic data gloves use a nine-axis sensor in the wrist for the absolute orientation of the hand as well as four sensors, one for each finger except the little finger, to measure the flexion and extension of the fingers. There is also a sensor to measure adduction and abduction of the thumb [16]. For force feedback, the data gloves use four modules to provide force in the direction of finger flexion at the fingertips. Furthermore, there are three actuators for vibrotactile feedback, one each for tips of the index finger and the thumb, while the third is located in the palm hub of the gloves.

The software application was programmed using the Unity engine 2021 (Unity Technologies, USA) In addition, the software wit.ai (Meta Platforms Inc., USA) was used to transform user voice commands into actions within the VR environment.

2.3 Qualitative Interviews (Design Loop 1)

Interview Guideline. A semi-structured interview guideline was developed in conjunction with MM and MT practitioners as well as teaching experts. The guideline was

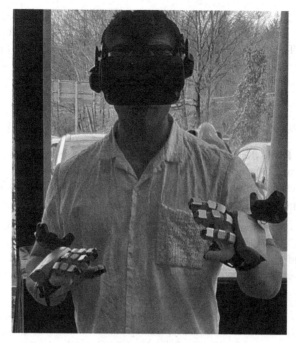

Fig. 1. The VR headset Valve Index used together with the SenseGlove Nova

constructed to ensure that each expert, teacher, and student would get the same overarching topics. Questions were framed in a manner to avoid bias, leading questions and to invite detailed responses from the participants.

Procedure of Interviews. The interviews were conducted with experts, teachers and students. The interviews with the experts and teachers were done in one-on-one sessions, while the students' interviews were done as focus group sessions. All sessions were conducted online and were recorded for later transcription and analysis. All participants received general information about the process and gave their written consent on the participation as well as recording beforehand.

The sessions started with a short introduction by the interviewer about the project and the general procedure of the interview. All participants were asked about the following topics:

- general teaching and training practices and weaknesses in MM and MT
- experience with digital solutions in teaching and training in MM and MT

For the last topic, the participants saw videos and some mockups of an early prototype of an application for MM and MT. The feedback on this early prototype concept was used for the next design loop. A session usually lasted about 120 min.

Sample of the Interviews. Five experts, in this case two doctors of MM and three teachers of MT at vocational colleges and further education institutions, were interviewed in one-on-one interviews. Eight students were interviewed in two focus groups of four students each. The first focus group consisted of one emergency medicine specialist with further education in MM, two students of MT at a university of applied sciences and one MT apprentice. The second focus group consisted of four trained MT that enrolled in medical studies after their training and were in their eighth semester at the time of the focus group session.

2.4 Quantitative Prototype Usability Testing (PUT, Design Loop 2)

Questionnaires from the PUT. The questionnaires used in the usability tests were the Igroup Presence Questionnaire (IPQ; [17]), the pretest and posttest versions of the Simulator Sickness Questionnaire (SSQ; [18]), the System Usability Scale (SUS; [19]) and the User Experience Questionnaire (UEQ; [20]).

IPQ. The IPQ is a 14-item questionnaire that is used to assess the feeling of presence in virtual reality. The IPQ is constructed out of the three subscales Spatial Presence, Involvement, and Experienced Realism and a single item on General Presence. The participant answers on a 7-point Likert scale, from 0 (strongly disagree) to 6 (strongly agree), on how much they agree or disagree with the given statements.

SSQ. The SSQ is a 16-item questionnaire, each item referring to a symptom commonly associated with simulator sickness and typically given both during the pretest and posttest phases of an experiment. For each of the 16 symptoms, the participants report how strongly the symptom currently affects them on a 4-point scale (none, slight, moderate, or severe).

SUS. The SUS is a 10-item scale used to assess the usability of a system. Participants use a 5-point Likert scale to rate how strongly they agree with the given statements about the system they are asked about.

UEQ. The UEQ is a 26-item questionnaire consisting of contrastive pairs of terms that can describe the user experience. For example, one of these items would be the pair of "attractive" and "unattractive". These pairs are scaled in seven steps, from -3 to $+3$, with $-$ being the most negative, 0 being a neutral and $+3$ is the most positive response. The UEQ is divided into six subscales: Attractiveness, Perspicuity, Efficiency, Dependability, Stimulation, and Novelty.

Procedure of the PUT. After incorporating some of the feedback from the interviews and testing several versions of a prototype VR application internally, a working version was tested in the field. The working prototype had a patient in the examination room as the setting. Participants had to do an examination of the patient's CTJ mobilization.

The PUT started with a pretest questionnaire about what technical devices they had and if they have any prior experience with VR. After filling out this questionnaire, the participants completed a small online course on the cervicothoracic transition which was used as a precursor to the patient examination in VR.

Before starting the VR application, participants were fitted with the Meta Quest 2 HMD and the SenseGlove Nova. The data gloves was then calibrated using the SenseGlove calibration app. The participants opened the prototype VR application and started the examination after a brief introduction on the general control scheme by the experimenters.

The VR examination began with the virtual patient sitting on a MT treatment table (Fig. 2). The participants then had to examine several joints and their mobilization both through haptic examination using the data gloves and through voice commands. The joints that needed to be examined were both highlighted on the patient's body (Fig. 2 top) and written down on a checklist visible in the VR application. The joints were highlighted as gray dots on the spine that turned red when touched by the participants' hands in VR. The examination could be done in any order and without a time limit. Voice commands were used to let the VR patient move their head to the right, to the left, tilt it forwards as well as tilt the head backwards. A voice command was also required to trigger the ability to perform an active MT exercise with the patient.

After completing the examination application in VR, the participants had to answer a short quiz about the examination in the online course. After this quiz, the participants had to answer a posttest questionnaire about their user experience using the UEQ and the SSQ, the usability of both the application and the data gloves using the SUS, their immersion in VR using the IPQ as well as demographic questions, e.g., age, occupation, and education.

Sample of the PUT. Thirty-two participants (13 male (40.62%), 19 female (59.38%), 0 diverse/non-binary (0.00%)), ranging in age from 20 to 79 years (M = 36.56 years, SD = 15.3 years, Md = 32.00 years) tested the VR prototype. Of the 32 participants, 15 were students (46.88%), twelve were teachers (37.50%) and five were practitioners (15.62%). Of these 32 participants, four had prior experience with VR (12.50%), 25 had no prior experience with VR (78.12%), and three did not answer this question (9.38%). Prior to the VR part of the testing, the SSQ showed no significant problems with symptoms of simulator sickness.

2.5 Analysis

R 4.3.1 was used to analyze all questionnaires except for the UEQ. For the analysis of the UEQ, the UEQ Analysis Tool Excel spreadsheets, as available on their website [21], were used.

3 Results

3.1 Results of Interviews (Design Loop 1)

Experts and Focus Groups on the Topic of Current Practices and Weaknesses. The experts mentioned several aspects of the current practices in teaching MT. A major part of teaching is teaching the different manual techniques. According to the experts, this is mainly done by showing the techniques to the students, then letting the students repeat the techniques and giving them feedback on what needs to be improved. One of the experts also said that they want.

"more variety in their teaching methods" than what they currently have.

One of the weaknesses in this regard, according to the experts, is that there are terminologies and concepts that vary between the different educational institutions which in turn makes communication and work more difficult. The students in the focus groups agreed on this point. One of the students in the focus groups said that.

"there are differences in each of the schools [...] differences in ordering of the courses, but also in material and content".

Furthermore, both the focus groups and the experts mentioned that the large size of classes tends to make it more difficult to learn and teach properly and to practice techniques. One of the students of the focus groups stated that *"The size of groups or courses was enormous".*

The students also wanted more connection to the real work, such as working on typical cases instead of exotic cases during the courses, as one of them stating that.

"there's an extreme lack of relation to the reality" in some of the courses.

Experts and Focus Groups on the Topic of Using Digital Technologies in Teaching and Learning MT. Both experts and focus groups said that digital technologies can help in teaching and learning if done correctly. While they said they already use video conferencing, learning management systems and have a wiki-style database of different manual techniques, there are things and procedures that can be further digitalized. The experts and teachers mentioned they could envision parts of the curriculum, e.g., fundamentals of joints and anatomy as well as practicing techniques, in VR and AR.

Experts and Focus Groups on the Early Concept of the Prototype. Concerning the early concept of the prototype shown in screenshots, experts pointed out that a structured approach based on the different steps is a meaningful way to use AR and VR in teaching in MM and MT. The experts said that the prototype should show the different steps as an overlay and indicate if the correct part of the body is being gripped or not. One expert reiterated the idea of using it to showcase the anatomy of the body and how the different joints actually work and move after being shown the early concept.

The focus groups also thought that the prototype could be used to show the anatomy. Another use case for them was to use it to practice some of the rarer cases to be prepared when they occur.

Both experts and focus groups agreed that a VR or AR application similar to the early concept prototype can help with practice and feedback in teaching and learning. Both also agreed that haptic feedback is needed to use it in a meaningful and sustainable way.

3.2 Results of Implementation of Prototype VR Application

The early-stage mockups were iteratively adapted, considering the results of the interviews mentioned in Sect. 3.1. Based on this, a realistic treatment room, an interactive virtual patient and a tablet for the VR environment were implemented, which are presented in detail in the following.

Treatment Room. Using the identified professional and technological requirements, a 3D VR environment was developed to replicate a treatment room (Fig. 2). This VR environment provides the flexibility to control various elements, including an adjustable therapy table and an integrated tablet for managing and displaying information.

Fig. 2. VR environment that replicates a MT treatment room

Tablet for Control and Display Functionalities. Furthermore, a tablet was integrated into the VR environment for control and display functionalities. Hand tracking was integrated using the data gloves, eliminating the need for a touch controller. The interaction with the tablet and other objects, such as the control function of the therapy table, is done by touch through the virtual hands of the hand tracking.

The tablet was iteratively equipped with additional functions during the course of the project. A login function allows users to log in during the evaluations with preconfigured user accounts. A checklist was used to keep track of all the steps carried out and their progress.

Movement in the virtual environment can be done either by moving around in the real room if sufficient space is available or by interacting with the tablet. For this purpose, certain areas of interest have been defined in relation to the virtual patient, to which the user can teleport by touching input on the tablet. The tablet always stays close to the user so that it is within reach even if the user teleports or moves.

Virtual Patient. A virtual patient has been developed to perform various MT diagnostic and treatment procedures (Fig. 3). These include passive examinations (cervical spine flexion/extension/rotation/lateral tilt) as well as an active preliminary examination to mobilize the CTJ and check the isometric resistance of the cervical spine. In addition to the haptic interactions in the environment, the VR application also allows voice interaction with the virtual patient, e.g. for the patient to perform the cervical spine rotation.

For passive examination tasks, the user must instruct the virtual patient to move his head in a certain way and in the correct order to visually see movement restrictions of the cervical spine and correctly diagnose the underlying issue (Fig. 3 bottom).

To check the isometric resistance of the cervical spine, the user has to perform certain grip techniques on the patient's head and tell him to resist against his own movement. The haptic feedback of the data gloves should allow the user to determine if there are any underlying issues with a weak resistance of the cervical spine.

For the CTJ, the user must touch the correct vertebral segments of the cervical spine and then instruct the virtual patient to move his head to one of the possible directions (forward, backward, left, right). By moving the head and the corresponding moving of the vertebral segments, the user should be able to visually see and physically feel abnormalities of specific segments.

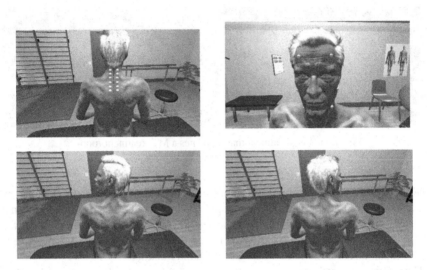

Fig. 3. Sketch of the vertebrae and vertebral segments of the virtual patient as a preliminary test for mobilization of the CTJ (top). Illustration of head rotation with full (bottom left) and limited (bottom right) range of motion.

3.3 Results of the PUT

There were no noticeable problems with simulator sickness according to the posttest SSQ, similar to the pretest SSQ.

The results of the IPQ by subscales are shown in Table 1. According to Melo et al. [22], the General Presence in the VR application can be considered *excellent* (grade *A*). While the Spatial Presence and Experienced Realism subscales could still be considered *marginally acceptable* (grade *E* and *D*, respectively), the grading of Melo et al. would describe the Involvement as *unacceptable* (grade *F*).

Regarding user experience, the SUS and the UEQ were analyzed. The SUS was used for the data gloves exclusively, while the UEQ was used for both the VR application and the data gloves.

The SUS scores for the SenseGlove Nova, $M = 58.44\ SD = 15.42\ Mdn = 61.25$, can be considered *ok* or grade *D* according to Bangor et al. [23].

Figure 4 and Fig. 6 show the mean values per item of the UEQ for the VR application and the data gloves, respectively. Items belonging to the same subscales are color-matched. In both cases, the UEQ values are on the positive spectrum of the opponent pair items. Figure 5 and Fig. 7 show the UEQ results for the VR application and

Table 1. Descriptive Statistics for the 7-point Likert scales version of IPQ

IPQ Subscale	N	M	SD	Mdn	Min	Max
General Presence	32	4.50	1.57	5.00	1	7
Spatial Presence	32	4.13	0.99	4.20	1.6	6
Involvement	32	3.34	0.92	3.25	1.75	5.25
Experienced Realism	32	3.15	0.7	3.00	2	4.25

the SenseGlove Nova, respectively, and compare these results to the UEQ benchmark data set. Compared to the benchmark data, the VR application can be considered *good* regarding Attractiveness, Stimulation and Novelty, but *below average* regarding Perspicuity, Efficiency and Dependability. The SenseGlove Nova, on the other hand, can be considered *above average* in Attractiveness, Perspicuity, Efficiency and Dependability, *excellent* in Stimulation and *good* in Novelty.

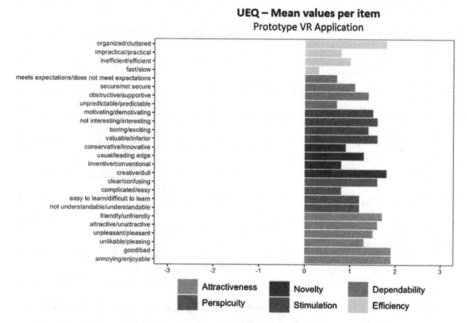

Fig. 4. Means per UEQ item on the experience of using the prototype VR application

In addition to the results of the questionnaires, some participants also gave free text feedback on the application and the hardware. When writing about the VR application, some participants mentioned the possibility of *"going or touching through the patient"* and the *"lack of feedback"* as confusing and bad, while also mentioning that "*it would be nice if it was more realistic*". Another participant said that they would like their avatar in VR to have legs. Concerning the data gloves, they said that "*the vibration mode of*

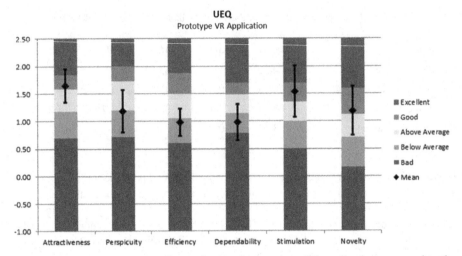

Fig. 5. UEQ results on the experience of using the prototype VR application compared to the UEQ benchmark dataset

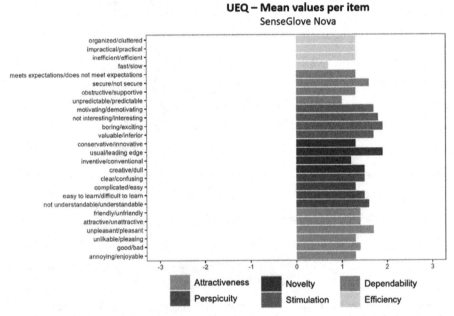

Fig. 6. Means per UEQ item on the experience of using the SenseGlove Nova for interacting in the prototype VR application

the gloves was partially inappropriate", that they *"wanted to have resistance in [their] fingers"* and that they would have liked *"more precision in their coordination"* of the hand movements.

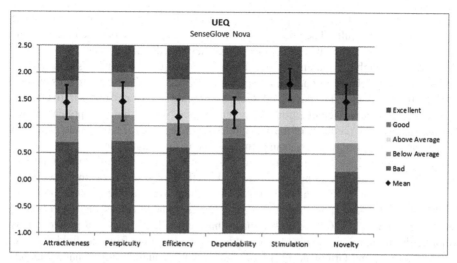

Fig. 7. UEQ results on the experience of using the SenseGlove Nova for interacting in the VR application compared to the UEQ benchmark dataset

4   Discussion

An iterative design process with in-between evaluations was used. The aim was to ensure that the iterations achieved the desired effect and that the prototype met the requirements of the target group. The first design loop consisted of semi-structured interviews with the target group, i.e. MM teachers and learners, in which they were asked about the requirements for a potential VR application. Furthermore, they were asked to evaluate a very early concept prototype in terms of its suitability for MT learning scenarios. The second design loop started with the implementation of a working VR application prototype showing a patient examination. The VR application utilized haptic data gloves to attempt to replicate the haptics in MM. Following implementation, this prototype was tested for usability and user experience of both the VR application itself and the data gloves. The results of the questionnaires showed promising results in terms of the general presence in VR and the user experience of the SenseGlove Nova. However, opportunities were also identified to optimize both technologies, the VR application and the SenseGlove Nova, concerning certain aspects of presence and user experience.

The UEQ results of the SenseGlove Nova showed above-average suitability of the gloves for the VR application. The VR application, on the other hand, was rated lower on average by the participants. However, the SUS results, which only rated the usability of the gloves as 'ok', must be taken into account when interpreting the results.

A possible explanation for the rating of the VR application could therefore lie not in the VR application itself, but in the interaction with the Sense Glove Nova. Beese et al. [24] compared two kinds of VR controllers and found differences in user preference but not in performance. They argued that it is about more than just the design of a controller. They also noted that the interplay of assets and the kind of interactions you want to enable in VR could play a bigger role in some cases. Reviewing the comments of the participants in the usability test of this study provides further insight into the possible causes of the differences in the results. The comments pointed to an imbalance between interactions in the physical and virtual worlds. For example, they stated that it was possible to move their hands through the patient. In addition, they stated that in some cases they were confused by the lack of feedback and inappropriate vibrations. These comments explain why the Involvement and Experienced Realism subscales were rated comparatively low.

Concerning the implementation of the SenseGlove Nova in the VR application, we found that the haptic feedback of the data gloves should be able to let the participants feel if there are issues with weak resistance in the spine in the examination. However, some participants pointed out the unrealistic feedback. One reason for this could be that the data gloves are either not good enough for the task or that some forms of implementation are not possible in the current state. Potentially, the gloves are the biggest limitation of this study, as the haptic capabilities of a human hand, such as the resolution of haptic detections [25, 26], are higher than what SenseGlove Nova can provide. This is particularly important to consider when dealing with a topic from the fields of MM and MT. Müller and Grunwald [27] have shown that manual therapists have a higher perceptual performance in terms of haptics. They argued that daily training in MM may have led to higher performance and a slower decline in this performance in older therapists. They also concluded that training programs for people with inherently low sensitivity could lead them to have higher haptic perception. Combined with our results from the questionnaires as well as the comments of the participants, the SenseGloves Nova in its current state could not satisfy all aspects needed in the MT setting in this study, which is in accordance with the argument made by Certinelli et al. [14] that the technology is still lacking.

Studies show that haptic data gloves may not need to realistically mimic human hands to train certain actions. Zhao et al. [28] found in their meta-analysis that the use of VR applications in medical education resulted in a higher pass rate for learners than for learners using traditional training approaches. They mentioned that learners have more confidence by gaining more hands-on experience and a better understanding of the procedures being practiced [28].

Regarding the effects of a realistic learning experience, Hekele et al. [29] found no differences in learning outcomes between a 2D video and a non-interactive 360° video shown in VR. Niedermayr et al. [30] found no significant differences in learning in VR when comparing interaction with realistic tools versus non-realistic tools in VR. However, they also stated that their qualitative evaluation showed higher engagement when using the realistic variants. This is also in accordance with the comments in our study that they wished the hand interactions and feedback would be more realistic. Then again, our study was only focused on usability for the time being.

In conclusion, the mixed-methods approach combined with iterative feedback and usability testing design loops helped to identify the target group's requirements for the VR application to practice MM and MT learning scenarios, and the main areas in which there is currently room for improvement to realize the full potential of this type of application. Further research should focus on the interaction between VR and data gloves. Special attention should be paid to the involvement of MM and MT teachers in the development process of haptic data gloves to meet the high requirements of this professional group. With respect to the current state of the art of haptic data gloves, it should be further evaluated for which learning scenarios in MM and MT the use of immersive VR applications already represents a real added value for learners and what impact the use of such technologies has on learning outcomes.

Acknowledgments. The study was part of the research projeject SmartHands and funded by the German Federal Ministry of Education and Research (Bundesministerium für Bildung und Forschung, BMBF, grant number # 01PG20006). We would like to thank the entire SmartHands consortium (Universitätsklinikum Halle, Alice Salomon University of Applied Science Berlin, imc information multimedia communication AG and the haptic research laboratory of the University Leipzig) for their collaboration, expertise, and support. We would also like to thank all study participants for providing expertise and feedback for the development of the VR application.

Disclosure of Interests.   The authors declare that they have no known competing financial interests or personal relationships that could have appeared to influence the work reported in this article.

References

1. Kamei, R.K., Cook, S., Puthucheary, J., Starmer, C.F.: 21st century learning in medicine: traditional teaching versus team-based learning. Med. Sci. Educ. **22**, 57–64 (2012). https://doi.org/10.1007/BF03341758
2. Izard, S.G., Juanes, J.A., Peñalvo, F.J.G., Estella, J.M.G., Ledesma, M.J.S., Ruisoto, P.: Virtual reality as an educational and training tool for medicine. J. Med. Syst. **42**, 50 (2018). https://doi.org/10.1007/s10916-018-0900-2
3. Kyaw, B.M., et al.: Virtual reality for health professions education: systematic review and meta-analysis by the digital health education collaboration. J. Med. Internet Res. **21**, e12959 (2019). https://doi.org/10.2196/12959
4. Tamim, R.M., Bernard, R.M., Borokhovski, E., Abrami, P.C., Schmid, R.F.: What forty years of research says about the impact of technology on learning: a second-order meta-analysis and validation study. Rev. Educ. Res. **81**, 4–28 (2011). https://doi.org/10.3102/0034654310393361
5. Scavarelli, A., Arya, A., Teather, R.J.: Virtual reality and augmented reality in social learning spaces: a literature review. Virt. Real. **25**, 257–277 (2021). https://doi.org/10.1007/s10055-020-00444-8
6. Radianti, J., Majchrzak, T.A., Fromm, J., Wohlgenannt, I.: A systematic review of immersive virtual reality applications for higher education: design elements, lessons learned, and research agenda. Comput. Educ. **147**, 103778 (2020). https://doi.org/10.1016/j.compedu.2019.103778
7. Alzahrani, N.M.: Augmented reality: a systematic review of its benefits and challenges in e-learning contexts. Appl. Sci. **10**, 5660 (2020). https://doi.org/10.3390/app10165660
8. Caeiro-Rodríguez, M., Otero-González, I., Mikic-Fonte, F.A., Llamas-Nistal, M.: A systematic review of commercial smart gloves: current status and applications. Sensors **21**, 2667 (2021). https://doi.org/10.3390/s21082667
9. Ozioko, O., Dahiya, R.: Smart tactile gloves for haptic interaction, communication, and rehabilitation. Adv. Intell. Syst. **4**, 2100091 (2022). https://doi.org/10.1002/aisy.202100091
10. Smith, S.M., Vela, E.: Environmental context-dependent memory: a review and meta-analysis. Psychon. Bull. Rev. **8**, 203–220 (2001). https://doi.org/10.3758/BF03196157

11. Krakauer, J.W., Mazzoni, P., Ghazizadeh, A., Ravindran, R., Shadmehr, R.: Generalization of motor learning depends on the history of prior action. PLoS Biol. **4**, e316 (2006). https://doi.org/10.1371/journal.pbio.0040316

12. Barteit, S., Lanfermann, L., Bärnighausen, T., Neuhann, F., Beiersmann, C.: Augmented, mixed, and virtual reality-based head-mounted devices for medical education: systematic review. JMIR Serious Games **9**, e29080 (2021). https://doi.org/10.2196/29080

13. Wan, T., Liu, K., Li, B., Wang, X.: Validity of an immersive virtual reality training system for orthognathic surgical education. Front. Pediatr. **11**, 1133456 (2023). https://doi.org/10.3389/fped.2023.1133456

14. Cerritelli, F., et al.: The challenges and perspectives of the integration between virtual and augmented reality and manual therapies. Front. Neurol. **12**, 700211 (2021). https://doi.org/10.3389/fneur.2021.700211

15. Field, T.: Massage therapy research review. Complement. Ther. Clin. Pract. **24**, 19–31 (2016). https://doi.org/10.1016/j.ctcp.2016.04.005

16. Find out about our Nova Haptic Glove. https://www.senseglove.com/product/nova/

17. Schubert, T.W.: The sense of presence in virtual environments: a three-component scale measuring spatial presence, involvement, and realness. Zeitschrift für Medienpsychologie **15**, 69–71 (2003). https://doi.org/10.1026//1617-6383.15.2.69

18. Kennedy, R.S., Lane, N.E., Berbaum, K.S., Lilienthal, M.G.: Simulator sickness questionnaire: an enhanced method for quantifying simulator sickness. Int. J. Aviat. Psychol. **3**, 203–220 (1993). https://doi.org/10.1207/s15327108ijap0303_3

19. Brooke, J.: SUS: A quick and dirty usability scale. Usability Eval. Ind. 189, (1995)

20. Laugwitz, B., Held, T., Schrepp, M.: Construction and evaluation of a user experience questionnaire. In: Holzinger, A. (ed.) HCI and Usability for Education and Work, pp. 63–76. Springer, Heidelberg (2008). https://doi.org/10.1007/978-3-540-89350-9

21. UEQ User Experience Questionaire. https://www.ueq-online.org/

22. Melo, M., Gonçalves, G., Vasconcelos-Raposo, J., Bessa, M.: How much presence is enough? qualitative scales for interpreting the igroup presence questionnaire score. IEEE Access **11**, 24675–24685 (2023). https://doi.org/10.1109/ACCESS.2023.3254892

23. Bangor, A., Kortum, P., Miller, J.: Determining what individual SUS scores mean: adding an adjective rating scale. J. Usabil. Stud. **4**, 114–123 (2009)

24. Beese, N.O., Reinhard, R., Lachmann, T.: The right tools for the job: towards preference and performance considerations in the design of virtual reality interactions. Behav. Inf. Technol. **42**, 278–288 (2023). https://doi.org/10.1080/0144929X.2022.2125831

25. Louw, S., Kappers, A.M.L., Koenderink, J.J.: Haptic detection thresholds of Gaussian profiles over the whole range of spatial scales. Exp. Brain Res. **132**, 369–374 (2000). https://doi.org/10.1007/s002210000350

26. Louw, S., Kappers, A.M.L., Koenderink, J.J.: Haptic discrimination of stimuli varying in amplitude and width. Exp. Brain Res. **146**, 32–37 (2002). https://doi.org/10.1007/s00221-002-1148-z

27. Müller, S., Grunwald, M.: Haptische Wahrnehmungsleistungen. Man. Med. **51**, 473–478 (2013). https://doi.org/10.1007/s00337-013-1068-y

28. Zhao, G., Fan, M., Yuan, Y., Zhao, F., Huang, H.: The comparison of teaching efficiency between virtual reality and traditional education in medical education: a systematic review and meta-analysis. Ann. Transl. Med. **9**, 252–252 (2021). https://doi.org/10.21037/atm-20-2785

29. Hekele, F., Spilski, J., Bender, S., Lachmann, T.: Remote vocational learning opportunities—a comparative eye-tracking investigation of educational 2D videos versus 360° videos for car mechanics. Br. J. Edu. Technol. **53**, 248–268 (2022). https://doi.org/10.1111/bjet.13162
30. Niedermayr, D., Wolfartsberger, J., Maurer, M.: Virtual reality for industrial assembly training: the impact of tool interaction realism on learning outcomes. In: 2023 IEEE International Symposium on Mixed and Augmented Reality Adjunct (ISMAR-Adjunct), pp. 183–190. IEEE, Sydney (2023)

Game Engine Technology in Cultural Heritage Digitization Application Prospect–Taking the Digital Cave of the Mogao Caves in China as an Example

Ruiguang Tan[✉], Bingnan Jiang, Shujie Liu, and Jie Zhang

East China University of Science and Technology, Shanghai, China
rgtan@ecust.edu.cn

Abstract. Taking the digital caves of the Mogao Grottoes in Dunhuang as an example, this paper explores the prospects for the application of game engine technology in the digital preservation and utilization of cultural heritage, and highlights the benefits of cultural heritage digitization in preservation, protection and dissemination. Digital technologies, especially game engine technologies, provide immersive and interactive experiences that overcome the limitations of space and time. This paper discusses the potential of game engine technologies to enhance the narrative, educational value and public engagement of cultural heritage, including a questionnaire survey to analyze public attitudes towards digital cultural heritage and the use of game engines in it. The study concludes that while game engine technologies hold great promise for cultural heritage applications, challenges remain in terms of marketing, economic costs and public understanding. In addition, the paper emphasizes the importance of balancing authenticity and entertainment in the process of digital gamification of cultural heritage, and calls for the resolution of intellectual property rights and ethical issues in the field to further promote the use of game engine technology in the field of cultural heritage preservation and access.

Keywords: Digitization of cultural heritage · Cultural heritage · Game engine · Digital preservation and utilization

1 Introduction

Cultural heritage embodies a profound wealth inherited by human society through the intricate tapestry of historical development and evolution [1]. It stands as an irreplaceable and renewable resource, encompassing both tangible cultural heritage [2] and intangible cultural heritage [3], which is transmitted from generation to generation. With substantial historical, artistic, scientific, and social value, cultural heritage not only represents the cultural essence of

J. Y. C. Chen and G. Fragomeni (Eds.): HCII 2024, LNCS 14708, pp. 170–188, 2024.
https://doi.org/10.1007/978-3-031-61047-9_11

a country and its people but also serves as a vital lens through which humanity comprehends its past. It acts as a pivotal link connecting a nation's past, present, and future, fostering national cohesion and a sense of belonging. The exploration, preservation, transmission, and adaptive utilization of cultural heritage are imperative not only for cultivating new avenues of economic growth and advancing national and regional economic development but also for safeguarding the traditional cultures of nations. Moreover, these endeavors contribute to nurturing mutual exchanges, respect, and integration among diverse cultures.

In the current era of rapid urban expansion, accelerated changes in the natural environment, and swift social and cultural transformations, numerous cultural heritages face natural erosion and human-induced damages. The protection and preservation of cultural heritages confront serious threats, emphasizing the urgency and necessity of risk prevention and protective utilization of cultural heritages [4]. Fortunately, with the rapid development of digital technology in recent years, cultural heritage is transcending the limitations of time and space, becoming a permanent digitalized memory for humanity [5]. Various emerging digital technologies, including 3D scanning, drone tilt photography, big data, artificial intelligence, digital twin platforms, social media platforms [6], virtual reality, and augmented reality, provide diverse solutions and flexible approaches for the protection, preservation, and utilization of cultural heritage. These include 3D laser scanning technology and drone tilt photography technology for information collection and acquisition, digital twin platforms for information storage and management, and artificial intelligence technology for information dissemination and sharing. Additionally, virtual reality, augmented reality, and game engine technology play roles in information dissemination and sharing.

Existing research primarily targets intangible cultural heritage, with tangible cultural heritage receiving less systematic theoretical and technical support [7]. Digital technology applications in this field are mainly focused on online exhibitions and AR displays, which face limitations such as small screen sizes and insufficient immersion, or require costly equipment [8]. Diverse participant backgrounds challenge traditional narrative methods in evoking emotional responses. Theoretical frameworks like multimodal interaction [9], immersive learning [10], and cognitive load theories [11], along with immersion theory and experience design [12,13], support enhancing interactive and immersive experiences. Game engine technology emerges as a promising tool for cultural heritage digitization, offering immersive experiences that engage emotions and improve narrative effects, thus fostering public participation and preserving collective memory [14–16]. Ubisoft's Assassin's Creed, especially its initiative following Notre Dame's fire damage, highlights the potential of using games to explore cultural heritage, receiving positive societal feedback [17].

In summary, this paper takes the Dunhuang Mogao Grottoes Digital Cache as a case study. Through a questionnaire survey to understand public attitudes, this paper explores the significance of integrating game engine technology into cultural heritage digitization, preservation and utilization, and draws inspiration from similar cases. In addition, this paper analyzes the advantages of game engine technology in comparison with traditional narrative methods. The paper also looks forward to the future application of the technology and delves into its potential value in the field of cultural heritage digitization, preservation and utilization.

2 Digital Technology and Cultural Heritage

The UNESCO-initiated "Memory of the World" project was launched in 1992, aiming to globally promote the process of digital preservation of cultural heritage [18]. In the same year, UNESCO employed Geographic Information System (GIS) technology to assist the Cambodian government in safeguarding the Angkor Wat [19]. By 2003, the "Charter on the Preservation of Digital Heritage" was enacted, calling for global attention and emphasis on the protection of digital cultural heritage [20]. In 2005, the European Union introduced the "Faro Convention" as a framework concerning the values of social and cultural heritage, clearly stating that heritage is significant based on the meanings and uses assigned to it by people and its representative values [21]. The European Commission released the "European Cultural Heritage Strategy for the 21st Century" in 2017, making demands on aspects such as data security, accessibility, and digital collaboration platforms in heritage protection [22]. During the International Council on Monuments and Sites (ICOMOS) General Assembly in 2017, the theme of "Cultural Heritage Conservation and Interpretation in the Digital Empowerment Era" was presented [23], highlighting the crucial role of digital technology in various aspects of cultural heritage, including recording, protection, community engagement, interpretation, communication, and disaster management. As of 2021, the "Impact of Information Technology" has become the foremost topic among the twelve global initiatives of the "Our World Heritage Initiative" [24]. This progression, from widespread advocacy to increasingly specific requirements, demonstrates that the digital preservation of world heritage is gradually evolving into an independent research field.

In practical applications, historical castles in Turin, Italy, employ Building Information Modeling (BIM) for information preservation and utilize VR applications for the promotion of architectural heritage conservation and utilization [25]. In the densely touristic environment of Timurid dynasty architectural complexes in Uzbekistan and Tajikistan, 3D scanning methods have been applied [26]. In Spain, knowledge of European silk heritage is presented through an interactive map [27]. Unmanned Aerial Vehicle (UAV) photogrammetry and Terrestrial Laser Scanning (TLS) integration have been used for the digital modeling and restoration of watchtowers in the challenging environments of the Qinghai-Tibet Plateau in China [28]. Ancient opera stages in Shanxi, China, employ knowledge visualization technology for digital display [29]. Various digital technologies, such as the Three-Dimensional Visualization Management System Platform for the Ming City Wall in Nanjing [30] and the Historical Building Information Management Platform in Shanghai [31], contribute novel approaches and inject vitality into the protection of cultural heritage.

2.1   Digitizing Chinese Cultural Heritage

Since 2016, China has prioritized the preservation and utilization of cultural heritage, shifting towards "promoting preservation through utilization" as evidenced by twenty policies [32]. The "Thirteenth Five-Year Plan" introduced the "Guiding Opinions on Promoting the Deep Integration of Culture and Technology" by six departments, aiming to merge culture with technology to spur cultural and technological innovation, transforming cultural development modes to better fulfill the cultural and spiritual needs of the population [33]. Furthermore, the "Opinions of the Ministry of Culture and Tourism" focuses on digital transformation in the cultural sector, advocating for the use of exceptional cultural resources to improve digitization quality and efficiency [34]. In 2022, the "Opinions on Promoting the Implementation of the National Cultural Digitalization Strategy" outlined eight key tasks for converting cultural resources into productive factors, marking the cultural heritage sector's elevation to a national priority during the "Fourteenth Five-Year Plan" period [35]. This series of policies underscores the Chinese government's commitment to enhancing cultural heritage protection and utilization through digital transformation.

From an academic perspective, with the development of digital technology, the digital preservation and utilization of cultural heritage have become prominent research topics in recent years [36]. A search for academic journals on the China National Knowledge Infrastructure (CNKI) using the keywords "cultural heritage" and "digitization" yielded a total of 727 relevant documents. Among them, the literature volume in the past five years, starting from 2019 and ending on November 22, 2023, amounted to 394 papers, constituting more than half of the total publications. In recent years, research and projects in the field of digital preservation and utilization of cultural heritage have expanded from the initial phases of informatization, database construction, and digital restoration to encompass the digital exhibition and dissemination of cultural heritage [7]. The year 2023 marks the 51st anniversary of the adoption of the "Convention Concerning the Protection of the World Cultural and Natural Heritage," where digital protection has become one of the most crucial topics in the field of World Heritage in the 21st century [24]. Broadly, we can categorize the application of digital technology in heritage protection into three types: (1) Information collection and acquisition technologies; (2) Information storage and management technologies; (3) Information dissemination and sharing technologies [37]. By clearly categorizing the application of digital technology in the field of landscape heritage protection, this classification provides a coherent framework for research and practice in related fields, facilitating more targeted and efficient protection and management of different types of cultural heritage.

From a market perspective, the digital revitalization of cultural heritage in China is gaining momentum, marked by initiatives like the "Chinese Intangible Cultural Heritage Gene Database," which offers a big data-based platform for sharing knowledge on intangible cultural heritage through the collaboration of the Qicheng Research Institute and others [38]. This project and others, such as the "Digital Forbidden City" and the "Digital Great Wall," leverage digital technology for preserving, interpreting, and disseminating cultural heritage, with the latter being the first to apply game engine technology for immersive digital restoration on a large scale [39,40]. In 2023, the collaboration between the Dunhuang Research Institute and Tencent led to the launch of the "Transcendental Participatory Museum," showcasing high-precision, 3D reconstructions of the Dunhuang Mogao Grottoes, a pioneering effort in digital cultural heritage presentation [41]. These efforts underscore the innovative approaches to cultural heritage protection and highlight the significant role of digital technology in the creative transformation and development of Chinese culture [24].

Digitizing cultural heritage offers significant benefits for its preservation, conservation, and sharing. Digital tools like Virtual Reality (VR), Augmented Reality (AR), and 3D technologies bridge the gap between traditional preservation and modern engagement, harmonizing the need to safeguard cultural heritage with the desire for public access and interaction. This approach enables global dissemination of Chinese culture, offering digital narratives, virtual tours, and immersive experiences that transcend geographical and temporal boundaries. It fosters new ways of exploring Chinese culture, leveraging technology to highlight its richness and uniqueness, thereby enhancing cultural confidence and international influence.

2.2 Protection and Utilization of Cultural Heritage

The relationship between the preservation and utilization of cultural heritage is dialectical [42], characterized by complexity and multifaceted dynamics. When dealing with cultural heritage, it is not sufficient to focus solely on preservation without activating utilization. Cultural heritage that remains preserved but lacks activation does not align with the trends of the times and lacks vitality. Such heritage, devoid of renewed vitality, will ultimately fade away in the course of history. Similarly, placing excessive emphasis on activation while neglecting preservation is also inappropriate. Activation and utilization should be built upon a foundation of sound preservation. Without proper preservation, cultural heritage cannot be fully activated and utilized. Blind utilization might even have counterproductive effects, exacerbating the degree of damage and hastening the process of disappearance. Balancing the preservation and utilization of cultural heritage requires careful and thoughtful planning by professionals [43]. It is essential to ensure effective preservation of cultural heritage while enabling it to adapt to the contemporary social, environmental, and natural contexts, thereby rejuvenating its value.

Traditional Methods of Conservation and Utilization. Traditional methods of cultural heritage protection mainly include the following: Documentary Records; Material Restoration and Maintenance; Defining Protection Zones and Controlling Visitor Numbers.

Inadequacies and Shortcomings of the Traditional Approach. The protection and utilization of cultural heritage have always been significant tasks in the cultural domain. However, traditional methods of cultural heritage protection have exhibited certain flaws and limitations in their long-term practical application [44], facing formidable challenges, such as:

Limited Scope and High Costs. Traditional documentation methods for cultural heritage, such as photography, written records, and drawings, necessitate substantial professional manpower and offer limited opportunities for public engagement, potentially hindering adequate protection due to subjective biases. Moreover, the data produced is static and cannot be readily updated, failing to reflect the dynamic nature of cultural heritage. Additionally, post-restoration, cultural heritage requires significant ongoing maintenance, entailing considerable human, material, and financial resources.

Restricted Participation and Limited Utilization. To preserve cultural heritage, many sites enforce protective measures like establishing protected areas, capping visitor numbers, and restricting visiting hours, which, while protective, limit visitor engagement and participation. These restrictions can hinder visitors' cultural experiences and education, potentially reducing public interest and support for cultural heritage. Moreover, the predominantly static nature of cultural heritage presentations, often limited to informative exhibits with explanations, animations, and demonstrations, lacks interactive and immersive elements, impeding deeper visitor understanding of cultural heritage.

Environmental Threats. The traditional model of cultural heritage protection often relies on passive defense against damage caused by natural environmental factors or human activities. Reactive measures make it challenging to achieve substantive prevention and protection.

2.3 Summary

Digital preservation and utilization are essential for overcoming the limitations of traditional cultural heritage methods. Digital technologies enable the creation of accessible databases for both online and offline access, ensuring dynamic and updated information sharing. Technologies like VR, AR, and XR enhance interactive experiences and public engagement by vividly presenting cultural heritage's historical and emotional context. Digital integration of environmental data and AI algorithms for disaster prediction and damage prevention facilitates proactive protection. Moreover, digital management platforms significantly reduce labor and maintenance costs, promoting sustainable cultural heritage conservation.

Digitization, recognized as a pivotal strategy for bridging cultural supply and demand [45] and fostering cultural industries' growth [46], caters to the increasing demand for immersive digital experiences among younger audiences [47]. The application of game engine technology in cultural heritage digitization not only transforms physical heritage into virtual data, creating new value but also ensures its perpetual preservation and dynamic transmission.

3   Game Engine Technology in the Field of Cultural Heritage

3.1   Game Engine Technology Development Overview

Game engine technology, notably through platforms like Unreal Engine and Unity, has emerged as a significant force in computer graphics and game development, offering versatile and scalable solutions for cultural heritage digitization [48]. These engines facilitate the detailed recreation of historical sites and artifacts, utilizing advanced rendering for realistic visuals and supporting VR and AR applications. This technology enables lifelike experiences of historical and cultural heritage through immersive devices, allowing for dynamic and interactive educational exhibits.

The adoption of game engine technology in cultural heritage, such as the 3D digitization of the Mogao Grottoes by the Dunhuang Academy [49], showcases its potential to bring cultural heritage to wider audiences online. Despite its advantages, challenges remain, including complex data handling [50], high costs of equipment [51], and navigating ethical and intellectual property considerations [52].

3.2   Game Engine Technical Features

Unreal Engine (UE), developed by Epic Games, initially supported the "Unreal" game development and has since expanded across multiple sectors, including gaming, film, television, and architectural visualization. Since its 1998 debut, UE has evolved through several versions, enhancing its versatility and functionality. Key milestones include UE2 in 2002, introducing console support; UE2.5 in 2004, adding physics and AI features; UE3 in 2006, with a new visual editor and advanced graphics; and UE4 in 2014, which made game development more accessible through the Blueprint visual programming system. The latest, UE5, launched in 2022, brought groundbreaking features like Nanite virtualized geometry and Lumen global illumination, revolutionizing the creation of detailed and realistic virtual environments.

Blueprint Programming, introduced by Epic Games in UE4, is a visual scripting language that encapsulates code written in traditional programming languages. It utilizes visual programming nodes to present a concrete representation of the code, which is then interpreted and executed by the computer. The advent of the Blueprint programming system allows individuals with non-programming backgrounds, such as artists and designers, to actively participate in game and application development. Simultaneously, it provides programmers with a more intuitive, rapid, and concrete working method, thereby increasing development efficiency and reducing barriers to entry.

Nanite, a feature of Unreal Engine 5, aims to render highly detailed 3D models with minimal impact on hardware performance. Traditional game development used Level of Detail (LOD) adjustments based on the viewer's distance to manage model complexity, often leading to visual discontinuity. Nanite innovates by partitioning model triangles into clusters and automatically generating LODs, avoiding noticeable transitions. This technology removes the need for manually creating LODs, streamlining development workflows and enabling the use of high-resolution models without significant resource consumption. Nanite's capabilities enhance visual quality in applications like cultural heritage digitization, film production, and virtual reality, facilitating the creation of detailed virtual environments more efficiently.

Lumen, UE5's real-time global illumination system, dynamically simulates light interactions within game environments, producing realistic lighting that responds to environmental changes. Unlike traditional methods requiring artists to pre-calculate lighting into static lightmaps, Lumen offers dynamic, real-time lighting, enhancing development flexibility and efficiency. This advancement allows for more realistic material textures and lighting in cultural heritage digitization, enabling immersive narrative experiences with minimal hardware performance impact. Lumen's capabilities facilitate the creation of detailed and interactive virtual reproductions of cultural heritage on both small and large scales.

In summary, the developmental trajectory of the Unreal Engine (UE) reflects the advancements in gaming and visual content creation technologies. Each version has brought significant innovations and improvements in graphic rendering, user-friendliness, multi-platform support, and has paved the way for new applications, especially in the realm of cultural heritage preservation and activation. As technology continues to evolve, it is foreseeable that game engine technologies will play an increasingly prominent role in creating more enriching, interactive, realistic, and educationally meaningful digitized representations of cultural heritage.

3.3   Game Engine Technology Application Case: Digital Scripture Cave of Mogao Grottoes, China

From a geographical perspective, the Mogao Caves are located on the western edge of the Hexi Corridor, adjacent to Xinjiang and the Qinghai-Tibet Plateau. Since the opening of the Silk Road during the Han Dynasty, it has been a crucial node and commercial center for cultural exchange between the East and West. Various cultures and religions converged here, engaging in mutual exchanges and integration. It is generally accepted by scholars that the caves were initially carved by the monk Le Zun in the second year of the Jianyuan era of the Former Qin dynasty (366 AD). Subsequently, due to frequent wars, changes of political regimes, especially during the Song Dynasty when northern territories of China were occupied by ethnic minorities, and the decline of the Silk Road, the Mogao Caves gradually fell into neglect and remained relatively unknown during the Ming Dynasty. In 1890, Taoist priest Wang Yuanluo arrived at the Mogao Caves during his travels and decided to settle there. He became the guardian of the grottoes and sought funds for the restoration and maintenance of the Mogao Caves temples.

The Mogao Caves represent the world's largest and most content-rich repository of Buddhist art, encapsulating the developmental evolution of Chinese cave art [53]. The caves comprise 735 grottoes, featuring over 45,000 square meters of murals, more than 2,400 color sculptures, five wooden-structured cave eaves from the Tang and Song dynasties, and a scripture cave covering 7 square meters containing over 60,000 ancient documents that record various aspects of Chinese civilization. These vast and diverse collections provide invaluable materials for studying ancient Chinese and Central Asian history, geography, religion, economy, politics, ethnicity, language, literature, art, and technology.

In June 2022, the "Tencent Interactive Entertainment × Digital Dunhuang Cultural Heritage Digital Creative Technology Joint Lab" was established with the vision of creating the "Digital Scripture Caves" project. This initiative aims to provide the public with a digital platform and channel to understand Chinese cultural relics such as the Mogao Caves Library. In 2023, the Dunhuang Academy and Tencent jointly launched the "Time-Space Participatory Museum - Digital Scripture Caves." Utilizing game engine technology, this project opens up the culturally rich world that has been sealed for centuries. It marks the first global comprehensive application of high-definition digital scanning, game engine physics rendering, global dynamic lighting, and 3D sub-millimeter modeling game technology to recreate and present the Mogao Caves Library in a digital format. This project accurately reproduces the spatial information of the Mogao Caves Library, benefitting from millimeter-level high-definition scanning. The dust at the joints of bricks and stones is meticulously preserved, and the sculptures of eminent monks in the scripture caves are composed of over 10 million triangles. Through PBR (Physically Based Rendering) technology and 4K virtual texture mapping, authentic restoration of material texture and structure is achieved, and ancient damaged documents are repaired, restored, and displayed. Additionally, the project incorporates interactive narrative gameplay, allowing participants to embody the "guardians of the scripture caves," engaging in dialogues with historical figures and experiencing the entire process of the caves, from excavation and sealing to the dispersal and reassembly of artifacts, across time and space.

Questionnaire Design. This study focuses on digital Dunhuang caves as a case study, utilizing surveys for investigation and analysis. The research aims to collect data to understand the public's perceptions and attitudes towards aspects such as the digitization of cultural heritage, the integration of game engine technology with cultural heritage, and related digital products. A total of 125 surveys were collected in this questionnaire survey, providing valuable guidance. To explore the dissemination and impact of digital Dunhuang caves and similar cultural products within the general population, a structured questionnaire was employed for systematic data collection. The questionnaire gathered basic information from respondents to ensure the relevance and accuracy of the data. Additionally, the questionnaire was divided into different modules, each addressing specific research questions. Respondents' answers to these modules determined subsequent survey content, ensuring accuracy and relevance for each participant. The questionnaire design, illustrated in Fig. 1, primarily utilized a "Five-Point Likert Scale" for measuring participants' attitudes and opinions on specific issues.

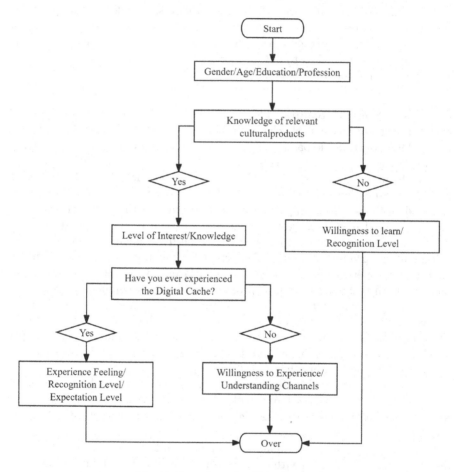

Fig. 1. Questionnaire Flow Design

As shown in the figure, the first key decision point in the questionnaire involves determining whether respondents are familiar with relevant cultural products. If respondents are unfamiliar or lack knowledge of such products, they are categorized as Group A. The focus is primarily on understanding their willingness to learn and their level of appreciation for cultural education. For those familiar with relevant cultural products (Group B), further investigation is conducted into their level of interest and understanding. The second key decision point involves querying Group B about their experiences with digital Dunhuang caves or related digital cultural products. If they haven't experienced these, the survey explores how they learned about these cultural products and assesses their willingness to experience them. For respondents who have experienced digital Dunhuang caves or related products (Group C), the survey delves into aspects such as game process, style, immersion, interactivity, educational significance, and expectations for similar digital cultural products, completing the questionnaire data collection.

With a carefully designed survey flow, ensuring the inclusivity of respondent groups, the study aims to obtain more accurate data for in-depth analysis, providing a rich and detailed perspective.

Analysis of Survey Results. This survey collected a total of 125 responses, and both the reliability (Cronbach's alpha coefficient = 0.897) and validity (KMO value = 0.926) of the scale passed the tests. The majority of the 125 respondents were in the age range of 18–38, constituting 66.4%. In terms of education background, the majority held a bachelor's degree or below, accounting for 93.6% of the overall respondents.

Based on the key decision points in the questionnaire, the collected responses were categorized into three groups. Group 1 consisted of 104 respondents who had neither knowledge nor experience with digital Dunhuang caves or related digital cultural products. Group 2 comprised 16 respondents who were familiar but had not experienced these products, and Group 3 included 5 respondents who were both familiar with and had experienced digital Dunhuang caves.

For Group 1, representing 83.2% of the total respondents, the survey focused on investigating their willingness to learn and their general attitudes towards cultural products. Seven scale questions were designed to analyze this group's overall views on understanding digital Dunhuang caves and related cultural products, as well as the barriers they face (Table 1).

Group 2, consisting of 16 respondents, was surveyed to analyze their level of interest, knowledge sources, and willingness to experience digital Dunhuang caves. Seven scale questions were designed, and the results were tabulated (Table 2).

Group 3, with only 5 respondents who had both knowledge and experience, was surveyed on satisfaction with the experience, game style and immersion, evaluation of educational value, improvement suggestions, and expectations. Twelve scale questions were designed, and the results were tabulated (Table 3).

Furthermore, by comparing the average scores of common questions across the three groups (Fig. 2), the following conclusions were drawn from the survey results: 1. Group 3 (those familiar with and experienced with digital Dunhuang caves) generally scored higher than Group 1 and Group 2, indicating that related digital products contribute to sparking public interest and recognition of cultural heritage. 2. All three groups showed lower average scores for understand-

Table 1. Respondent Group 1 Scale Topics and Mean Scores.

Question	Options (1–5 points from left to right)	Average
You are interested in cultural heritage	*Strongly Agree/Agree/Neutral/Disagree/Strongly Disagree*	3.26
You know cultural heritage	*Strongly Agree/Agree/Neutral/Disagree/Strongly Disagree*	3.39
You know about digital preservation and utilization of cultural heritage	*Strongly Agree/Agree/Neutral/Disagree/Strongly Disagree*	2.94
You believe that digitization can effectively transmit and promote cultural heritage	*Strongly Agree/Agree/Neutral/Disagree/Strongly Disagree*	4.23
You believe that digitization of cultural heritage has important educational significance	*Strongly Agree/Agree/Neutral/Disagree/Strongly Disagree*	3.00
You are interested in experiencing cultural heritage digitization products	*Strongly Agree/Agree/Neutral/Disagree/Strongly Disagree*	3.91
You believe that digitization can contribute to a better understanding of cultural heritage	*Strongly Agree/Agree/Neutral/Disagree/Strongly Disagree*	3.09

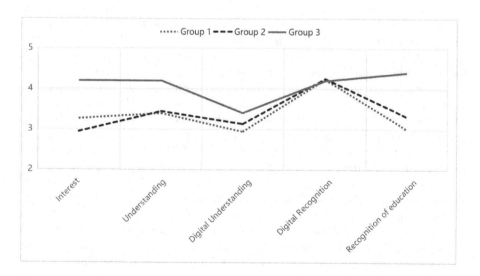

Fig. 2. Comparison of Average Scores

Table 2. Respondent Group 2 Scale Topics and Mean Scores.

Question	Options (1–5 points from left to right)	Average
You are interested in cultural heritage	*Strongly Agree/Agree/Neutral/Disagree/Strongly Disagree*	2.94
You know cultural heritage	*Strongly Agree/Agree/Neutral/Disagree/Strongly Disagree*	3.44
You know about digital preservation and utilization of cultural heritage	*Strongly Agree/Agree/Neutral/Disagree/Strongly Disagree*	3.13
You believe that digitization can effectively transmit and promote cultural heritage	*Strongly Agree/Agree/Neutral/Disagree/Strongly Disagree*	4.25
You believe that digitization of cultural heritage has important educational significance	*Strongly Agree/Agree/Neutral/Disagree/Strongly Disagree*	3.31
You are willing to try to experience digital caves or related digital products	*Strongly Agree/Agree/Neutral/Disagree/Strongly Disagree*	4.13
You believe that digitization of cultural heritage can effectively promote the public's interest in cultural heritage	*Strongly Agree/Agree/Neutral/Disagree/Strongly Disagree*	4.06

ing cultural heritage digitization and utilization, while their approval ratings were relatively high, indicating a noticeable gap. Groups 1 and 2 exhibited lower interest levels, suggesting a lack of proactive willingness and limited channels for the public to understand cultural heritage digitization. 3. In Groups 1 and 2, the level of recognition for the educational significance of cultural heritage digitization products was significantly lower compared to Group 3, suggesting that those who have experienced such products find them more educationally valuable. 4. Group 3 respondents expressed higher satisfaction with the immersion, game style, and overall gaming experience of digital Dunhuang caves and related cultural heritage digitization products. However, they noted that the process was lengthy, and the atmospheric creation was somewhat lacking. 5. Among the survey respondents, 83.2% had neither knowledge nor experience with digital Dunhuang caves or related cultural heritage digitization products, and there were no clear correlations with age, education background, gender, etc.

Additionally, in open-ended opinion questions, respondents emphasized the historical accuracy, realism, and accessibility of related digital products.

Table 3. Respondent Group 3 Scale Topics and Mean Scores.

Question	Options (1–5 points from left to right)	Average
You are interested in cultural heritage	*Strongly Agree/Agree/Neutral/Disagree/Strongly Disagree*	4.20
You know cultural heritage	*Strongly Agree/Agree/Neutral/Disagree/Strongly Disagree*	4.20
You know about digital preservation and utilization of cultural heritage	*Strongly Agree/Agree/Neutral/Disagree/Strongly Disagree*	3.40
You believe that digitization can effectively transmit and promote cultural heritage	*Strongly Agree/Agree/Neutral/Disagree/Strongly Disagree*	4.20
You believe that digitization of cultural heritage has important educational significance	*Strongly Agree/Agree/Neutral/Disagree/Strongly Disagree*	4.40
What do you think about the game flow of Digital Sutra Cave?	*Too Long/Long/Moderate/Short/Too Short*	4.00
You think the game flow of Digital Sutra Cave is smooth and easy to understand	*Strongly Agree/Agree/Neutral/Disagree/Strongly Disagree*	4.00
You think the visual effects of Digital Cave of Sutras are very good	*Strongly Agree/Agree/Neutral/Disagree/Strongly Disagree*	4.20
You think the atmosphere of Digital Sutra Cave is good	*Strongly Agree/Agree/Neutral/Disagree/Strongly Disagree*	3.80
You think Digital Cave of Sutras effectively protects and passes on cultural heritage	*Strongly Agree/Agree/Neutral/Disagree/Strongly Disagree*	3.80
You are willing to recommend the Digital Cave of Tibetan Scriptures to people around you	*Strongly Agree/Agree/Neutral/Disagree/Strongly Disagree*	4.80
You are looking forward to more similar cultural heritage digitization products	*Strongly Agree/Agree/Neutral/Disagree/Strongly Disagree*	4.60

Summary. The Digital Dunhuang Caves project, through the integration of advanced game engine technology and digitization methods, effectively addresses the limitations of traditional approaches to the preservation and utilization of cultural heritage. This enables a highly realistic digital restoration of tangible cultural heritage, offering a new interactive experience for the dissemination of intangible cultural heritage. This technological approach allows traditional cultural heritage to transcend temporal and spatial constraints, making it more accessible and understandable to a global audience. The presentation of cultural heritage is no longer confined to traditional museums and book introductions but transforms into a dynamic, interactive, and immersive experience. This approach significantly enhances the unique appeal and dissemination efficiency of cultural heritage, especially targeting younger audiences and those in the digital age.

However, despite receiving unanimous acclaim from users and showcasing innovation and educational value in the fusion of game engine technology with cultural heritage, survey results indicate a relatively low market penetration for such products. This reflects evident shortcomings in promotion and popularization. Simultaneously, respondents exhibit a moderate level of awareness and willingness to engage with such products. Although there is potential interest and demand, understanding remains relatively limited. Additionally, the survey's respondents are predominantly aged between 18 and 38, constituting 66.4% of the total, with only 34.4% having an educational background below the undergraduate level. Consequently, the data generated from this survey possesses certain limitations.

4 Conclusion

Tangible cultural artifacts, buildings, as well as intangible traditions and customs, constitute valuable treasures left behind in the course of human history. These irreplaceable resources carry profound historical, artistic, scientific, and social values. They are the crystallization of national culture and serve as bridges connecting the past, present, and future. In an era of rapid urban expansion, accelerating natural environmental changes, and dynamic socio-cultural transformations, the protection and revitalization of cultural heritage face a series of formidable challenges. Fortunately, the rapid development and innovation of game engine technology have injected new vitality into the preservation and revitalization of cultural heritage, providing multiple avenues and methods. The integration of advanced digital technology with the protection and utilization of cultural heritage is currently a prominent focus in relevant professional research. The digitization of cultural heritage not only rejuvenates with the evolving times, creating new economic growth points, but also fosters cultural exchanges and integration among nations, regions, and countries. It facilitates the realization of cultural heritage protection and revitalization in the new era.

This article, primarily focusing on the Digital Cave Project, explores the application value of game engine technology in the field of digital preservation and activation of cultural heritage through a questionnaire survey. Analysis of the collected survey data indicates that the "Digital Cave" project has, to a certain extent, realized its initial vision of providing a novel and efficient channel and platform for the public to understand artifacts and their historical backgrounds. It also demonstrates that game engine technology exhibits innovativeness and educational value in the domain of digital preservation and utilization of cultural heritage, receiving a considerable level of recognition. However, there is still a lack of public understanding regarding digital preservation and utilization of cultural heritage, with the majority of respondents having not experienced the Digital Cave or similar products. The author analyzes this phenomenon with the following three reasons: (1) Currently, research outcomes related to game engine technology in the field of digital cultural heritage are mostly concentrated in the realm of intangible cultural heritage, with limited applications in the protection and utilization of tangible cultural heritage [7]. (2) The application of game engine technology in the digitalization of large-scale heritage sites requires handling a significant amount of complex data and scenes, imposing higher demands on technology and resources. Additionally, immersive and interactive cultural heritage experiences rely on facilities and equipment that are relatively expensive, immobile, and require regular maintenance. The high cost and requirements of these facilities and equipment are not conducive to the promotion and popularization of related products. (3) The application of game engine technology in the field of digital preservation and utilization of cultural heritage raises questions about how to ensure a balance between accuracy, authenticity, and entertainment in the digitization process. Furthermore, issues related to intellectual property rights, ethics, cultural sensitivity, and relevant technical standards still need to be addressed.

Moreover, based on the questionnaire data collected in this study, the following issues persist: The age range is concentrated between 18–38 years old, failing to cover all age groups completely. The majority of respondents have a bachelor's degree, while respondents with other educational backgrounds are relatively scarce. Very few respondents have experienced the Digital Cave or similar digital cultural heritage products. Therefore, the data collected in this questionnaire has certain limitations, as the attitudes of the main group of respondents, who show a positive attitude toward the digitization of cultural heritage, may not fully represent the attitudes of the general public across different educational backgrounds and age groups.

In conclusion, the Digital Cave project has successfully protected fragile original murals from environmental and human damage, significantly enhancing public awareness and interest in this world cultural heritage. The application of game engine technology in the cultural heritage field demonstrates great potential. With this technology, we can not only better protect and preserve precious cultural heritage but also provide education and experiences to the public in novel ways. However, due to various factors, the popularization and promotion of game engine technology in the field of digital preservation and utilization of cultural heritage still face challenges. Public recognition is limited, but there is potential interest and demand among the public. Improving public awareness and experience of these products will require more efforts from various professionals, with the hope that game engine technology can bring even more possibilities for the protection and activation of cultural heritage in the future.

References

1. Li, Z., Zou, H., Yi, Q., et al.: Study on the assessment of tourism resource potential of terraced agricultural cultural heritage. Econ. Geogr. **35**(06), 198–201 (2015)
2. Aikawa, N.: An historical overview of the preparation of the UNESCO International convention for the safeguarding of the intangible cultural heritage. Museum Int. **56**(1–2), 137–149 (2004)
3. He, X.: Preservation of intangible cultural heritage and modernization of national culture. Ethnicity Today **2**, 55–57 (2005)
4. Zhang, X., Zhi, Y., Xu, J., et al.: Digital protection and utilization of architectural heritage using knowledge visualization. Buildings **12**(10), 1604 (2022)
5. Dou, J., Zhang, B., Qian, X.: A review of AI-empowered cultural heritage: visualization analysis based on CiteSpace. Packag. Eng. **44**(14), 1–20 (2023)
6. Liang, X., Lu, Y., Martin, J.J.S.: A review of the role of social media for the cultural heritage. Sustainability **12**(10), 1055 (2022)
7. Xu, J.: Research on the current status and development trends of digital research on intangible cultural heritage in China. China-Arab States Sci. Technol. Forum **01**, 59–63 (2024)
8. Paliokas, I., Patenidis, A.T., Mitsopoulou, E.E., et al.: A gamified augmented reality application for digital heritage and tourism. Appl. Sci. **10**(21), 7868 (2020)
9. Long, J.: An exploration of experience-based interaction design of preschool children's books in AR forms. China Publish. J. **16**, 38–41 (2017)
10. Cai, S., Wang, P., Yang, Y., Liu, E.: Review on augmented reality in education. J. Dist. Educ. **35**(05), 27–40 (2016)
11. Zhang, H., Zhang, D., Huang, R.: The development, application and reflection of cognitive loading theory in the intelligent era-a review for the 11th International Cognitive Load Theory Conference. Mod. Distance Educ. Res. **06**, 37–44 (2018)
12. Cheng, J., Zhu, X.: Review on educational game researching between china and foreign country. Mod. Educ. Technol. **07**, 72–75 (2007)
13. He, J., Liang, R., Han, G., Xian, X., et al.: Research on construction of deeper learning field model based on virtual reality. e-Educ. Res. **40**(01), 59-66 (2019)
14. Liu, T., Zhang, Y.: The game road to digital humanities: the representation and the procedural rhetorical mechanisms of traditional cultural symbols in game narratives. Nanjing J. Soc. Sci. **11**, 123–136 (2023)
15. Jeffrey, S., Jones, S., Maxwell, M., Hale, A., Jones, C.: 3D visualisation, communities and the production of significance. Int. J. Herit. Stud. **26**(09), 885–900 (2020)
16. Psomadaki, O.I., Dimoulas, C.A., Kalliris, G.M., Paschalidis, G.: Digital storytelling and audience engagement in cultural heritage management: a collaborative model based on the digital city of Thessaloniki. J. Cult. Herit. **36**, 12–22 (2019)
17. O'Connor, S., Colreavy-Donnelly, S., Dunwell, I.: Fostering engagement with cultural heritage through immersive VR and gamification. Vis. Comput. Cult. Herit. 301–321 (2020)
18. Chen, Z., Fan, J.: Application of cultural and technological convergence in cultural heritage protection - a case study of the digitalization of the Mogao Grottoes. Dunhuang Res. **02**, 100–107 (2016)
19. Xing, J.: Original exploration on high-tech trend in modern landscape. Chinese Doctoral dissertations and Master's thesis Full-text Database (Master) (2004)
20. The UNESCO character on the preservation of digital heritage. https://unesdoc.unesco.org/ark:/48223/pf0000380295. Accessed 20 Nov 2023

21. Chen, X., Dong, F.: The authenticity of living heritage: take the conservation of Sri Dalada Maligawa in Sri Lanka as an example. World Archit. **09**, 18–22 (2023)

22. Guo, Y., Ji, T., Tian, Q.: A study of design for digital cultural innovation under the integration of culture and technology: a knowledge graph analysis based on citespace. J. Zhejiang Univ. (Human. Soc. Sci.) **53**(01), 30–43 (2023)

23. Guo, X., Yang, C., Han, F.: Research on digital record and innovative conservation of cultural landscape heritage. Chin. Landsc. Archit. **36**(11), 84–89 (2020)

24. Yang, C., Chen, Z.: Digital conservation of world cultural and natural heritage and new international trends thereof. Landsc. Archit. **30**(10), 96–102 (2023)

25. Osello, A., Lucibello, G., Morgagni, F.: HBIM and virtual tools: a new chance to preserve architectural heritage. Buildings **8**(1), 12 (2018)

26. Milosz, M., Kęsik, J., Montusiewicz, J.: 3D scanning and visualization of large monuments of timurid architecture in central Asia - a methodical approach. J. Comput. Cult. Herit. (JOCCH) **14**(1), 1–31 (2020)

27. Sevilla, J., Casanova-Salas, P., Casas-Yrurzum, S., Portalés, C.: Multi-purpose ontology-based visualization of spatio-temporal data: a case study on silk heritage. Appl. Sci. **11**(4), 1636 (2021)

28. Chen, S., Yang, H., Wang, S., Hu, Q.: Surveying and digital restoration of towering architectural heritage in harsh environments: a case study of the millennium ancient watchtower in Tibet. Sustainability **10**(9), 3138 (2018)

29. Zhang, X., Xu, J., Wang, Y.: Study on digital revitalization of ancient opera stage in Shanxi based on knowledge visualization. Art Des. (Theory) (2022)

30. Jin, L.: Application and prospect of digitalization on cultural heritage conservation in Nanjing city wall. Study Nat. Cult. Herit. **4**(08), 39–43 (2019)

31. He, S., Zheng, H., Tang, Z.: Research on the construction of urban historical and cultural heritage management information system based on geographic information system (GIS). J. Guangdong Univ. Technol. **35**(05), 38–44 (2018)

32. Bai, G., Yang, W.: From image to images pedigrees: production and protection of image cultural heritage in China. J. South-Central Minzu Univ. (Human. Soc. Sci.) **43**(11), 86–94+184 (2023)

33. Hu, Z.: Get through the "last mile" of convergence: Six departments including the Ministry of Science and Technology of PRC, Publicity Department of the Communist Party of China etc. issued the "Guidance on promoting in-depth convergence of culture". Sci. Technol. China Broadcasts (09), 6 (2019)

34. Chen, D., Zhang, J.: Promoting high-quality development of digital culture industry. Chin. Natl. Conditions Strengths **06**, 61–63 (2021)

35. Xie, Z., Chen, Y.: Analysis on the direction of digital construction of public cultural services in China: interpretation of opinions on promoting the implementation of the national cultural digitization strategy digitization strategy. Library (10), 16–21+45 (2023)

36. Dou, J., Li, C.: Research status, hotspots and trends of domestic smart public cultural services based on knowledge graphs. Packag. Eng. **44**(20), 97–107 (2023)

37. Zhang, R., Zhang, C.: Classification and application of digital technologies in landscape heritage protection. Land **11**(10), 1699 (2022)

38. Zhao, Y., Wu, X., Duo, T., et al.: Embracing cultural digitization strategies: a review and foresight of non-heritage digitization practices. Libr. Dev. 1–10

39. Feng, N.: Thoughts about the future of the digitalized palace museum. Palace Museum J. (02), 126–134+163 (2018)

40. Sun, R.: From the "Digital Great Wall" to see the cultural heritage of the digitalization of commitment. Packag. Eng. **06**, 4–7 (2022)

41. Tencent SSV Program homepage. https://tanyuan.qq.com/tanyuan-plan-2023/. Accessed 22 Jan 2024

42. Cai, X.: Dialectical reflection on the safeguarding and utilization of intangible cultural heritage. Hundred Sch. Arts **36**(05), 205–209+22 (2020)

43. Xia, J., Ye, Z.: Research on the integration and development of cultural heritage and digital technology from the perspective of symbiosis theory. Adm. Reform **10**, 14–24 (2023)

44. Dong, J.: Study on digital protection of intangible cultural heritage of minority nationality in Xiangxi autonomous prefecture. Resourc. Dev. Market **29**(12), 1298–1301 (2013)

45. Ma, B., Chen, X., Chen, F.: Multi-scale temporal and spatial differentiation characteristics of Dunhuang tourism flow based on social big data. Econ. Geogr. **41**(03), 202–212 (2021)

46. Liu, Y., Hu, A.: Research on the design and automatic generation of interactive digital art collection of characteristic national culture: a case study on Buddstorm project. Art Des. **06**, 80–85 (2023)

47. Yang, Y.: Cultural digitalization and digital culturalization-rethinking the future of digital culture. Frontiers **01**, 82–90 (2023)

48. Li, M., Wang, Y.: The development foundation and future direction of visual industrial internet. Frontiers **16**, 104–107 (2023)

49. Liu, F., Wu, Z.: Analysis and application suggestions on digital narrative phenomenon of cultural heritage. Digit. Libr. Forum **19**(11), 46–52 (2023)

50. Chen, J., Wang, P., Wang, X.: Semantic service of digital cultural heritage resources—a case study of mapping manuscript migrations (MMM) project. Libr. Tribune **43**(09), 132–141 (2022)

51. Wen, Z., Li, P., Wang, X., et al.: Mixed reality based visual analytics. J. Comput.-Aided Des. Comput. Graph. **34**(06), 821–829 (2022)

52. Tan, Z., Li, H.: The logical mechanism and innovative path of digital technology enabling the protection and inheritance of non-heritage. Nanjing J. Soc. Sci. **01**, 142–150 (2024)

53. Meng, X., Yang, R., Per, Q., et al.: A preliminary study on the decorative art of the architectural color paintings in Mogao Cave 361. Dunhuang Res. **01**, 87–98 (2022)

VAMR Applications and Development

A Virtual Reality Based Therapeutic Approach for Stuttering Intervention

J. Cecil[1(✉)], John A. Tetnowski[2], and Sriram Kumar Tentu[1]

[1] Department of Computer Science, Center for Cyber-Physical Systems,
Oklahoma State University, Stillwater, OK, USA
{j.cecil,stentu}@okstate.edu
[2] Communication Sciences and Disorders, Oklahoma State University, Stillwater, OK, USA
john.tetnowski@okstate.edu

Abstract. Stuttering, a speech disorder with far-reaching effects on communication and emotional well-being, has long posed challenges for those affected. This study introduces a novel approach to address this issue by harnessing the potential of Virtual Reality (VR)-based therapy, specifically designed for teenagers who stutter. In this paper, the overall approach underlying this innovative therapy is discussed along with the outcomes of this pilot project. By immersing participants in simulated scenarios closely resembling real-life speaking situations, we aimed to provide an innovative and engaging platform for therapy. The VR environments were designed using advanced 3D engines and VR software tools, offering a realistic and interactive experience. Participants engaged in therapy sessions equipped with VR headsets and controllers, allowing them to navigate and interact within these immersive environments.

The outcomes of this pioneering study revealed a positive trend, with a significant majority of participants exhibiting a notable reduction in stuttering frequency. Beyond the quantitative improvements, participants reported that the VR-based therapy was not only effective but also intriguing and beneficial. This research showcases the potential of VR technology to transform stuttering therapy by replicating authentic speaking scenarios, thus offering a more engaging and impactful avenue for enhancing communication skills and emotional well-being among individuals who stutter. Through this innovative approach, we open new doors for addressing the multifaceted challenges of stuttering, ultimately fostering improved communication and overall quality of life for those affected.

Keywords: Virtual Reality (VR) · stuttering therapy · speech disorders · immersive technology · communication skills enhancement · Human-Computer Interaction (HCI) · Mixed Reality (MR) · simulation-based learning

1 Introduction

Stuttering, a complex speech disorder affecting millions worldwide, significantly impacts their ability to communicate effectively, often leading to emotional and social challenges [4]. Traditional therapeutic interventions have made strides in addressing the behavioral

J. Y. C. Chen and G. Fragomeni (Eds.): HCII 2024, LNCS 14708, pp. 191–203, 2024.
https://doi.org/10.1007/978-3-031-61047-9_12

aspects of stuttering. However, they frequently fall short of comprehensively addressing the multifaceted nature of this condition. Consequently, there is an urgent need to explore innovative approaches to provide more holistic and effective treatment for individuals who stutter. Virtual Reality (VR) technology has emerged as a promising tool with the potential to revolutionize stuttering therapy [3]. This paper delves into the design of an innovative therapeutic intervention approach where the central component is an immersive Virtual Reality based simulation environment. This study explores the potential of using such innovative approaches as a therapeutic intervention for adolescents who stutter, shedding light on its immersive capabilities and impact on reducing stuttering frequency, affective responses, and cognitive reactions.

Virtual Reality environments [8] can be described as 3D graphics intensive environments created using software tools that enable a user to 'immerse' themselves into a target environment and interact with this environment in a realistic manner; such interactions are possible with the help of controllers, sensors and 3D headsets which enable the users to see a stereoscopic scene which mimics a target or real environment. VR based environments have been created for a range of process contexts, from advanced manufacturing [9] to medical simulators [11]. They have also be used to treat anxiety and phobias [13–23] such as acrophobia; other contexts include designing space systems immersively and for training astronauts for the Moon Mission [7]. In the area of cyber-physical systems and Internet-of-Things (IoT), such VR based approaches have been integrated as part of a link between distributed cyber and physical components [10, 11].

In healthcare and educational settings, Human-Computer Interaction (HCI) related research has witnessed the robust introduction of Virtual Reality and Mixed Reality (MR) technology as part of enhancing training experiences for medical professionals, veterinarians, and surgeons; other efforts have explored ways to support Science Technology Engineering Mathematics (STEM) learning for individuals with autism spectrum disorders [5, 6]. Researcher have also investigated the impact of such VR and MR based environments on a user's cognition, comprehension and skills acquisition [12]. These applications have underscored the potential of VR and MR environments to simulate real-world scenarios, offering controlled and immersive experiences for therapy and interventions. In [17], researchers have investigated the role of cognitive behavioral therapy to address public speaking anxiety. Building upon this foundation, our research explores the potential of VR-based mediums in helping adolescents who stutter enhance their communication skills. By replicating real-life speaking situations within a 3D cyber-based environment, we aim to provide a novel and engaging platform for stuttering therapy. We offer participants a unique opportunity to practice and apply their speech modifications.

Critical insights from previous studies by researchers such as Brundage (2004) [3], Al-Nafjan et al. (2021) [2], and Tetnowski et al. (2023) [1] have demonstrated the positive impact of VR in speech therapy, particularly in reducing stuttering frequency and addressing affective aspects of stuttering, such as anxiety. However, the long-term goal of this research is to focus on adolescents who stutter and introduces the concept of at-home VR simulation environments, allowing participants to engage with VR scenarios independently. Through a comprehensive methodology that assesses stuttering skills, affective and cognitive responses, and lived experiences, we aspire to contribute to the growing body of knowledge surrounding VR-based interventions for stuttering. Our goal in this preliminary study is to pave the way for more extensive research, envisioning a future where VR becomes a standard and highly effective therapeutic tool for individuals who stutter, offering them improved communication skills and an enhanced quality of life.

2   Related Work

Stuttering is a pervasive speech disorder that affects millions of individuals worldwide, impacting both their ability to communicate effectively and their emotional well-being. Traditional therapeutic interventions have made commendable progress in addressing the behavioral aspects of stuttering but have often fallen short in providing comprehensive solutions to the multifaceted nature of this condition. This section explores the existing research and studies related to the application of Virtual Reality (VR) technology in stuttering therapy, shedding light on the promising potential of this innovative approach.

2.1   Previous Studies on VR-Based Stuttering Therapy

Researchers such as Brundage (2004), Al-Nafjan et al. (2021), and Tetnowski et al. (2023) have pioneered the exploration of VR-based interventions in the field of speech therapy. Their studies have shown encouraging results, particularly in reducing stuttering frequency and addressing affective aspects of stuttering, such as anxiety. Brundage (2004) introduced VR as an exciting tool to enhance stuttering treatment, acknowledging the potential of immersive environments to provide realistic scenarios for therapy. Al-Nafjan et al. (2021) delved into the application of VR technology and speech analysis for individuals who stutter, highlighting the role of VR in providing precise feedback and analysis. Tetnowski et al. (2023) extended the research into adolescents who stutter and introduced the concept of at-home VR simulation programs, demonstrating the feasibility of participants engaging with VR scenarios independently [1–3].

2.2   VR Applications in Healthcare and Education

Beyond stuttering therapy, Human-Computer Interaction (HCI) has witnessed significant advancements in the use of Virtual Reality (VR) and Mixed Reality (MR) in healthcare and educational settings. VR and MR have been effectively employed to enhance training experiences for medical professionals, including surgeons, and have shown promise in supporting individuals with autism spectrum disorders in educational settings [6, 7]. These applications underscore the potential of VR and MR environments to simulate real-world scenarios, offering controlled and immersive experiences for therapy and interventions, which aligns with the objectives of stuttering therapy.

Building upon this existing body of research, our study focuses on harnessing the immersive capabilities of VR technology to provide adolescents who stutter with a unique and engaging platform for therapy. By replicating real-life speaking situations within a 3D cyber-based environment, we aim to contribute to the growing body of knowledge surrounding VR-based interventions for stuttering, ultimately envisioning a future where VR becomes a standard and highly effective therapeutic tool for individuals who stutter.

In the subsequent sections, we detail our methodology, present our research findings, and discuss the implications and contributions of our study to the field of stuttering therapy.

3 Methodology

The process of creating such VR based environment is complex and involves an interdisciplinary approach comprising of 3D simulation environment designers, software implementation team members, and speech therapy experts. Using an information modeling approach, the first phase is to create a functional model which serves as the planning and design foundation to design, build and validate such an environment. Based on the software design details and architecture of the simulation environment, the next phase is to build this 3D environment using software engines such as Unity 3D and programming various elements using C# scripts. This environment was integrated with the Oculus Quest 2 platform. In this study, we employed a comprehensive methodology to assess the impact of Virtual Reality (VR) simulations on heart rate and user experience in a simulated restaurant ordering scenario at "Bob's Burger Palace [1]." Our primary objective was to understand how this VR simulation environments influenced participants' physiological responses and their subjective perception of the simulated experience. An overview of the assessment approach follows.

We recruited ten normal, healthy individuals to participate in the study. These participants were selected to represent a diverse range of demographics [1, 3]. Each participant wore a heart rate monitoring device while engaging and interacting with the VR simulation environment. The heart rate data was collected continuously throughout the user interactions, providing insights into the participants' physiological responses during the food or burger ordering process [1]. The VR simulation environment was implemented on the Oculus Quest 2 VR platform, which allowed us to create an immersive simulation environment mimicking an interactive food ordering scenario and process [1].

The VR simulation environment included a target scenario of a burger restaurant ("Bob's Burger Palace") aimed to replicate a real-world ordering experience as closely as possible [1]. Participants were instructed to order as they would in an actual restaurant, using the VR environment. Avatars of human customers and server, as well as resources one would see in a typical burger restaurant were included including ovens, the ordering kiosk, food price displays, etc. As the users interacted with the virtual cashier and made their choices, their heart rate data was recorded in real time. This allowed us to measure any variations in heart rate, potentially indicative of stress or excitement, as a response to the interactions with the VR simulation environment. Views of the VR scenarios can be seen in Figs. 1 and 2 shows views of participants wearing 3D headsets and interacting with the VR environments.

3.1 The Process of Creating VR Simulation Environments for Stuttering

One of the thrusts in this research is to explore the role of information models as a foundational basis for understanding the target process and activities to be simulated inside the VR environment; subsequently, this understanding is used to design, build and validate the VR based simulation environment.

The information model can be created using a function modeling language (such as IDEF-0) or the engineering Enterprise Modeling Language (eEML). eEML was used to understand the relationships within the target activities to be simulated. It captured both the functional and temporal relationships of the target process, which in this case was a delineation of the various interactions in the stuttering therapy scenarios. While the detailed discussion of this eEML is beyond the scope of this paper, an overview of the information captured in this model follows.

The eEML modeling activity begins with identifying the modeling perspective, the modeling scope and the modeling objective. The various steps in a target scenario are represented as verb phrases; each step can be depicted as a task or activity; using precedence relationships (which can be represented as AND or OR or XOR junctions), the overall flow of the activities can be modeled and simulated. For example, a customer walks up the counter, reviews the menu options, and places an order. The service person then responds, asks for the payment, hands over the receipt and then later the ordered food. This can be modeled as a flow chart with 4 distinct associated entities: (1) the data/information or physical triggers or inputs to begin or initiate a task (2) the resources associated with accomplishing or performing that task (for example, for a given task, is the human model performing that task, or a robot or some other object) (3) there may be controlling factors or data/information which may influence the accomplishment of that given task (for example, a certain time limit type of constraint may be imposed on the completion of a task or a quality control rule needs to be observed, etc.) (4) the outcome of a task or activity being completed (this then initiates the next step in that simulated process or procedure). These can be viewed as information centric flow charts that can

Fig. 1. (a): The eating area inside the burger restaurant. The menu displays, the server, customers in a line, etc. can be seen within the VR environment

be modeled at various levels of abstraction or detail. A top level task can be 'place your food order' can be decomposed into sub tasks: walk to the counter, greet the server, order the needed food'. In a simulation scenario such as in Fig. 1, there may be several activities occurring simultaneously; these can be modeled as asynchronous or synchronous activities (they can start or end in such a manner). Creating such an information intensive process model enables the design and model building team to understand the context and enabling them to give feedback so that changes can be made to the VR environment being created.

The VR environment was created based on the design of the software environment; first, the CAD models of the various Objects of Interest (OOI) are crated using a CAD tool such as Solidworks; subsequently, these models are brought into the Unity 3D engine; here the various behavioral attributes to the various objects (avatars, customers, etc.) are added using C# scripts. The immersive capabilities that allow a user to zoom, move around and navigate, allows them to pick up object, press a virtual button or display a human or object movement are programmed during this phase. For the stuttering therapy VR environment, this involved ensuring that the Unity based environment was interfaced with the Oculus Rift platform (Fig. 2) (Figs. 3 and 4).

Fig. 2. b. A view of the VR based Therapeutic Intervention scenario (this view shows other employees in the inner room preparing the burgers, etc.)

To complement the physiological data, we designed a survey containing several questions to assess the participants' subjective experiences during their interactions with the VR simulation environment [1]. The survey included inquiries related to the realism of the scenario, the effectiveness in simulating communication challenges, the clarity of instructions and prompts, the quality of interaction with the virtual cashier, comfort, and ease of use of the VR system, as well as strengths and weaknesses of the simulation. Each question in the survey had a 5-point ordinal rating scale with options ranging from

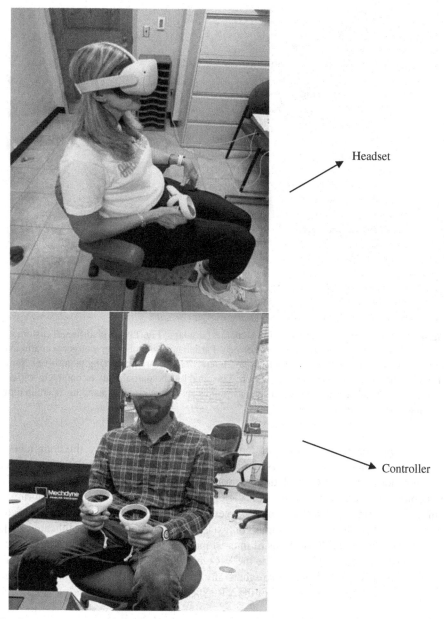

Fig. 3. (a, left) and (b, right): participants interacting with the VR simulation environment using Oculus Rift; they are holding controllers which help them pick up objects, navigate within the VR environment, etc. The headset provides a stereoscopic view of the target environment.

"Not Good" to "Very Satisfactory," allowing participants to express their opinions and impressions about the VR experience [1].

Fig. 4. c: Close-up of one of the ordering scenarios (similar to Fig. 1 but with different customer): Avatars of servers and a participant can be seen. Participants can observe a target scenario and become comfortable with the various tasks and interactions before immersing themselves. Some of the interaction menu buttons can be seen. This enables the participants to complete various interactions, repeat a certain process or step as well as get help with understanding a certain term or step in the interaction process.

Combining heart rate data and participant feedback through surveys, this comprehensive approach enabled us to understand better the physiological and subjective aspects of interactions with a VR simulation environment [1]. The data collected in this study was analyzed to assess the impact of VR on heart rate and user experience during a simulated ordering scenario at "Bob's Burger Palace," contributing valuable insights to the field of VR applications in various contexts, including training and healthcare [6, 7].

Some of the research questions of interest include: does the heart rate of the participants during the talking tasks inside the VR environment comparable to normal heart rate for college age participants? Are there any conclusions based on the survey model related to effectiveness and reality of the VR experience?

4   Results and Discussion

The feedback and responses obtained from participants who participated in the VR simulation study aimed to assess the effectiveness of the virtual reality ordering scenario at "Bob's Burger Palace." Participants included individuals from various age groups, genders, and academic majors. Their responses were categorized based on several criteria, including the realism of the scenario, effectiveness in simulating communication challenges, clarity of instructions and prompts, interaction with the virtual cashier, and comfort and ease of use of interacting with the VR environment.

To analyze the central tendency and spread of the data, we calculated the median and range for each of the criteria (Table 1):

Table 1. Median and Range of Participants' Feedback on the interactions with the VR simulation environment and scenarios

Criteria	Median	Range
Realism of the Scenario	Good	Very Satisfactory to Average
Effectiveness in Simulating Communication Challenges	Very Satisfactory	Very Satisfactory to Average
Clarity of Instructions and Prompt	Good	Very Satisfactory to Below Average
Interaction with the Cashier	Good	Very Satisfactory to Average
Comfort and Ease of Use	Very Satisfactory	Very Satisfactory to Good

Descriptive statistics provide an overview of the participants' overall responses. The median values suggest that, on average, participants found the interactions with the VR environment to be "Good" regarding realism, clarity of instructions, and interaction with the cashier. The effectiveness in simulating communication challenges received a higher median rating of "Very Satisfactory," indicating that the VR scenario was successful in this aspect. The comfort and ease of use were generally rated as "Very Satisfactory." The range in responses indicates individual differences in perception, emphasizing the need for further exploration of factors that influenced participants' experiences.

The results of the heart rate measurement (of the participants) during the VR environment interactions yielded a mean heart rate of 72.4 beats per minute, with a standard deviation 10.01. This was compared to a normal heart rate for young adults and analyzed using a one sample t-test. The results of the analysis yield a t-value of 2.463 with 9 degrees of freedom, resulting in a p-value of 0.036 ($p < .05$). Pre-analysis revealed that the distribution of responses was normal without significant outliers.

The feedback from participants in this pilot project indicated a generally positive perception of the VR based therapy and interactions. This suggests that, overall, participants found the simulation effective, clear, and a valuable tool for addressing communication challenges [1]. The fact that the responses spanned from negative to highly positive indicates a spectrum of experiences, which is valuable for understanding the potential benefits and limitations of the technology [1].

It is important to note that the power of this study is that heart rate could be effectively monitored. The fact that the heart rate for this group of participants did not fall within the normal range (as noted by the one sample t-test) encourages us to explore this and other biological markers that may be related to anxiety and other affective conditions. The implications for a population of individuals that stutter is warranted, since this is a population that typically experiences anxiety in speaking situations [1, 5]. This aligns with the goal of creating a more comprehensive approach to stuttering therapy. Given these promising findings, it is a worthy endeavor to continue along the lines of this research.

The overall outcomes of this research innovation indicate positive potential to help individuals who stutter (with the data showing a normal distribution and no outliers. This suggests that VR simulation-based intervention was well-received across diverse participants. Moreover, a strong case exists for expanding the participant pool to include individuals of different age groups, both younger and older, and those who stutter [1]. This broader demographic representation would enhance the applicability of the research findings and contribute to a deeper understanding of how VR-based therapy can be tailored to diverse populations.

In conclusion, the results of this pilot project have laid a solid foundation for further research into using such VR based environments as part of stuttering therapy. The positive feedback, and the potential to address speech-related anxieties underscore the importance of continuing this research. This project holds promise for individuals who stutter and represents a valuable step forward in pursuing more effective and inclusive therapeutic interventions.

5 Contributions

Our research findings throw more light on the potential of this VR based therapeutic approach contributions, which encompass both novel insights and practical advancements:

5.1 Novel Therapeutic Approach

One of the primary contributions of this research lies in introducing a novel therapeutic approach for adolescents who stutter. By harnessing the immersive capabilities of VR, a unique platform was created that replicates real-life speaking scenarios within a 3D cyber-based environment. This approach offers an unprecedented level of engagement and interaction, allowing individuals who stutter to practice and apply their speech modifications in a controlled and supportive setting. This 3D environment can be enhanced and enriched while also being scalable at different levels of abstraction. More details and specific aspects can be added at lower levels of abstraction; at the same time, given the 3D modeling capabilities, the scope of the interactions can be expanded by adding other interactive scenarios, with other humanoid characters or avatars, objects and procedures. Additional guidance on interacting with the VR scenarios can also be incorporated.

5.2 Evidence of Effectiveness

Our study provides empirical evidence of the effectiveness of VR-based therapy in reducing stuttering frequency and addressing affective aspects of stuttering, such as anxiety. The results from our research demonstrate that most of the participants showed a decrease in stuttering after engaging in VR therapy sessions. This empirical validation reinforces the potential of VR technology as a valuable tool in stuttering therapy.

5.3 Feasibility of At-Home VR Programs

The proposed approach was implemented on the Oculus platform; the VR environment can be created using software tools (Unity 3D and CAD modeling tools) and a computer. Once the VR environment is created, it can be used at home or other locations. The VR based therapy setup can be moved to different locations as desired. Such VR simulation environments can be viewed as an 'at-home' therapy tool for individuals who stutter. Our findings showcase the feasibility of participants independently engaging with the VR scenarios, highlighting the flexibility and accessibility of this therapeutic approach. This contribution opens new avenues for stuttering therapy, allowing individuals to access treatment conveniently and effectively from their own homes.

5.4 Advancements in HCI for Healthcare

Our research also contributes to the broader field of Human-Computer Interaction (HCI) by demonstrating the applicability of VR technology in healthcare settings. While VR has been extensively utilized in medical training, our study showcases its potential in speech therapy, emphasizing the versatility of VR across various healthcare domains.

This research provides a key insight on the potential of VR-based stuttering therapy, presenting novel insights, empirical evidence of effectiveness, and practical advancements that have the potential to enhance the quality of life for individuals who stutter. These contributions lay the groundwork for further research and the integration of VR technology as a standard and highly effective therapeutic tool in the field of speech therapy.

The study of such 3D scenarios on participants perception, cognition and comprehension can also be studied as part of future research. Another area of research which can be explored is the cognitive load on the participants' when they are interacting with 3D data and information rich VR environments. Other measures such as visual and haptic affordance enable to improve the effectiveness and human centric aspects of such VR environments.

6 Conclusion

In conclusion, our study employed a comprehensive methodology to investigate the impact of Virtual Reality (VR) simulations on participants' heart rate and user experience during a simulated restaurant ordering scenario at "Bob's Burger Palace." The initial activities included designing, building and validating the VR based therapeutic environment. An interdisciplinary team of 3D VR design experts, software implementation specialists and speech communication experts were involved in this research activity. Assessment activities conducted helped through more light on the potential of such innovative technology based therapeutic approaches to help individuals who stutter. The combination of physiological data and subjective feedback helped gain a deeper understanding of the effects of VR technology in this context. Some of the tests conducted revealed a statistically significant difference in heart rates during the VR simulation interactions, indicating that the technology can influence participants' physiological responses. Furthermore, participants' subjective feedback reflected a range of experiences, highlighting the potential benefits and limitations of this VR based approach. These findings suggest that VR based interventions has promise as a tool for engaging individuals and eliciting physiological responses, underscoring its potential applications in fields such as training, education, and healthcare.

Acknowledgment. Funding for this research project was received from the National Stuttering Association (NSA), which is gratefully acknowledged.

References

1. Tetnowski, J.A., Brock, K., Cecil, J., Sedeghi Milani A.: Virtual reality-based simulation environments to investigate carryover in adolescents who stutter. Paper Presented at the Annual Conference of the American Speech-Language-Hearing Association, Boston, MA (2023)
2. Al-Nafjan, A., Alghamdi, N., Almudhi, A.: Virtual reality technology and speech analysis for people who stutter. EMITTER Int. J. Eng. Technol. **9**(2), 326–338 (2021)
3. Brundage, S.B., Graap, K.: Virtual reality: An exciting new tool to enhance stuttering treatment. Perspect. Fluen. Fluen. Disorders **14**(2), 4–9 (2004)
4. Tichenor, S.E., Yaruss, J.S.: Stuttering is defined by adults who stutter. J. Speech Lang. Hear. Res. **62**(12), 4356–4369 (2019)
5. Cecil, J., Sweet-Darter, M., Cecil-Xavier, A.: Exploring the use of virtual learning environments to support science learning in autistic students. In: IEEE Conference on Proceedings of the 2017 Frontiers in Engineering FIE, Indianapolis, 18–20 October 2017 (2017)
6. Gupta, A., Cecil, J., Pirela-Cruz, M., Ramanathan, P.: A virtual reality enhanced cyber-human framework for orthopedic surgical training. IEEE Syst. J. **13**, 3501–3512 (2019)
7. Cecil, J., Krishnamurthy, R., Gupta, A.: Exploring immersive simulation-based design frameworks in support of the moon mission. In: Proceedings of the 13th Annual IEEE International Systems Conference, Orlando, Florida, 8–11 April 2019 (2019)
8. Cecil, J., Kanchanapiboon, A.: Virtual Engineering Approaches in product and process design. Int. J. Adv. Manuf. Technol. **31**(9–10), 846–850 (2007)
9. Cecil, J., Jones, J.: An advanced virtual environment for micro assembly. Int. J. Adv. Manuf. Technol. **72**(1), 47–56 (2014)
10. Cecil, J., Albuhamood, S., Cecil-Xavier, A., Ramanathan, P.: An advanced cyber physical framework for micro devices assembly. IEEE Trans. Syst. Man Cybern. Syst. **49**(1), 92–106 (2017)
11. Cecil, J., Gupta, A., Pirela-Cruz, M., Ramanathan, P.: A Network based Virtual Reality Simulation Training Approach for Orthopedic Surgery. ACM Trans. Multimed. Comput. Commun. Appl. (TOMM) **14**(3), 1–21 (2018)
12. Gupta, A., Cecil, J., Pirela-Cruz, M.: A multi-level HXRI-based approach for XR-based surgical training. In: Proceedings of the IEEE Systems Man Cybernetics (SMC) Conference, Hawaii, USA, 1–4 October 2023 (2023)
13. Parsons, T., Rizzo, A.: Affective outcomes of virtual reality exposure therapy for anxiety and specific phobias: a meta-analysis. J. Behav. Ther. Exp. Psychiatry **39**, 250–326 (2008)
14. Glantz, K., Rizzo, A.: Virtual reality for psychotherapy: current reality and future possibilities. Psychotherapy **40**, 55–67 (2003)
15. Krijn, M., Emmelkamp, P.M., Olafsson, R.P., Biemond, R.: Virtual reality exposure therapy of anxiety disorders: a review. Clin. Psychol. Rev. **24**, 259–281 (2004)

16. Pull, C.B. (ed.): Current status of virtual reality exposure therapy in anxiety disorders: editorial review. Curr. Opin. Psychiatry **18**, 7–14 (2005)
17. Anderson, P.L., Zimand, E., Hodges, L.F., Rothbaum, B.O.: Cognitive behavioral therapy for publics speaking anxiety using virtual reality for exposure. Depress. Anxiety **22**, 156–158 (2005)
18. Bouchard, S., Cote, S., St-Jacques, J., Robillard, G., Renaud, P.: Effectiveness of virtual reality exposure in the treatment of arachnophobia using 3D games. Technol. Health Care **14**, 19–27 (2006)
19. Cote, S., Bouchard, S.: Documenting the efficacy of virtual reality exposure with psychophysiological and information processing measures. Appl. Psychophysiol. Biofeedback **30**, 217–232 (2005)
20. Emmelkamp, P.M., Bruynzeel, M., Drost, L., van der Mast, C.A.: Virtual reality treatment in acrophobia: a comparison with exposure in vivo. Cyberpsychol. Behav. **4**, 335–339 (2001)
21. Emmelkamp, P.M., Krijn, M., Hulsbosch, A.M., de Vries, S., Schuemie, M.J., van der Mast, C.A.: Virtual reality treatment versus exposure in vivo: a comparative evaluation in acrophobia. Behav. Res. Ther. **40**, 509–516 (2002)
22. Klinger, E., et al.: Virtual reality therapy versus cognitive behavior therapy for social phobia: a preliminary controlled study. Cyberpsychol. Behav. **8**, 76–88 (2005)
23. Krijn, M., Emmelkamp, P.M., Biemond, R., de Wilde de Ligny, C., Schuemie, M.J., van der Mast, C.A.: Treatment of acrophobia in virtual reality: the role of immersion and presence. Behav. Res. Ther. **42**, 229–239 (2004)

Thirteen Hongs of Canton: An Immersive Virtual Reality Game for Exploration of Cultural Heritage

Guangdai Chen[1] ⓘ, Xintong Xie[1] ⓘ, Zhimin Chen[3] ⓘ, and Chaoguang Wang[1,2](✉) ⓘ

[1] Guangdong University of Finance and Economics, Guangzhou, China
[2] Bournemouth University, Poole, UK
wangc@bournemouth.ac.uk
[3] Guangdong Polytechnic Normal University, Guangzhou, China

Abstract. Recent advancements in virtual reality (VR) technology have made it possible to effectively recreate traditional historical environments, allowing users to immerse themselves in real history and culture. The objective of this study is to develop a virtual experience of the commercial culture of the Thirteen Hongs of Canton, a significant trading site between China and Europe during the Qing dynasty. The game development involved creating an animated character navigating the streets of the Thirteen Hongs, surrounded by merchants, vendors, and tourists. The main goal of the game is for players to use VR controllers to purchase various products, while facing challenging tasks that require focus on different visual and auditory cues. The educational aspect of the game aims to enlighten players about the significant historical role of the Thirteen Hongs as a bustling trade hub, and to educate them about the diverse range of Chinese goods that were exported to European nations. This research explores the integration of digital games and VR technologies in order to enhance cultural heritage education, providing an engaging and effective learning experience. The findings of this study contribute to interdisciplinary research on VR technologies, cultural heritage education, and game design, opening up possibilities for future investigations in this field.

Keywords: Virtual Reality · VR games · Cultural Heritage · Thirteen Hongs of Canton

1 Introduction

With the development of the economy and the acceleration of urbanization, the pressure on cultural heritage conservation has become increasingly significant. In some areas where cultural heritage is located, the process of economic development and urbanization may lead to the destruction and disappearance of cultural heritage, as well as inevitable damage caused by natural disasters such as earthquakes, floods, and fires. As a result, some historical buildings and sites, such as the Thirteen Hongs of Canton, have disappeared without proper protection. Due to the long absence of certain cultural elements in certain regions and the incomplete transmission of information, cultural conservation work faces enormous difficulties and challenges. However, recent advancements in virtual reality (VR) technology have made it possible to effectively recreate traditional historical environments, allowing users to immerse themselves in real history and culture. Especially, VR environments can contribute to enhancing the communication of cultural heritage to the younger generation described as the Digital Natives (Ch'Ng, Li, Cai, & Leow, 2020).

1.1 VR Game for Cultural Heritage

VR technology is an integration of various technologies such as computer digital image processing, big data, multimedia, sensing technology, and artificial intelligence (Sherman, & Craig, 2018). It utilizes computer systems to create a realistically immersive three-dimensional virtual environment that incorporates auditory, tactile, visual, olfactory, and gustatory sensations. Through the fusion of multiple information sources, it generates dynamic 3D visual effects, allowing individuals to immerse themselves in a virtual environment using interactive devices and experience sensations equivalent to those in the real world. VR employs computer simulation to create a virtual environment, providing users with a 360° panoramic experience. Interaction within the virtual environment enables users to feel a strong sense of immersion. With the advancement of technological capabilities, VR devices have become increasingly sophisticated, and the application of virtual reality technology has expanded across various fields. In recent years, the use of VR technology in the preservation of digital culture has become one of the most crucial application areas (Selmanović, et al., 2020). In the virtual world, users can engage with historical buildings, artifacts, and events.

The fusion of cultural and artistic design with virtual reality technology not only demonstrates technological advancement, but also showcases the true potential of virtual reality for cultural preservation. Fang and Chen explored the use of VR for enhancing history learning and provided a VR version of the seven significant scenes in the Port of Canton including Thirteen Hongs (Fang, & Chen, 2018). However, their VR application only provides viewers with still images without any further user interactive content. Liarokapis et al. developed an immersive VR educational game that assesses two maritime archaeological methods for search and underwater archaeological sites in Europe (Liarokapis et al., 2020). Liu et al. designed a VR game named RelicVR that trains players to take away the earth gradually without hitting the artifact itself and learn how archaeological discovery happens in real life, in which they need to unearth artifacts hidden in a clod enclosure by using available tools and physical movements (Liu, Lin, Shi, Luo, & Liang, 2021).

The restoration of scenes is challenging due to the fragmented or missing artifacts, resulting in a relatively low degree of restoration. The existing cultural heritage restoration plans can only partially restore cultural relics and historical sites. However, VR technology can use 3D modeling techniques to restore cultural objects more easily and cheaply. For instance, early researchers used VR engines to reconstruct of cultural heritage of the Roman villa, allowing full exploration of the space (Rua, & Alvito, 2011). Ferdani et al. provided a workflow for the production of historically accurate 3D VR products, supporting by a case study of reconstructing the Forum of Augustus in Rome

(Ferdani et al., 2020). In addition to restoring buildings and historical artifacts from various eras, VR technology can also recreate famous figures from different dynasties, historical legends, and cultural events. In China, Zhang et al. developed the VR Terracotta Warriors Serious Games that combines the live experience of the audience, creating an immersive journey to learn the history and culture of Qinshihuang's Mausoleum (Zhang et al., 2018).

Moreover, during and after the pandemic, there is a strong need for cultural heritage to find new ways to engage the public. VR technology can support engagement with cultural content for remote audiences and contribute to the recovery of tourist destinations when travelling is restricted in real life. During pandemic's period, Vercelli el al. Launched a serious game in VR called Puzzle Battle 2.0 to teach art history at a distance, which required user to complete all the proposed paintings to collect them in a personal museum (Vercelli, Iacono, Vallarino, & Zolezzi, 2021). The use of virtual technology for cultural experiences can transcend the limitations of time and space, providing a comprehensive display of historical factors and cultural significance.

It was demonstrated by neurophysiological measurement of user experience that VR application for cultural heritage would sustain high levels of presence, immersion, and engagement (Škola, et al., 2020). The captivating quality of VR allows individuals to fully immerse themselves and actively interact with the people and objects within the virtual environment. This is made possible through the use of controllers, data gloves, and other sensory devices. Rather than simply receiving audio-visual information, learners become active participants in the learning process by directly communicating with the virtual environment.

1.2 The History of Thirteen Hongs

The Thirteen Hongs of Canton, also known as the Thirteen Factories or the Canton Factories, is an important cultural heritage in Chinese history, holding significant historical significance, especially as a crucial institution in the history of Sino-Western interactions. Established during the Ming Dynasty (founded in 1368), the Thirteen Hongs were an official trade organization set up by the government in Guangzhou, representing the government's management of foreign maritime trade. Western traders were required to work through Chinese merchants of the Thirteen Hongs who would guarantee their good behavior and tax obligations.

In 1757, the Qing Dynasty closed all ports to control trade with the West within its own country by focusing all trade on the southern port of Canton (now Guangzhou). This business system made Guangzhou the only open trade port for Europe and America in China, turning the city into one of the most prosperous trade centers globally, fostering the development of Sino-foreign trade. From the late 17th century to the early 19th century, merchants from the Thirteen Hongs managed all trade in the port of Canton. During that time, the Thirteen Hongs accounted for over half of the China's foreign trade, dealing primarily in commodities such as silk, tea, porcelain, spices, and medicinal herbs. The Thirteen Hongs experienced unprecedented prosperity, engaging in trade across Asia, Europe, and the Americas. Simultaneously, the cultural influence of Thirteen Hongs promoted the spread and impact of Chinese culture internationally, with Guangzhou ceramics, embroidery, and traditional Chinese crafts becoming representatives of "Chinese style" in fashion trends in Europe and America (Van Dyke, 2018).

After the First Opium War in 1841, China's closed foreign trade policy came to an end, marking the conclusion of the trade model of Thirteen Hongs. In the Second Opium War of 1856, British forces bombarded Guangzhou, leading to the furious destruction of Thirteen Hongs by enraged citizens, reducing the buildings to ashes. Despite their disappearance, the cultural influence of Thirteen Hongs has had a significant and enduring effect on China's history and cultural progress. Some historical buildings of Thirteen Hongs in Guangzhou, such as Yongqing Square and Baohua Middle Lane in Liwan District, have been rigorously protected and restored in recent years. In 2016, the Guangzhou Thirteen Hongs Museum was inaugurated on the site of the Thirteen Hongs area, covering an area of 3,060 square meters with a total construction area of 6,090 square meters, housing over 4,800 cultural artifacts. Additionally, Guangzhou actively promotes the application for World Heritage status for the Maritime Silk Road, with Thirteen Hongs being a vital component. As a crucial historical site in Guangzhou, Thirteen Hongs attracts numerous tourists for sightseeing, contributing significantly to the city's tourism industry.

In summary, the rise and development of Thirteen Hongs had profound impacts on China's economy, culture, and history. It stands as an important cultural heritage of the ancient Maritime Silk Road in China, holding high cultural and heritage value, deserving of effective inheritance. Despite the various measures taken by the municipal government to protect and pass on the culture of Thirteen Hongs, many representative cultural relics and historical buildings have disappeared, making it challenging for people to appreciate their historical charm. Moreover, while the municipal government has organized numerous cultural festivals and exhibitions, opportunities for ordinary citizens to understand and participate in these cultural activities remain limited. Therefore, we hope to integrate the latest VR technology to better promote and inherit this valuable cultural heritage.

2   VR Game Development

We aimed to create an interactive VR game designed for unique use by cultural heritage education, particularly for young generation. This new and unique area of game design bridged the gap between VR technology and cultural heritage. The challenge of creating games for educational purpose must take into account not only any entertainment aspects, but also an educational dimension that determine how to integrate the game as a learning environment.

2.1   Game Outline

Games are complex systems comprising of a diversity of pieces and parts, and a number of framework has been created to map out the main elements in the design of games. The Mechanics-Dynamics-Aesthetics (MDA) model is a well-known framework that describes the game in terms of three mutually-dependent layers: Mechanics (M), Dynamics (M) and Aesthetics (A) (Hunicke, LeBlanc, & Zubek, 2004). The mechanics are the basic components that defined the game, such as rules, goals and control options. The dynamics are the player behaviors resulted from applying game mechanics, while the aesthetics are the subjective experience of the player among the game playing.

In the present project, we decided to use MDA model as a framework to organize game ideas and guide the game design and implement as shown in Table 1. Many existing models examined game elements from a very academic perspective, more concerned with a philosophical analysis than with one framework that is useful for the practical game design. In contrast, MDA model has evident implication in the design and analysis of game elements, and its' substance resides on viewing games from the perceptive of the game design process and a development studio. The MDA arises as a suitable candidate also because it has been proven to be a powerful tool for educational games design (Kusuma et al., 2018).

Table 1. Game Outline

Name	Thirteen Hongs of Canton
Genre	Action game
Art style	Realistic painting style
Platform	Virtual reality device
Operations	Walking—Navigate through the streets of the Thirteen Hongs Purchase—Pick up the items you want to buy Avoidance—Steer clear of items you don't want to purchase
Game Level	In a limited time frame, using 3,000 silver coins, purchase as much silk, tea, and porcelain as possible while avoiding mistakenly buying other goods. Each successful purchase will cost 10 silver coins, but each time a wrong purchase is made, 50 silver coins will be deducted. If the silver coins reach 0, the level ends

2.2 Game Development

Mechanics. Mechanics are the rules and procedures of the game, describing in which way players can achieve the goal and what happens when they play. The game mechanics involved creating an animated character navigating the streets of the Thirteen Hongs, surrounded by merchants, vendors, and tourists. The main goal of the game is for players to use VR controllers to purchase various products, while facing challenging tasks that require focus on different visual and auditory cues. By training playing in this way, we will attempt to simulate the trade activities in the Thirteen Hongs through an immersive way.

Scoring in the game is recorded on a time basis. The required time to purchase goods listed is the basis of scoring, with users attempting to improve the speed at which they complete the task. A decrease in time correlates to increased focus and improvement at the task, therefore an increased ability in operation. The aim is to encourage the user to keep lowering the time it takes to complete each level, as this equates to acquiring more knowledge about Thirteen Hongs of Canton.

Dynamics. We learnt from the experiences of Thirteen Hongs Museum and existing history literatures to refine the user experience. Utilizing this information to better understand how Thirteen Hongs built their communities and created a commercial culture is essential in creation of our game as shown in Fig. 1.

Fig. 1. Shops at Thirteen Hongs

Thirteen Hongs of Canton provides a virtual environment tailored to building historical streets, facilitating real-time interaction and information about the history of Thirteen Hongs (including audio, video, and websites). It creates an engaging, easy to use 3D VR environment to participate in encourages exploration of cultural heritage. Within this virtual world, player can build their own presence, participate in playing, and discover environments created by designers. The drive to compete and get the best score possible is one of the main reasons people will keep playing the game, whether it is against friends and family or for self-improvement.

Having a clearly designed game map allows players to find what they are looking for almost instantly, while allowing for simple travel rather than constant exploration and movement through the virtual world. To avoid clutter and confusion within the world, we modeled the game layout so that it resembled more of a 3D platform game that is easy to navigate and explore.

Aesthetics. Aesthetics describe how the game looks and sounds, such as graphics, sound and music. We used VR technology to accurately recreate historical scenes and characters. The historical and cultural scenes related to the Thirteen Hongs include the Whampoa Anchorage, Pazhou Tower, Tongwen Street, Nanhai God Temple, Yue Customs, and other locations. To ensure the virtual scene closely resembles the authentic setting, the construction of models must adhere to the empirical data recorded in the preliminary research, including the appearance, motion structure, and dimensions of the models.

Firstly, terrain drawing was initiated, envisioning the virtual experience scene of the Thirteen Hongs in Guangzhou as a 5 km * 6 km terrain. Unity3D's Terrain tool was employed to sketch out the basic topography. Following this, common trees in Guangzhou, such as the kapok and banyan trees, were imported to enhance the environmental ambiance. Next, individual models, textures, and animations were constructed and baked using 3ds Max. These were then imported into Unity3D, where they were strategically placed on the terrain drawn in Unity3D. Lastly, to enhance the authenticity and immersion of the scene, a skybox is added to the VR camera in Unity3D, rendering an atmosphere of blue skies and white clouds. Subsequently, a lighting system was created in Unity3D to enhance the overall illumination effects of the game scene as shown in Fig. 2.

Fig. 2. Thirteen Hongs in Historical Painting (left) and VR Restoration (Right)

Simultaneously, we created animated characters in the game, allowing users to exist in the virtual world from a first-person perspective, enhancing the immersive experience of the game. The rendering style of the characters needs to be designed according to the social background, local customs, and cultural traditions of that time. After the construction of the character models is completed, UV unwrapping is necessary. Splitting the UVs was done based on material properties. For instance, the skin of the character model was treated as a whole, and the hair of the character model is considered another entity. Once UV splitting is done, the model needs to be textured to complete the rendering process as shown in Fig. 3.

The environmental sound effects for the virtual experience scene of the Thirteen Hongs in Guangzhou mainly consist of bustling urban sounds, including the calls of vendors and the clattering of horse-drawn carriages. Additionally, sounds from traditional Lingnan instruments such as the yangqin, pipa, and erhu were added to capture the distinctive musical ambiance of the region. This not only created a vibrant environmental atmosphere but also enhanced the commercial characteristics of Guangzhou as shown in Fig. 4. Finally, sound effects were synthesized using Audition software.

Fig. 3. Game Characters Modelling

Fig. 4. Thirteen Hongs' Tongwen street in Historical Painting (left) and VR Restoration (Right)

3 Conclusion

Our research developed a game demo focusing on a 3D explorative world of Thirteen Hangs, and it was discovered that experience is engaging in this scenario. Respecting historical facts is essential for VR technology for cultural heritage, which should be based on reliable historical data to accurately recreate historical scenes and figures. Objectivity is crucial, and VR technology should present historical scenarios and characters without subjective bias (Ferdani et al., 2020). We focused on to aesthetic detail of Thirteen Hongs to enhance the credibility and realism of the historical reconstructions. The unique value of VR technology lies in its ability to provide users with an immersive experience, aiding in a deeper understanding of cultural heritage. VR Graphical environments are more effective in providing a context for experiencing, interacting and engaging in cultural heritage. It offers an effective means for the protection and inheritance of cultural relics. Additionally, VR enhances learning experiences, providing users with vivid and realistic educational experiences, improving learning outcomes. VR technology also facilitates the digital preservation and dissemination of cultural heritage, overcoming limitations imposed by physical space and time, allowing more people to appreciate and understand cultural heritage.

The educational games we develop using VR technology are easily accessible in museums, schools, and other public spaces. These games are convenient for maintenance, subsequent feature development, and continuous release of new gameplay and levels (Vercelli, Iacono, Vallarino, & Zolezzi, 2021), incorporating additional cultural heritage education content. Upon validation of development process, expansion to other cultural heritage projects for education and promotional purposes is feasible. Given that today's youth grow up with games and digital products, VR educational game can enhance their knowledge of cultural heritage, and increase their awareness of cultural heritage protection, as well as assist teachers a in teaching and guiding this knowledge (Ch'Ng, Li, Cai, & Leow, 2020).

Our research focuses on the development of educational games through VR platforms, offering experiential and interactive displays of cultural heritage, fostering the integration of traditional culture with technological advancements. The findings contribute to interdisciplinary research on VR technologies, cultural heritage education, and game design, paving the way for future studies in this field. It provides VR technology with an opportunity to explore new issues that arise from "serious applications" of video game to cultural heritage education.

Acknowledgment. This study was supported by the grant of "The Education of Cultural Heritage for Teenagers Based on Virtual Reality Technology" (Ref No.: PDJH2023B0214) from the 2023 Guangdong Provincial Science and Technology Innovation Strategy Special Fund, the grant of "Narrative Design Analysis of Overseas Published Chinese Games" (Ref No.: GD23CXW05) from the Guangdong Social Science Foundation, and has received funding from the European Union's Horizon 2020 research and innovation programme under the Marie Skłodowska-Curie grant agreement No. 900025 (CfACTs).

References

Ch'Ng, E., Li, Y., Cai, S., Leow, F.T.: The effects of VR environments on the acceptance, experience, and expectations of cultural heritage learning. J. Comput. Cult. Heritage **13**(1), 1–21 (2020)

Fang, L., Chen, S.-C.: Enhancing the learning of history through VR: the thirteen factories icube experience. In: Väljataga, T., Laanpere, M. (eds.) Digital Turn in Schools—Research, Policy, Practice. LNET, pp. 37–50. Springer, Singapore (2019). https://doi.org/10.1007/978-981-13-7361-9_3

Ferdani, D., Fanini, B., Piccioli, M.C., Carboni, F., Vigliarolo, P.: 3D reconstruction and validation of historical background for immersive VR applications and games: the case study of the Forum of Augustus in Rome. J. Cult. Herit. **43**, 129–143 (2020)

Hunicke, R., LeBlanc, M., Zubek, R.: MDA: a formal approach to game design and game research. In: Proceedings of Nineteenth AAAI Conference on Artificial Intelligence and Interactive Digital Entertainment, vol. 4, p. 1722. The AAAI Press, Washington, DC, USA (2004)

Kusuma, G.P., Wigati, E.K., Utomo, Y., Suryapranata, L.K.P.: Analysis of gamification models in education using MDA framework. Procedia Comput. Sci. **135**, 385–392 (2018)

Liarokapis, F., Vidová, I., Rizvić, S., Demesticha, S., Skarlatos, D.: Underwater search and discovery: From serious games to virtual reality. In: Stephanidis, C., Chen, J.Y.C., Fragomeni, G. (eds.) HCII 2020. LNCS, vol. 12428, pp. 178–197. Springer, Cham (2020). https://doi.org/10.1007/978-3-030-59990-4_15

Liu, Y., Lin, Y., Shi, R., Luo, Y., Liang, H.N.: RelicVR: a virtual reality game for active exploration of archaeological relics. In: Proceedings of the Extended Abstracts of the 2021 Annual Symposium on Computer-Human Interaction in Play, Online, pp. 326–332. ACM (2021)

Rua, H., Alvito, P.: Living the past: 3D models, virtual reality and game engines as tools for supporting archaeology and the reconstruction of cultural heritage–the case-study of the Roman villa of Casal de Freiria. J. Archaeol. Sci. **38**(12), 3296–3308 (2011)

Selmanović, E., et al.: Improving accessibility to intangible cultural heritage preservation using virtual reality. J. Comput. Cult. Herit. **13**(2), 1–19 (2020)

Sherman, W.R., Craig, A.B.: Understanding Virtual Reality: Interface, Application, and design. Morgan Kaufmann, Burlington (2018)

Škola, F., et al.: Virtual reality with 360-video storytelling in cultural heritage: study of presence, engagement, and immersion. Sensors **20**, 5851 (2020)

Zhang, L., Qi, W., Zhao, K., Wang, L., Tan, X., Jiao, L.: VR games and the dissemination of cultural heritage. In: Streitz, N., Konomi, S. (eds.) DAPI 2018. LNCS, vol. 10921, pp. 439–451. Springer, Cham (2018). https://doi.org/10.1007/978-3-319-91125-0_35

Van Dyke, P.A.: Merchants of Canton and Macao: Success and Failure in Eighteenth-Century Chinese Trade. Hong Kong University Press, Hong Kong (2018)

Vercelli, G.V., Iacono, S., Vallarino, M., Zolezzi, D.: Puzzle Battle 2.0: a revisited serious game in VR during pandemic's period. In: de Rosa, F., Schottman, I.M., Hauge, J.B., Bellotti, F., Dondio, P., Romero, M. (eds.) GALA 2021. LNCS, vol. 13134, pp. 252–257. Springer, Cham (2021). https://doi.org/10.1007/978-3-030-92182-8_25

Research on Immersive Virtual Reality Interactive Design for Dyeing and Weaving Process in Tang Dynasty

Chenchen Ge[✉]

Wuhan University of Technology, 122 Luoshi Road, Wuhan, Hubei,
People's Republic of China
1398871119@qq.com

Abstract. With the arrival of the digital era and the national promotion of non-heritage culture, traditional handicraft techniques are gradually becoming known to the public, and the dyeing and weaving crafts of the Tang Dynasty are famous for their unique technical standard and artistic value. However, due to the complexity and scarcity of the craft, there are certain difficulties in the traditional way of learning and preservation, and the development of immersive virtual reality technology provides an opportunity for the public to recognize and understand the Tang Dynasty dyeing and weaving craft. The greatest academic contribution of this paper is to reproduce and protect the traditional history and culture of China, to provide innovative interaction design concepts and to promote the application of virtual reality technology in the field of cultural heritage.

First of all, through the methods of literature review and field study, this paper conducts an in-depth research on the dyeing and weaving craft of the Tang Dynasty, including its historical background, technical characteristics and artistic value, which is of great significance for the protection and education of history and culture. Through immersive virtual reality technology, the details and processes of Tang Dynasty dyeing and weaving craft can be reproduced. Through clear visual effects and dynamic interactive experience, users can feel the unique charm of Tang Dynasty dyeing and weaving craft immersively. This immersive experience can better convey the artistic value and aesthetic emotion in history and culture to users, and inspire their interest in traditional culture and awareness of protection. In addition, immersive virtual reality interaction design can also provide a new way for the promotion and dissemination of Tang Dynasty dyeing and weaving craft. Virtual reality technology can present the Tang Dynasty dyeing and weaving craft globally, so that more people can understand and appreciate the uniqueness of our traditional culture. Through channels such as the Internet and mobile terminals, users can participate in the immersive virtual reality experience anytime, anywhere, so that the Tang Dynasty dyeing and weaving craft can enter thousands of households, and make positive contributions to the protection and education of China's history and culture.

Secondly, this study proposes a new interaction design concept through in-depth exploration of immersive virtual reality technology and interaction design. This concept emphasizes the user's subjective experience and emotional perception in the virtual environment, thus providing a new way to enhance the user's sense of participation and immersion. The concept focuses on the interaction and

J. Y. C. Chen and G. Fragomeni (Eds.): HCII 2024, LNCS 14708, pp. 214–223, 2024.
https://doi.org/10.1007/978-3-031-61047-9_14

empathy between the user and the virtual environment, and enhances the user's understanding and perception of history and culture by creating empathy and emotional resonance. First, designers can create an immersive experience through multi-sensory interaction design. Using virtual reality technology, it is possible to simulate the craft scenes, environmental sounds, and even smells and tactile sensations of the Tang Dynasty, allowing users to immerse themselves in the real atmosphere of Tang Dynasty dyeing and weaving craftsmanship. Through tactile feedback and stereo sound effects, users can personally experience the texture and sound of the dyeing and weaving process, enhancing the subjective sense of participation and experience. Secondly, designers can try emotion-oriented design to guide users to deeper experience. In the design process, some emotional elements can be incorporated, such as cultural background music and emotionally-intended storylines, to create an emotional connection that makes it easier for users to empathize. Through well-designed plots and characters, create an experience with emotional tension and guidance, triggering users to think about the historical and cultural background and emotional resonance. Third, designers can use social interaction design to promote communication and sharing between users and others. Through virtual reality interactive design, it can provide users with the opportunity to communicate with other users and jointly explore and experience the Tang Dynasty dyeing and weaving process. Designers can introduce social interaction elements, such as virtual communities and online cooperation modes, to enable users to communicate and share with other users, and to experience and pass on this historical and cultural heritage together. In conclusion, in the study of immersive virtual reality interaction design for Tang Dynasty dyeing and weaving craft, innovative interaction concepts that emphasize users' subjective experience and emotional perception in virtual environments can be realized through multi-sensory interaction, emotion-oriented design, and social interaction design.

Finally, this research is conducive to promoting the application of virtual reality technology in the field of cultural heritage, and its research results not only help to enrich the application field of virtual reality technology, further deepen the understanding of Tang Dynasty dyeing and textile technology and the perfection of simulation technology, but also promote the development of virtual reality technology in the field of cultural heritage. At the same time, virtual reality technology can realize large-scale user interaction and sharing, through the Internet and social media and other channels, so that more people can participate in the Tang Dynasty dyeing and weaving craft experience and learning, and can promote cross-border cooperation and cultural exchanges, and promote the interaction and sharing between different regions and cultures. In conclusion, the study of immersive virtual reality interaction design for Tang Dynasty dyeing and weaving crafts can promote the application of virtual reality technology in the field of cultural inheritance, realize the innovative protection and inheritance of traditional crafts by providing immersive experience, enriching the inheritance of traditional culture, promoting the interactive participation and learning experience of users, and promoting the popularization and sharing of cultural inheritance, and at the same time encouraging more people to use this technology to study and spread our traditional history and culture.

Keywords: Virtual Reality · Tang Dynasty Dyeing and Weaving · Interaction Design · Heritage Communication Generation of meta smart city

1 Introduction to the Paper

1.1 Research Background

In the wave of the digital era, traditional handicraft technology has gradually received widespread attention as a precious heritage of Chinese culture. Among them, the dyeing and weaving technology of the Tang Dynasty is famous worldwide for its unique technical standard and outstanding artistic value. The dyeing and weaving technology of the Tang Dynasty is an old craft in the history of clothing technology, and after inspiring various later printing processes, it should have been replaced by other technologies and died out. But this did not happen. The "backward" technology, with its own unique charm, has always been accepted and loved by people in the torrent of craft evolution.

With the promotion of intangible cultural heritage by the State, traditional handicraft techniques have gradually become the focus of public research and understanding. However, this traditional craft faces the dual challenges of complexity and scarcity, which bring certain difficulties to its study, inheritance and protection. In 2005, the State Council issued the Circular of the General Office of the State Council on Strengthening the Protection of China's Intangible Cultural Heritage, which aroused widespread social attention to China's rich intangible cultural heritage. In recent years, all sectors of society have conducted in-depth discussions on the transmission and dissemination methods of intangible cultural heritage, and have come to the realisation that the one-sided and unitary transmission methods can no longer meet the needs of social development. Digital media have begun to be applied as a new inheritance carrier, gradually replacing the traditional paper-based form of inheritance. The application of digital technology in the collection and display of cultural heritage is increasing, and it has become an imperative trend to take digital virtual reality technology as the core means to protect the endangered intangible cultural heritage.

1.2 Research Purpose

In recent years, with the rapid development of digital technology, virtual reality technology has been widely used in military, aerospace and other fields, and gradually penetrated into all aspects of production and life. This paper aims to explore the feasibility and necessity of digital technology in the inheritance and dissemination of intangible cultural heritage by taking virtual reality technology as the main technical path, taking Tang Dynasty dyeing and weaving technology as the main research subject and practical object, and using the visualisation platform as the communication medium. Through the use of virtual reality technology to reproduce the Tang Dynasty dyeing and weaving technology, users can experience the traditional dyeing and weaving process and processing methods in an immersive way, and explore other new modes of intangible cultural heritage transmission and dissemination in a point-to-point manner.

Therefore, the research purpose of this paper is embodied in the following three aspects: firstly, to explore the application methods and paths of virtual reality technology in the inheritance and dissemination of intangible culture; secondly, to study the technical means of virtual reality technology in the inheritance and dissemination of Tang Dynasty dyeing and weaving technology; and lastly, to construct a visualisation platform of Tang Dynasty dyeing and weaving technology.

1.3 Research Content

This study takes the inheritance and dissemination method of Tang Dynasty dyeing and weaving technology as the main research content, and takes virtual reality technology as the tool of analysis and research, and takes Tang Dynasty dyeing and weaving technology as the core object for in-depth research. Through the analysis of digital protection paths and methods, it aims to explore the feasibility and necessity of virtual reality technology in Tang Dynasty dyeing and weaving technology. Based on the research conclusions, the virtual engine technology is used to integrate and develop a new visualisation platform in order to promote the inheritance and promotion of Tang Dynasty dyeing and weaving technology.

The research content mainly includes:

1. Overview of the definition, development and characteristics of virtual reality technology and other aspects.
2. In-depth analysis of the feasibility of applying virtual reality technology to the inheritance of Tang Dynasty dyeing and weaving technology, introduction of the basic functions and characteristics of virtual reality, and its ultimate value appeal in the inheritance of intangible cultural heritage.
3. Introducing the cultural and artistic value of Tang Dynasty dyeing and weaving technology, elaborating the necessity and positive effect of using virtual reality technology to inherit Tang Dynasty dyeing and weaving technology, and proposing the realisation method and process of virtual Tang Dynasty dyeing and weaving technology according to the conclusion.

This study focuses on the inheritance of Tang Dynasty dyeing and weaving technology in digital space, emphasising the living inheritance of the production process. In terms of design content, it presents the traditional craft process by displaying the living craft and providing immersive experience; in terms of display content, more emphasis is placed on the interactive experience process. In terms of promotion and application, it can be used in various fields such as teaching, processing and science popularisation.

2 Theoretical Research on the Application of Virtual Reality Technology to Cultural Inheritance

2.1 Definition of Virtual Reality Technology

The terms "virtual" and "reality" are clearly defined in Chinese dictionaries. Reality refers to "things that exist objectively", while virtual means "things made up by imagination". The combination of these two opposing words into "virtual reality" refers to the high-tech means of allowing the audience to get a feeling similar to the real experience in the virtual scene. Zhao Qinping, a professor at Beijing University of Aeronautics and Astronautics, explains: "Virtual reality (VR) is a digital environment that takes computer technology as its core, combines relevant science and technology, and generates a digital environment that is highly similar to the real environment in terms of vision, hearing, and tactile sensation, etc. Users interact with the objects in the digital environment through the necessary equipment and influence each other, thus generating a feeling as if they were in the real world. Interact with each other, thus generating feelings and experiences as if they were in the real environment."

Therefore, virtual reality technology based on computer technology can simulate real things or build virtual things, which is a major breakthrough in the history of human civilisation. With the help of this digital technology, people can immersively re-experience history, feel reality and experien.

The future meta smart city should emphasize the construction of humanistic contexts. People do not exist in isolation, but must live in a certain context. According to habit theory, we can presume that the construction of the future meta-universe will not be beyond the real world, and the habits formed by people in the socialization process will be brought from the real world to the meta-universe, which will also produce a context similar to the real society [6]. The reason why the meta-universe is called the universe is that there must be various scenarios of human life presented. And contextuality is also common between the meta-universe and the real world. In the real world, urban services need to analyze the problems of service recipients from the context, and also solve problems from the context.

A humanistic smart city is not a simple pile of top technology, but a collection of livable places built with the core of serving the resident. Therefore, the construction of a meta smart city should start from the interests of the resident, fully consider the cultural and spiritual needs of the resident, and adopt reasonable and advanced technology to build this new city. Only when technology and humanities are coordinated, the power of technology is brought into play to the utmost. Combining the technological path of the metaverse into the physical city scene provides residents with a new type of leisure and entertainment place where virtual and reality interact. The virtual scene should be constructed based on the local cultural lineage of the city as well as specific realistic scenes.

2.2 The Significance of Virtual Reality Technology Used in Cultural Heritage

In the Convention for the Safeguarding of the Intangible Cultural Heritage, UNESCO specifies that "safeguarding" of the intangible cultural heritage refers to "measures relating to archiving, research, conservation, protection, promotion, promotion, transmission and revitalisation". "Since the 18th Party Congress, General Secretary Xi Jinping has made a series of important expositions on cultural innovation. Xi Jinping emphasised the importance of attaching great importance to cultural innovation, committing to its development, and placing it at the heart of the overall national development situation. Innovation is an important driving force for the development of intangible cultural heritage, and is also the basis for the promotion of cultural prosperity and development, and will surely become a major highlight of cultural development during the 13th Five-Year Plan period.

In recent years, with the rapid development of network digital media, people's cultural level has been significantly improved, so that the public began to re-examine the value of traditional culture, and through new means of protection, the use of innovative technology for inheritance, so that China's intangible cultural heritage to re-attract people's attention. In a big data survey on intangible cultural heritage, it is shown that most users prefer to understand intangible culture through "experience", and think that personal experience is more intuitive and interesting, which provides a broad market prospect for virtual intangible cultural heritage experience.

With the continuous development of science and technology, information technology, image processing and virtual reality (VR) technology is showing a unique charm for the inheritance of intangible cultural heritage provides a more advanced and excellent means of protection. Currently, panoramic virtual reality technology has achieved many application examples in entertainment, news and other fields, and has made substantial progress in the digital protection of intangible cultural heritage. For example, the Nantong Plate Harrier Kite in Jiangsu Province uses digital programming and VR technology to demonstrate its production process, enabling people to watch the whole process on the Internet. The Digital Palace Museum in Beijing provides people with the opportunity to view the Palace's collections online, while Shaanxi has established a digital display of the Terracotta Warriors and Horses of the First Qin Emperor through a digital museum, and Sichuan Opera face-changing explores the use of virtual reality to allow viewers to experience the performance, among other things. Numerous research results show that the display and dissemination of non-fraditional culture through virtual reality technology is a product of the development of information in modern society, and at the same time has become a new direction for the protection of non-fraditional culture. The use of virtual reality technology to develop and enhance intangible cultural heritage is not only the implementation of national strategies, but also a key way to promote the innovative development of intangible heritage inheritance and dissemination work. The clever combination of virtual reality technology and intangible cultural heritage is of great significance to make up for the insufficiency of intangible cultural heritage inheritance and dissemination, the innovation of cultural heritage protection methods, and to help people gain a deeper understanding of intangible cultural heritage.

3 Application of Virtual Reality Technology to the Inheritance of Dyeing and Weaving Crafts in the Tang Dynasty

3.1 Overview of Tang Dynasty Dyeing and Weaving Crafts

The Tang Dynasty was a powerful dynasty in Chinese history, a splendid and marvellous flower in the long river of Chinese history. The country was strong, the society was stable, the nation was united, the economy was prosperous, the culture was splendid, and the international communication was frequent. Tang Dynasty due to the unprecedented economic prosperity, with diversified cultural characteristics, people live in affluence, commerce, handicrafts flourished, the aristocrats live a life of luxury and focus on enjoyment, dress competition for luxury, these have promoted the development of textile technology. Tang Dynasty dyeing and weaving process, under the supervision of the feudal central government has a weaving and dyeing department, specialising in the management of production. Dyeing and weaving of the division of labour is very fine, according to the "Tang six canon" records: "Weaving society work has ten. Group ribbon work has five. Dyeing work has six." And silk and linen weaving production almost all over the country, and the output is very large, enough to prove that the Tang Dynasty textile technology is developed.

3.2 Analysis of the Integration of Virtual Reality Technology and Tang Dynasty Dyeing and Weaving Crafts

Virtual reality technology is introduced into the Tang Dynasty dyeing and weaving craft, based on the design concept of craft protection as the basis, inheritance and innovation, and with the help of digital science and technology to find the most effective methods and techniques for the dissemination of Tang Dynasty dyeing and spinning techniques. In terms of the dyeing and weaving process, in the virtual scene, all aspects of the dyeing and weaving process, whether it is the preparation of dyes, the weaving of fabrics or the drawing of patterns, can be easily viewed through the zoom in and zoom out of the view without any dead angle. The use of computer three-dimensional software to simulate the functions of dyeing, weaving and spinning can easily solve the technical difficulties encountered in the traditional dyeing and weaving process. Computer-aided design software is similar to traditional dyeing and weaving methods, which are carried out through different process tools. The inheritors of the skills can simulate the textile process through virtual dyeing and weaving tools, and judge and experience the operation results through the virtual environment, so as to make the operation of the dyeing and weaving process more innovative and flexible. In terms of resource utilisation, as different dyed textiles have different needs for raw materials and dyes, we can digitally sample and analyse the raw materials and dyes, and use computer software to carry out virtual design, model cutting and data analysis to find more sustainable and efficient dyeing and weaving methods, so as to improve the utilisation rate of the raw materials and dyes, and to maximise the savings of resources and reduce costs. Through virtual operation, the dyeing and weaving artists are able to show all aspects of the Tang Dynasty dyeing and weaving process in its entirety, realising the immersion, reversibility and interactivity of the operations of selecting materials, designing and dyeing, making the Tang Dynasty dyeing and weaving process more intuitive and the means and methods of designing more diversified with the support of virtual reality technology. Its unique advantages provide a new breakthrough for the inheritance and development of Tang Dynasty dyeing and weaving craft.

Based on the application of virtual reality technology to Tang Dynasty dyeing and weaving craft, we can analyse the existing problems through reverse design. Although natural raw materials for dyeing and weaving are in different forms, through digital acquisition, we are able to graphically analyse all aspects of fibres and dyes, so as to establish a scientific design and dyeing and weaving method, in order to ensure the maximum use of raw materials. Combining virtual reality and other computer technologies to conceptualise, design, 3D modelling and virtual demonstration of Tang Dynasty dyeing and weaving processes in a virtual environment is a brand new attempt. The application of virtual reality technology in the traditional dyeing and weaving process, in addition to the characteristics of intuitiveness, reversibility and interactivity, can also predict and optimise the emergence of problems in the dyeing and weaving process, improve the success rate of dyeing and weaving, shorten the design cycle, and reduce the development cost and creative risk. Through the support of digital technology, the Tang Dynasty dyeing and weaving process can usher in a more efficient, precise and innovative development, injecting new vitality into the cultural heritage.

3.3 The Realisation and Process of Virtual Technology of Tang Dynasty Dyeing and Weaving Process

The core of the virtual Tang Dynasty dyeing and weaving process lies in the development of a virtual reality interactive system based on a PC platform. Developers are able to realise the simulation effect through personal computers or workstations, and influence the user's senses through the computer's input and output devices, so that they are immersed in the virtual three-dimensional simulation system. The virtual environment can change with the subject changes, so that the user experiences the immersive feeling. The virtual Tang Dynasty dyeing and weaving process adopts the interaction method of "haptic feedback". The user wears VR glasses, faces the computer screen, and is able to browse the virtual space and preset tools in an all-round way. The virtual dyeing and weaving interactive experience is realised through the VR handle, and the process operation mainly relies on buttons and vibration feedback, two-handed discrete and six-degree-of-freedom spatial tracking interactive devices. The sensors of the data handle track the position of each finger in the virtual scene in real time, and the operation actions such as picking up, releasing, moving, dyeing and weaving are realised through the trigger keys, touch panels and gripping handles. The virtual Tang Dynasty dyeing and weaving process is characterised by the ability of the user to be fully immersed in the world of virtual dyeing and weaving. The computer feeds back into the dyeing scene according to the user's movement trajectory, gesture and technical operation data, making the user feel immersed and fully engaged. This technology is very suitable for the Tang Dynasty dyeing and weaving process, which is high-cost, highly technical and difficult to realise.

The means of obtaining images are mainly through cameras, video cameras, scanners and other equipment, but these methods can only produce two-dimensional images of the scanned object, that is, a single-sided profile two-dimensional plane information. However, nowadays, with the progress of science and technology, more and more three-dimensional scanning technology has gradually replaced the traditional scanning methods to fill the two-dimensional scanning in the expression of spatial data, can more accurately reflect the entity in the real space data information.

Three-dimensional scanner as a scientific instrument for detecting and analysing the shape and appearance data of objects, can accurately obtain the three-dimensional coordinates of the outer surface of the object in space and digital model. The current 3D scanning technology has developed to the fourth generation of handheld scanning technology. For the textile original model acquisition in dyeing and weaving technology, the use of handheld laser scanner can obtain complete textile data, with accurate, efficient, flexible, easy to use and so on. The scanner and the computer update the recorded data in real time through the data interface, providing a basic guarantee for further processing of textiles.

In virtual reality design, there are five main steps involved in designing, cutting, finishing, polishing and outputting the scanned textile model. Firstly, the scanned textile is analysed from multiple angles, and the design is carried out on the model through 2D graphic software, which can assist in the drawing of the artwork with the help of convenient tools such as copying and mirroring, and the matching of the graphic with the textile is adjusted through repeated adjustments. Then, the textile is preliminarily processed using the corresponding tools, and finally the model is imported into the virtual environment for human-computer interaction through different software.

In the textile processing process, the use of virtual technology for design, simulation, modelling, interaction and other operations can be simulated in advance of the product shape, cost, process and other aspects. This not only brings predictability to the dyeing and weaving technology, but also adds more artistic creativity. The virtual reality design model creates a fundamental change in the traditional mode of dyeing and weaving production, enabling designers, customers and students to understand more intuitively the design concepts, values and processing of Tang Dynasty dyeing and weaving technology, and providing a maximised application of this technology in the fields of creation, processing, production, sales and training.

4 Conclusion

Based on the digital transmission and dissemination of intangible cultural heritage, this paper explores the application in the field of Tang Dynasty dyeing and weaving technology by using the interactive method of virtual experience. The project not only provides a practical sample for the digital inheritance of Tang Dynasty dyeing and weaving techniques, but also provides a reference for the digital inheritance of other intangible heritage traditional handicrafts and techniques.

The significance, advantages, principles and measures of virtual reality in the protection of non-heritage culture are summarised through the argumentation and sorting out of non-heritage digital inheritance and dissemination methods. Taking Tang Dynasty dyeing and weaving technology as an example, the necessity and feasibility of applying virtual reality-based technology to dyeing and weaving process are elaborated, and its innovative process and effect are comparatively analysed and studied. The following main research conclusions are finally drawn:

1. Constructing a visualisation platform for dyeing and weaving technology based on virtual reality technology, realising a complete industrial chain with teaching, processing and production in one. This helps to accelerate the training of talents in dyeing and weaving technology, improve the production cycle and efficiency, achieve reversible modification of the process and results, reduce the loss of processing materials, and clear the obstacles for the inheritance and dissemination of non-heritage culture.
2. Virtual reality technology realises the permanent preservation of traditional handmade techniques. By having effective image data, 3D model database and simulated spatial structure resources, it is an innovative mode of digital preservation of intangible cultural heritage by preserving endangered traditional handcraft techniques in real time, scientifically and accurately.
3. Integrate the 3D modelling technology and digital technology into the dyeing and weaving process, and develop a new operation platform through the integration of virtual engine technology. This makes the processing process virtualised and imaged to achieve interactive and dynamic participation, breaks the limitations of space and geography, and promotes training, innovation and scientific research.
4. Dyeing and weaving visualisation platform is a human-computer interaction system that perfectly combines knowledge and technology. It makes the traditional dyeing

and weaving and virtual dyeing and weaving perfectly integrated, and constructs the virtual dyeing and weaving processing process through vivid and effective means, tools and carriers, which provides a new medium and a new path for the inheritance of dyeing and weaving craft.

In a comprehensive view, virtual reality technology has given birth to a subversive new concept of visual communication, challenging the traditional static visual communication form. In the field of dyeing and weaving technology, the research of visualisation platform realises the combination of technicality and inheritance, which makes the communication of traditional crafts more efficient. The display and dissemination of Tang Dynasty dyeing and weaving technology through digital media and digital platforms further realises the cultural inheritance of non-heritage in digital space.

References

1. Bian, F., Jiang, M., Sang, Y.: Advances in virtual reality and its applications. Comput. Simul. (6), 1–4+12 (2007). (in Chinese)
2. Li, D.: Design of plane image interaction system based on virtual reality technology. Mod. Electron. Technol. **43**(8), 158–160+165 (2020). (in Chinese)
3. Hu, Q.-Y., Kung, W.-L., Hu, Y.-X., et al.: Inverse modelling based on 3D laser scanning point cloud. Beijing Surv. Mapp. **34**(3), 352–355 (2020). (in Chinese)
4. Li, M.: Design and Implementation of Bronze Wine Vessel Display in Jin Hou Tomb Based on Mobile Devices. Beijing University of Technology, Beijing (2014). (in Chinese)
5. Xue, Y.: Analysis of urban culture communication based on algorithmic city. J. News Res. **12**(13), 239–241 (2021). (in Chinese)
6. Kitch, C.: Twentiet century tales: news magazines and American memory. J. Commun. Monogr. **1**, 119–120 (1999)
7. Green, A.: Overview of networking cultural heritage initiatives in the United States and Canada, 11 April 2011. http://archive.ifla.org/IV/ifla71/papers/018e-Green.pdf
8. Kozan, J.M.: Virtual Heritage Reconstruction: The Old Main Church of Curitiba, Brazil. University of Cincinnati (2004)

Comparing Different Methods for Remote Configuration of Pervasive Augmented Reality Experiences: A User Study in Logistics Procedures

Rafael Maio, Bernardo Marques$^{(\boxtimes)}$, Paulo Dias, and Beatriz Sousa Santos

IEETA, DETI, LASI, University of Aveiro, Aveiro, Portugal
bernardo.marques@ua.pt

Abstract. Augmented Reality (AR) is a promising technology in Industry 4.0, improving industrial procedures and reducing errors. Using a Human-Centered Design methodology, a Pervasive AR tool was initially created to support logistics tasks in the shop floor. To benefit from the tool, a prior configuration of the AR environment is required. This work proposes a remote tool to configure AR content in the industrial scenario, replacing the current in-person configuration. Therefore, we developed three methods (based on different environments and materials): non-immersive virtual reality with keyboard and mouse, hands-free AR and immersive virtual reality with controllers. A user study with 24 participants was conducted to compare their usability and performance. Results show that users can easily perform the configuration remotely. The immersive virtual reality method presented a better accuracy and higher preference. However, the AR method proved to be efficient and a more natural solution.

Keywords: Industry 4.0 · Pervasive Environments · Remote Configuration · Authoring Tool · Virtual Reality · Augmented Reality · 3D Reconstruction · User Study · Logistics Procedures

1 Introduction

Industry 4.0 refers to the fourth industrial revolution where technologies are changing industry, connecting digital and physical worlds. The integration of smart sensors, embedded systems and cyber-physical systems into the manufacturing processes created a new generation of factories, the smart factories [1]. Logistics is an industrial field where human intervention is not replaceable, since workers carry the necessary abilities to perform these tasks efficiently [9]. Mixed-model assembly is an example where this applies, operators must identify, locate and collect different components to assemble distinct kits, depending on the product being complemented [8].

Augmented Reality (AR), one of the pillars that smart factories will rely on, is employed for additional guidance and faster decision-making, while improving

© The Author(s), under exclusive license to Springer Nature Switzerland AG 2024
J. Y. C. Chen and G. Fragomeni (Eds.): HCII 2024, LNCS 14708, pp. 224–234, 2024.
https://doi.org/10.1007/978-3-031-61047-9_15

work processes. AR technologies are able to add digital context on top of the real operators workspace [11], assisting assembly tasks [14], indoor localization [15], data visualization and interaction [13], context-aware issues [3], maintenance applications [7] or quality control [2]. Improved work safety, successful learning and training, as well as increased task efficiency and effectiveness are examples of the advantages of technological industrialization supported with AR [6]. In kit assembly processes, paper manuals are commonly used for conveying information. Voice, light and Head-Up Displays (HUD) are other strategies replacing traditional paper manuals [4], besides, with Industry 4.0, AR is also introduced for supporting the task [8].

Despite the advantages of applying AR in industry use-cases, most solutions are limited to markers or other tracking materials that hinder the proper functioning and restrict spatial boundaries [5]. Therefore, Pervasive AR was conceived to overcome such limitations. Taking advantage of its ability to seamlessly adapt with to the user's surroundings and integrate their movements, it has the potential to revolutionize the way we interact with technology and the world around us [12]. Pervasive AR-based applications demand a preliminary phase, in which the AR environment is configured and its virtual objects require a prudent and accurate placement in the scene [10]. Different applications use distinct devices to perform the scenario configuration. Studies indicate that performing such configuration using a computer in a Non-Immersive Virtual Reality (N-IVR) environment can be more accurate and practical than with a mobile device in AR [10]. Besides, [10] computer method has the advantage of being remote, avoiding the need for physical on site presence. However, N-IVR environment is not the only way of performing configurations remotely, Immersive Virtual Reality (IVR) and different AR displays can also be adopted as possible solutions.

In this paper, we propose a remote configuration using three different methods: N-IVR with keyboard and mouse, AR with hands-free and IVR with controllers. This tool was designed through a Human-Centered Design (HCD) methodology focused on creating a Pervasive AR prototype for training logistics operators in kit assembly procedures requiring order picking. A user study was conducted to evaluate and compare three distinct remote methods, the main goal being to verify whether the tool fulfills its purpose and identify which method is preferred. Then, the obtained results are presented and discussed. Finally, concluding remarks and future research opportunities are drawn.

2 Materials and Methods

This section presents the logistics environment and the task performed by operators. Next, the requirements defined by a HCD approach are listed. The developed Pervasive AR tool for supporting the industrial operators is then summarized, giving more context to the study. Finally, we detail the remote configuration procedure and the methods for handling it.

2.1 Shop Floor Scenario

The line where the picking of components occurs is centrally located in a factory enveloped with transitable corridors and other production lines. It consists of seven shelves, each subdivided into various crates with multiple components inside. Each crate is labelled based on the line location where it rests (shelve, column and row numbers). This label is the main information that logistics operators use for finding the crate containing the components they need to collect. Although the line composition remains unchanged during long periods of time, changes occur (add, remove and relocate crates) and they need to be acknowledged by the system and the operators. It is also frequent to have *rare crates*, with rarely picked components, that are added when they will be useful and removed when no longer needed.

Four operators work in parallel on this production line. They transport large carts to facilitate and accelerate the picking process, occupying most of the line space. Their task is summed up as: depending on the kit (set of components) requiring preparation, the corresponding kit will be printed in a paper sheet, so operators can identify the components locations, perform the picking and pack them to accompany the final product for distribution worldwide.

2.2 Requirements Elicitation

Through the use of a HCD methodology, the project team was able to gain a deeper understanding of the specific needs and difficulties faced by the stakeholders. As a result of the need for effective communication and idea generation, together with our industrial partners, we held a combination of in-person and virtual meetings, including several sessions focused on touring the logistics line. The meetings included representation from various industrial departments, such as data engineers, process development engineers, line operators, and line managers. From these meetings and discussions we came up with a set of requirements:

- **Support mixed-model assembly** - Acknowledge the kit requiring assembly at a given moment and identify the components constituting the corresponding kit and their real world locations;
- **Assist the picking task** - Increase the user performance and decrease the work load, by presenting visual AR cues overlaying the crates where the components need to be picked from;
- **Validate picking** - Verify that all of the required components for a particular kit were properly collected;
- **Adapt to changes** - The technology must quickly comprehend the modifications in the physical line;
- **Study different technology alternatives** - Consider the hardware and software options available, evaluating the technology performance, the workload it would impose on users and the overall users' performance increase.

2.3 Pervasive AR Tool for Picking Tasks

In order to meet the previously identified requirements, a Pervasive AR tool was developed (Fig. 1). As the tool requires a prior step for establishing the Pervasive AR environment it is divided into two modules: *configuration* and *visualization*. The *visualization* was built for supporting two distinct display technologies: Head-Mounted Displays (HMDs) (Fig. 1 - Left) and Handheld Devices (HHDs) (Fig. 1 - Right).

Fig. 1. Pervasive AR tool *visualization module*: Responsible for helping the picking task, by visually showing the components locations. Left - HMD version - the blue balloon represents the picking validation. The directional arrow points to the next picking location. Right - HHD version - the white balloon represents the component that needs to be picked. (Color figure online)

The *configuration module* allows the association of virtual boxes to physical crates. Accordingly, for each existing crate, a user needs to manually place a virtual box on top of it and select the component inside it. After having the environment configured, changes are only needed when the physical line is rearranged. The *visualization module* is responsible for assisting the industrial picking task. The operator selects the kit to be assembled and virtual balloons will be displayed above the relevant crates. These balloons incorporate pertinent information about the crate components. The picking will be validated when the user's hand enters the crate to grab the component (HMD) or pressing the device screen (HHD). A directional arrow helps operators in locating the next crate more quickly.

In order for the virtual balloons to be automatically placed above the correct crates, the *visualization module* uses the stored configuration to align the virtual scene. This alignment process is performed at the application launching and can be performed in two ways. The virtual information placement can be based on real-world mapping created during an in-person configuration. Alternatively, it can rely on a physical static marker for aligning the virtual content. The latter alignment process opens up the possibility for a remote configuration mechanism.

2.4   Remote Tool for Creation of Pervasive AR Scenarios

To provide a better response to the *"adapt to changes"* requirement, we proposed a remote tool for configuring Pervasive AR scenarios, allowing the acknowledgment of real-world changes, from anywhere and without disturbing the line workers. The tool uses a 3D model of an industrial line captured using a BLK360 Imaging Laser Scanner. This configuration procedure requires an additional step. Before associating the virtual boxes to the corresponding real-world crates, using the virtual model for matching, a virtual marker needs to be placed overlaying the real-world marker, physically placed in an well-known pose. The virtual boxes coordinates are then computed and stored in relation to the marker pose. The configuration result is device-independent, which means that it can be imported by distinct devices that support the Pervasive AR tool. Three different methods for achieving the remote configuration were considered: N-IVR with keyboard and mouse, hands-free AR and IVR with controllers.

The N-IVR method (Fig. 2 - Top) is performed in a computer using keyboard for moving the camera and the secondary mouse button for the camera orientation. For the object manipulation, it uses the primary mouse button for translating them parallel to the ground and the mouse wheel to control their height. Pressing the *CTRL* key while moving the mouse, the objects can be rotated (circular movement) or scaled (inward/outward movement). Users can switch between rotation and scaling actions and choose the rotation axis in the UI. Alternatively, more experienced users in object manipulation may use a second technique based on the *Transform Gizmo*. Once the object is correctly placed, the corresponding component can be associated using a scroll menu. The second method, hands-free AR (Fig. 2 - Center), unlike the other two methods which use the real-world scale of the line, uses a scale model on top of a table. Its camera control is only dependent on the HMD motion. Using the pinch gesture, users are able to translate and rotate virtual objects as they will follow their hands. The scaling process is identical, performing the pinch gesture with both hands and using the inward/outward technique. The components can be associated by turning the left-hand palm up and selecting it from the list displayed all at once. Finally, IVR with controllers (Fig. 2 - Bottom), combines the device camera control with joystick movement. The left joystick is used for panning the camera horizontally and the right joystick for rotating it. The virtual object copies the controller motion, while pressing the *hand trigger button* inside it. For scaling, the buttons are simultaneously pressed on both controllers and the controllers are moved inward or outward. To associate the corresponding real-world component, a scroll menu is opened on the left controller, and the right controller is used to select the component.

3   User Study

In this section, we present the methodology of the user study conducted, which aimed to evaluate the remote configuration tool and verify the performance and preference of users regarding different aspects of the three methods.

Fig. 2. Remote configuration tool user study. Participants manipulating blue cubes to make them match the orange ones in three conditions (within different environments and using distinct materials): N-IVR application using keyboard and mouse (C1); AR application with hands-free (C2); IVR application using controllers (C3).

3.1 Experimental Setup

Three methods were evaluated: C1 - *N-IVR with keyboard and mouse* using a desktop computer (Asus VivoBook 15); C2 - *AR with hands-free* using a HMD (Microsoft HoloLens 2) and C3 - *IVR with controllers* using a HMD (Oculus Quest 2). In condition C2 a table was used as a base for the virtual model to rest on.

3.2 Experimental Design

The null hypothesis (H0) was considered, i.e., all experimental conditions are equally usable, effective and acceptable to perform the configuration remotely of a Pervasive AR scenario. The independent variables were the tool methods, corresponding to the experimental conditions (C1, C2 and C3). The dependent variables were participants' opinion about each condition, as well as time and accuracy for each virtual object placement. As secondary variables, participants' demographic data, previous experience with AR, IVR and with object manipulation software were considered. A within-subjects experimental design was used, meaning that all participants used every condition. The order in which conditions were presented across the group of participants was counterbalanced, minimizing learning effects.

3.3 Task and Procedure

Adopting each condition, participants were asked to place eight blue cubes, one by one, making them match target cubes (Fig. 2). The target cubes location was uniform between conditions. After the placement of each cube, participants had to associate a component to the cube. Each set of two cubes required different geometric transformations: translation, rotation, scaling and all transformations, respectively.

Data was collected in two categories. Participants' performance, which consists in the average time for the cube placement and component association, as well as, the average accuracy errors: distance, orientation and scale discrepancy to the target cubes. This allows to validate the tool utility in use-cases where the virtual object orientation and scale is relevant. The second category is participants' opinion, gathered through a post-task questionnaire, collecting the following dimensions: Easiness in the object placement - Translation, Rotation and Scale (D1, D2 and D3); Level of physical and mental effort and satisfaction (D4, D5 and D6). Dimensions data was collected using a Likert-type scale: 1 - Low; 7 - High. Moreover, users' challenges, suggestions and observations were registered.

Initially, participants gave their informed consent and were introduced to the study through instructional videos. . Before each condition, participants had an adaptation period to the environment, materials and manipulation techniques. When prepared, they performed the tasks described above. At the end, a post-task questionnaire was filled.

4 Results and Discussion

We recruited 24 participants (6 female, 18 male), whose ages ranged from 22 to 47 years old (M = 26.3, SD = 5.6), 58.3% had previous experience with object manipulation software, 54.2% with IVR and 62.5% with AR. All participants were able to accomplish the task successfully with all conditions. The remote configuration tool was perceived as useful and its methods were considered intuitive and adequate. Figure 3 presents the results of the participants' performance regarding the four measures recorded. The accuracy errors represent the discrepancy between the actual and desired pose when visualizing the virtual content in the real-world industrial line (*visualization module*). Accordingly, as condition C2 adopted a reduced scale model, its distance and scale errors were normalized. The top left boxplot chart depicts the average distance error of the cubes requiring translation for the 24 participants in each condition. Condition C3 was the most effective, followed by condition C1 and C2 (0.016 m, 0.031 m and 0.049 m). The top right chart, concerning the average orientation error, also illustrates that condition C3 was the most effective, followed by condition C1 and C2 (16.5º,

17.2º and 19.7º). The average scale error chart shows an identical error between condition C1 and C3, significantly lower in comparison to condition C2 (0.008 m, 0.011 m and 0.076 m). The last chart reveals the average cube configuration time (placement time and component association time). Condition C2 and C3 show similar efficiency, but substantially lower configuration time than condition C1 (71.6 s, 74.6 s and 110.7 s). Hence, condition C3 was the method which facilitated a better overall users' performance, allowing more accuracy than condition C1 and C2 while also resulting in a beneficial level of efficiency, which was slightly worse than C2 and significantly better than C1.

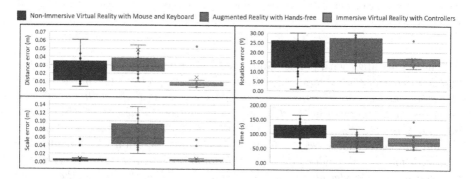

Fig. 3. Overview of participants' performance in each condition, regarding distance error, orientation error, scale error and time for the cube placement and component association.

Assessing the dimensions evaluated through the post-task questionnaire (Fig. 4) we report the following findings. Regarding the top chart, illustrating the *easiness in the object placement*, condition C3 was rated higher in every dimension (translation (D1): median = 7, sum = 155; rotation (D2): median = 7, sum = 149 and scale (D3): median = 7, sum = 157). Condition C2 follows C3 in translation and rotation (D1 and D3) and was rated lower in scaling (D3) (D1: median = 6, sum = 136; D2: median = 5, sum = 117 and D3: median = 6, sum = 129). Lastly, condition C1, was rated lower in dimensions D1 and D2 and slightly higher in dimension D3 (D1: median = 5, sum = 113; D2: median = 3, sum = 82 and D3: median = 6, sum = 130). Concerning the effort and satisfaction chart, in the level of physical effort (D4), condition C1 was rated lower (median = 1, sum = 41), then condition C2 (median = 2, sum = 61) and condition C3 (median = 2, sum = 64). As for the level of mental effort (D5), condition C2 was rated lower (median = 2, sum = 62), followed by condition C3 (median = 3, sum = 82) and condition C1 (median = 4, sum = 100). With respect the level of satisfaction (D6), condition C3 (median = 6, sum = 144) was rated higher, then condition C2 (median = 6, sum = 129) and condition C1 (median = 4, sum = 97). When questioned about their preference, condition C3 (median = 6, sum = 146) was selected as the preferred alternative, followed by condition C2 (median = 6, sum = 135) and lastly, condition C1 (median = 4, sum = 90).

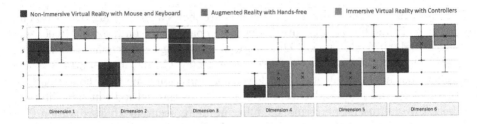

Fig. 4. Overview of participants' preference in each condition. On the top regarding object manipulation (Dimensions 1 - Translation, 2 - Rotation and 3 - Scale) and on the bottom concerning effort and satisfaction (Dimensions 4 - Physical, 5 - Mental and 6 - Satisfaction).

The results align with participants' feedback. Regarding condition C1, *"it is harder to control the camera and get the desired perspective"* (11 participants), *"the manipulation of 3D objects in 2D environments is more challenging"* (7), *"requires more mental effort as there are more controls to memorize"* (5), *"rotating one axis at a time is more complicated than all axis simultaneously"* (7) *"... but can deliver more accuracy"* (3). Concerning condition C2, *"on the cube release, it followed the index finger while undoing the pinch gesture, furthermore, the reduced scale model also made the method less accurate"* (14), *"the limited field of view makes it difficult to visualize the virtual environment"* (9), *"the projection and tracking do not have the required quality, causing confusion"* (7), *"it felt more natural, as it was a real scale model assemble"* (6). Respecting condition C3, *"the environment and the controllers deliver easier accuracy"* (7), *"the speed of the camera could be adjustable and its rotation more fluid, reducing motion sickness"* (9), *"having commands to control the camera height can help the object manipulation"* (10), *"the arms motion with controllers, increases the physical effort"* (5).

5   Concluding Remarks and Future Work

All methods considered seemed appropriate for setting up Pervasive AR scenarios, each possessing its own strengths and limitations, being more suitable depending on the use-case. The IVR with controllers method, although requiring a higher level of physical effort, was preferred by the majority of participants for its immersion and easier control. This method was found to have higher accuracy and satisfactory efficiency, however, needing further improvements in the camera control. The AR with hands-free is convenient when accuracy is not priority as it provides efficiency and a more natural task experience. It could be enhanced for more refined pinch detection and elaborated projections. Lastly, N-IVR with keyboard and mouse presented poorer results, as participants reported more difficulties in its usage. Nevertheless, implementing participants' suggestions, has potential to provide faster and more accurate configurations.

To improve this study, the level of symmetry among the methods considered must be addressed. Different approaches can be further studied, merging the most advantageous features of each method. The tool flexibility can also be deepen, studying its functioning in other scenarios. This work is also being expanded by investigating co-located configuration.

Acknowledgments. To everyone involved in discussion sessions and user studies, thanks for your time and expertise. This research was supported by IEETA, in the context of project [UIDB/00127/2020].

Disclosure of Interests. The authors have no competing interests to declare that are relevant to the content of this article.

References

1. Al-Maeeni, S.S.H., Kuhnhen, C., Engel, B., Schiller, M.: Smart retrofitting of machine tools in the context of industry 4.0. Procedia CIRP **88**, 369–374 (2020)
2. Alves, J.B., Marques, B., Dias, P., Santos, B.S.: Using augmented reality for industrial quality assurance: a shop floor user study. Int. J. Adv. Manuf. Technol. **115**(1), 105–116 (2021)
3. Aromaa, S., Väätänen, A., Aaltonen, I., Goriachev, V., Helin, K., Karjalainen, J.: Awareness of the real-world environment when using augmented reality head-mounted display. Appl. Ergon. **88**, 103145 (2020)
4. Battini, D., Calzavara, M., Persona, A., Sgarbossa, F.: A comparative analysis of different paperless picking systems. Ind. Manage. Data Syst. **115**(3), 483–503 (2015)
5. Boonbrahm, S., Boonbrahm, P., Kaewrat, C.: The use of marker-based augmented reality in space measurement. Procedia Manuf. **42**, 337–343 (2020)
6. Bottani, E., Vignali, G.: Augmented reality technology in the manufacturing industry: a review of the last decade. IISE Trans. **51**(3), 284–310 (2019)
7. Gavish, N., et al.: Evaluating virtual reality and augmented reality training for industrial maintenance and assembly tasks. Interact. Learn. Environ. **23**(6), 778–798 (2015)
8. Hanson, R., Falkenström, W., Miettinen, M.: Augmented reality as a means of conveying picking information in kit preparation for mixed-model assembly. Comput. Ind. Eng. **113**, 570–575 (2017)
9. Jwo, J.S., Lin, C.S., Lee, C.H.: Smart technology-driven aspects for human-in-the-loop smart manufacturing. Int. J. Adv. Manuf. Technol. **114**(5), 1741–1752 (2021)
10. Madeira, T., Marques, B., Neves, P., Dias, P., Santos, B.S.: Comparing desktop vs. mobile interaction for the creation of pervasive augmented reality experiences. J. Imaging **8**(3), 79 (2022)
11. Marino, E., Barbieri, L., Colacino, B., Fleri, A.K., Bruno, F.: An augmented reality inspection tool to support workers in industry 4.0 environments. Comput. Ind. **127**, 103412 (2021)
12. Marques, B., Carvalho, R., Alves, J., Dias, P., Santos, B.S.: Pervasive augmented reality for indoor uninterrupted experiences: a user study. In: Adjunct Proceedings of the 2019 ACM International Joint Conference on Pervasive and Ubiquitous Computing and Proceedings of the 2019 ACM International Symposium on Wearable Computers, pp. 141–144. Association for Computing Machinery, London (2019)

13. Martins, N.C., Marques, B., Alves, J., Araújo, T., Dias, P., Santos, B.S.: Augmented reality situated visualization in decision-making. Multimed. Tools Appl. **81**, 1–24 (2021)
14. Mourtzis, D., Zogopoulos, V., Xanthi, F.: Augmented reality application to support the assembly of highly customized products and to adapt to production re-scheduling. Int. J. Adv. Manuf. Technol. **105**(9), 3899–3910 (2019)
15. Saeedi, S., et al.: Navigating the landscape for real-time localization and mapping for robotics and virtual and augmented reality. Proc. IEEE **106**(11), 2020–2039 (2018)

A Novel Approach for Software 3D-Debugging in Virtual Reality

Sven-Tizian Mauer[1], Laura Ködel[1], Lukas Ertl[1], David Flaig[1], Martin Hedlund[2], and Gerrit Meixner[1,2(✉)]

[1] UniTyLab, Heilbronn University, Max-Planck-Str. 39, 74081 Heilbronn, Germany
lukas@l-ertl.de, david.flaig@hs-heilbronn.de,
gerrit.meixner@hs-heilbronn.de
[2] Media Technology and Interaction Design, KTH Royal Institute of Technology, Stockholm, Sweden
marthed@kth.se, meixner@kth.se

Abstract. This paper introduces a novel concept of virtual 3D debugging in software development, motivated by mental model research in information studies and cognitive design elements. The main goal is to improve the debugging process by allowing programmers to navigate and visualize code in a virtual 3D environment, thereby supporting the construction of the programmers mental model during software exploration. The paper also present the findings of an exploratory study of participants mental models of an academic information system. Participants used our 3D debugging prototype for a debugging procedure as part of the process of making sense of their experiences.

Furthermore, software developers often struggle with debugging. Comprehension of the program structure or the underlying processes can be problematic especially as programs become more complex, or if a person is unfamiliar with the source code. Debugging is an essential part of the software development process, and this paper aims to address this challenge using innovative methods.

Keywords: Unity · 3d Debugging · Virtual reality · Debugging · Programming

1 Introduction

"Our reasoning processes - learning, understanding, problem solving - are largely dependent on our mental modelling mechanisms. ... A model is not a merely simplified version of a certain reality. The main characteristic of a model is that it is a reality of its own. ... Being structurally unitary and autonomous, the model very often imposes its constraints on the original and not vice versa!" [7]

The concept of sense-making is one of the most prevalent in contemporary research on *human-computer interaction* [6]. The idea of sense-making holds that the human experience is, in part, an intentional, socially anchored process of producing sense or meaning out of informational issues, discontinuities, and disconnections that we all deal with on a daily basis in both our personal and professional lives [6].

The users level of comprehension of a system or process from which they are expected to get information corresponds to the effectiveness of their mental models. These models could be limited; they might merely represent analogies, which frequently function rather effectively. People adopt mental models that are partial and/or inaccurate yet nonetheless work with varying degrees of effectiveness and efficiency [7].

Programmers devote a significant amount of their time to debugging their systems. Using commands like step, continue, and goto. The programmer may set breakpoints, check storage, and control execution. The programmer then studies the execution of these instructions in detail, trying to figure out where the program deviates from the expected behavior and why.

The difficulty of debugging increases considerably when software becomes increasingly complex. The interweaving of different modules and the increase in dependencies make it more difficult to identify errors. Especially in large code bases, the lack of familiarity with the entire source code can significantly hinder debugging. In addition, certain types of errors can easily be overlooked in modern integrated development environments (IDEs). For example, simple syntax errors such as the absence of a semicolon are often only indicated by a small red line and are therefore easy to overlook. Poor collaboration support in debugging tools further hinders the efficiency of the debugging process. Team members may be working on different parts of the code, and communication about bugs found and their solutions can be inefficient, leading to longer downtimes. Improved collaboration of tools and practices could make a significant contribution here.

In order to uncover interesting future directions for debugging assistance, our research examines the potential for various techniques of displaying code and managing the control flow in a virtual environment. We did so by developing a prototype for a debugging tool, and conducted an initial exploratory study to understand the strength and limitations of the prototype. We designed the prototype based on programmers information-seeking strategies and the *Cognitive Design Elements* [6], and used Virtual Reality (VR) to improve the debugging process.

2   Theoretical Background

The concept of mental models stems from Kenneth Craik, whom in 1943 characterized mental models as "small scale models" [5] of reality. According to cognitive psychologist Philip Johnson-Lairds, people use mental models to infer linkages, anticipate outcomes, comprehend the systems they interact with, decide a course of action, regulate that action, and experience events 'by proxy' [5]. This reason-centered understanding of mental models contrasts with Normans physically centered approach, which depicted mental models as constrained internal diagrams that only apply to physical activities, like moving pulleys around the same time [3, 7]. Many scholars have used observation and experiments to study how programmers comprehend programs. As a result of this research, numerous cognitive theories to characterize the understanding process have been developed. Although the cognitive theories differ in style and content, many aspects and concepts that characterize fundamental actions in program comprehension are shared by them.

In the context of software engineering, many cognitive models have been presented during the last 20 years to describe how programmers interpret code throughout software maintenance and evolution. Debugging can be comprehensive when a programmer can build a mental model that corresponds to the actual world [6]. This motivated us to create a 3D-debugging prototype that aids comprehension by integrating mental models and includes temporal visualization.

Exaggerated or severe assertions regarding the importance or nature of mental models have occasionally prevented a more in-depth analysis of their function in information seeking. Mental models can aid in understanding user behavior when considered as one significant aspect of sense-making rather than as the exclusive basis for system design. They are no more difficult in their application than any other internalized human phenomena [7]. Models often contain a considerable deal of what is accurate since they are developed based on what has worked in practice; yet, people rarely review their mental models for defects. The complexity of the job and the performance, increase with the number of models needed for a task. However, the enigma of the individual mind is where the main challenge in using mental model theory to enhance information system design resides. Utilizing interviews, observations, and think-aloud procedures, the grounded-theory sense-making approach from communication and information studies reduces this challenge [7].

A user's mental representation of the program to be understood is described as a mental model. A cognitive model explains the mental model's cognitive processes and informational framework. Storey et al. [6] proposes cognitive design elements for program comprehension. They categorize information-seeking as strategies: top-down and bottom-up. Programmers that utilize a top-down strategy focus on understanding the big picture first, and those who prefer bottom-up started with local information (e.g. reading source code) and later integrates their local knowledge into a holistic picture. In other words, programmers first create a low-level abstraction of the program that captures the program's sequence of operations before creating a mental model that incorporates knowledge of the data flow. In the next section we describe how we designed a 3D-debugging tool inspired by the Cognitive Design Elements.

3   System Design

In this section we describe how our 3D-debugging prototype for VR was designed. We designed the prototype for the JavaScript programming language, but our proposed concepts could theoretically be used in any procedural programming context. We used a bottom-up strategy, described by Storey et al. [6], to aid users program understanding while debugging. Bottom-up comprehension requires reading program statements and structures and dissecting them into higher-level abstractions until a thorough understanding of the program is gained. The three main tasks involved in bottom-up understanding are (i) identifying software objects and the relationships among them, (ii) examining code in delocalized plans, and (iii) producing abstractions (by chunking from lower-level units). A debugging tool that supports bottom-up comprehension should support these tasks [6]. A starting point for supporting bottom-up comprehension is that the fundamental components of the program, such as the code or visual representations of it, should be accessible immediately while starting to understand a program (to support ii). We also assume it is necessary to visualize software objects and the relationship between them (to support i and iii). Therefore, VR was used to provide adequate physical space for visualizing the objects and relationships.

Furthermore, Storey et al. [6] describe several cognitive design elements to assist in building a mental model for software exploration. Some of these design elements were considered in the implementation of our 3D-debugging prototype. They are intended to provide the user with the most intuitive user interface possible and to assist in the process of program comprehension and sense-making.

3.1   Reduce Disorientation

When navigating larger programs or trying to solve more complex problems, disorientation can easily occur. In order for the user to focus on solving the problem, it is essential to prevent this disorientation. Storey et al. proposed, that "disorientation can be alleviated by removing some of the unnecessary cognitive overhead resulting from poorly designed user interfaces and by using specialized graphical views for presenting large amounts of information" [6].

In our implementation we used a Chrome Debugger for traversing JavaScript code. This debugger contains redundant information for debugging purposes. Therefore, we decided not to use all control elements the Chrome Debugger offers. This reduction of elements prevents the user from being overwhelmed and ensures full concentration on the actual problem. The two main elements that the Chrome Debugger feeds into the 3D-debugging environment are (i) the code window, and (ii) the call stack (Fig. 1).

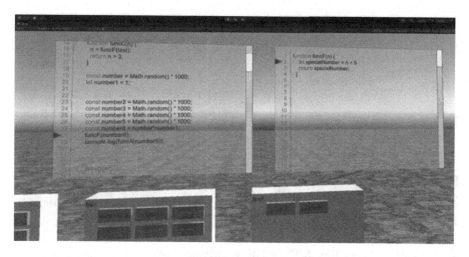

Fig. 1. Screenshot of the virtual 3D debugger prototype showing the code windows and the call stack

Code Window: The code window refers to the display of the source code currently being debugged. In our prototype, the code window floats in three-dimensional space in front of the user and allows the player to inspect the code relevant to the current debug process. Similar to traditional debuggers, the current line of code is highlighted with a green arrow on the side of the window. For a better overview, programming language specific keywords are highlighted, and the code lines are numbered. If the code to be debugged is spread over several files, there are several instances of the code window lined up next to each other. A colored line between call stack and code window indicates in which file the debugger is currently working. This line further prevents user disorientation.

Call Stack: In addition to the code windows, the current call stack is also displayed to the user. Here the called functions are listed from bottom to top. A function is graphically represented as a three-dimensional cube. On the top left of the cube the name of the function is displayed and on the rest of the cube the variables of the function are displayed in the form of red boxes. These red boxes contain the name and the currently assigned value of the variable.

3.2   Show the Path that Led to the Current Focus

To help the user understand complex problems, it is useful to store and visualize small pieces of temporary information, such as the path that led to the current focus. On the World Wide Web, this design element is often represented in the form of breadcrumbs, which make it clear to the user which path he or she has already taken and how it led to the current focus [6]. In this project, the path the user has already taken is represented in the form of a timeline (Fig. 2).

This timeline is formed by different call stacks that represent the current program state of different points in time in the past. Since this takes place in

Fig. 2. Virtual 3D debugging timeline

three-dimensional space, users can, if necessary, simply turn their heads to the left or even walk to the desired location to explore the program path that has been taken.

Navigation: In order to provide the user with the most intuitive navigation possible within the system, we let the user simply walk and interact as in the physical world to interact with the system. Movements like walking in a room or moving the hands are transferred to the virtual reality. This allows the user to change the position within the application by walking in the physical world, and thus, for example, to be able to examine the timeline more accurately, which helps understanding the problem to be solved. If the user walks in the timeline at a past point in time, he sees the current call stack with the variables set at that time and their assigned values. Furthermore, the code windows follow the user along the timeline. These also adapt to the targeted time in the past and visualize which file was in focus at that time and in which code line the user was. In this way, the user can examine his past steps, as in a kind of time travel, and thus better understand the current program status (Fig. 3).

Since users are likely to use the application indoors, and thus also have limited movement options, the use of teleportation was resorted to in addition to physical movement. If the desired time point in the timeline is too far away to walk to, the user can teleport to the respective location using the controller. Teleportation platforms are placed on the floor for every fifth debug step, the space in between is only reachable by walking there.

3.3   Indicate the Maintainers Current Focus

Several design elements are implemented to provide guidance and show the users where they currently are in the code and give the ability to set the focus in the code [6]. The user's focus is enhanced in two ways. Firstly, an arrow marks the

Fig. 3. Teleportation platforms in virtual 3D debugging

position of the active step in the code window. Secondly, the current focus of the user within the call stack on the timeline is indicated by the user's position. When walking around on the timeline, the focus changes according to the position in relation to the call stack block that is in front of the user.

4   Integration in Software Development Workflow

To optimize the added value of using 3D-debugging in virtual reality, it is crucial to seamlessly integrate this technology into the software development workflow. The following are potential application areas of this technology in the software development process:

Integration into New or Existing Projects: The versatility of 3D-debugging in virtual reality extends to both new and existing projects. This inclusivity ensures that developers can harness the benefits of this immersive technology at any stage of the development process. By seamlessly integrating virtual 3D debugging, teams can maintain a consistent approach to problem-solving and debugging throughout the software life-cycle.

Error Analysis in 3D: The immersive capabilities of the technology empower developers to conduct in-depth error analyses. By visually representing bugs and the related code in all three dimensions on a timeline, the technology provides a comprehensive understanding of how errors originate and evolve during the software development process. This visual approach not only facilitates error identification but also enhances the overall comprehension of error patterns, leading to more effective and targeted bug resolution.

Refactoring of Programs: During the refactoring of existing software architectures, 3D-debugging technology could play a crucial role. Visualizing the existing software structure could provide developers with a better understanding of the code's structure. Bugs and errors could be depicted in an immersive environment in all three dimensions on a timeline, allowing for a thorough analysis of error development. This representation extends across various software components, facilitating precise error localization and promoting efficient refactoring. Through immersive visualization, developers could not only fix errors but also better comprehend how the existing architecture interacts. This contributes to making the refactoring process more transparent and enables well-informed decisions to improve software quality.

Training and Onboarding: The interactive nature of VR technology becomes particularly valuable during the onboarding phase for new team members. Creating an immersive training environment allows new developers to explore the code and project architecture, fostering a quicker and more intuitive understanding of the existing system. This hands-on approach to learning can significantly reduce the learning curve and improve the efficiency of new team members.

Documentation and Presentation: The dynamic 3D visualizations produced by the technology serve as powerful tools for documentation and presentations. Developers can articulate complex relationships with clarity, making it easier to convey intricate details to both internal team members and external stakeholders. The visual nature of these representations enhances communication and comprehension, contributing to more effective collaboration and decision-making.

Collaboration in the Virtual Space: The collaborative potential of VR 3D-debugging is a cornerstone of its utility in the software development process. Enabling multiple users to work simultaneously on a problem in a virtual environment fosters real-time collaboration. With the freedom to move and manipulate code snippets, developers can share insights and collectively solve problems, creating a collaborative and immersive environment that transcends the limitations of traditional collaboration tools. This approach not only enhances teamwork but also promotes a sense of shared understanding and collective problem-solving.

5   Technical Implementation

Technical Equipment: To use the 3D-debugging prototype, users need VR glasses and one VR-controller. It is important that the VR glasses support the tracking of the physical world, so movements, such as walking, can be interpreted by the system and transferred to the virtual world. For this prototype we used the Oculus Quest 2.

Frontend Implementation: Unity is used as IDE for developing and visualizing the virtual environment. Unity is a real-time 3D engine with an integrated development environment that is typically used for game development [4].

The code developed in Unity mainly takes care of visual things, such as displaying the code in 3D space, interpreting the user's movements, or providing various interaction options for the user. Besides visual things, the frontend code also takes care of things like storing the debug history or communicating with the backend part of this project (Fig. 4).

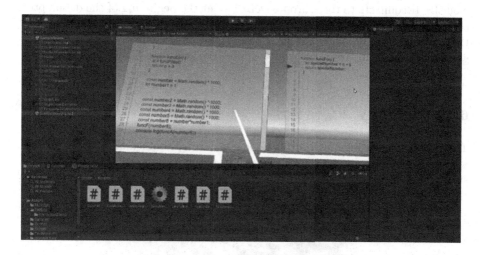

Fig. 4. Screenshot of the Unity 3D engine during development

Backend Implementation: For necessary functions of a debugger, such as step-into, information about variables or occurring errors we relied on the Google Chrome Debugger. The available API makes it possible to interact with the debugger and to get information about the debug process. The Google Chrome Debugger is sufficient for debugging JavaScript code. Since this project is based on this debugger, only debugging of JavaScript code is currently possible in the 3D debugger. To make the Google Chrome Debugger API available, the Chrome browser must be started via command line. Afterwards, the web page or file on which the code to be debugged is located must be called and the Chrome Debugger must be opened. Now, a WebSocket interface is available to interact with via a WebSocket connection (Fig. 5).

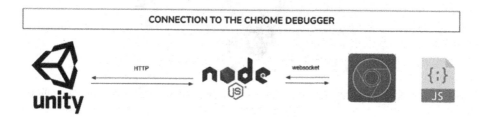

Fig. 5. Visualization of mapping the WebSocket API into an HTTP API

To avoid having to maintain a persistent WebSocket connection via the VR glasses, an additional server application was developed that converts the WebSocket interface to an HTTP interface. This application was implemented in NodeJS. It connects to the Chrome Debugger at the beginning of the debug process, waits for requests via its HTTP interface and converts the sent data into the required format. This way it is possible to send commands to the debugger and receive data from the Unity application without having to maintain a constant connection.

6　User Study

To test the 3D-debugging prototype and derive recommendations for further actions, a small exploratory user study with 6 participants was conducted. The study offers a first impression about the acceptance of 3D-debugging as well as the feeling and usability of the prototype (Fig. 6).

Fig. 6. Photo of a participant in the user study using the VR glasses and controllers.

6.1   Participants

The 6 participants in the study were required to already have some programming and debugging experience, but it was not necessary for them to have previous experience with virtual reality applications. As the group of participants was small, it also was a homogeneous group of mostly male participants in the age of 18 to 25.

6.2   Task and Procedure

The study consisted of a faulty program that participants had to debug in order to identify the problem. They were also encouraged to try out all functionalities offered by the prototype. The test program itself was a small JavaScript program consisting of a main function calling some sub-functions with input and return values. The included error originates in one of the sub-functions so the user can observe how the functions are called and how the step-into feature is used. We formulated a small set of questions that were answered before or after the execution of the test program. The questions being asked beforehand covered expectations of a 3D-debugging application as well as possible advantages that could be provided by such a solution (without knowing it). After the test program was completed, participants were asked about details that should assess how the environment covered their mental model. Those questions covered individual experiences regarding intuitive navigation, problems during execution, suggestions for improvement or extensions, as well as personal opinion about virtual 3D-debugging and the prototype.

6.3   Results

With an introductory explanation and some guidance offered by the interviewers, all participants managed to debug through the test program and finally find the cause of error and test out all the functionalities the prototype offers. Thereby it could be determined that participants with prior experience in virtual reality applications managed to familiarize themselves more quickly with the 3D debugging environment and therefore needed less guidance.

The main purpose of the user study was to get some general feedback about 3D-debugging and the application as well as to collect suggestions for improvements. Even if none of the participants ever tried 3D-debugging before, the overall impression of this approach was positive. The possibilities offered by using the three-dimensional space and other benefits of virtual reality could be used to make debugging more interesting and enjoyable. Like the possibility of better virtual collaboration. This seems to be less significant as it is a non-functional advantage with a hard measured impact (in contrast to efficiency), but considering that software developers spend most of their time debugging programs, making this task more enjoyable is a desirable goal. Additionally, 3D-debugging could potentially speed up the debugging process, which we aim to explore in future iterations of this prototype. Conclusively, all participants agreed on the statement that they can imagine using a more advanced 3D-debugging application in their future working environment.

Regarding the current state of the tested application itself, the participants emphasized the navigation positively. The feeling of walking around in the code along a timeline highly supports program comprehension, the added teleportation functionality encourages fast navigation over longer distances and benefits usability. Furthermore, highlighting of the current step in focus inside the overall context was pointed out being positive for the users. They especially mentioned the arrow as marker for the current code position as well as the line connecting the call stack information to the code file. To summarize the impressions of the tested application, all participants were unanimous that it provides a valid starting point for further research and development of 3D-debugging.

As mentioned, the tested application provides a starting point and is therefore still limited in its functionalities. Some suggestions for improvement of the application were collected during the user study. Regarding the code windows in the background of the visualization, file names could be displayed for better orientation. In the foreground, where the call stacks are located, testers suggested to mark the variables which have changed from the previous to the current step. Feedback to the overall application included to show the hierarchy of the whole project. This function especially comes into effect when debugging larger projects. Furthermore, the participants wanted to drag and move the blocks around. When implementing this feature, attention must be paid to the arrangement of the code blocks on the timeline as this can result in confusion and unstructured visualization quickly. Generally, it was suggested to provide some color coding for several, important information to highlight the crucial content or changes to support program comprehension. Building on this, more customizations could be offered in general so each user can influence the design and representation of information in a way that suits them best. For increasing the contrast and readability of the visualized items, one participant suggested to change the position of the light source within Unity. This leads to a movement of the shadows and visible changes in the overall illumination of the application.

The results of the user study are summarized in Fig. 7.

Some of the drawbacks of the prototype were related to the concept of mental models. As explained earlier, mental models are build up individually and are needed for the comprehension of a system. Even if there are some system design concepts that generalize to mental models, the process of sense-making is very individually. Conclusively, each user of the prototype builds their own mental model according to the system, which is used to try to understand what is presented. In practice, this showed up during the user study as various aspects of navigational elements or code representations were clear and intuitive for some users as they were confusing and unclear for others. The observed effects naturally correlate with the level of expertise. More experienced programmers find it easier to understand the software architecture or the components of the debugging process whereas people familiar with virtual reality have fewer problems with navigation. This leads to the conclusion, that the individual level of

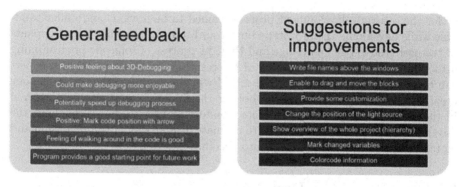

Fig. 7. List of general feedback and suggestions for improvement.

experience is another factor influencing the personal mental model and therefore system comprehension.

According to the described distinctions corresponding to various users and likewise the different levels of expertise, multiple sub-tasks within the process of system comprehension can also result in distinct mental models. Regarding the sense-making of a debugging process within a virtual 3D environment, the relevant sub-tasks to be understood could be navigation and orientation, software architecture as well as the debugging process itself. As the user studies have shown, understanding differs throughout these components, indicating that there are different mental models build up. In line with the aforementioned conclusion, the level of experience in each of the sub-tasks influences the respective mental model.

The proposed project with the developed prototype focuses on debugging, which is an inevitable task within the software development process. However, this implementation transfers the task of debugging to a new environment while the remaining software development process is conducted in a classical IDE. This workflow requires developers to switch between the IDE they're used to and the new virtual 3D environment to accomplish the different challenges. Both development environments represent very different concepts for the representation of code structure and architecture. According to the aforementioned sub-tasks, switching development environments concludes in a change of mental models. This means that the mental models existing for the comprehension of the software architecture could look differently throughout software development in a classical IDE compared to the debugging process conducted in virtual reality. This phenomenon was not observed directly while conducting the user study as the tests focused on the 3D debugging process, but it is a logical conclusion when the participants thought about integrating this application in the software development process.

Another discrepancy in mental models originates when comparing the perspective of the prototype developers to the perspective of the prototype users. Some elements, either in terms of usability, regarding the software architecture, or for the software development process seemed to be obvious and understandable while developing the prototype but proved to be unclear to the participants of the user study. The knowledge and thought process of someone programming a tool influences the comprehension of the resulting tool. Conclusively, this person builds up a very specific mental model which naturally differs from the one created by someone who uses the tool for the first time and was not involved in the development process. Therefore, conducting user studies throughout the development process is unavoidable to evaluate usability and comprehension and to take the mental model of users into account.

7   Limitations and Drawbacks

While 3D debugging offers significant advantages over traditional debugging, it also comes with its own limitations and drawbacks. This must be taken into account in the further development of 3D debugging.

Virtual Reality Sickness of Users. An existing problem with VR is that virtual reality sickness can occur when using VR glasses and motion sickness-like symptoms can occur. The most common symptoms are "eye fatigue, disorientation, and nausea". [2] The focus should be on minimizing these effects.

The Space Required for the Use of VR. A basic feature of 3D debugging is to display the debugging in 3D space. Navigation in space is achieved by the user walking and teleporting in space. This requires a safe physical area in which the user can move undisturbed and safely.

Media Disruption from Programming to Debugging. The current 3D debugging model only provides for debugging with VR glasses. This means that the user must leave the workstation used for programming and use the VR workstation for debugging. This media break could lead to users being reluctant to use 3D debugging.

Accessibility of 3D Debugging. In the current model of 3D debugging, it is only possible to move in space by moving in physical space or teleporting to teleportation platforms located every 5 debugging steps. This could lead to users who cannot do this being excluded and there should preferably be a mode that allows this without physical movement.

Hardware Requirements. The use of 3D debugging requires VR glasses. Which is not part of the standard equipment and would have to be purchased for this purpose. In addition, the physical VR area should be appropriately designated and secured in a professional environment.

Integration with Existing Tools. Currently, only an integration with the Google Chrome Debugger is implemented, which limits the potential use. The integration of other debuggers would require the provision of an API or other cooperation.

Learning Curve. 3D Debugging was designed with ease of use by the user in mind. Nevertheless, it is a novel idea of debugging and should be introduced and taught to potential new users.

Isolation from Reality. While using 3D debugging in the VR environment, the user is shielded from the outside world by the VR glasses and therefore only experiences very limited sensations from the real world. Depending on the environment, this can lead to safety concerns, for example if there is no secure VR area. The use of VR glasses can lead to the user feeling isolated, as the use of VR glasses impairs interaction with other people

8 Future Work

As the prototype provides basic functionalities to give an impression of 3D-debugging, the user study pointed out that continuing this work might result in a product that will be accepted by software developers. Combining the results of the user study together with our own experiences during the process of developing and testing the 3D-debugging tool, some ideas for future work could be derived.

Aside from this, some general ideas for improving the debugging experience were formulated. For example, user-defined backgrounds could be provided. Furthermore, personalization of the content is another important area of improving the user experience. Users want to be able to control which colours are used or which size the code blocks and writing are. Moreover, it can be thought about providing different layouts for the organization of the different elements within the visualization. This would provide more freedom to the user through fulfilling the need for personalization as well as for moving the blocks around, which was pointed out during the user study. Nonetheless this approach keeps the elements in a fixed order avoiding the risk of confusion as the call stack blocks still are attached to the timeline.

To make 3D debugging applicable in the work life of professional software developers, the visualization must be able to display the contents of a larger code base in an understandable and accessible way. Therefore, a concept must be developed consisting of different design elements to provide the relevant information. The user must be able to keep orientation within the program all the time and furthermore must keep track of the changes that happened during the previous debugging steps. Presenting a large program in a comprehensive way will be one of the major challenges when conceptualizing 3D debugging for usage in the daily life of software developers. Here, the topic of customization comes into action again. To avoid overwhelming the user with all the information, it must be possible to hide parts of the content so that the user can expand and view them if needed. Because everyone has a different strategy of program comprehension, it is important to focus on the overview and overall context at first and provide deeper, more detailed information when it is required. This can be done with design elements for visualization and navigation as well as by using colours and textual or even acoustical descriptions. Ideas like that are accompanied by having a more interactive solution where the user has more possibilities as well as more room for making decisions as it is provided in the current prototype version.

As being said, the prototype version of 3D-debugging opens up a wide space of possibilities for ongoing work. Especially when the requirements for displaying larger programs alongside with usability and customizability are regarded during further development, 3D-debugging could greatly improve the debugging experience of software developers.

9   Conclusion

In this paper, we have demonstrated how a 3D-debugging prototype for virtual reality can be used to comprehend a program and effectively debug it. As a part of this work, we have opened up the field for future study and research in the development and debugging of software in virtual 3D environments.

It's a known fact that an obstacle to software engineering education and training is a lack of fundamental knowledge about how programs are executed [1]. The majority of the time, traditional methods of code debugging are challenging. Our findings indicates that 3D-debugging tools might be developed to directly help in thorough comprehension of programs.

During the study, we discovered that participants had favourable opinions of the application's general user interface, navigational flow, and information visualization inside the prototypes. The participants emphasized the navigation as a strong point of the evaluated application's present condition. The experience of moving through the code along a timeline greatly aids in understanding programs, and the addition of teleportation capabilities promotes quick movement across long ranges so that the application may be utilized even when there is just a small amount of physical area available. Furthermore, it was also beneficial for the participants to highlight the current debugging-step in focus within a larger context.

On the other hand, it is acceptable that, the current prototype has a lot of room for improvement. Functionalities like drag-and-drop repositioning, color-coding, highlighting important information to draw attention to content that is important, could all be added in future iterations.

In summary, we have demonstrated that creating a debugging tools in a virtual 3D environment is both feasible and potentially advantageous.

Acknowledgment. We are grateful to Bhanu Chandan Machenahalli Vishweswaraiah for his constructive contributions. We also want to express our appreciation to everyone who took part in the user study for testing of the model.

References

1. Atkinson, R., McBeath, C., Soong, S.K.A., Cheers, C. (eds.): ICT: Providing Choices for Learners and Learning. Centre for Educational Development, Nanyang Technological University, Singapore, 2–5 December 2007. http://www.ascilite.org.au/conferences/singapore07/procs/
2. Chang, E., Kim, H.T., Yoo, B.: Virtual reality sickness: a review of causes and measurements. Int. J. Hum.-Comput. Interact. **36**(17), 1658–1682 (2020). https://doi.org/10.1080/10447318.2020.1778351
3. Ford, M., Johnson-Laird, P.N.: Mental models: towards a cognitive science of language, inference, and consciousness. Language **61**(4), 897 (1985). https://doi.org/10.2307/414498. http://dx.doi.org/10.2307/414498
4. Hussain, A., Shakeel, H., Hussain, F., Uddin, N., Ghouri, T.: Unity game development engine: a technical survey. Univ. Sindh J. Inf. Commun. Technol. **4**, 73–81 (2020)
5. Johnson-Laird, P.: Mental models in cognitive science. Cogn. Sci. **4**, 71–115 (2010). https://doi.org/10.1207/s15516709cog0401_4
6. Storey, M.A., Fracchia, F., Muller, H.: Cognitive design elements to support the construction of a mental model during software visualization. In: Proceedings Fifth International Workshop on Program Comprehension, IWPC 1997. WPC 1997. IEEE Computer Social Press. https://doi.org/10.1109/wpc.1997.601257. http://dx.doi.org/10.1109/wpc.1997.601257
7. Westbrook, L.: Mental models: a theoretical overview and preliminary study. J. Inf. Sci. **32**(6), 563–579 (2006). https://doi.org/10.1177/0165551506068134

SpaceXR: Virtual Reality and Data Mining for Astronomical Visualization

Mikhail Nikolaenko[⊠] and Ming Tang

Extended Reality Lab, Digital Futures, University of Cincinnati, Cincinnati,
OH 45011, USA
nikolamv@mail.uc.edu

Abstract. This paper presents a project named "SpaceXR" that harmonizes data science, astronomy, and Virtual Reality (VR) technology to deliver an immersive and interactive educational tool. It is designed to cater to a diverse audience, including students, academics, space enthusiasts, and professionals, offering an easily accessible platform through VR headsets. This innovative VR application offers a data-driven representation of celestial bodies, including planets and the sun within our solar system, guided by data from the NASA and Gaia databases. The VR application empowers users with interactive capabilities encompassing scaling, time manipulation, and object highlighting. The potential applications span from elementary educational contexts, such as teaching the star system in astronomy courses, to advanced astronomical research scenarios, like analyzing spectral data of celestial objects identified by Gaia and NASA. By adhering to emerging software development practices and employing a variety of conceptual frameworks, this project yields a fully immersive, precise, and user-friendly 3D VR application that relies on accurate, publicly available databases to map celestial objects.

Keywords: Virtual Reality · Interactive Learning · Astronomical Visualization

1 Introduction

1.1 Background

Technological advancements are continually transforming and enhancing current systems. One such system, education, has seen perpetual improvements following global technological advancements. As an illustration, the widespread adoption of computers transformed basic instructional tools into advanced, interconnected systems, which broadened educational reach and opened new avenues for communication and collaborative learning [1]. A closer examination of education in the subsequent sections reveals how technology influences its effectiveness and the overall learning process of an individual.

Education, by definition, is the process of passing skills, knowledge, or traits to others, typically in a formal setting such as a school or university, to reach a particular

J. Y. C. Chen and G. Fragomeni (Eds.): HCII 2024, LNCS 14708, pp. 252–267, 2024.
https://doi.org/10.1007/978-3-031-61047-9_17

learning outcome. This learning outcome can be achieved through various learning methods described by popular theoretical models and frameworks, such as those proposed by Kolb, Bergsteiner, Avery, and Neumann. From these theoretical models, three main senses can be derived that facilitate learning based on human perception: visual, auditory, and kinesthetic learning [2]. Despite the lack of evidence supporting the meshing hypothesis, which suggests that focusing on one sense leads to better learning outcomes over another, the incorporation of all three, referred to as cross-modal processing [3], will be implemented by utilizing immersive learning.

Immersion is defined as an objective measure of vividness offered by a system, based on the number of senses that are activated by technology, and the extent to which a system can shut out the outside world [4]. Simply put, you are more immersed as the simulated reality converges with reality. Take learning from a textbook as an example. The experience of reading instructions on fishing from a textbook yields a lower degree of immersion, compared to if you were to go to a physical body of water and experience fishing first-hand. The latter yields a high or full degree of immersion, as you are physically present in the environment and engaging in the actions personally. The idea is that a more immersive experience may lead to improved factual, conceptual, and procedural knowledge acquisition, including transfer of learning and improved learning outcomes [4]. Cross-modal processing does not always mean high immersion, but high immersion typically always includes the use of all sensory inputs.

1.2 XR as a Tool

A technology that has grown exponentially in the past decade is known as extended reality (XR). Extended reality is an umbrella term that encompasses three main branches: virtual reality (VR), augmented reality (AR), and mixed reality (MR). VR is defined as facilitating immersion in a simulated 3D virtual environment. The most common system used for VR is the head-mounted display (HMD). As the name suggests, individuals mount a display onto their heads for visual feedback, frequently paired with speakers on the HMD for auditory feedback, as well as complementary holdable controllers to mimic hand movement and interaction for interactive feedback [5]. In this way, VR can hit all three human senses, effectively enabling cross-model processing and making it an exceptionally immersive tool. Most often, the simulated environment seen through an HMD is created using computer graphics. Expanding on the interaction aspect of VR, interactive elements have shown to be vast. This allows for the cultivation of interactive experiences whilst simultaneously handing the power to the user [6]. Moving on, AR is quickly defined as augmenting the current reality, typically using digital elements overlayed over the physical space, where they are fully independent of one another. MR, on the other hand, like AR, is defined as overlaying digital elements over the physical space, but the elements do interact with the physical environment [5].

XR can be effective in spatial scenarios and visualization. It opens the opportunity to visualize and interact with different kinds of data [7]. It introduces spatial orientation and awareness, which allows for sensing of scale and space. XR's proficiency in this concept is particularly pertinent to fields that rely heavily on visualizing complex, multidimensional data [8], such as astronomy. Astronomical data is vast, ranging from close-to-home solar system information like orbits and orientation of different planets, to spectrum data of distant stars and galaxies, making astronomy a great candidate to test XR's capabilities.

Each branch of Extended Reality (XR)—Virtual Reality (VR), Augmented Reality (AR), and Mixed Reality (MR)—has unique applications depending on the context. This research focuses specifically on VR as the primary modality. The choice of VR over AR or MR is influenced by two main factors. First, considering the project's goal of visualizing and interacting with celestial objects, VR was deemed more suitable than AR/MR, which might conflict with the intended immersive environment. Second, among the three modalities, VR is currently the most advanced in terms of development and available support. While the potential for incorporating AR or MR exists in the future, the scope of this research is confined to VR applications.

The discussion thus far suggests that VR, when adeptly utilized and tailored for specific use cases, can serve as a potent tool. It offers a platform for crafting experiences that are not only immersive but also interactive, effectively facilitating cross-modal processing to enhance learning outcomes. Considering optimal areas for applying this technology, the focus shifts to a notable intersection. The inherent adaptability of educational systems to technological changes, coupled with the extensive datasets available in astronomy, posits VR's conceptual framework as a key component. This combination raises an intriguing question: Can the integration of VR technology into educational and academic disciplines, using astronomy as a guiding example, yield significant benefits and advancements in these fields?

1.3 Objectives

This research is committed to developing a multi-disciplinary immersive VR software tool that assesses the feasibility and utility of real-time or imported data interaction within educational and astronomical domains. The focus is on exploring the capabilities of VR in enhancing 3D visualization and improving instructional methods in education. The application is designed to be a versatile tool that not only addresses the immediate requirements of data interaction and visualization in these fields but also delves into the intricacies of VR's interactive design. This exploration aims to establish the application as an innovative solution that strengthens the way complex concepts are visualized and taught, thereby contributing significantly to both educational and astronomical disciplines. The primary objectives are:

Development of a comprehensive. VR application. To develop a versatile and user-friendly VR application that integrates data from multiple astronomical databases for diverse educational and academic use cases.

Astronomical Data Visualization. To effectively visualize a wide range of celestial objects and astronomical phenomena, leveraging data from NASA, Gaia, and other databases, thus facilitating a deeper understanding of space science.

Interactivity and User Control. To implement and refine interactive features such as teleportation, scaling/time manipulation, and object highlighting within the VR environment, ensuring that the application meets the specific needs of various users.

Assessment of Application Performance and Limitations. To evaluate the application's performance, identify and address the challenges faced, such as optimizing for a larger number of celestial objects, and laying the groundwork for future enhancements.

2 Related Works

The intersection of education, astronomy, and Virtual Reality (VR) has been explored in previous works, providing foundational insights into the development of immersive educational tools. Early studies, although not employing immersive VR in the contemporary sense with Head-Mounted Displays (HMDs), have demonstrated the educational benefits of conceptualizing astronomical phenomena in three-dimensional (3D) spaces through non-immersive VR applications. These applications, operating on computer-based interactive windows, underscore the potential of 3D spatial representations in enhancing students' comprehension of complex astronomical concepts. The engagement facilitated by these 3D models, coupled with the perspective shift they offer, serves as a precursor to the development of more immersive experiences [9, 10].

Building on these insights, this project leverages the advantages of real data importation from publicly available databases, enhancing user's engagement using HMDs and controllers. This approach not only introduces spatial awareness and kinesthetic interaction but also utilizes cross-modal processing to foster a comprehensive understanding of celestial bodies and their dynamics. Contrasting with the screen-based methodologies of previous works, this research incorporates real-time solar system data and imported celestial information, offering an interactive exploration environment enriched with scientific metadata.

A notable progression in this field is the advent of immersive VR applications that gamify astronomical education, such as a recent game-app integrating external data to visualize deep sky objects from Earth's perspective [11]. This application highlights the role of VR in mitigating the constraints imposed by light pollution, enabling users worldwide to experience the night sky in its entirety. Comparatively, the application created in this research distinguishes itself by offering an overhead perspective for user-driven exploration and manipulation, integrating the solar system and extraterrestrial objects into a singular, data-driven VR experience.

In summary, this research synthesizes the core aspects of these pioneering works into a modern, immersive VR application. By combining accurate data visualization, interactive engagement, and educational gamification, it aims to revolutionize the learning experience in astronomy, offering a unique platform for exploring the cosmos.

3 Technical Development

3.1 Hardware

In the realm of current VR technology, there is a wide array of options available, each with its unique strengths and applications. For the purposes of this research, the Meta Quest 2 [12] was chosen for its combination of affordability and functionality. This choice aligns with the goal of preparing for a broad dissemination of the application, where a cost-effective Head-Mounted Display (HMD) is more pragmatic. The Quest 2 stands out for its versatility and ability to meet the minimum standards required for this research. Alongside the HMD, the Quest 2 controllers were essential in introducing interactive elements into the application, enabling users to engage directly with the VR environment and manipulate various aspects of the celestial visualization effectively.

Additionally, a personal Windows computer was essential for the development phase and running the application via PC-VR, rather than as a standalone system. The distinction between standalone and PC-VR system setups is significant in this context. Standalone VR is self-contained, offering convenience and ease of use without the need for external hardware. However, it is often limited by its in-built processing power. On the other hand, PC-VR system setups, while requiring a connection to a computer, offer enhanced graphical fidelity and processing capabilities. This is particularly crucial for the application in question, which demands high-performance computing for rendering detailed 3D environments and specialized data processing tasks.

The decision to utilize PC-VR in this research was driven primarily by the need for higher graphical fidelity, as personal computers generally provide superior performance compared to standalone VR. Furthermore, the data streaming process integral to the application necessitates custom processes only feasible on a PC platform. This approach allowed for a more detailed and immersive visualization of celestial objects, leveraging the advanced computational power available through PC-VR system setups.

3.2 Software

The software infrastructure of the project was built on Unreal Engine 5 [13], a free source-available game engine renowned for its exceptional graphical fidelity and advanced computer graphics capabilities [14, 15], including real-time lighting effects, raytracing, and realistic textures. These features allow developers to focus on application creation without being bogged down by the intricacies of computer graphics, which was particularly beneficial in this research. The engine, primarily based on the C++ programming language, offers a robust framework for developing intricate and visually appealing environments.

A significant aspect of Unreal Engine 5's utility in this project was its integrated visual programming system known as Blueprints. Blueprints facilitated rapid prototyping and interactive design, allowing for a streamlined development process. Most of the application's coding was achieved through this node-based interface, which proved crucial for efficiently implementing the interactive features of the VR environment.

In addition to its core programming capabilities, Unreal Engine 5 played a pivotal role in porting the developed environment onto the Meta Quest 2 HMD. This process involved adapting the 3D environment and interactive elements to be compatible with the VR headset, ensuring seamless integration and user experience. The engine's compatibility with VR hardware, particularly the Quest 2, enabled a smooth transition of the virtual environment onto the headset, providing users with an immersive and responsive VR experience.

Moreover, the capacity for custom C++ coding in Unreal Engine 5 opened avenues for future enhancements, such as integrating live data streaming. The potential for implementing real-time celestial data streams, utilizing technologies like Inter-Process Communication (IPC), a technique used for dynamic data sharing between processes, can significantly elevate the application's interactive and educational value. This dual-language support—combining the rapid development of Blueprints with the customizability of C++ —ensured that the software infrastructure was not only apt for the current scope of the project but also adaptable for future expansions and technological integrations.

Software Development Protocols. The software development for the application was guided by common-day software development models, adapting a strategy that best fit the project's requirements and team structure. Given the project's nature of incremental additions and a small development team, a combination of agile and DevOps methodologies was employed [16].

3.3 Data Research

External Data. This section refers to data on celestial objects outside of the solar system.

Database Analysis. An integral component of this research was the selection and analysis of appropriate astronomical data.

The objective to develop a data-driven VR application with accurate celestial visualizations necessitated a thorough understanding of the available astronomical data landscape. Initial efforts focused on extensive online research to identify major publicly available databases in the field of astronomy. This exploration revealed several key databases, including Gaia [17–19], the Sloan Digital Sky Survey (SDSS) [20], and the Dark Energy Survey [21].

Gaia, an observatory mission led by the European Space Agency, emerged as a primary data source. It aims to construct the most extensive 3D map of the Milky Way galaxy, containing information on nearly 2 billion celestial objects, representing about 1% of the Milky Way galaxy. The SDSS provides detailed information on distant stars and galaxies using spectral imaging and spectroscopy, while the Dark Energy Survey focuses on mapping celestial objects to enhance the understanding of dark energy.

For the data visualization component of the application, Gaia's Data Release 3 (DR3) was chosen due to its comprehensive range and consistent data on celestial objects. Additionally, consultations with Dr. Bischoff and Dr. Bayliss, associate professors at the University of Cincinnati's astrophysics department, further reinforced the selection of Gaia. Their expert insights aligned with the research's focus and supported the inclusion of Gaia's data in the application.

These discussions also touched on the concept of 'cross-matching' celestial objects between different databases—a common practice in astronomy to combine data from multiple sources [22]. While the Gaia database includes a section for cross-matched objects from other databases, for simplicity, this project focused solely on Gaia-specific objects. However, the potential for implementing custom cross-matching algorithms in future expansions of the project was acknowledged, though it was beyond the scope of the current phase of research.

The process of database analysis and selection was a crucial step in ensuring the application's success. By choosing Gaia DR3 for its extensive and reliable data, the project laid a solid foundation for creating accurate and immersive visualizations of celestial objects.

Data Integration. Following the selection of a suitable data source, the next step was to develop methods for integrating this data into the application.

A critical distinction was made between live or real-time data and imported data. Real-time data involves streaming, filtering, and manipulation during the application's runtime, whereas imported data is pre-loaded and static, without the capability for additional data input during runtime.

To extract information from the Gaia database, the Astronomical Data Query Language (ADQL) was utilized. This programming language allows for querying the Gaia database effectively. While programmatic access to Gaia data in Python was available, it would have required additional work to create an Inter-Process Communication (IPC) between Python and Unreal Engine 5's C + + environment. This integration, although feasible, was earmarked for future development.

For this project, data was queried in advance from the Gaia archive. The algorithm developed for this purpose extracted desired attributes while filtering out non-essential data. Key information such as parallax, inclination, and declination were targeted, enabling the computation of object positionality, which will be described in the following section. Approximately 1000 celestial objects were selected based on these attributes.

It's important to note that the Gaia database provides a wealth of data beyond the selected attributes, including astrometric solutions, G magnitudes, astrophysical parameters from BP/RP spectra, and more. This variety of data can be highly beneficial for individuals interested in visualizing specific astronomical data in a three-dimensional space.

With the celestial positions computed and embedded within a data table, including additional metadata, Unreal Engine 5's Blueprint code completes the mapping process. By parsing the table, each celestial object's positional and metadata are dynamically integrated into the VR environment, enabling an accurate and interactive representation of the astronomical data. This integration empowers the application with the capability to not only depict celestial bodies in their precise locations but also to associate each with its unique data profile, enriching the user's exploratory and learning experience.

Mathematical Conversion. Unreal Engine 5 (UE5) operates within a Cartesian coordinate system, using X, Y, and Z coordinates to define the positioning of objects in three-dimensional space. This system is fundamental for creating realistic and accurately scaled virtual environments.

To translate the celestial data from the Gaia database into this coordinate system, specific mathematical conversions were required. The raw data from Gaia provides the positions of celestial objects in terms of celestial coordinates, which include right ascension, declination, and parallax. These coordinates are based on spherical geometry and need to be converted to Cartesian coordinates for use in UE5.

Despite the robustness of the Gaia dataset, users should be aware that distances obtained through this method are estimates and subject to potential errors inherent in the parallax inversion process and the assumptions made in the conversion formulas. This approximation serves the project's scope for a feasibility study, but for precise scientific applications, additional error analysis and data validation would be necessary [23].

The process begins by calculating the distance of the celestial object from Earth in parsecs using the formula:

$$Distance(parsecs) = \frac{1}{Parallax(arcseconds)} \tag{1}$$

Once the distance is known, the next step is to convert it into X, Y, and Z components. This conversion involves trigonometric calculations that consider the declination and inclination (right ascension) of the object. The formulas used for this conversion are:

$$X = Distance \times \cos(Declination) \times \cos(Inclination) \tag{2}$$

$$Y = Distance \times \cos(Declination) \times \sin(Inclination) \tag{3}$$

$$Z = Distance \times \sin(Declination) \tag{4}$$

After calculating the distance of a celestial object in parsecs from the inversion of its parallax, this distance is then converted into lightyears by multiplying by a factor of 3.262. This step is crucial as it translates the astronomical distance into a more universally recognized unit. Subsequently, to align with the Unreal Engine 5 (UE5) environment that operates in kilometers, this value in lightyears is further multiplied by 30,856,775,812,800, the number of kilometers in one lightyear. These calculations transform the spherical astronomical coordinates into Cartesian coordinates that can be directly used in the virtual environment of UE5. The data from Gaia, while extensive, was capped at a certain distance to ensure celestial objects remain visible within the application (Fig. 1).

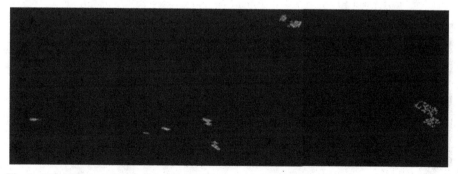

Fig. 1. Visualization of celestial objects with capped distances for enhanced UX, based on Gaia data

Internal Data. This section refers to data on celestial objects within the solar system.

In the exploration of data pertinent to solar system objects, the research uncovered the utility of NASA's Spice Toolkit (NST) [24, 25]. Recognized within the planetary science and engineering communities, NST stands as a comprehensive information system designed to furnish precise observation geometry. It offers custom application programming interfaces (APIs) that facilitate many functionalities, including but not limited to, time system conversions, precise location and orientation of spacecraft and celestial bodies, transformations of reference frames, and calculation of illumination angles. For instance, consider the NST's application in trajectory planning for space missions. The toolkit's sophisticated algorithms enable researchers to input specific parameters for a spacecraft and project its orbital path around celestial bodies. This functionality extends to the anticipation of spacecraft interactions with planetary bodies, such as gravity-assist maneuvers which are critical for interplanetary missions. Such predictive modeling is theoretical and can be dynamically represented in UE5, offering a visual and interactive experience of the mission's potential trajectory within a virtual reality setting. This wealth of high-precision data renders NST an invaluable resource for solar system mapping applications.

The integration of NST with Unreal Engine 5 (UE5) is facilitated through the MaxQ plugin [26]—a wrapper that enables the seamless implementation of NST's computations within UE5's development environment. Whether utilizing UE5's native Blueprint scripting or the more traditional C++ programming, MaxQ empowers developers to incorporate NST data directly into their virtual creations. This synergy between NST and UE5 paves the way for accurate representations of celestial timing and positioning, enriching the application with interactive elements that enhance user engagement and learning. Key data points, including the position, orientation, and scale of solar system objects are extracted using NST, through MaxQ, and brought into virtual reality. This application inclusively models all planets in the solar system, along with the sun and Earth's moon, thereby offering users a comprehensive and interactive exploration of our celestial neighborhood (Fig. 2). This holistic approach underscores the project's aim to enhance user engagement and educational value through precise, dynamic visualizations of solar system objects.

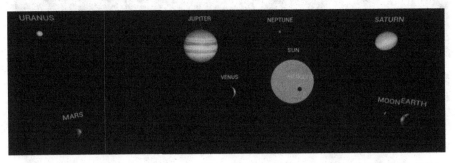

Fig. 2. Representation of solar system objects as integrated using NASA's Spice Toolkit

Differences. Here, it is important to highlight the differences between how external and internal data is treated once within Unreal Engine 5.

The NASA Spice Toolkit (NST) operates on a dynamic data model, forecasting astronomical events based on real-time calculations. For instance, it can predict Earth's relative position to the solar system's barycenter at any given moment. This is a quintessential example of real-time data processing, where predictions are made concurrently with the running application. In stark contrast, external data sources like the Gaia database offer a snapshot perspective. The data from Gaia was collected over a 34-month period, spanning from July 25, 2014, to May 28, 2017. This distinction between real-time predictive data and static historical data is crucial. It influences user interaction with the celestial objects in the VR application and dictates the structural design of the application's framework, enabling users to experience and understand the dynamic nature of celestial mechanics in contrast to the static historical observations.

3.4 Interaction and UX Design

This section delves into the interaction dynamics and user experience (UX) design of the application, focusing on how users engage with the imported astronomical data.

Current Interactive Elements. The application incorporates four key interactive elements, each tailored to enhance the user's exploratory experience within the virtual environment. These elements, detailed below, are currently applicable to internal celestial objects due to specific constraints, which will be elaborated on subsequently.

Teleportation. Activated through a tablet-like interface in the VR space, this feature enables users to instantaneously travel to any celestial object within the simulation. For instance, selecting 'Earth' transports the user to its virtual location. This element effectively addresses VR's inherent limitation of physical space, allowing expansive exploration within a confined area.

Scale Manipulation. Accessible via the same interface, this feature empowers users to adjust the solar system's scale through a slider mechanism. By sliding left or right, the user can alter the solar system's size from smaller to larger scales. This tool is invaluable for comprehending the relative sizes and distances of celestial bodies, offering a tangible sense of the vastness of space.

Time Manipulation. Also housed within the interaction window, this function grants users control over the temporal frame of the solar system. Leveraging the NST's real-time data computations, this feature allows users to select a reference time, prompting NST to calculate and display the current or future positions and orientations of celestial bodies. With three distinct modes of time manipulation, users can either observe significant time shifts or focus on more minute temporal changes. This dynamic exploration tool enables users to witness the motion of planets in their orbits and other celestial phenomena in a three-dimensional space.

Highlighting. By directing the controller towards a celestial object, users can activate a detailed information panel adjacent to the selected object. This panel provides comprehensive details about the object, including descriptive metadata. This feature enriches the user's experience by offering in-depth insights into each celestial body they choose to examine.

These interactive elements are designed not only for engagement but also for educational enrichment, allowing users to gain a deeper understanding of astronomical concepts through direct manipulation and exploration. By providing these tools, the application fosters a more immersive and informative experience, enhancing the user's connection with the vastness of space and the intricacies of our solar system.

User-Centered Design Approach. This approach emphasizes understanding the users' needs, preferences, and limitations to create an experience that is both intuitive and engaging (Fig. 3).

Teleportation was designed to address VR's spatial constraints. Recognizing that physical movement in VR is limited, this feature allows users to navigate vast cosmic distances effortlessly, thus overcoming a fundamental challenge in virtual space exploration.

Scale manipulation responds to the educational need to comprehend the relative sizes and distances in space, which are often difficult to grasp. This tool empowers users to adjust the scale of the solar system, facilitating a hands-on understanding of astronomical scales, and bringing abstract concepts to life.

Time manipulation enables users to interact with celestial dynamics over time, a key aspect in understanding astronomical phenomena. This feature not only enhances the immersive experience but also serves an educational purpose by allowing users to observe and comprehend the movement of celestial bodies and their positional changes over time.

Highlighting was incorporated to satisfy the curiosity-driven nature of learning. By providing detailed information about celestial objects on demand, this feature supports exploratory learning, allowing users to delve deeper into subjects of interest.

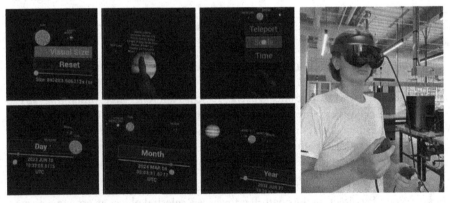

Fig. 3. User Interface with VR headset and motion controllers.

Impact on Learning and Engagement. The interactive features of the application significantly enhance its educational value.

Teleportation engages users by making space exploration accessible and exciting, encouraging exploration and discovery.

Scale manipulation offers a practical tool for visual learning, helping users visualize and understand the vastness of space and the relative sizes of celestial bodies—concepts often challenging to convey through traditional educational methods.

Time manipulation provides an interactive way to understand celestial mechanics. By observing the movement of planets and other celestial bodies over different time frames, users gain a dynamic understanding of the solar system, fostering a deeper grasp of astronomical concepts.

Highlighting enhances engagement by catering to the user's immediate curiosity. It serves as an on-demand educational resource, enabling users to learn more about specific celestial objects, thereby supporting individualized learning paths.

Overall, these interactive elements enrich the learning experience by fostering an environment of exploration and active participation. They encourage users to engage deeply with the content, leading to a more profound understanding of complex astronomical concepts, and enhancing the overall educational impact of the application.

4 Discussion

4.1 Implications and Challenges

In reviewing the development, architecture, and user experience of the VR application created in this research, several key implications and challenges emerge:

Data Integration Complexity. The process of integrating data into the application has proven to be highly context dependent. Databases, particularly in astronomy, exhibit a diverse range of structures and formats. This diversity necessitates a tailored approach for effective cross-integration within each specific application context. In this project, the distinction between 'external' and 'internal' data sources required meticulous development to ensure seamless integration. The foundational principle for data validity in this context hinged on the commonality of three-dimensional spatial representation, allowing for the unique projection of each data point within Unreal Engine 5 (UE5).

Technological Limitations and Opportunities. UE5, while a powerful tool, imposes limitations on the number of objects that can be simultaneously represented in a spatial environment. Considering the extensive scope of the Gaia database, which contains over 2 billion objects, the limitation to approximately 5000 objects through instanced meshes poses a significant challenge. Alternative, more optimized approaches, such as using UE5's Niagara particle system, may offer viable solutions for representing large-scale data in future project phases.

User Experience and Learning Engagement. The interactive elements integrated into the VR application significantly enhance user engagement, aligning with the principles of cross-modal processing. The application's immersive environment offers an innovative approach to learning, potentially transforming traditional educational methods. An initial comparative study to assess the application's effectiveness against conventional teaching methods in astronomy education was envisaged. However, time constraints precluded this analysis within the current research phase. Future studies focusing on this comparative analysis could provide empirical evidence on the impact of VR in educational settings, offering insights into its pedagogical efficacy.

Preliminary User Feedback and Future Directions. Early user feedback indicates high levels of engagement and interest in the application, which may be attributed to the novelty of VR or other factors. Without a formal evaluation in an educational context, definitive conclusions about the application's impact on learning outcomes remain elusive. However, this initial response suggests a promising direction for future research. Future studies should focus on evaluating the application's effectiveness in enhancing learning outcomes and user engagement, potentially harnessing VR's novelty to elevate the educational experience.

In conclusion, while this research has laid a strong foundation in developing a VR application for astronomical education, it opens avenues for further exploration in understanding the full implications of immersive learning technologies in educational settings.

5   Future Work and Direction

As this research project progresses into its next phases, several areas of future work have been identified, each presenting opportunities to enhance the application's capabilities and impact. These areas can be categorized into immediate priorities and broader, exploratory objectives.

5.1   Immediate Priorities

Evaluating Educational and Visualization Effectiveness. A critical next step involves empirically assessing the application's impact in educational settings and its effectiveness in astronomical visualization. This evaluation could include studies comparing the VR application's learning outcomes against traditional teaching methods, focusing on user engagement, comprehension, and retention of astronomical concepts.

Optimization of Data Representation. Improving the application's ability to handle and display large datasets, such as those from Gaia, is essential. This includes enhancing data processing efficiency and exploring more effective visualization techniques for representing vast numbers of celestial objects.

Enhanced Interaction with Imported Data. Developing methods to allow interactive engagement with imported data, such as that from Gaia, will enrich the user experience. This could include features that enable users to query, manipulate, and explore this data dynamically within the VR environment.

Expansion of Interactive Elements. Introducing more comprehensive and diverse interactive elements can significantly improve the application's educational and exploratory value. This includes tools for data analysis, simulation controls, and narrative-driven educational experiences.

Incorporating Story-Driven Teaching. Utilizing narrative techniques and story-driven approaches to present astronomical concepts can enhance user engagement and make learning more impactful and memorable.

Upgrading Graphical Fidelity for Immersion. Investing in higher-quality graphics and more detailed visualizations will enhance the overall immersion and realism of the virtual environment, making the educational experience more compelling.

5.2 Broader, Exploratory Objectives

Integration of a ChatGPT Bot Helper. Incorporating an AI assistant like ChatGPT [27], which users can interact with via voice commands and receive responses through text-to-speech, would add a new dimension of interactivity and support within the application.

Exploring AR/MR Integration. Expanding beyond VR, integrating augmented reality (AR) and mixed reality (MR) could offer alternative ways of experiencing and interacting with astronomical data. This could involve overlaying celestial data onto physical environments or blending virtual and real-world elements.

These future directions aim to not only refine and expand the current capabilities of the VR application but also to explore new frontiers in interactive learning, user engagement, and data visualization within the realms of education and astronomy.

6   Conclusion

This research project embarked on a journey to harness the transformative power of Virtual Reality (VR) in the realm of education and astronomy. By developing a multidisciplinary immersive VR software tool, the project aimed to revolutionize how celestial data is visualized and interacted with, thereby enhancing the learning experience in educational and astronomical studies.

Throughout this journey, the project navigated the complexities of integrating vast astronomical datasets, like those from Gaia, into an interactive VR environment. This integration was pivotal in creating an immersive platform where users could engage with celestial objects, experiencing the vastness of space in a tangible and meaningful way. The development process underscored the necessity of a tailored approach to data integration, emphasizing the uniqueness of each dataset and its requirements for effective visualization.

The Unreal Engine 5 (UE5) served as the backbone of this endeavor, providing the necessary tools and frameworks to bring celestial data to life in a virtual space. Integrating the NASA Spice Toolkit (NST) via the MaxQ plugin further augmented the application, allowing for precise and dynamic representations of celestial objects within the solar system.

The VR application, enhanced by its interactive elements like teleportation, scale manipulation, time manipulation, and highlighting, successfully bridged the gap between complex astronomical concepts and user-friendly educational tools. These features were not only instrumental in enhancing user engagement but also played a crucial role in fostering a deeper understanding of astronomical phenomena.

Reflecting on the project's journey, it is evident that the application has set a strong foundation for future exploration in immersive educational technologies. The initial user feedback has been promising, indicating high levels of engagement and interest.

However, a formal evaluation in an educational context remains a future goal and is vital for understanding the full impact of this VR tool on learning outcomes.

Looking ahead, the project has outlined several avenues for future work. These include empirical studies to assess the educational effectiveness of the application, optimization of data representation for larger datasets, expansion of interactive elements, and exploration of narrative-driven teaching methods. Additionally, the integration of technologies like ChatGPT and the expansion into Augmented Reality (AR) and Mixed Reality (MR) realms hold the potential to further revolutionize the user experience.

In conclusion, this research has not only demonstrated the feasibility of integrating complex astronomical data into an immersive VR environment but also opened the door to a new era of interactive learning. The journey of this project highlights the endless possibilities that lie at the intersection of technology, education, and space science, inspiring future endeavors in these dynamic fields.

Acknowledgments. This study was funded by the University of Cincinnati Space Research Institute for Discovery and Exploration (SRIDE). We want to thank the guidance received from Prof. Matthew Bayliss and Prof. Colin Bischoff, and various feedback from participants of 2023 Undergraduate Scholarly Showcase at the University of Cincinnati.

This work has made use of data from the European Space Agency (ESA) mission Gaia (https://www.cosmos.esa.int/gaia), processed by the Gaia Data Processing and Analysis Consortium (DPAC, https://www.cosmos.esa.int/web/gaia/dpac/consortium). Funding for the DPAC has been provided by national institutions, in particular the institutions participating in the Gaia Multilateral Agreement.

Disclosure of Interests. The authors have no competing interests to declare that are relevant to the content of this article.

References

1. Zawacki-Richter, O., Latchem, C.: Exploring four decades of research in computers and education. Comp. Educ. **122**, 136–152 (2018). https://doi.org/10.1016/j.compedu.2018.04.001
2. Bergsteiner, H., Avery, G.C.: The twin-cycle experiential learning model: reconceptualising Kolb's theory. Stud. Contin. Educ. **36**(3), 257–274 (2014). https://doi.org/10.1080/0158037X.2014.904782
3. Aslaksen, K., Lorås, H.: The modality-specific learning style hypothesis: a mini-review. Front. Psychol. **9**, 1538 (2018). https://doi.org/10.3389/fpsyg.2018.01538
4. Makransky, G., Petersen, G.B.: The cognitive affective model of immersive learning (CAMIL): a theoretical research-based model of learning in immersive virtual reality. Educ. Psychol. Rev. **33**, 937–958 (2021). https://doi.org/10.1007/s10648-020-09586-2
5. Rauschnabel, P.A., Felix, R., Hinsch, C., Shahab, H., Alt, F.: What is XR? Towards a framework for augmented and virtual reality. Comput. Hum. Behav. **133**, 107289 (2022). https://doi.org/10.1016/j.chb.2022.107289
6. Rubio-Tamayo, J., Barrio, M.G., García, F.G.: Immersive environments and virtual reality: systematic review and advances in communication, interaction and simulation. Multimodal Technolo. Interact. **1**(4), 21 (2017). https://doi.org/10.3390/mti1040021

7. El Beheiry, M., Doutreligne, S., Caporal, C., Ostertag, C., Dahan, M., Masson, J.-B.: Virtual reality: beyond visualization. J. Mol. Biol. **431**(7), 1315–1321 (2019). https://doi.org/10.1016/j.jmb.2019.01.033

8. Çöltekin, A., et al.: Extended reality in spatial sciences: a review of research challenges and future directions. ISPRS Int. J. Geo-Inf. **9**(7), 439 (2020). https://doi.org/10.3390/ijgi9070439

9. Mintz, R., Litvak, S., Yair, Y.: 3D-Virtual reality in science education : an implication for astronomy teaching, J. Comput. Math. Sci. Teach., vol. 20, no. 3, pp. 293–305, (2001). Retrieved Feb 1, 2024, from https://www.learntechlib.org/primary/p/9543/

10. Barnett, M.: Using virtual reality computer models to support student understanding of astronomical concepts," J. Comput. Math. Sci. Teach., vol. 24, no. 4, pp. 333–356, (2005). Retrieved Feb 1, 2024, from https://www.learntechlib.org/primary/p/6025/

11. Cecotti, H.: A serious game in fully immersive virtual reality for teaching astronomy based on the messier catalog, In Proceeding of the 8th International Conference of the Immersive Learning Research Network (iLRN), Vienna, Austria, pp. 1–7, (2022), doi: https://doi.org/10.23919/iLRN55037.2022.9815994

12. Meta Platforms, Inc., Meta Quest 2 Virtual Reality Headset (2020)

13. Epic Games, Unreal Engine 5.1 [Software], (2022). Available at: https://www.unrealengine.com. Accessed 11 Nov 2022

14. Vohera, C., Chheda, H., Chouhan, D., Desai, A., Jain, V.: Game engine architecture and comparative study of different game engines In 2021 12th International Conference on Computing Communication and Netwoking Technologies, pp. 1–6, (2021). https://doi.org/10.1109/ICCCNT51525.2021.9579618

15. Lambru, C., Morar, A., Moldoveanu, F., Asavei, V., Moldoveanu, A.: Comparative analysis of real-time global illumination techniques in current game engines. IEEE Access **9**, 125158–125183 (2021). https://doi.org/10.1109/ACCESS.2021.3109663

16. Jabbari, R. bin Ali, N. Petersen, K. Tanveer, B.: What is DevOps? A systematic mapping study on definitions and practices, In Procedings of the Science. Workshop Proc. of XP2016, Edinburgh, Scotland, UK, Art. No. 12, pp. 1–11, (2016). https://doi.org/10.1145/2962695.2962707

17. Prusti, T., et al.: The Gaia mission, Astron. Astrophys., vol. 595, A1, pp. 1–36, Nov. (2016). https://doi.org/10.1051/0004-6361/201629272

18. Gaia Collaboration, A.G.A., et al.: Gaia early data release 3. Summary of the contents and survey properties (Corrigendum), Astron. Astrophys., vol. 650, C3, pp. 1–7, June (2021). https://doi.org/10.1051/0004-6361/202039657e

19. Babusiaux, C., et al.: Gaia data release 3: catalogue validation. Astron. Astrophys. **674**, A32 (2023). https://doi.org/10.1051/0004-6361/202243790

20. The Sloan Digital Sky Survey, (2023). https://www.sdss4.org/, Accessed 31/1/2023

21. Dark Energy Survey, (2023). https://www.darkenergysurvey.org/, Accessed 31/1/2023

22. Budavári, T., Szalay, A.S.: Probabilistic cross-identification of astronomical sources. Astrophys. J. **679**, 301–309 (2008). https://doi.org/10.1086/587156

23. Bailer-Jones, C.A.L.: Estimating distances from parallaxes. Publ. Astron. Soc. Pac. **127**(956), 994 (2015). https://doi.org/10.1086/683116

24. Acton, C.H.: Ancillary data services of NASA's navigation and ancillary information facility. Planet. Space Sci. **44**(1), 65–70 (1996). https://doi.org/10.1016/0032-0633(95)00107-7

25. Charles Acton, N., et al.: A look toward the future in the handling of space science mission geometry," Planet. Space Sci., (2017). https://doi.org/10.1016/j.pss.2017.02.013

26. Gamergenic, MaxQ: Spaceflight Toolkit for Unreal Engine 5, (2022). Available at: https://www.gamergenic.com/project/maxq/. Accessed: 2/1/23

27. OpenAI, ChatGPT (Jan 10 version) [Large language model], (2024). Available at: https://chat.openai.com

VR-Enhanced Teleoperation System for a Semi-autonomous Mulitplatform All-Terrain Exploration Vehicle

Daniel Scholl[✉] , Jannis Meier , and Michael Reke

The Mobile Autonomous Systems and Cognitive Robotics Institute,
FH Aachen University of Applied Science, Aachen, Germany
{d.scholl,meier,reke}@fh-aachen.de

Abstract. This paper presents a research on the integration of a virtual reality (VR) enhanced teleoperation system within the semi-autonomous multi-platform all-terrain exploration vehicle (MAEV). The main objective is to improve the operator's control and situational awareness when exploring difficult terrain. The methodology includes an in-depth analysis of the MAEV project, describing the configuration of the teleoperation system and careful VR integration processes.

In the section on system development and implementation, the details of the step-by-step construction of the VR-based teleoperation system and the MAEV vehicle are explained. This includes the careful selection of VR hardware, the harmonization of VR with the control systems of the MAEV, and the resolution of challenges encountered during the integration process.

The key findings highlight the benefits of the VR system, such as increased immersion for operators, improved precision in remote control, increased safety through remote operation in hazardous environments and the potential for realistic training and simulation scenarios. These findings contribute significantly to the further development of teleoperation systems, especially in the context of all-terrain vehicles.

Keywords: teleoperation · remote control · telepresence · virtual reality · collaborative control · HMI · behaviour planner · Robot Operating System (ROS2) · semi-autonomous · UGV

1 Introduction

Many areas within open pit mines and underground mines are hard and dangerous to reach for human workers, because the occupational safety can not be guaranteed, the environment is polluted or the spatial access is limited. Potential areas of application include rough terrain, mining above and below ground, climate, environmental and occupational safety and construction sites.

As an alternative in this paper we will present a versatile teleoperated, semi-autonomous exploration vehicle with modular platforms to reach such areas to

© The Author(s), under exclusive license to Springer Nature Switzerland AG 2024
J. Y. C. Chen and G. Fragomeni (Eds.): HCII 2024, LNCS 14708, pp. 268–285, 2024.
https://doi.org/10.1007/978-3-031-61047-9_18

fulfill different tasks. The modular platform aims to include robotic arm-powered sampling, drone-assisted exploration, enhancing resource efficiency via digitization and monitoring parameters related to climate, environment, and occupational safety as well. For the vehicle we examined different types of feedback for improved teleoperation performance. In particular, the focus is on the question of whether the integration of virtual reality (VR) provides added value for teleoperation. The work was realised within the public funded project MAEV[1] (Mulitplatform All-Terrain Exploration Vehicle). Figure 1 shows the vehicle with the sampling module attached.

Fig. 1. MAEV vehicle equipped with the sampling module

First, the requirements and the concept for such a vehicle are developed. The design of the vehicle and the implementation of the software in the vehicle and on the teleoperation stand are then described in detail. Finally, various test scenarios are carried out to validate the entire system with the VR extension.

2   State of the Art

While the level of autonomy in vehicles and robots continues increasingly, there is also growing awareness of the value of manual teleoperation. Especially when dealing with challenging tasks or operating vehicles in unfamiliar environments. A combination of manually controlled and autonomous vehicles results in a teleoperated semi-autonomous vehicle [11]. The vehicle assists the operator in control through its own actions. However, the tasks performed by the vehicle are

[1] Funded by the German Federal Ministry of Education and Research, 033RK086D.

less extensive than those of autonomous systems. The focus of semi-autonomous teleoperation is more on collaboration between the operator and the vehicle. So that each side can carry out independent tasks that contribute to better task fulfillment. The operator's situational awareness is a crucial key factor for the effective operation of the remotely operated vehicle [3,5]. This means that the operator must receive good feedback from the vehicle about its current location, surroundings, current movement, and future movement [7]. The VR supported teleoperation was investigated in various papers for different applications [4,6,9,10] using different kind of interfaces [1,8]. The immersion of the operator within the teleoperated application can be described by the telepresence, which is defined in [2].

The innovation of this project is the development of a teleoperation system for a modular vehicle with an additional VR system to improve the environmental awareness and telepresence.

3   Requirements and Concept

The tracked vehicle must meet the requirements of an underground operation within a mine. The control should be possible from a distance via a teleoperation stand. To ensure the safety and functionality of the overall system, there are various requirements. The tracked vehicle is designed to be configurable for three different modules. This leads to different areas of application and boundary conditions for the teleoperation system. In the following, the requirements are first generally related to the vehicle and the control system and then tailored to the individual boundary conditions by the modules.

3.1   Teleoperation Stand and Vehicle

The teleoperation stand must provide the teleoperator with information in order to assess the tracked vehicle's surroundings. For this purpose, a camera stream is set up from the vehicle to the teleoperation stand. The teleoperator has the option of using an output system, such as monitors or virtual reality glasses, to capture the vehicle's surroundings and react to them. This requires a good network connection between the vehicle and the teleoperation stand. As this interface is essential for the teleoperated operation of the vehicle, this connection must be continuously monitored from both sides. The system must react to delays or failures in the connection. If the connection between the teleoperation station and the vehicle fails, the vehicle must switch to a safe state. If the delay in transmission increases, operation via the teleoperation stand must also be adapted. To ensure safe operation, the teleoperator must always be able to stop the vehicle in sufficient time, even if the image data or the control command to be executed arrives with a delay. Depending on the delay, warnings are displayed on the screen for the teleoperator or control commands are restricted. If the latency is too long, the vehicle must have partially automated operation. In addition, the tracked vehicle will have its own collision detection and will over-write or not implement the teleoperator's control command in the event of an imminent collision with the surroundings. The teleoperator is given the option of deactivating this function if it is recognized that the collision avoidance system has made an incorrect assumption. For semi-automated operation, the vehicle uses its environment sensors to create a map of its surroundings and localizes itself within this map. The created map of the environment should be displayed in a 3D environment, so that the teleoperator has the possibility to view the created map in a more immersive presence and make better decisions regarding navigation. VR glasses will be used to view the environment.

3.2   Sampling Module

The sampling module has a robotic arm. This arm should be able to collect samples in the form of drill holes. This situation places further requirements on the vehicle and its navigation by the teleoperator. The vehicle must know that the Sampling module is in use. The robot arm extension changes the geometry of the overall system. The control of the vehicle via the teleoperation system will also change due to the different center of mass. The teleoperation must be adapted to this change. The previously mentioned collision avoidance must also be adapted to the situation. Approaching a wall to take a sample must not be avoided. However, the system is not switched off, but adapted to the situation. When approaching a wall, a reduced speed is permitted depending on the distance. In addition, the vehicle and the robot arm will exchange information about the current status of the system. The vehicle must not be authorized to move as long as the robot arm is moving. In contrast, the robot arm must not move if the vehicle is in motion. The teleoperator is given the opportunity to form a picture of the environment by virtually mapping the system and transmitting the camera stream. The mapping of the environment allows the environment can also be viewed retrospectively using VR glasses. This will help the teleoperator to determine the location of the sample.

3.3   Monitor Module

Monitor module: The monitor module is equipped with measurement technology for the environment and a landing platform for a monitoring drone. The mea-surement technology should display the various environmental parameters in a meaningful way for the teleoperator. With regard to the landing platform for the drone, the vehicle must be able to recognize the orientation of the platform and react to it. The vehicle either aligns itself or refuses to land the drone if the inclination is above a defined threshold value.

3.4   Rescue Module

The rescue module is used to transport people. In this mode, the vehicle should only have a limited speed. While the rescue module is in use, the preferred control of the vehicle should be via an external remote control and not via the teleoperation station. This serves to protect the person on the stretcher, but also the people in the vicinity of the Rescue Module. The Rescue Module.

3.5 Hardware Concept

The following illustration shows the underlying hardware concept. The teleoperation stand is equipped with high-performance hardware to meet the graphical requirements for mapping the environment. Three monitors are used for the graphical output to provide a good overview. VR glasses are also used to analyze how such a system can help the teleoperator. A stick controller from the flight simulator sector is used to control the tracked vehicle via the teleoperation stand. Stick controllers offer the advantage of many degrees of freedom and are therefore often used in the construction sector. The stick controller will have two separate thrust controls to enable the vehicle's tracks to be controlled separately. In addition, various buttons and switches must be available that can be assigned individual functions, such as switching lights on and off. VR controllers with tracking sensors are used to extend the operation of the vehicle via the VR goggles. These controllers make it possible to interact with the virtually generated world and, for example, set target coordinates or paths for the tracked vehicle. For the connection to the tracked vehicle, an outdoor WLAN access point is used to achieve the necessary range (Fig. 2).

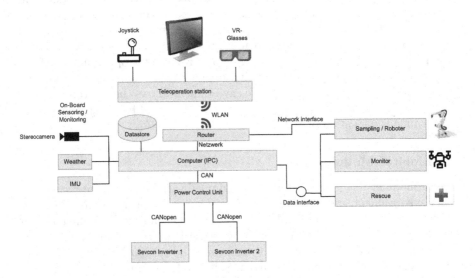

Fig. 2. Hardware concept

The following list shows the selection of the main components for the implementation of vehicle navigation. When selecting the computers, particular attention was paid to performance. The ZBOX for the vehicle and the Magnus One for the teleoperation stand have sufficient processor and graphics performance to perform the software calculations. The ZED2 from Stereolabs is used as a stereo camera for the front and rear of the vehicle. The factory-calibrated stereo lenses enable distortion-free images. These are used to calculate and map a spatial image of the surroundings. Two Dell monitors are used to provide a good overview at the teleoperation stand. The output is enhanced with Vive Pro2 VR glasses. This will make it possible to display the mapped environment for the teleoperator in retrospect. Two WLAN access points from Mikrotik will establish a secure connection between the teleoperation stand and the vehicle.

Description	Manufacturer	Item
1x Teleoperation stand computer	Zotac	MAGNUS ONE ECM
1x vehicle computer	Zotac	ZBOX QK7P3000
2x Front and rear camera	Stereolabs	ZED2
2x WLAN access points	Mikrotik	OmniTIK5ac
3x Teleoperation stand monitor	Dell	S2721HN
1x Stick Controller	Logitech	G X56
1x VR-glasses with tracking controller	HTC	Vive Pro 2

3.6   Software Concept

In order to design the software for the overall system, we must first determine the basis on which the software can be developed. The functional software must be developed for a total of three system components. The three components are the teleoperation station, the navigation computer and the drive control unit. The drive control unit is an embedded controller with an HSC08 chip that is programmed in C90. The navigation computer and the teleoperation computer are X86 computers. Ubuntu was selected as the operating system for the navigation computer and Windows for the teleoperation computer. For the development of the software, the framework to be used was initially selected depending on the requirements. Operation with a teleoperation stand and a vehicle involves several computer systems. For this reason, the Robot Operating System 2 (ROS2) is used as the underlying framework. The framework offers the possibility of quickly and efficiently establishing UDP-based communication between different computers via an API. The Unity graphics engine was chosen for the graphical representation in the teleoperation stand. This engine offers a direct ROS2 connection and can also be extended with additional plug-ins. Once the frameworks had been determined, a software architecture was developed to meet all the specified requirements. This is shown schematically in the following figure. The graphic can be divided into two parts. The upper part shows the software architecture of the teleoperation stand with Unity and the ROS2 interface. The lower, larger block represents the software architecture of the base vehicle. These are now considered separately (Fig. 3).

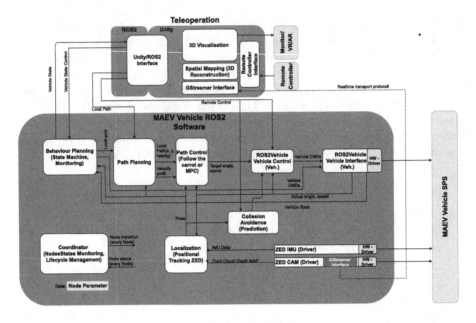

Fig. 3. Software architecture

Base Vehicle. The individual blocks, hereinafter referred to as nodes (ROS2 terminology), are now described in more detail. The "ROS2Vehicle Interface" is located on the right-hand side of the MAEV Vehicle ROS2 software. This interface controls the driver for CAN communication and represents a mapping of the vehicle commands to the CAN side. On the one hand, commands are sent for vehicle control and on the other hand, status and sensor values are received from the drive control unit. The "ZED CAM (Driver)" and "ZED IMU (Driver)" nodes represent further interfaces to the base vehicle. The camera driver node is responsible for capturing the video streams from the individual lenses of the stereo cameras. It also calculates a 3D point cloud from the stereo information in order to generate an environment model of the vehicle's surroundings. A special feature is an additional connection to the teleoperation computer via the real-time transport protocol (RTP). In a proof of concept test, it was established that the ROS2 framework is not suitable for the transmission of image data in teleoperated mode. The image data had a big time delay, even under ideal connection conditions. To solve this problem, the RTP protocol is used via the GStreamer API. Many configuration parameters allow this stream to be configured without interruption. This allows us to reduce the resolution and thus increase the throughput if the delay times, which have to be measured continuously, degrade. The quality of the image becomes blurrier in the teleoperation state, but the time delay is greatly reduced. This option is also used for the vehicle's driving dynamics. This means that the resolution of the video stream is reduced at higher speeds, thus increasing the number of images per second. The

ZED2 stereo cameras have integrated IMU sensors. These are used to monitor the acceleration and orientation of the vehicle and react to this depending on the operating mode. This is implemented in the "ZED IMU (Driver)" node.

Once a 3D point cloud has been generated from the stereo images, it is further processed in the "Localization" node. The 3D point cloud represents an image of the environment from the perspective of the stereo cameras at a fixed point in time. This means that each stereo camera only records a part of the environment. In the "Localization" node, these point clouds are initially assembled according to fixed time intervals. After each additional measurement, this accumulation of point clouds is further added. This creates a mapping of the surroundings. The IMU values from the "ZED IMU (Driver)" node support the composition of the individual point clouds by providing information on the orientation and movement of the vehicle. While the mapping is continuously added and corrected, the most recent point cloud measurement value can be used to localize itself in this mapping. This process is also known as SLAM for Simultaneous Localization and Mapping.

The "Collision Avoidance" node picks up the data from the surroundings and uses a size model of the vehicle to avoid imminent collisions with the surroundings. In teleoperated mode, the module uses the control commands of the teleoperator and the delay times of the connection to assess whether the control is compatible with collision avoidance. If a collision is imminent, the teleoperator commands are overwritten.

The control and implementation of the control commands on the individual tracks is implemented in the "ROS2Vehicle - Vehicle Control" node. A vehicle model for a chain drive is used for this in order to convert the control inputs to the drive in a meaningful way. The control of the individual chains is then sent to the Vehicle Interface Module after a plausibility check of the data.

In certain cases, it may not be possible for the teleoperator to control the vehicle directly. For example, the delay time of the image and control data during transmission is too long. In this case, another option is for the teleoperator to define a target point in the vicinity of the vehicle. The vehicle can then calculate a suitable path to this point and, if the teleoperator agrees to this path, follow it. These functions are implemented in the "Path Planning" and "Path Control" nodes.

The last module, "Behavior Planning", contains the vehicle's logic. Depending on the state of the vehicle, a decision must be made here as to whether the vehicle is released for driving or whether it must remain stationary because, for example, a drilling operation is taking place. This node also reconfigures various parameters depending on the modules. As described in the specifications, for example, the speed of the vehicle must be reduced if a person is being transported with the rescue module. This means that the module must monitor the entire status information of the vehicle and react accordingly.

The "Coordinator" is being developed to ensure additional monitoring of the individual nodes. This manages the individual nodes and monitors the cycle times of the individual connections between the nodes. If a threshold value is exceeded, the coordinator can prevent the vehicle from being controlled.

Teleoperation Stand. The software for the teleoperation stand is developed with the Unity engine. A Unity/ROS2 interface makes it possible to obtain all the vehicle's status data via an existing network connection. Control commands can also be sent to the vehicle via this connection. The control commands are fed into the software via the G X56 control element from Logitech. Sensible mapping of the axes and control elements ensures the best possible implementation of the control system on the tracked vehicle. Several views are available to the teleoperator. On the one hand the video streams from the stereo cameras and on the other hand a 3D reconstructed virtual world from the video stream data. The Unity Engine uses the Spatial Mapping algorithm for this. This puts the individual image data as textures over the mapped point cloud and creates a 3D model of the environment. The teleoperator can move freely in this 3D model without having to control the vehicle. This opens up exciting new fields of application. For example, measurement data of the surroundings can be visually linked to the respective location. The teleoperator can use this technology with VR glasses to select a nearby destination for the vehicle, for example, and the vehicle drives to this point semi-automatically. Further possibilities arise in combination with the various modules. The teleoperator will be able to select and mark positions for drill holes in walls and floors more easily.

As in the basic vehicle, Unity is equipped with a Gstreamer interface for the real-time transport protocol. This enables the video stream to be received and the teleoperation station has the option of configuring the stereo cameras. The video stream is displayed with an overlay for controlling the vehicle. This overlay offers the option of making settings for the vehicle or the sensors via menu navigation. A typical problem with a transmitted video stream is the estimation of sizes. The user of the teleoperation stand finds it difficult to estimate whether the vehicle will fit through the tunnel or not. For this reason, the system has been enhanced with auxiliary lines. The guide lines are calibrated and display the width and height of the vehicle. The distance to objects in front of the camera can also be read off.

To enable more precise control using the joystick, a colored circle is also displayed in the video stream. This circle indicates the current position or target for steering. This serves as an aid for steering execution.

4 System Development and Implementation

In the following, the realization of the teleoperation stand is explained first. The control system and the graphic visualization are described. It is then shown how the control system was improved by mapping the surroundings and how the communication between the vehicle and the teleoperation stand was set up.

Control of Teleoperation Stand and Graphical User Interface: A joystick, which is often used in flight simulations, was selected to control the vehicle via the teleoperator station. The advantage lies in the high number of degrees of freedom. Since the MAEV vehicle has differential drive kinematics, the joystick can be better used for control.

The Fig. 4 shows the control and its assignment. The pure joystick on the right-hand side is used for the steering and turning movements of the vehicle. The kinematics make it possible to move the vehicle to the right or left on the spot by moving the joystick to the right or left. The throttle lever on the left-hand side allows the vehicle to be set to a basic speed. The position of the throttle lever is assigned to a speed in m/s and sent to the drive control unit, which regulates the specified speed.

If the teleoperator wishes to limit the maximum speed of the vehicle, a rotary control below the throttle lever can be used for this purpose. This has proven to be particularly useful in narrow sections.

First, the various driving modes are selected using the 3-way switch at the bottom left. The top position is "safe mode", in which no control commands are passed on to the vehicle. This is followed by the middle position for "manual mode", which enables direct control of the vehicle. The lowest position is intended for "extended semi-autonomous mode". This enables indirect control of the vehicle by allowing the vehicle to drive specified short sections independently.

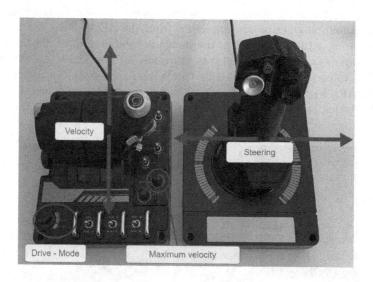

Fig. 4. Joystick

Figure 5 shows the overlay for the camera's video stream. This is intended to give the teleoperator a better overview of the status of the vehicle and its surroundings via menus and additional information displayed.

Initially, two camera perspectives are displayed. The middle main display shows the camera image of the left lens of the real stereo camera. At the top right, the 3rd person orbit camera is displayed, which moves with the vehicle and can be rotated around the vehicle by holding down the left mouse button and dragging the mouse.

The windows with the red title bars can be shown and hidden using the corresponding buttons in the title and footer bar. They can also be moved freely on the interface. The camera settings window allows changes to be made at runtime. Particular attention should be paid to the "Exposure" setting, as this contributes to a longer display delay.

Spatial mapping enables the creation of a colored point cloud of the environment. This can also be paused and resumed by starting it again. "Hide" allows you to temporarily hide the point cloud. Recording continues in the background even in hidden mode. The red and gray distance lines in the middle of the main camera are projected onto the camera image of the real stereo camera. The red dot in the center of the screen represents the deflection of the joystick to the right or left. On the one hand, this helps to estimate the size of the steering command and, on the other, together with the fixed green dot in the middle of the screen, it provides a kind of "manual" tracking control. On the left-hand side, the deflection of the throttle lever is displayed as a percentage. The center position is 0%, upwards to 100% and downwards to -100%. Additional status information is displayed in the header and footer. The values: camera model, resolution used, depth and sensing mode used, camera connection status, tracking status and spatial mapping status are requested from the ZED SDK. The latency is measured using a timestamp when the image is created and a timestamp when the image arrives. The current network transmission rate and signal strength of the routers to each other is queried by the WLAN router via the corresponding MikroTik API. Figure 6 shows the entire teleoperation station. The teleoperator uses the joystick in front of the monitors to control the vehicle. The monitor on

Fig. 5. Graphical user interface of the teleoperation station (Color figure online)

Fig. 6. Teleoperation station with VR and digital twin of the vehicle

the right side shows the main display for driving the vehicle. It consists of the live video feed overlaid with additional information and auxiliary lines for better depth perception. The leftmost monitor displays the mapped and explored area of the environment as a colorized pointcloud with the digital twin localized in it.

Another option for experiencing the virtual replication of the real world is provided by using the VR headset. This enables the user to immerse in the environment and examine additional details.

Fig. 7. Precise control of the MAEV on a garage door

Localization and Environment Mapping: Simple teleoperation is theoretically also possible without a localization system of the vehicle, but localization opens up some additional possibilities to optimize the teleoperation experience. For example, the extension of partial autonomy through indirect control. Because only if the vehicle can localize itself in the "world" can it also follow a predefined path independently. The "Spatial Mapping" process allows a map of the surroundings to be generated via the stereo camera using vision algorithms and the integrated IMU sensor. In addition, the camera and thus also the vehicle localize themselves within this map. By mapping and localizing in real time, a MAEV model can be superimposed on the current position as a digital twin. This has the advantage that the user can use this information to steer the vehicle more precisely. For example, in Fig. 7, the MAEV vehicle is steered precisely into the vicinity of a garage door.

5   Evaluation

The previous chapters have shown that the development of a teleoperated semi-autonomous tracked vehicle with a VR interface is highly complex. The validation of the entire system is based in particular on predefined test scenarios that are conducted by different people for each scenario. This makes it possible to use the user experience through the control with extended VR interface to evaluate the overall system. The following test scenarios were carried out for the evaluation.

Digital Twin and Mapping: In this scenario, the MAEV was controlled by two people. The actual teleoperator and another person who used the VR glasses to analyze the recorded environment. The teleoperator used the joystick to drive the vehicle through the environment. The second person observed how the spatial mapping generated the 3D environment and was able to provide assistance to the teleoperator if a part of the environment was not mapped correctly. The second person, wearing VR goggles, observed the digital twin, which moved exactly like the original vehicle. Using this method, the person did not need to be near the vehicle and could assist the teleoperator in mapping the environment. This led to better results in the creation of digital 3D maps.

Cooperative Teleoperation: In this test scenario, communication between the person with the VR interface and the teleoperator was intensified. The teleoperator responded to direct driving commands from the VR observer and steered the vehicle into the hall. This was possible with precision and the observer had a continuous overview of the current situation. It has been shown that this type of teleoperation is particularly advantageous in tight spaces (Figs. 8 and 9).

Fig. 8. Digital Twin

Fig. 9. Cooperative Teleoperation

Precise Control of Vehicle: In the next scenario, the vehicle was steered towards the wall at low speed. The vehicle was supposed to come to a stop exactly one meter in front of the wall. Initially, the teleoperator only used the guide lines of the overlay for the control. The actual distance was then measured. It turned out that the error in the control was approx. 10 cm. It was only with the help of the VR observer that the vehicle could be controlled within an error range of a few centimeters.

VR PointerControl: In another scenario, the VR pointers were used to set various markers for the teleoperator to position the vehicle. These markers were added precisely using the VR controllers. This allowed the teleoperator to follow instructions from the VR observer, even though there was no direct communication between the people (Figs. 10 and 11).

Fig. 10. Precise control

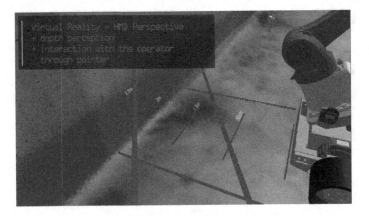

Fig. 11. VR Pointer Control

Sampling: In order for the vehicle to take drill samples with the robot arm, it must approach a marked point and drill into this position with the robot arm. For this scenario, a Styrodor wall was used as the drilling object. The VR observer marked a position on the Styrodor with the pointer and the teleoperator moved to the position using the joystick. The drilling mode was then activated and the vehicle could no longer move from the spot. Kuka's robot arm with the drilling attachment drilled a hole in the Styrodor at the correct position.

Pick Up: In the "Pick up" scenario, a tool bag was prepared so that the gripper on the Kuka robot arm could pick it up. To do this, the teleoperator moved to a position near the vehicle. The robot arm was then moved manually to the position of the tool bag. Another person with a VR interface was able to assist in positioning the gripper. This enabled the case to be lifted successfully (Figs. 12 and 13).

Fig. 12. Sampling

Fig. 13. Pick up

6   Conclusion

In this paper, the requirements for a teleoperated semi-autonomous vehicle with VR enhancements were first worked out. A complex system consisting of a vehicle and a teleoperation stand was then developed which can fulfill these requirements. A prototype was built and its functionality validated using various test scenarios.

The benefits of a VR system, as used in the MAEV project, include:

- Increased immersion and situational awareness: VR allows operators to experience a more realistic and immersive experience of the vehicle environment, leading to better understanding and responsiveness in complex scenarios.
- Improved remote control: VR technology allows operators to control the vehicle more effectively and intuitively than would be possible with conventional remote control systems.
- Safety: VR systems can reduce the risk to operators as they work remotely and do not need to be physically in dangerous or inaccessible areas.
- Training and simulation: VR offers excellent opportunities for training and simulating operational scenarios without endangering the real vehicle or environment.

These advantages help to increase the effectiveness and safety of remote control of semi-autonomous vehicles in challenging environments. The conclusion of the validation of the MAEV project underlines the transformative effect of integrating virtual reality (VR) into the teleoperation of semi-autonomous vehicles. It highlights the improvements in operational precision, user engagement and situational awareness, representing a significant leap forward in remote vehicle management. The research demonstrates the potential for wider application in various fields and points to a future where VR-enabled teleoperation becomes more widespread. It calls for continued innovation to overcome challenges such as latency and haptic feedback and to further bridge the gap between human operators and remote environments.

References

1. Fong, T., Thorpe, C.: Vehicle teleoperation interfaces. Auton. Robot. **11**(1), 9–18 (2001). https://doi.org/10.1023/A:1011295826834
2. Held, R.: Telepresence. J. Acoust. Soc. Am. **92**(4 Supplement), 2458 (1992). https://doi.org/10.1121/1.404500
3. Held, R., Durlach, N.: Telepresence, time delay and adaptation. In: Pictorial Communication in Virtual and Real Environments, pp. 232–246 (1991)
4. Kalinov, I., Trinitatova, D., Tsetserukou, D.: WareVR: virtual reality interface for supervision of autonomous robotic system aimed at warehouse stocktaking. In: 2021 IEEE International Conference on Systems, Man, and Cybernetics (SMC), pp. 2139–2145 (2021). https://doi.org/10.1109/SMC52423.2021.9659133
5. Kay, J.: Stripe: remote driving using limited image data, February 1997. https://doi.org/10.1145/223355.223426

6. Livatino, S., et al.: Intuitive robot teleoperation through multi-sensor informed mixed reality visual aids. IEEE Access **9**, 25795–25808 (2021). https://doi.org/10.1109/ACCESS.2021.3057808
7. Moniruzzaman, M., Rassau, A., Chai, D., Islam, S.M.S.: Teleoperation methods and enhancement techniques for mobile robots: a comprehensive survey. Robot. Auton. Syst. **150**, 103973 (2022). https://doi.org/10.1016/j.robot.2021.103973
8. Nielsen, C.W., Goodrich, M.A., Ricks, R.W.: Ecological interfaces for improving mobile robot teleoperation. IEEE Trans. Rob. **23**(5), 927–941 (2007). https://doi.org/10.1109/TRO.2007.907479
9. Stotko, P., et al.: A VR system for immersive teleoperation and live exploration with a mobile robot. In: 2019 IEEE/RSJ International Conference on Intelligent Robots and Systems (IROS), pp. 3630–3637 (2019). https://doi.org/10.1109/IROS40897.2019.8968598
10. Tzafestas, C.S.: Virtual and mixed reality in telerobotics: a survey, chap. 23. IntechOpen, Rijeka (2006). https://doi.org/10.5772/4911
11. Winfield, A.: Future directions in tele-operated robotics, September 2009

Interactive Visualizations for Crime Data Analysis by Mixed Reality

Sharad Sharma[1]([✉]) [ID], Sri Chandra Dronavalli[1], Maruthi Prasanna Chellatore[2], and Rishitha Reddy Pesaladinne[2]

[1] Department of Information Science, University of North Texas, Denton, TX, USA
sharad.sharma@unt.edu, srichandradronavalli@my.unt.edu
[2] Department of Computer Science, University of North Texas, Denton, TX, USA
{maruthiprasannachellatore,rishithareddypesaladinne}@my.unt.edu

Abstract. Crime data visualization plays a key role in understanding and dealing with criminal activities. This paper focuses on the integration of mixed reality (MR) and crime data analysis. There are many barriers and challenges when developing MR three-dimensional (3D) environments for visualization and inspection. The main problem is the lack of commonly shared data structures and interfaces between them. The rise in crime rates over the past few years is a huge source of issue for police departments and law enforcement organizations. As the crime rates significantly changed throughout time, both upward and downward, these changes are then compared to external factors, such as population, unemployment, and poverty. There is a need for visualizing the multiple crime datasets in multiple states with external factors. This work proposes a novel interactive approach for loading crime datasets into the HoloLens 2 device and displaying them in a mixed-reality setting for data analysis. By allowing people to engage and analyze datasets in a 3D space, the suggested system seeks to close the gap between data analysis and machine learning. Users can import many datasets, such as spatial, category, and numerical data, into the HoloLens 2 device and interactively visualize crime data for different states simultaneously. The system offers user-friendly capabilities for interactive data visualization in mixed reality once the data has been imported. The dataset is manipulated and transformed by users, who can also rotate, scale, and position it in 3D. To depict various characteristics and dimensions of the data, the system also supports a variety of visual encoding techniques, such as color mapping, size scaling, and spatial layout with the use of the imported datasets and the HoloLens 2's visualization capabilities, users can discover new insights and intricate linkages within the data. Natural movements and voice instructions allow users to engage with the visible data, enabling a hands-free and immersive data exploration experience. This paper also visualizes the crime data for four different cities: Chicago, Baltimore, Dallas, and Denton. Analyzing crime against factors such as population, employment, unemployment rate, and poverty rates provides information about the complex relationship between social factors and criminal behavior. The results and outcomes of this work will help the police department and law enforcement organizations better understand crime issues and supply insight into factors affecting crime that will help them deploy resources and help their decision-making process.

© The Author(s), under exclusive license to Springer Nature Switzerland AG 2024
J. Y. C. Chen and G. Fragomeni (Eds.): HCII 2024, LNCS 14708, pp. 286–303, 2024.
https://doi.org/10.1007/978-3-031-61047-9_19

Keywords: Data Visualization · Mixed Reality · Crime Data Analysis · Anomaly Detection

1 Introduction

The fusion of MR technology with crime data analysis is highlighted in this work and offers a fresh approach to data presentation and exploration. The suggested approach gives users the ability to engage spatially and interactively with datasets, creating new opportunities for education, cooperation, and data-driven decision-making across a range of fields, including science, engineering, and data-driven storytelling. With the increase in new VR/AR headsets and smartphone platforms, there has been an increasing interest in MR applications [1, 2]. Although there is a large variety of tools in AR/VR for design and development, there is less support available for evaluation. MR applications allow for interactions for user studies as well as usability evaluations [3]. This paper focuses on the integration of MR technology with crime data analysis, aiming to overcome barriers and challenges in developing MR environments for visualization and inspection. The rise in crime rates in recent years has posed significant challenges for police departments and law enforcement organizations. Understanding the dynamics of crime rates and their relationship with external factors, such as population, unemployment, and poverty, is crucial. There is a need for effective visualization of multiple crime datasets across different states, considering these external factors.

This work proposes a novel interactive approach that utilizes the HoloLens 2 device to load crime datasets and visualize them in a mixed-reality setting for data analysis. By leveraging the capabilities of MR technology, the suggested system aims to bridge the gap between data analysis and machine learning. Users can import various types of datasets, including spatial, category, and numerical data, into the HoloLens 2 de-vice and interactively visualize crime data for different states simultaneously. One of the key advantages of using MR technology for crime data analysis is the ability to create three-dimensional (3D) visualizations. Traditional two-dimensional (2D) charts and graphs often fall short of capturing the spatial aspects of crime patterns. By visualizing crime data in 3D, analysts can gain a better understanding of the geographical distribution of crime incidents, hotspots, and their relationships with other factors such as demographics or socioeconomic variables. The system offers user-friendly capabilities for interactive data visualization once the datasets are imported. Users have the flexibility to manipulate and transform the datasets, including rotating, scaling, and positioning them in a three-dimensional (3D) space. To represent different characteristics and dimensions of the data, the system supports a variety of visual encoding techniques, such as color mapping, size scaling, and spatial layout.

By utilizing the imported datasets and the visualization capabilities of the HoloLens 2 device, users can explore the data and uncover new insights and intricate linkages within the crime data as shown in Fig. 1. The system allows users to engage with the visible data using natural movements and voice instructions, creating a hands-free and immersive data exploration experience. Another benefit of MR technology is the ability to overlay crime data onto real-world environments. By using spatial mapping and aug-mented reality techniques, crime incidents can be visualized in their actual geographic locations, superimposed onto the physical world. This has practical implications for law enforcement agencies as they can better understand crime patterns in specific areas and make informed decisions about resource allocation and patrol strategies.

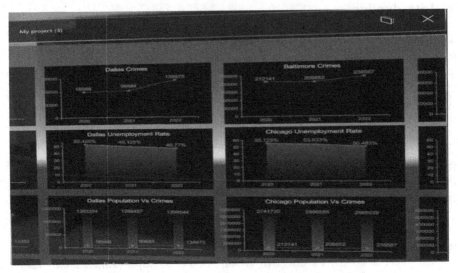

Fig. 1. Dashboard for crimes Vs factors affecting crime.

2 Related Work

Shama et al. [4–7] have developed an integrated situational awareness mobile augmented reality (AR) application for smart campus planning and emergency response by providing contextualized 3D visualizations that promote and support spatial knowledge acquisition and cognitive mapping. Microsoft HoloLens has also been used for providing contextualized 3D visualizations to support knowledge acquisition for indoor evacuation and emergency response [8–10]. Lately, immersive and MR environments have received increasing interest from researchers as well as developers. MR combined with spatially tracked mobile devices offers natural and embodied user interaction to support visual analysis of data.

The crime rate is a big concern for society living in large metropolitan cities worldwide. Based on the previous research done [11] in the United States based on COVID-19 on various racial demographics, the African American race is majorly impacted due to coronavirus, and also this analysis is majorly compared with the impact indexes such as infection rate, death rate, and death to infection ratio Latino population are there second most impacted with large infections. Furthermore, research [12] towards COVID-19 in comparison with crime data clearly stated that racial ethnic, and minority groups are disproportionally affected by COVID-19, especially in Baltimore City in 2019, and 62.4% of citizens were African American which determines while the city is disproportionally affected, had influenced to increase in the crime landscape of the city. According to [13], there was a decrease in crime as a result of the pandemic, more African Americans than Whites, Asians, Hispanics, and Indians were admitted to hospitals for COVID-19, 14.4% of African Americans lack health insurance, the median sale price of homes in Baltimore City increased by 11%, and 3.6% of occupied housing units designated as Black or African American were occupied. If there were better living circumstances, more access to healthcare, and better healthcare, the African American population may be affected more favorably. According to Walker et al. [12] researchers in the data analytics for crime data in different cities, there are some common data visualization techniques used to represent the data are line charts, bar charts, and maps.

In Baltimore due to the racial ethnic and minority groups, citizens belonging to the African American proportion is high, which is the major community affected by coronavirus. Jia et al. [14] have studied how African American race is impacted the most when comparing the infection rate impact index, death rate index, and the death to infection impact index, and other races less impact on the infection rate, but the highest death rate due to infection rate ratio is high in African American and Latino. Roth. et.al. [15] have described the current state of the science and practice of spatiotemporal crime analysis in medium to large law enforcement agencies in the northeastern United States. The study included a review of the literature in the areas of criminology/crime analysis and geoinformatics/mapping and interviews with seven law enforcement officials. Comparing science and practice provides insight and identifies four unmet needs. Improves access to government records, user interface design for crime mapping tools, integrates geographic and temporal representations for better analysis of criminal activity, and improves support for strategic crime analysis and policymaking. The results were reflected in the development of a spatiotemporal crime mapping application called GeoVISTA Crime Viz. Santos [16] has emphasized the importance of crime analysis ineffective policing tactics and suggests that police departments engage crime analysts to help with crime reduction initiatives. It also emphasizes the importance of additional research on crime analysis techniques and their impact on crime reduction [17]. Santos has further conveyed that GIS has a broader role than just being a mapping tool in the analysis of crime. This differs from the impression one might get from crime mapping research, which may unfairly limit the scope of GIS.

3 Data Visualization Using HoloLens

Data visualization using HoloLens, a mixed reality (MR) device, offers a unique and immersive way to interact with data in three-dimensional (3D) space. HoloLens can be used for Spatial Data Visualization which enables the visualization of data in a spatial context. Instead of traditional charts and graphs, data can be represented as holograms placed in the user's physical environment. For example, geographical data can be projected onto a map, allowing users to explore and analyze data points in their spatial context. It can be used for Interactive Manipulation where users can manipulate and interact with the data using gestures, voice commands, and gaze-based interactions. They can resize, rotate, and move visualized data elements, allowing for dynamic exploration and analysis. This interactive manipulation provides a hands-on experience and facilitates a deeper understanding of the data. HoloLens is used for the representation of complex relationships and multidimensional data. By leveraging holograms and spatial depth, users can gain insights into patterns, correlations, and trends that may not be easily apparent in traditional 2D visualizations Fig. 2.

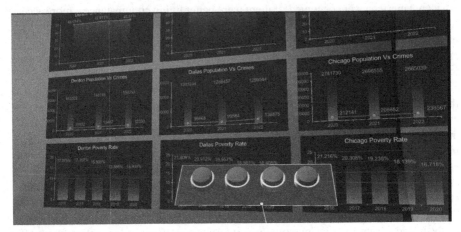

Fig. 2. GUI for Interaction

HoloLens allows for the overlay of data visualizations onto the user's real-world environment. For example, users can view real-time data overlays on physical objects or locations, providing context-rich visualizations. This capability is particularly useful for applications such as crime mapping or architectural design, where data can be super-imposed onto real-world objects or spaces. HoloLens also supports collaborative data visualization, allowing multiple users to share the same holographic environment. Users can see and interact with each other's visualizations, fostering collaboration, discussion, and knowledge sharing. This feature is particularly valuable for team-based data analysis and decision-making processes. It provides an immersive and engaging experience for data exploration. Users can step into the data environment and move around, gaining different perspectives and uncovering hidden insights. By leveraging spatial sound and visual cues, HoloLens creates an immersive environment that enhances the understanding and analysis of complex datasets. HoloLens enhances collaborative data analysis and decision-making processes in several ways like.

- Shared Holographic Environment: HoloLens allows multiple users to share the same holographic environment, enabling them to view and interact with data visualizations together. This shared experience promotes collaboration and facilitates real-time discussions and brainstorming sessions among team members.
- Co-located Collaboration: HoloLens enables users to see each other's avatars or representations within the shared environment, creating a sense of co-presence even if the collaborators are physically located in different places. This co-located collaboration fosters a more natural and immersive communication experience, facilitating effective teamwork and coordination.

- Simultaneous Data Exploration: Collaborators using HoloLens can simultaneously explore and manipulate data visualizations in real-time. They can interact with holographic elements, annotate or highlight specific data points, and discuss their findings with others. This simultaneous exploration promotes a deeper understanding of the data and allows for the identification of insights that may not be evident when working individually.
- Gesture and Voice-Based Interactions: HoloLens supports gesture and voice-based interactions, allowing collaborators to intuitively manipulate data visualizations and issue commands. This hands-free interaction frees up users' hands and enables more fluid collaboration, as they can focus on the data and communicate without the need for additional devices or tools.
- Remote Collaboration: HoloLens enables remote collaboration by leveraging mixed reality. Collaborators can connect from different locations and interact with the shared holographic environment, regardless of their physical distance. This capability is particularly beneficial for distributed teams, experts located in different regions, or situations where physical presence is challenging.
- Enhanced Data Communication: HoloLens provides a powerful medium for data communication. Instead of relying solely on verbal descriptions or static visualizations, collaborators can use holographic elements to represent data, relationships, and insights. This visual and interactive representation enhances comprehension and facilitates effective communication of complex data concepts among team members.
- Decision-Making Support: HoloLens can support decision-making processes by enabling collaborators to analyze data, compare scenarios, and visualize potential outcomes. By immersing themselves in the data environment, collaborators can gain a holistic understanding and make more informed decisions based on shared insights.

In summary, HoloLens offers a powerful platform for data visualization, enabling spatial data exploration, interactive manipulation, and collaboration. By leveraging the capabilities of mixed reality, HoloLens provides a novel and immersive way to interact with data, facilitating deeper insights and more informed decision-making. While HoloLens is not a dedicated data analysis tool like traditional statistical software, its capabilities as a mixed reality device provide unique opportunities for visualizing, exploring, and collaborating on data analysis tasks. It offers a more immersive and interactive approach to data analysis, enabling users to engage with data in new ways and derive meaningful insights.

3.1 Interactivity

HoloLens provides seamless integration with the Unity game development engine, enabling developers to create interactive mixed reality experiences. Unity is a popular and powerful platform for building 3D applications, and it offers extensive support for HoloLens development. Here are some key aspects of the interactivity between HoloLens and Unity:

- Spatial Mapping: HoloLens uses spatial mapping to understand the surrounding environment. Unity provides APIs and tools to access and utilize spatial mapping data. Developers can use this data to create interactive experiences that respond to the physical world, such as placing virtual objects on real surfaces or detecting collisions with the environment.

- Gesture Recognition: HoloLens supports gesture recognition, allowing users to interact with holograms using hand gestures. Unity provides gesture recognition APIs that can be utilized to detect and respond to gestures like air tap, bloom, or pinch. Developers can implement gesture-based interactions to manipulate objects, trigger actions, or navigate through the application.
- Voice Commands: HoloLens includes a built-in microphone and supports voice commands. Unity integrates with the HoloLens voice recognition system, enabling developers to create voice-controlled interactions within their applications. Developers can define voice commands and associated actions, allowing users to interact with holograms using voice input.
- Gaze Interaction: HoloLens tracks the user's gaze direction, and Unity provides APIs to access gaze information. Developers can use gaze tracking to create interactive experiences where the user's gaze can trigger actions or provide input. For example, activating an object by looking at it or displaying additional information when the user gazes at a specific location.
- Spatial Sound: HoloLens allows for spatial sound, meaning that audio can be positioned in 3D space to create a more immersive experience. Unity supports spatial audio integration, enabling developers to incorporate realistic 3D audio effects that match the position and movement of virtual objects in the mixed reality environment.
- Input Management: Unity provides an input management system that abstracts the different input methods available on HoloLens, such as gaze, gestures, voice, and controllers. Developers can utilize this system to handle different input sources and create unified interactivity within their applications.
- UI Elements and Interactions: Unity offers a wide range of UI development tools and frameworks. Developers can create interactive user interfaces (UI) for HoloLens applications using Unity's UI system, which includes buttons, sliders, panels, and other UI elements. These UI elements can respond to user interactions, such as gaze or gesture inputs.
- Application Lifecycle: Unity provides hooks and events that allow developers to handle the application lifecycle on HoloLens. This includes events for application startup, pause, resume, and shutdown. Developers can use these events to manage the state of their applications and implement custom behaviors based on the application lifecycle.

Figure 3 shows a high-level overview of a system that uses Unity and Visual Studio to create mixed reality (MR) experiences. The user interacts with the MR experience using hand gestures. Unity is used to create the 3D world of the MR experience, including importing assets, designing the virtual environment, and defining interactions. Visual Studio is used to write the C# code that controls the behavior of the MR experience, including handling hand gestures input, managing virtual objects, and implementing desired functionality. The C# code is compiled into machine code, transforming it into a format that the computer or MR device can execute. The XChart Asset, a custom Unity asset, is utilized to display charts and graphs within the MR experience, providing visual representations of data. The Mixed Reality Toolkit (MRTK) simplifies the development process by offering pre-built scripts, input handling, interaction models, and other utilities for creating immersive MR applications.

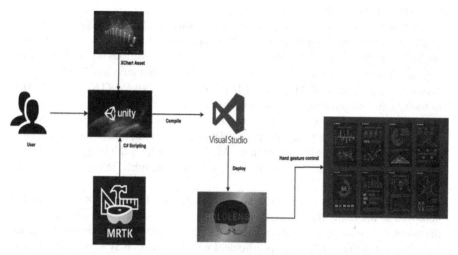

Fig. 3. User Interactivity with HoloLens

The MR experience is packaged and deployed to the target device, such as a HoloLens headset, following the specific deployment process for the platform and device. The deployed MR experience is ready for the user to interact with, utilizing hand gestures to control and manipulate virtual objects within the 3D environment. Below is a detailed description of each component.

1. User: The user is the person who will be experiencing the MR application. They interact with the MR experience using hand gestures, which provide a natural and intuitive way to control and interact with virtual objects.
2. Hand Gesture Control: Hand gesture control is a component of the MR experience that enables the user to interact with virtual objects or elements within the 3D world using hand gestures. This can include gestures like air tap, pinch, swipe, or hand tracking for manipulating objects, selecting options, or triggering actions.
3. Unity: Unity is a powerful game engine commonly used for creating interactive 3D applications, including MR experiences. It provides a visual development environment where developers can design and build the 3D world, import assets, define interactions, and create the overall user experience. Unity supports scripting in C#, allowing developers to write code to control the behavior of the virtual objects and handle user interactions.
4. Visual Studio: Visual Studio is an integrated development environment (IDE) that provides a comprehensive set of tools for software development. In the context of creating an MR experience, Visual Studio is used to write the C# code that controls the behavior of the virtual objects and handles user input. It offers features like code editing, debugging, and project management, making it easier for developers to create and maintain their MR applications.

5. Compile: After writing the C# code in Visual Studio, the code needs to be compiled into machine code that can be executed by the computer or the MR device. Compilation translates the human-readable code into a format that the computer can understand and execute.
6. XChart Asset: The XChart Asset is a custom Unity asset specifically designed for displaying charts and graphs within the MR experience. It provides convenient tools and functionality for creating, customizing, and rendering various types of charts and graphs, allowing developers to present data visually within the virtual environment.
7. Mixed Reality Toolkit (MRTK): The Mixed Reality Toolkit (MRTK) is a collection of tools, components, and APIs that simplify the development of MR experiences in Unity. It offers pre-built scripts, input handling, interaction models, and other utilities that accelerate the development process and provide common functionalities required for creating immersive MR applications. MRTK streamlines the integration of hand gesture recognition, spatial mapping, spatial sound, and other MR-specific features into the Unity project.
8. Deploy: Once the MR experience is created and tested, it needs to be packaged and deployed to the target device, such as a HoloLens headset. This involves preparing the application files, assets, and dependencies, and transferring them to the device for installation and execution. The specific deployment process may vary depending on the target platform and device requirements.

3.2 GUI Elements

In the MR application created using Unity and Visual Studio, various GUI elements are incorporated to enhance the user experience and provide different modes of interaction. Below are the GUI components that are utilized:

1. Buttons: Buttons are a common GUI element used to trigger actions or perform specific functions within an MR application. Unity provides a UI system that allows developers to create and customize buttons with different visual styles, such as 3D buttons or holographic buttons. Users can interact with these buttons using hand gestures, such as air tapping or pressing and releasing a virtual button using hand tracking. On a click of these buttons, the graphs can be displayed and hidden.
2. Voice Commands: Voice commands provide a hands-free mode of interaction in an MR application. By integrating voice recognition capabilities, users can control the application by speaking specific commands. Unity, along with the HoloLens platform, supports voice recognition, allowing developers to define voice commands and associate them with corresponding actions or functionalities within the application. Users can simply speak the voice command, and the application will respond accordingly.
3. Laser Pointer: A laser pointer is an interactive tool that allows users to point and interact with virtual objects or UI elements in the MR environment. It can be simulated using hand gestures, where the user's hand is recognized as a laser pointer. As the user moves their hand or finger, a virtual laser pointer is projected in the direction of the user's gaze, enabling precise selection and interaction with objects or UI elements. The laser pointer can be used to activate buttons, select menu options, or manipulate virtual objects. Using the laser pointer, button on click and off-click events are triggered.

4. Gesture-based Interactions: In addition to buttons and voice commands, the MR application can incorporate gesture-based interactions. Unity, combined with HoloLens, supports hand gesture recognition, enabling users to interact with virtual objects or UI elements through predefined hand gestures such as air tap, pinch, swipe, or grab. These gestures can be used to manipulate objects, navigate menus, or trigger specific actions within the application. With this gesture control, movement of the graph is achieved, and the graph can be zoomed in and zoomed out. The distance between the graph and the eye was adjusted using this control. Figure 4 shows the UI interactions using hand gestures.

5. Spatial UI Elements: Spatial UI elements refer to user interface components that are positioned in 3D space in the MR environment. Unity provides tools and frameworks for creating spatial UI elements, such as panels, tooltips, or information displays that can be anchored to virtual objects or positioned relative to the user's gaze. These spatial UI elements can provide additional information, options, or visual feedback to enhance the user experience and improve interaction within the application.

Fig. 4. User interaction using hand gestures

By incorporating these GUI components, users get an interactive experience in the MR application. Users can interact with virtual objects, trigger actions through buttons or voice commands, use hand gestures for manipulation, and receive visual feedback through spatial UI elements. This combination of GUI elements expands the range of interaction possibilities and makes the MR experience more intuitive and engaging for users.

4 Analysis of Crime Comparison with Factors

Analyzing crime against factors such as population, unemployment, and poverty rates provides valuable information about the complex relationship between social factors and criminal behavior. Unemployment is a factor that can affect crime rates. A high unemployment rate can create an environment conducive to crime, as people with financial difficulties and limited employment opportunities may turn to illegal means to support themselves. Unemployment can also affect the general economic conditions of an area and affect the availability of resources, social services, and community well-being, all of which can indirectly affect crime rates. The poverty rate is also closely related to crime.

4.1 Analysis of Crime with Population

Crime is often high in areas with higher poverty rates. Poverty can create social and economic inequality, lack of access to education and health care, and limited opportunities, leading to frustration, hopelessness, and an increased likelihood of engaging in criminal activity. Poverty can perpetuate the cycle of crime, so it is critical to address economic inequalities and provide support systems to rebuild disadvantaged communities.

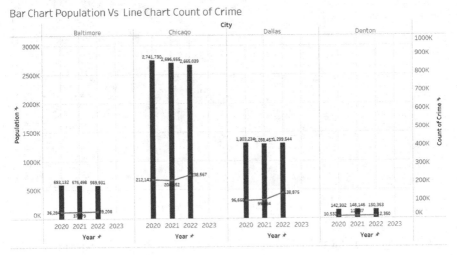

Fig. 5. Population Vs Crime in 4 Cities from 2020 to 2022.

Figure 5 shows the population dynamics of Baltimore, Chicago, Dallas and Denton show interesting trends compared to crime in 2020–2022. Despite the population decline, Baltimore experienced an increase in crime during the same period. This shows an alarming trend where crime has increased even as the population has decreased. The rate of change in crime is significant, with an increase of 8.05. This suggests that despite population declines, other factors such as socioeconomic conditions, community dynamics, or changes in police strategies may be contributing to crime growth. Chicago experienced a similar pattern of population decline followed by a decline in crime in

2020–2021. However, crime increased in 2021–2022. Resulting in a 12.45 increase in crime between 2020 and 2022. This indicates a variable crime trend, suggesting that some factors such as population dynamics, socioeconomic conditions, or changes in police strategies can influence the level of crime in Chicago. Dallas experienced a population decline in 2020–2021 followed by an increase in 2021–2022. At the same time, crime has continuously increased in the same period; the rate of change is 43.3. This shows that despite changes in population size, crime has increased in Dallas. Understanding the factors that influence crime growth is critical to effective crime prevention and community safety. Denton's population grew from 2020 to 2022, in line with crime growth at a rate of change of 17.26. The increase in crime indicates that a growing population can affect community dynamics and crime patterns in Denton.

4.2 Population Comparison with Employment

By analyzing the relationship between population and employment, we can better understand the labor force participation rate and possible effects on economic conditions. A higher employment-to-population ratio indicates a healthier labor market and better job opportunities. On the other hand, lower employment-to-population may indicate a less favorable labor market, where job opportunities are limited. Analyzing population and employment together can help identify areas of potential labor market imbalances. In addition, understanding the relationship between population and employment can inform workforce development strategies and policies. In summary, comparing population and employment provides valuable information about labor market dynamics, labor force participation rates, and economic conditions. By analyzing these factors together, decision-makers and stakeholders can better understand the labor market, identify potential challenges, and develop strategies to promote employment growth and overall economic well-being.

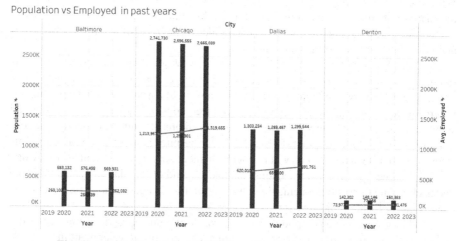

Fig. 6. Count of Population Vs Employed in 4 Cities from 2020 To 2022.

Figure 6 shows that despite the population decline, employment in Baltimore initially declined in 2020–21, but then increased in 2021–22. This suggests an unstable labor market where there may have been some instability in working conditions. The change in employment levels in the face of population decline indicates that background factors influencing these trends, such as changes in industries, economic conditions, or local politics, require further investigation. Despite the population decline, Chicago showed employment growth from 2020 to 2022. This suggests a resilient labor market that has managed to create opportunities despite population decline. Increases in employment during times of population decline may be due to factors such as industrial diversification, economic development initiatives, or changes in the composition of the workforce. Understanding these dynamics can provide valuable insight into the causes of Chicago's employment growth.

Dallas experienced a population decline in 2020–2021, followed by an increase in 2021–2022. At the same time, employment increased over the same period. This indicates a positive development, where both population and employment are increasing. Rising employment rates combined with demographic changes point to a growing job market and potentially expanding job opportunities in Dallas. Denton's population grew between 2020 and 2022, consistent with rising employment levels over the same period. This suggests that population growth was accompanied by job growth and expanded job opportunities. Employment growth combined with population growth means a healthy job market in Denton.

4.3 Population Comparison with the Unemployment Rate

Comparing the population with the unemployment rate gives an idea of the dynamics of the labor market and the unemployment rate of a certain population. By studying the relationship between population and unemployment, we get a better understanding of the availability of job opportunities and the economic well-being of the population. When comparing the population with the unemployment rate, it is imperative to consider the share of the unemployed in the workforce. This metric helps measure the extent of unemployment in the population and gives an idea of the level of economic difficulties and potential socio-economic challenges.

A higher unemployment rate indicates a weaker labor market and fewer job opportunities relative to the available workforce. This shows that a significant part of the population is actively looking for work but is unable to find a suitable job. Higher unemployment rates can lead to financial stress, reduced consumer spending, and potential social consequences. Figure 7 shows that in Baltimore, the unemployment rate rose initially in 2020–2021, but then fell in 2021–22, despite the population decline. This suggests a volatile labor market, where unemployment conditions fluctuated somewhat. Changes in unemployment rates against the background of population decline indicate that background factors influencing these trends, such as changes in industries, economic conditions, or local politics, need to be further investigated.

In Chicago, although the population decreased, the unemployment rate showed a general decrease from 2020 to 2022. This indicates a positive development in the labor market, where job opportunities expanded, or unemployment decreased despite a population decrease. A decrease in the unemployment rate indicates a relatively healthier labor market in Chicago, which may be due to factors such as economic development initiatives, changes in the labor force share, or industry dynamics.

Population vs Unemployment rate in past years

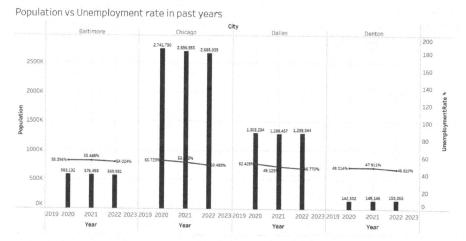

Fig. 7. Count of Population Vs Employed in 4 Cities from 2020 to 2022.

Dallas experienced a population decline in 2020–2021, followed by growth in 2021–2022. At the same time, the unemployment rate decreased during the same period. This indicates a positive development, where both the population and unemployment have improved. A decline in the unemployment rate amid population fluctuations indicates an improvement in the Dallas job market and possibly an expansion of job opportunities. Denton's population increased between 2020 and 2022, consistent with a decrease in the unemployment rate over the same period. This shows that the growth of the population was accompanied by a decrease in unemployment. Lower unemployment combined with population growth means a healthier job market in Denton.

4.4 Crime Comparison with Unemployment Rate

An analysis of the relationship between crime and the unemployment rate provides insight into the possible influence of economic conditions on criminal behavior. By examining the relationship between these two factors, we can better understand the complex dynamics between socioeconomic factors and crime.

When comparing the crime rate with the unemployment rate, it is important to consider the possible causal relationship between the two. High unemployment can increase the likelihood of criminal activity for several reasons. Economic pressures, economic desperation, and limited job opportunities can push people to illegal livelihoods or lead to greater frustration and social unrest, which can lead to an increase in crime. On the other hand, a decrease in unemployment can be a sign of an improvement in the economic situation and an improvement in legal employment opportunities. This can potentially lead to a reduction in crime as individuals have better prospects for financial stability and are less likely to resort to criminal activity.

However, it is important to understand that the relationship between crime and unemployment is complex and influenced by many other factors. Socioeconomic differences, educational attainment, community resources, and cultural factors influence crime rates and unemployment rates. Therefore, a comprehensive analysis that takes into account multiple variables is necessary to accurately understand the interaction between unemployment and crime.

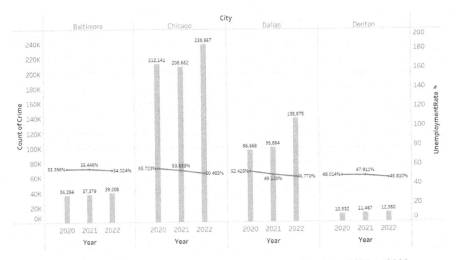

Fig. 8. Count of Crime Vs Unemployment Rate in 4 Cities from 2020 to 2022.

Figure 8 shows that the unemployment rate in Baltimore is expected to decrease by about 1 percent between 2020 and 2022, there is a slight increase in reported crime. This suggests that the drop in unemployment is not necessarily correlated with the drop in crime in Baltimore. Other factors such as socioeconomic conditions, systemic challenges, or community dynamics can also contribute to crime growth. Similarly, Chicago, with an unemployment rate of about 5 % between 2020 and 2022 but a slight increase in reported crime, is 12.4 %. This shows that the drop in unemployment does not directly translate to a drop in crime in Chicago. Other factors such as neighborhood dynamics, social inequality, or other causes may also contribute to the increase in crime.

Although the unemployment rate in Dallas decreased by about 6 percent between 2020 and 2022, reported crime increased slightly. This suggests that a reduction in unemployment alone does not guarantee a crime reduction. Other factors such as social factors, community resources, or changes in criminal behavior patterns may contribute to the increase in crime in Dallas.

Similarly, in Denton, while the unemployment rate decreased by about 3% between 2020 and 2022, reported crime increased slightly. This shows that the drop in unemployment does not directly correspond to the drop in crime in Denton. To fully understand the drivers of crime growth, it is important to consider other factors such as demographic changes, community dynamics, or changes in police strategies.

4.5 Population Below the Poverty Rate

The percentage of people living in poverty provides valuable insight into the socioe-conomic conditions within a population. Comparing the poverty rates in Baltimore, Chicago, Dallas, and Denton reveals variations in the prevalence of poverty across these cities. However, it still indicates a significant portion of the population experiencing poverty. Efforts to address poverty in Chicago, Baltimore, Dallas, and Denton should focus on creating economic opportunities, promoting affordable housing, and strength-ening social programs. Supporting initiatives that foster economic empowerment and provide resources to individuals and families in need can help alleviate poverty.

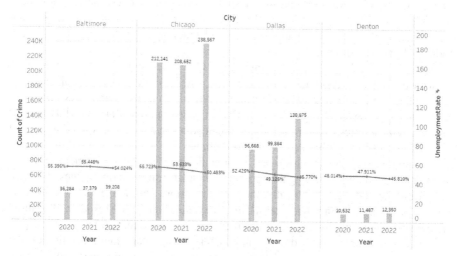

Fig. 9. Population Below Poverty Level Status in 4 Cities from 2016 to 2020.

Figure 9 shows that the analysis of poverty rates in Baltimore, Chicago, Dallas, and Denton from 2016 to 2020 shows some interesting trends and differences in the prevalence of poverty in these cities. A decrease in the poverty rate indicates possible improvements in economic conditions, resource availability, and socioeconomic support systems in Baltimore. However, it is important to note that the initial poverty rate in Baltimore was relatively high in 2016, indicating significant economic challenges that require attention and targeted action. It refers to efforts to fight poverty and improve the economic conditions of the city. The general trend indicates a change in the level of poverty during this period. The initial decline in the poverty rate indicates a positive development in poverty reduction efforts and improving economic conditions in Dallas. The overall trend indicates that poverty levels in Denton fluctuate during this period.

An initial increase may indicate socioeconomic challenges, but a subsequent decline followed by an increase indicates a dynamic socioeconomic landscape and possible changes in economic conditions in the city. In contrast, Denton had the lowest poverty rate in 2019 at 13.886%, indicating relatively better socioeconomic conditions. In general, a lower-level analysis of poverty rates in these cities shows a decrease or change in poverty rates.

5 Conclusions

The integration of MR technology with crime data analysis presents a promising approach for enhancing crime data visualization, analysis, and interpretation. This paper utilizes the HoloLens 2 device to import and visualize multiple crime datasets in a mixed-reality environment. The system enables users to engage with the data spatially and interactively, bridging the gap between data analysis and machine learning. The user-friendly capabilities of the system allow for the importation of diverse crime data types, including spatial, category, and numerical data, into the HoloLens 2 device. Once imported, users can manipulate and transform the datasets, providing flexibility in exploring the data from different perspectives. Visual encoding techniques, such as color mapping, size scaling, and spatial layout, facilitate a comprehensive understanding of the data, revealing intricate crime patterns and trends that may be challenging to discern in traditional 2D visualizations.

The immersive and hands-free nature of the system sets it apart, as users can interact with the data using natural movements and voice instructions. This enhances the data exploration experience and enables users to focus on analysis and discovery without the need for physical input devices. The proposed approach also extends beyond law enforcement, offering interdisciplinary applications in education, collaboration, and data-driven decision-making across various domains.

The practical benefits of this work are significant for police departments and law enforcement organizations. By gaining a better understanding of crime issues and mapping crime incidents geographically, these organizations can derive valuable insights into the factors influencing crime rates. This knowledge can inform resource allocation, strategic planning, and decision-making processes, leading to more effective crime prevention measures and improved community safety. In summary, the integration of MR technology with crime data analysis provides an innovative and promising solution for data presentation and exploration. It empowers users to engage spatially and interactively with crime datasets, opening new opportunities for understanding crime patterns, making data-driven decisions, and fostering collaboration.

Acknowledgments. This work is funded in part by the NSF award 2321539 and Sub Award No. NSF00123–08 for NSF Award 2118285. The authors would also like to acknowledge the support of NSF Award 2319752, and NSF Award 2321574.

References

1. Milgram, P., Kishino, F.: A taxonomy of mixed reality visual displays, IEICE Trans Inf. Syst. 77, **12** (1994), 1321–1329, (1994)
2. Speicher, M., Hall, BD., Nebeling, M.: What is mixed reality?. In: Proceedings of the 2019 CHI Conference on Human Factors in Computing Systems May 2019, Paper No.: 537, pp 1–15, (2019)
3. Dünser, A., Billinghurst, M.: Evaluating augmented reality systems. In: Furht, B. (ed.) Handbook of Augmented Reality, pp. 289–307. Springer New York, New York, NY (2011). https://doi.org/10.1007/978-1-4614-0064-6_13

4. Sharma, S., Pesaladinne, R.R.: Spatial analysis and visual communication of emergency information through augmented reality. J. Imaging Sci. Technol. **67**(6), 1–9 (2023). https://doi.org/10.2352/J.ImagingSci.Technol.2023.67.6.060401

5. Pesaladinne, R., Chellatore, M.P.,Dronavalli,S., Sharma, S.: Situational awareness and feature extraction for indoor building navigation using mixed reality In: Proceedings of the IEEE International Conference on Computational Science and Computational Intelligence, (IEEE-CSCI), Research Track on Big Data and Data Science (CSCI-RTBD), Las Vegas, USA, December, pp.13–15,(2023)

6. Sharma, S.: Mobile augmented reality system for emergency response.In: Proceedings of the 21st IEEE/ACIS International Conference on Software Engineering, Management and Applications (SERA 2023), Orlando, USA, May 23–25, (2023)

7. Sharma, S., Engel, D.: Mobile augmented reality system for object detection, alert, and safety. In: Proceedings of the IS&T International Symposium on Electronic Imaging (EI 2023) in the Engineering Reality of Virtual Reality Conference, Jan, pp.15–19, (2023)

8. Sharma, S., Bodempudi, S.T., Scribner, D., Grynovicki, J., Grazaitis, P.: Emergency Response Using HoloLens for Building Evacuation. In: Chen, J.Y.C.., Fragomeni, G. (eds.) Virtual, Augmented and Mixed Reality. Multimodal Interaction: 11th International Conference, VAMR 2019, Held as Part of the 21st HCI International Conference, HCII 2019, Orlando, FL, USA, July 26–31, 2019, Proceedings, Part I, pp. 299–311. Springer International Publishing, Cham (2019). https://doi.org/10.1007/978-3-030-21607-8_23

9. Stigall, J., Bodempudi, S.T., Sharma, S, Scribner, D., Grynovicki, J., Grazaitis, P.: Use of Microsoft HoloLens in indoor evacuation In: Int. J. Comput. Their Appl. IJCA, Vol. 26, No. 1, March (2019)

10. Sharma, S., Bodempudi, S.T., Scribner, D.: Identifying anomalous behavior in a building using HoloLens for emergency response. Electron. Imaging **32**(13), 224-1–224-7 (2020). https://doi.org/10.2352/ISSN.2470-1173.2020.13.ERVR-224

11. Rayan, T., et al.: The effect of COVID-19 on various demographics by race in the united states In: 2020 International Conference on Computational Science and Computational Intelligence (CSCI), pp. 364–368, (2020)

12. Walker, S., Sharma, S.: Data visualization of Covid-19 and crime data. In: Proceeding of the IEEE International Conference on Computational Science and Computational Intelligence, (CSCI'21), Symposium of Big Data and Data Science (CSCI-ISBD), Las Vegas, USA, December, pp. 15–17, (2021)

13. Walker, T., Sharma, S.: Data analysis of crime and rates of hospitalization due to COVID-19. In Proceeding of the IEEE International Conference on Computational Science and Computational Intelligence, (CSCI'21), Symposium of Big Data and Data Science (CSCI-ISBD), Las Vegas, USA, December, pp.15–17, (2021)

14. Jia, Z., Shen, C., Chen, Y., Yu, T., Guan, X., Yi, X.: Big-data analysis of multi-source logs for anomaly detection on network-based system, In: Proceedings 13th IEEE Conference Automation Science Engineering (CASE), Xi'an, China, pp.1136_1141, Aug. 2017

15. Roth, R.E., Ross, K.S., Finch, G.B.G., Luo, W., MacEachren, A.M.: Spatiotemporal crime analysis in U.S. law enforcement agencies: current practices and unmet needs. Gov. Inf. Q. **30**(3), 226–240 (2013)

16. Santos, R.B.: The effectiveness of crime analysis for crime reduction: cure or diagnosis? J. Contemp. Crim. Justice **30**(2), 147–168 (2014). https://doi.org/10.1177/1043986214525080

17. Murray, A.T.: Exploratory spatial data analysis techniques for examining urban crime: implications for evaluating treatment. Br. J. Criminol. **41**(2), 309–329 (2001). https://doi.org/10.1093/bjc/41.2.309

HoloAAC: A Mixed Reality AAC Application for People with Expressive Language Difficulties

Liuchuan Yu[1]([⊠]) [iD], Huining Feng[1] [iD], Rawan Alghofaili[1,2] [iD],
Boyoung Byun[1] [iD], Tiffany O'Neal[1] [iD], Swati Rampalli[1] [iD], Yoosun Chung[1] [iD],
Vivian Genaro Motti[1] [iD], and Lap-Fai Yu[1] [iD]

[1] George Mason University, Fairfax, VA 22030, USA
{lyu20,hfeng2,ralghofa,cbyun2,toneal,srampall,ychung3,
vmotti,craigyu}@gmu.edu, rawan@utdallas.edu
[2] University of Texas at Dallas, Richardson, TX 75080, USA

Abstract. We present a novel AAC application, HoloAAC, based on mixed reality that helps people with expressive language difficulties communicate in grocery shopping scenarios via a mixed reality device. A user, who has difficulty in speaking, can easily convey their intention by pressing a few buttons. Our application uses computer vision techniques to automatically detect grocery items, helping the user quickly locate the items of interest. In addition, our application uses natural language processing techniques to categorize the sentences to help the user quickly find the desired sentence. We evaluate our mixed reality-based application on AAC users and compare its efficacy with traditional AAC applications. HoloAAC contributed to the early exploration of context-aware AR-based AAC applications and provided insights for future research.

Keywords: Augmentative and alternative communication · Mixed reality · Assistive technology · Object detection · Text-to-speech

1 Introduction

Augmentative and alternative communication (AAC) [5] is a communication mechanism for those with complex communication needs (CCN) [33], and existing AAC devices are forms of assistive technology (AT) comprising hardware and software that can support or replace natural speech entirely. On the other hand, augmented reality (AR), a user's visual perception supplemented with additional computer-generated sensory modalities, is rising in its ability to support AT through rehabilitation therapies that support people with disabilities. While immersive learning applications in AR have greatly supported individuals with disabilities, current AAC devices do not carry the contextual intelligence to prompt appropriate conversation choices or phrases based on a user's environment. This is particularly concerning for emergency situations where real-time communication is important for supporting AAC users who have to not

© The Author(s), under exclusive license to Springer Nature Switzerland AG 2024
J. Y. C. Chen and G. Fragomeni (Eds.): HCII 2024, LNCS 14708, pp. 304–324, 2024.
https://doi.org/10.1007/978-3-031-61047-9_20

only consider their accommodations but also navigate a crisis with heightened emotions. This prompts the need for an AI-driven AAC system aware of the environmental situation and demand. Because of the monumental shift in the nature of AAC, AAC has expanded its reach to include more people with a wider range of CCN [39].

Fig. 1. When the user wears HoloLens 2 and stands by the side of the cashier, the user clicks the camera button to capture current objects on the desk. In this scenario, there are three objects on the desk: soda, coffee, and water. After the captured image is processed on the PC, the detected objects, the generated keywords, and the generated sentences will be shown in front of the user via an AAC interface visualized by HoloLens 2. As the user clicks the *prices* keyword, the sentence "what are the prices of these groceries?" is shown. The user clicks this sentence to trigger our application to speak it accordingly.

AR is becoming popular in various fields such as teaching [42], learning [29], entertainment [19], defense [44], and marketing [36]. As an immersive technology, AR opts to observe the user's surroundings, understand the context, and synthesize context-aware content with the aid of computer vision and artificial intelligence algorithms. Moreover, head-mounted AR headsets feature egocentric vision, referring to being capable of seeing what the user sees. These factors make head-mounted AR headsets promising vehicles for delivering AAC applications in the future. Compared to current AAC devices that require users to operate an AAC application on a phone or tablet, an AAC app running on a head-mounted AR headset could be less distracting and more intuitive to provide in-situ conversation help, thanks to the advantage of AR in being able to incorporate a user interface into the physical environment, which reduces gaze switch and enhances eye contact.

To explore this direction, we propose HoloAAC, a computer vision-guided mixed-reality AAC application that helps AAC users in grocery shopping scenarios as shown in Fig. 1. First, we devise a computational approach to generate shopping-related sentences. Second, we use a mixed reality device to capture an image of the current context, based on which an object detection algorithm is applied. Third, we propose a natural language processing (NLP) based algorithm to help the user quickly find the desired sentence. Fourth, a text-to-speech engine will translate the entire sentence into speech upon the user's selection. To the best of our knowledge, HoloAAC is the very first application that explores using mixed reality and contextual awareness to provide AAC for users who have expressive language difficulties but possess good control over hand movements. The major contributions of this work include:

– Proposing a novel AAC interface that can be used on a mixed-reality headset;
– Devising an interactive approach based on object detection and text retrieval techniques to help AAC users quickly retrieve and speak desired sentences via text-to-speech;
– Evaluating our approach through experiments that mimic grocery scenarios and case studies conducted with people who have expressive language difficulties.

HoloAAC code is available at https://github.com/luffy-yu/HoloAAC.

2   Related Work

There are needs for just-in-time communication and context-aware technologies in the AAC community. In fact, this is an area of need that has been prevalent. We review some existing works.

2.1   Context-Aware AAC

Communication depends on context. People talk about things that are rooted in their environments [31]. A context-aware system decides what information and which service should be presented to the user [38].

TalkAbout [21] is a context-aware and adaptive AAC system that tailors its users' word list based on their current surroundings and the person they are conversing with. TryTalk [14] operates similarly, considering the user's location obtained through GPS or building QR code, as well as the day and time. Chan et al. [7] employed Bluetooth Low Energy beacons for precise indoor tracking and a micro-location context-aware AAC system to minimize the cognitive burden of user interaction. Moreover, Chan et al. [8] proposed a context-aware AAC system to enhance daily communication for nonverbal schoolchildren with moderate intellectual disabilities. On the other hand, Shen et al. [40] devised KWickChat for nonspeaking individuals with motor disabilities, which leverages a GPT-2 language model and context information to improve the quality of the generated responses. Rocha et al. [37] introduced a system to assist individuals with aphasia to achieve two-way communication.

Unlike the previous works, our application offers full sentences for users to select instead of a single word or a single phrase. Inspired by TryTalk [14], our application also prioritizes frequently clicked sentences relevant to the detected objects. Our application leverages the image capturing, hand tracking, visualization, and audio capabilities of the HoloLens 2 to realize a novel and integrated AAC interface in augmented reality.

2.2   Computer Vision-Based AAC

Computer vision has been applied for AAC. The computer vision-based AAC applications primarily lie on eye tracking, blink recognition, head tracking, facial detection, and sign language recognition [31].

Raudonis et al. [35] proposed an affordable eye-tracking system that uses a webcam and artificial neural classifiers to achieve precise eye-tracking. Al-Rahayfeh et al. [2] surveyed eye-tracking and head movement technologies, demonstrating their potential for enhancing the accuracy and reducing the costs of assistive technologies. Jen et al. [20] proposed a wearable, highly accurate and robust eye-gaze tracking system, which only required one single webcam mounted on the glasses. On the other hand, Al-Kassim et al. [1] designed an eye-tracking scanning keyboard to help individuals with paralysis. Moreover, Zhang et al. [45] developed GazeSpeak, an eye gesture communication system that operates on smartphones and benefits individuals with motor impairments. Fiannaca et al. [13] presented AACrobat, a Gaze-Based AAC to lower communication barriers and provide autonomy using mobile devices. For more recent research on eye-tracking, please refer to a recent review [23].

For other AAC applications based on blink recognition, head tracking, facial detection, and sign language recognition, please refer to this review [31].

Disparate previous AAC research that used computer vision for communication purposes, we leverage computer vision to drive our application: object detection analyzes the context in a scenario, and the detection result hints what items the user is probably concerned about, helping the user quickly generate context-aware sentences.

2.3   Augmented Reality for AAC

Augmented reality (AR) for AAC is a relatively new research field. Ramires et al. [34] proposed a system that utilizes AR and integrates AAC along with Applied Behavior Analysis (ABA) for aiding interventions with children diagnosed with Autism Spectrum Disorders (ASD). Kerdvibulvech et al. [22] proposed a three-dimensional augmented reality-based human-computer interaction application to assist children with special problems in communication. Also, other research works [3,9–11,17,26,27] show that AR can be used to improve language and communication skills in individuals with ASD and has positive outcomes such as increased motivation, attention, and learning new tasks.

The direction of using HoloLens for AAC applications is relatively unexplored. Zhao et al. [46] proposed an AAC application that runs on HoloLens to use eye-gaze technology to select words and make sounds. Krishnamurthy et al. [24] introduced HoloType, a prototype system aimed at enhancing communication outcomes for individuals with nonspeaking autism to deliver interactive educational content, enabling users to concurrently enhance their pointing skills.

Compared to previous works, HoloAAC not only aims to help AAC users in daily grocery shopping scenarios but also aims to speak a meaningful sentence rather than a word or a phrase.

2.4   User Interface and Interaction for AAC

Several design efforts focused on user interfaces and interactions to support AAC applications. Sobel et al. [41] found that higher-resolution displays enhance AAC applications. Gibson et al. [15] extracted design requirements from a clinical AAC tablet application. Kristensson et al. [25] proposed a design engineering approach for quantitatively exploring context-aware sentence retrieval. Besides, Obiorah et al. [30] developed meal-ordering prototypes for people with aphasia to dine in restaurants. Mitchell et al. [28] investigated a custom-designed optimized keyboard alongside the widely used QWERTY keyboard for three individuals experiencing dexterity impairments caused by motor disabilities.

Wearable devices, like smart glasses, offer convenience compared to handheld devices. In contrast to using a handheld AAC device, using an AAC app visualized through an AR headset allows the user to maintain better eye contact in face-to-face conversations. Additionally, an AR headset can sense the surroundings and provide scene-aware conversational assistance. Devices like HoloLens have provided a glimpse into the future prevalence of such devices. Thus, it is valuable to integrate AR with AAC. We devised HoloAAC as a prototype to explore realizing an AAC interface on smart glasses. We believe that combining computer vision, natural language processing, and text-to-speech technologies in AAC shows promise as an emerging research direction.

3   Interview with AAC Users

To devise a friendly, accessible, and practical application for AAC users, we interviewed 2 professional AAC users who have been using AAC devices for more than 3 years and also teaching people to use AAC devices. We obtained the following insights about the design of this application.

- This application should be portable and the device running the application should be untethered (A1).
- This application should be easy to use with minimal configurations and intuitive operations (A2).
- Considering that some AAC users are used to symbol-based or text-based AAC tools, it is preferable to use similar symbols in this application (A3).
- This application should be friendly to those AAC users with listening disabilities (A4).
- For the grocery shopping scenario, it would be convenient to automatically detect items and support the user in selecting items (A5).

We devise our augmented reality AAC application, HoloAAC, based on the above observations. The application runs on the Microsoft HoloLens 2 (A1). It comprises three windows: an entry window, a network setting window, and a main window (A2). In this application, we support setting voice speed, volume, and voice type (male voice/female voice). Besides that, since computer vision can be used in context-aware AAC to determine what objects of interest are in the environment [31], we use computer vision techniques to detect groceries and provide an optional way to select/deselect groceries (A5). In addition, the application also tracks the user's sentence selection history to prioritize previously selected sentences (A2). Our application employs the wireless network to realize the portable goal (A1). We choose mid-air tapping as the interaction method. To enhance intuitiveness, we add symbols in front of nouns (A3). In order to make this application more accessible, we use red color to denote being selected. What's more, we set the pressed sentence's color to red to indicate that it is being spoken, which is more friendly for people with listening disabilities (A4).

4   Technical Approach

4.1   Overview

Figure 2 shows our application workflow. First, the user wearing a HoloLens 2 takes a picture of the groceries in front. The picture is then sent to the server (a PC in our experiments) for processing: semantic segmentation, object detection, sentence retrieval, and text-to-speech. When HoloLens 2 gets the response from the server, the user can select one or more keywords to quickly locate the desired sentence and trigger the device to speak it.

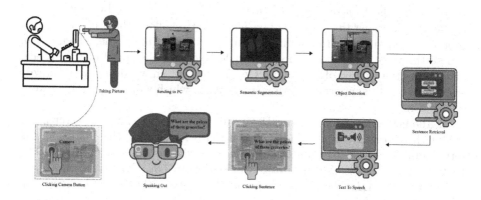

Fig. 2. Our application's overview

4.2   AR Tool and User Interface

As aforementioned, our application runs on Microsoft HoloLens 2. We use the Unity and the Mixed Reality Toolkit (MRTK) to develop the application. HoloLens 2 supports hand tracking so the user interface (UI) is movable in the 3D space. The UI primarily includes three parts: entry UI (Fig. 3(a)), network setting UI (Fig. 3(b)), and main UI (Fig. 3(c)).

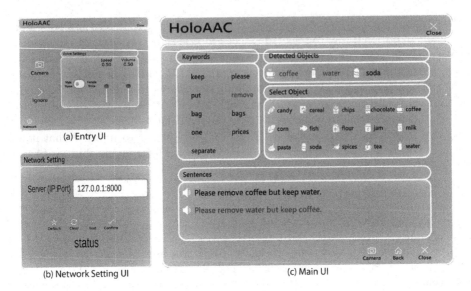

Fig. 3. HoloAAC UI

The entry UI will be displayed after launching our application on Microsoft HoloLens 2. The *Camera* button is for starting the prototype by capturing an image. It will trigger the main UI. The *Ignore* button allows the user to start the prototype without capturing an image. In the *Voice Settings* panel, the user can choose the voice type: male voice or female voice, set the speed of the speech, and change the volume of the sound. On the left bottom, we design the *Network* setting button to support network configuration, which will trigger the network setting UI.

In the network setting UI, the *Default* button is for setting the server input field with the default value. The *Clear* button is for clearing the content in the server input field. The *Test* button is for testing whether the server is accessible. If the server is accessible, the *status* will change to *OK*. Otherwise, the *status* will change to *FAIL*. The *Confirm* button is for setting the server configuration and closing this panel.

The main UI is where the detected objects, keywords, and sentences are shown. The top *Detected Objects* panel shows the detected objects in the captured picture. The left *Keywords* panel displays keywords related to the selected objects in the *Detected Objects* panel and the *Select Object* panel. The central *Select Object* panel lists all the objects that are supported. In case the object detection fails and therefore no object is detected and automatically selected, the user can still select any object in this panel manually. To enhance understanding, we add a symbol in front of each object's name. The bottom *Sentences* panel shows relevant sentences retrieved according to objects and keywords. When the user presses one sentence, the application will speak the sentence.

At the bottom right, there are three buttons: *Camera, Back,* and *Close.* This *Camera* button performs the same action as the camera button in the entry UI. The *Back* button is used to go back to the entry UI. The *Close* button is used to quit this application. We use a red color to denote the selected objects, keywords, and sentences in the *Detected Objects* panel, the *Select Object* panel, *Keywords* panel, and *Sentences* panel. Note that the *Detected Objects* panel, the *Select Object* panel, and the *Keywords* panel support multi-selection.

4.3   Object Detection

As aforementioned, we take the image captured by the HoloLens 2 as the input. The next step is to detect possible objects in the image.

Semantic Segmentation. Although object detection can be directly employed on grocery items, detection failure may happen in practice due to the difference between training images and captured images by HoloLens 2. Therefore, we apply semantic segmentation as a preprocessing step to improve object detection accuracy. In our approach, we first apply a semantic segmentation method (Deeplabv3+). It generates object masks that will be applied to crop the captured image into multiple smaller segments for object detection.

Object Detection. Inspired by the GroceEye[1], to perform object detection of grocery items, we fine-tune a YOLOv5 model with the Freiburg Grocery dataset. We use the processed Freiburg dataset which can be downloaded from Github.

4.4   Relevant Sentence Retrieval

We interviewed two professional AAC users, who have been using AAC devices for more than 3 years and also teaching people to use AAC devices, for their opinion regarding common conversations in grocery shopping scenarios. We abstracted them and made them extensible to support adding other sentences easily. We devise a sentence database to construct object-relevant sentences. Since the number of sentences with regard to every object is large, it is hard for a user to locate the target sentence. Therefore, we tokenize and stem sentences to get keywords, which are used to group sentences. Hence the user can select the target sentence through selecting keywords. We also consider historical data, that is, which sentences are selected by the user before, to sort the sentences. As a result, the more times one sentence is selected, the higher the precedence of showing that sentence is. After the sentences are confirmed, the text-to-speech engine will synthesize the corresponding audio of speaking the sentences.

---

[1] http://students.washington.edu/bhimar/highlights/2020-12-18-GrocerEye/.

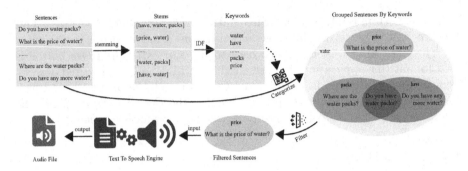

Fig. 4. Sentence retrieval overview

Overall Workflow of Sentence Retrieval. After detecting the objects on the image, our approach retrieves relevant sentences that the user may want to speak. As illustrated in Fig. 4, our method first retrieves all sentences containing the detected grocery names. After removing stop words and punctuations, it extracts the stems of each sentence. We use the IDF algorithm to obtain keywords. The sentences will then be categorized by the keywords. The user could click further keywords on the UI, which will then trigger our approach to filter out any irrelevant sentences. Those sentences that pass the filter will be processed by the text-to-speech engine to generate the audio files of the spoken sentences.

Keywords Generation for Locating Sentences. As we have the sentences of one or more items, the next step is to enable the user to quickly select the target sentence. First, for every sentence, we tokenize the sentence, removing punctuations and stopwords. In NLP, stopwords refer to those words that do not add much meaning to a sentence, such as "a" and "the". After that, we get the stem for every sentence. Then, we vectorize the sentences based on the occurrences of words. The result will be a count matrix. We apply the IDF algorithm to get the words with high frequency. In NLP, IDF means inverse document frequency. IDF is a common term weighting schema in information retrieval. A token with a higher IDF weight has a lower frequency, and vice versa. In our approach, we use the top-ten lower IDF weight tokens as the keywords. It will split sentences into several groups.

Sentence Filtering. After we get both the object name(s) and the keywords, we are able to filter the sentence database. First, we filter the subset of the entire sentence dataset using the object name(s). Sentences irrelevant to the objects will be removed, while those relevant will be kept. Then, we filter the subset again with the keywords. After that, we obtain several target sentences that the user may prefer. To adapt to the user and personalize our approach, we record the sentences the user has selected before. This data is a kind of prior knowledge. When the user selects the same objects and the same keywords next time, the

Table 1. Our seven participants (2 females and 5 males) had different years of experience using different AAC devices. Note that for P6 and P7, the years of AAC experience are counted as zero as they only used the conventional typing approach on cellphones/iPads for communication.

Participant	Gender	AAC Device	Years using AAC	VR/AR Experience
P1	F	Proloquo4Text	5	No
P2	M	ASL Interpreter	5	VR
P3	F	EZKeys	20	No
P4	M	Proloquo2Go	11	VR
P5	M	NovaChat 8	5	No
P6	M	Cellphone/iPad	0*	VR
P7	M	Cellphone	0*	No

sentences will be sorted according to this data. The more times a sentence has been selected, the higher precedence of appearance the sentence is given.

4.5   Error Handling

Computer vision techniques such as semantic segmentation and object detection could fail in some circumstances, for example, due to motion blur caused by the user's head movement or varying light conditions. We devise our application to tolerate such situations if semantic segmentation or object detection fails. In such situations, our approach leaves the *Detected Objects* panel empty and fills the sentences panel with sentences with no object specification. The user can select listed objects in the *Select Object* panel to retrieve relevant sentences.

5   Case Studies

As disability simulations might introduce negative stereotypes and fail to highlight infrastructural and social challenges [4], we recruited people with expressive language difficulties for case studies. According to the American Speech-Language-Hearing Association, about 0.60% of the population use AAC[2]. Inspired by AACrobat [13], we formed case studies where we observed a small group of people with expressive language difficulties who used HoloAAC to complete tasks. We then obtained the users' feedback. According to the local standards for sample size in computer-human interaction studies [6], considering the COVID-19 pandemic, the study setting, and the availability of participants, we recruited 7 participants. This sample size follows the highly expert recommendations ranging from 4 ± 1 to 10 ± 2 [6]. P1, P2, P3, and P4 are local, while P5, P6, and P7 are non-local. P1 is blind in her right eye. P2 is deaf. P4 has a lower-limb disability. P6 has aphasia. P7 has aphasia and hemiplegia. Table 1 shows their demographics.

---

[2] https://www.asha.org/njc/aac/.

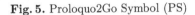

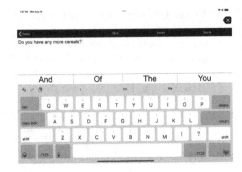

Fig. 5. Proloquo2Go Symbol (PS)   **Fig. 6.** Proloquo2Go Typing (PT)

Since Proloquo2Go[3] is a popular AAC application on iPhone and iPad for people with expressive language difficulties [12], we let participants complete the same tasks using it as a baseline to investigate the usability and feasibility of our application. Considering the comfort, IRB regulation, safety, convenience, and privacy of AAC users, we conducted the case studies in a simulated environment for P1, P2, P3, and P4. We used a private room inside a lab and set up an environment similar to a grocery store cashier. P5 lives 400 mi away, so we traveled to his home for the case study. Similarly, we drove to an aphasia rehabilitation center 100 mi away to conduct case studies for P6 and P7.

5.1   Implementation

We developed HoloAAC using a PC equipped with a Nvidia GTX 3070 GPU, running Unity 2020.3.20, Microsoft Visual Studio 2019, Anaconda3, and PyCharm 2021.2.3. The backend services such as image processing and sentence retrieval also run on this PC. The prototype runs on a Microsoft HoloLens 2. For fine-tuning the YOLOv5 object detection model, we used a PC with a Nvidia GTX 3090 GPU.

5.2   Procedure

Control Groups. We used two control groups: Proloquo2Go Symbol (Fig. 5) and Proloquo2Go Typing (Fig. 6) since these two modes are frequently used by AAC users. In our case study, Proloquo2Go runs on an iPad.

Warm-Up Session. We conducted a warm-up session to get participants familiarized with the basic operations of Proloquo2Go and our application as well. To let them get ready for the formal case study tasks, the warm-up session comprised of two tasks. The two warm-up tasks were the same, except that

---

[3] https://www.assistiveware.com/products/proloquo2go.

we assisted them in finishing the first task while they finished the second task independently. For counterbalancing, the participant did the tasks in different orders. For example, if the participant did Proloquo2Go Symbol, Proloquo2Go Typing, and HoloAAC for the first task, the participant would do the second warm-up task in a different order: e.g., HoloAAC, Proloquo2Go Symbol, and Proloquo2Go Typing.

Table 2. Target sentences used for the six tasks. To avoid confusion, we used *bag* in Proloquo2Go Typing and HoloAAC, and *plastic bag* in Proloquo2Go Symbol as the *bag* symbol in Proloquo2Go was not a plastic bag. Also, as Proloquo2Go did not have the plural form symbol of *bag* and *soda*, we used the singular form. Besides, in Proloquo2Go Symbol, we omitted the punctuations of the target sentences for simplicity.

Task	Item(s)	Proloquo2Go Typing and HoloAAC	Proloquo2Go Symbol
1	water	What is the price of water?	What is the price of water
2	soda	Do you have six-packs of soda?	Do you have six-packs of soda
3	coffee	Do you have any more coffee?	Do you have any more coffee
4	soda	Put all the sodas in one bag?	Put all the soda in one plastic bag
5	water, soda	Can you put the water and soda in one bag?	Can you put the water and soda in one plastic bag
6	water, coffee, soda	Can you put these groceries in separate bags?	Can you put these groceries in separate plastic bag

Table 3. Task completion times and time analysis (Unit: second) of the participants. HL, PS, and PT denote the HoloAAC, Proloquo2Go Symbol, and Proloquo2Go Typing conditions. SD denotes standard deviation.

Participant	Task 1			Task 2			Task 3			Task 4			Task 5			Task 6			Mean			SD		
	HL	PS	PT	HL	PS	PT	HL	PS	PT	HL	PS	PT	HL	PS	PT	HL	PS	PT	HL	PS	PT	HL	PS	PT
P1	18	63	20	12	32	19	30	47	16	21	90	15	11	84	20	18	81	23	18	66	19	7	23	3
P2	40	66	9	12	65	8	40	24	9	32	86	14	52	102	18	27	93	23	34	73	13	14	28	6
P3	33	84	34	15	137	22	78	48	23	39	147	23	15	147	30	39	114	43	37	113	29	23	40	8
P4	10	92	7	35	47	21	43	41	5	60	113	7	14	107	9	10	91	16	29	82	11	21	31	6
P5	27	134	23	15	116	32	33	143	27	33	214	24	14	190	38	19	211	51	24	168	33	9	47	11
P6	39	153	81	26	75	82	38	214	64	27	245	47	7	256	64	15	105	123	25	175	77	13	75	26
P7	12	156	16	31	206	29	35	100	22	30	221	50	41	84	38	17	119	57	28	148	35	11	56	16

Case Study Tasks. As shown in Table 2, we designed 6 tasks with different target sentences, which were also given with counterbalancing. Our application tracked the time spent on different operations (e.g., clicking keywords). However, as Proloquo2Go does not have a timing function, we employed an external timer to count the time for the Proloquo2Go Symbol and Proloquo2Go Typing conditions. For Proloquo2Go Typing, we ended the timer once the user had typed the entire sentence. For Proloquo2Go Symbol, we ended the timer once the user had typed the last symbol.

Questionnaire. After the last Proloquo2Go Symbol/Typing and the HoloAAC tasks, we asked the participants to finish a questionnaire to evaluate the workload, using the same iPad which they used to complete Proloquo2Go Symbol/Typing tasks. Besides, we asked them for general feedback. They typed their responses on their AAC devices or phones. We used the NASA Task Load Index (TLX) [16] to assess the subjective workload. It had six questions in total, which were answered using a 7-Likert scale.

Result Analysis. Table 3 shows the task completion times and time analysis of the participants. We can see that P1, P2, P3, and P4 show a more stable ability to type, probably because they type frequently in their daily life. During the case study, they sometimes chose the autocomplete words supplied by the tablet's input keyboard to speed up their input.

Table 4. Mean completion time for each task with HoloAAC.

Task	1	2	3	4	5	6
Mean Time(s)	26	21	42	35	22	21

P1 took similar time using HoloAAC or Proloquo2Go Typing. The completion times with HoloAAC are less than those with Proloquo2Go Typing in 4 out of 6 tasks (Task 1, 2, 5 & 6).

P2 took more time using HoloAAC than Proloquo2Go Typing. We found that it was hard for him to quickly manage to click the target sentence in AR. It took him many attempts to click one sentence to make it speak.

P3 took slightly more time using HoloAAC than Proloquo2Go Typing on average. However, she finished 4 out of 6 tasks (Task 1, 2, 5 & 6) faster using HoloAAC.

P4 took more time using HoloAAC than Proloquo2Go Typing probably due to his many years of experience with Proloquo2Go but no experience with AR.

P5 took less time in 3 out of 6 tasks (Task 2, 5 & 6) using HoloAAC than Proloquo2Go Typing. The mean and standard deviation (SD) show that using HoloAAC is faster than using Proloquo2Go Symbol or Typing. Proloquo2Go and HoloAAC are both new to him. The data shows that he becomes familiar with HoloAAC faster than with Proloquo2Go.

P6 took less time in all 6 tasks using HoloAAC compared to using Proloquo2Go Symbol or Proloquo2Go Typing. From the SD and mean, using HoloAAC is faster than using Proloquo2Go Symbol or Typing.

P7 took less time in 3 out of 6 tasks (Task 1, 4, & 6) using HoloAAC than Proloquo2Go Typing. From the SD and mean, using HoloAAC is faster than using Proloquo2Go Symbol or Typing. Because of hemiplegia, P7 felt hard clicking the sentence precisely and gradually became frustrated as the case study went by. As a result, in the NASA TLX, he gave the same ratings for all questions under

HoloAAC (7), Proloquo2Go Symbol (4), and Proloquo2Go Typing (1) to finish the case study quickly.

We note that the participants generally finished the tasks much faster using HoloAAC than using Proloquo2Go Symbol, even for P1 and P4 who are experienced with Proloquo2Go but not with AR. It seems that choosing keywords/symbols to finish a sentence exactly may take more time than typing especially for experienced typers.

Table 4 shows the mean completion time for each task. We can see that Task 3 and Task 4 are the top two in time consumption as they required the participant to click keywords in AR. More AR mid-air interactions generally resulted in more time needed.

5.3   User Feedback

General Feedback. About our HoloAAC application, all participants said that they liked the automatic popping up of relevant keywords and sentences with respect to the objects detected.

Table 5. NASA TLX workload assessment ratings given by the participants. HL, PS, and PT denote the HoloAAC, Proloquo2Go Symbol, and Proloquo2Go Typing conditions. Please refer to Sect. 5.3 for the findings and explanations.

Participant	Mental Demand			Physical Demand			Temporal Demand			Performance Dissatisfaction			Effort			Frustration		
	HL	PS	PT	HL	PS	PT	HL	PS	PT	HL	PS	PT	HL	PS	PT	HL	PS	PT
P1	4	5	1	3	1	1	4	5	2	3	3	1	3	5	1	1	1	1
P2	5	6	1	5	6	1	2	6	1	4	3	1	5	6	1	2	6	1
P3	7	2	1	7	2	2	3	1	1	3	1	1	7	2	1	2	2	1
P4	2	6	2	4	3	2	2	6	5	2	3	2	3	7	3	3	5	4
P5	7	7	1	7	4	1	2	7	1	4	1	1	7	7	1	7	7	6
P6	3	3	3	5	4	3	5	3	3	4	4	3	3	5	4	3	2	4
P7	7	4	1	7	4	1	7	4	1	7	4	1	7	4	1	7	4	1

P1 appreciated the camera feature for quicker expression but found interacting with the AR interface challenging due to her right eye's blindness.

P2 enjoyed automated sentence generation but found sentence clicking in AR challenging. His unfamiliarity with AR glasses presented some task difficulties but ultimately brought a sense of fulfillment upon completion.

P3 appreciated the automatic object detection and sentence generation functionalities but suggested improving user input responses and enhancing mid-air clicking for smoother interactions. During the case study, it took her multiple attempts to click target sentences but she found a sense of accomplishment after completing tasks. She also recommended extending HoloAAC for hospital use.

P4 appreciated HoloAAC's speed and efficiency but had three suggestions. First, he proposed extending the system to distinguish subtle item differences like colors and sizes. Second, he suggested instant picture-to-speech capabilities for situations like seeing a cute dog on the street. Third, he recommended personalizing response options based on contexts such as retrieving recent personal stories during conversations with friends.

P5 liked the new interaction approach and felt excited when clicking the expected sentence. However, he found the interaction challenging and time-consuming. He suggested using HoloAAC in schools.

P6 was highly enthusiastic about HoloAAC, seeing its potential for communication and time-saving. He expressed a desire for improved interaction accuracy and recommended broader uses in parks, shops, and schools.

P7 struggled with HoloAAC due to hemiplegia as he could only use his left hand for clicking. He recommended improving accuracy and sensitivity to benefit a wider range of users in the workplace.

NASA TLX. We used NASA TLX to measure the workload. It measures the workload from six aspects: mental demand, physical demand, temporal demand, performance dissatisfaction, effort, and frustration. Table 5 shows the original ratings and Fig. 7 shows the rating plots using the box and whisker plot. 1 represents very low and 7 represents very high. The lower, the better.

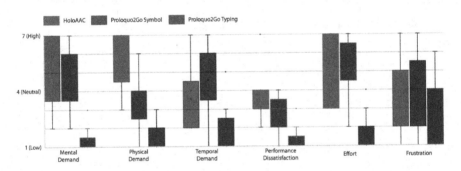

Fig. 7. NASA TLX workload assessment rating plots. Each box and whisker plot comprises six-number summary of the rating: minimum, lower quartile (Q1), median (line), mean (×), upper quartile (Q3), and maximum. Please refer to Sect. 5.3 for the findings and explanations.

P1, P2, and P4 found HoloAAC generally superior to Proloquo2Go Symbol in all aspects. P1 and P2 excelled with Proloquo2Go Typing due to their 5 years of AAC experience. P4 considered HoloAAC on par with Proloquo2Go Typing. P3 rated HoloAAC highly in mental demand, physical demand, and effort due to her 20 years with traditional AAC. P5 gave HoloAAC high ratings in various aspects but struggled due to myopia and the difficulty with sentence selection. P6's ratings were similar for both Proloquo2Go and HoloAAC as both were new to him. P7 assigned the highest ratings to HoloAAC, middle ratings to Proloquo2Go Symbol, and the lowest ratings to Proloquo2Go Typing due to his limited ability to use only his left hand for tasks. In comparison to other participants, mid-air AR interactions were more physically demanding for him.

Mental Demand. The average rating of HoloAAC is 5, and 4 out of 7 ratings are greater than 4. The reason is that participants needed to focus on the AR panel to be able to interact. On the other hand, all 7 participants hadn't used HoloLens 2 before, but they were more or less experienced in Proloquo2Go or similar devices/applications.

Physical Demand. The average rating of HoloAAC is 5.43, which is even higher than that of the mental demand. 5 out of 7 ratings are greater than 4. The reason is that the task was simple to understand, but the interaction required motion control. Some of the participants had disabilities besides speaking disabilities, which made the physical demand even higher. Another reason is, as Plasson et al. [32] pointed out, the mid-air interaction that HoloLens uses is less accurate than 2D touch and tends to result in physical fatigue.

Temporal Demand. The average rating of HoloAAC is 3.57, a little better than neutral (4); and 5 out of 7 ratings are less than or equal to 4. The reason is that participants didn't feel stressed when performing the tasks. On the other hand, few interactions were needed to complete the tasks using HoloAAC.

Performance Dissatisfaction. The average rating of Holo-AAC is 3.86, a little better than neutral (4). 6 out of 7 ratings are less or equal to 4. Note that only P7 gave a high rating (7) for this aspect. The reason is that P7 did attempt many times to interact with the AR interface because of his hemiplegia. We can say most participants tended to be satisfied with their performance.

Effort. The average rating of HoloAAC is 5, which is equal to the mental demand rating. 4 out of 7 ratings are greater than 4. The reason is that some participants had other disabilities in eyes or motion control, which means that it required more effort for them to finish tasks.

Frustration. The average rating of HoloAAC is 3.57, a little better than neutral (4). 5 out of 7 ratings are less than 4. Most participants didn't feel high frustration when performing tasks using HoloAAC.

In all six aspects, participants gave the lowest ratings to Proloquo2Go Typing. That is because 26-key keyboard-based typing is classic and the participants were more or less familiar with it. Compared to tablet-based AAC applications, HoloAAC running on a HoloLens 2 headset was new to the participants and might be rated unfavorably due to the participants' unfamiliarity with mixed reality. On the other hand, tablet-based AAC applications might have been favored due to the participants' familiarity with tablets.

5.4   Limitations and Future Work

Due to the small population size of AAC users and the challenge that few AAC users were willing to sign up for our case study, our study recruited only seven participants. Hence, we are unable to draw statistically significant conclusions.

We only demonstrate HoloAAC for simple grocery scenarios. The generalizability depends on the underlying object detection model. By using a more versatile model, HoloAAC can function in a wider range of scenarios. We chose to experiment with the grocery scenario for two reasons: 1) the conversations at a cashier tend to be more coherent; and 2) we can leverage contextual information based on grocery items recognized using off-the-shelf computer vision techniques. HoloAAC serves as an early prototype to explore and validate the possibility of integrating AR with AAC. The framework can be extended for other applications. It is technically feasible to enhance the generalizability by incorporating a virtual keyboard or replacing the backend models with contrastive language-image pre-training (CLIP) to satisfy the needs of specific users or application scenarios. Furthermore, the seamless integration of large language models (LLMs) such as ChatGPT into our approach is promising as AI-generated phrases can potentially lessen physical and cognitive sentence creation efforts during communication [43].

Another possible extension is to attach a 4G/5G communication module to enable HoloLens to work without Wi-Fi, which would allow our application to be employed in more scenarios such as supporting outdoor activities. Besides, due to the reality that a standard disabled experience rarely plays out in practice [18], it would be helpful to support multi-modal interactions considering multiple disabilities so as to better accommodate AAC users. For example, for those people with both expressive language difficulties and motion control disabilities, an interaction mechanism based on eye-tracking rather than hand-clicking is more accessible.

For those users who have not used HoloLens, it might take them some time to get familiar with the AR interactions. In our case study, some participants experienced difficulty in clicking the keywords or sentences shown in AR. We believe that improving the hand-tracking precision would make AR-based AAC applications more practical and favorable. Alternatively, instead of using mid-air interactions, using a controller (e.g., the clicker of HoloLens 1) could make interaction easier especially for users with body movement disabilities.

6   Conclusion

We presented HoloAAC, a novel mixed reality-based AAC application. We explored its usability and feasibility through a case study, which provided useful insights for future AR-based AAC applications. First, CV and NLP-based functionalities showed promise and were favored by our participants. Second, other disabilities of AAC users may be considered in designing an AR-based AAC application. Moreover, multi-modal interactions can be incorporated to improve the user experience.

Acknowledgments. We are grateful to the participants for their feedback on our application. This project was supported by NSF grants (award numbers: 1942531 and 2128867).

Disclosure of Interests. The authors have no competing interests to declare that are relevant to the content of this article.

References

1. Al-Kassim, Z., Memon, Q.A.: Designing a low-cost eyeball tracking keyboard for paralyzed people. Comput. Electr. Eng. **58**, 20–29 (2017)
2. Al-Rahayfeh, A., Faezipour, M.: Eye tracking and head movement detection: a state-of-art survey. IEEE J. Transl. Eng. Health Med. **1**, 2100212 (2013)
3. Bai, Z., Blackwell, A., Coulouris, G.: Using augmented reality to elicit pretend play for children with autism. IEEE Trans. Vis. Comput. Graph. **21**, 598–610 (2015). https://doi.org/10.1109/TVCG.2014.2385092
4. Bennett, C.L., Rosner, D.K.: The promise of empathy: design, disability, and knowing the "other". In: Proceedings of the 2019 CHI Conference on Human Factors in Computing Systems, pp. 1–13 (2019)
5. Beukelman, D.R., Mirenda, P., et al.: Augmentative and Alternative Communication. Paul H Brookes, Baltimore (1998)
6. Caine, K.: Local standards for sample size at CHI. In: Proceedings of the 2016 CHI Conference on Human Factors in Computing Systems, pp. 981–992 (2016)
7. Chan, R.Y.Y., Bai, X., Chen, X., Jia, S., Xu, X.h.: IBeacon and HCI in special education: micro-location based augmentative and alternative communication for children with intellectual disabilities. In: Proceedings of the 2016 CHI Conference Extended Abstracts on Human Factors in Computing Systems, CHI EA 2016, pp. 1533–1539. Association for Computing Machinery, New York (2016)
8. Chan, R.Y.Y., Sato-Shimokawara, E., Bai, X., Yukiharu, M., Kuo, S.W., Chung, A.: A context-aware augmentative and alternative communication system for school children with intellectual disabilities. IEEE Syst. J. **14**, 208–219 (2020)
9. Chen, C.H., Lee, I.J., Lin, L.Y.: Augmented reality-based self-facial modeling to promote the emotional expression and social skills of adolescents with autism spectrum disorders. Res. Dev. Disabil. **36**, 396–403 (2015). https://doi.org/10.1016/j.ridd.2014.10.015
10. Chen, C.H., Lee, I.J., Lin, L.Y.: Augmented reality-based video-modeling storybook of nonverbal facial cues for children with autism spectrum disorder to improve their perceptions and judgments of facial expressions and emotions. Comput. Hum. Behav. **55**, 477–485 (2016)
11. Cihak, D.F., Moore, E.J., Wright, R.E., McMahon, D.D., Gibbons, M.M., Smith, C.: Evaluating augmented reality to complete a chain task for elementary students with autism. J. Spec. Educ. Technol. **31**(2), 99–108 (2016). https://doi.org/10.1177/0162643416651724
12. DongGyu, P., Song, S., Lee, D.: Smart phone-based context-aware augmentative and alternative communications system. J. Central South Univ. **21**, 3551–3558 (2014). https://doi.org/10.1007/s11771-014-2335-3
13. Fiannaca, A., Paradiso, A., Shah, M., Morris, M.R.: AACrobat: using mobile devices to lower communication barriers and provide autonomy with gaze-based AAC. In: Proceedings of the 2017 ACM Conference on Computer Supported Cooperative Work and Social Computing, pp. 683–695 (2017)
14. Ghatkamble, R., Son, J., Park, D.: A design and implementation of smartphone-based AAC system. J. Korea Inst. Inf. Commun. Eng. **18**(8), 1895–1903 (2014)

15. Gibson, R.C., Dunlop, M.D., Bouamrane, M.M., Nayar, R.: Designing clinical AAC tablet applications with adults who have mild intellectual disabilities. In: Proceedings of the 2020 CHI Conference on Human Factors in Computing Systems, pp. 1–13 (2020)
16. Hart, S.G.: Nasa task load index (TLX) (1986)
17. Hayden, C.M., et al.: Augmented reality for speech and language intervention in autism spectrum disorder. Ph.D. thesis (2017)
18. Hofmann, M., Kasnitz, D., Mankoff, J., Bennett, C.L.: Living disability theory: reflections on access, research, and design. In: Proceedings of the 22nd International ACM SIGACCESS Conference on Computers and Accessibility, pp. 1–13 (2020)
19. Hung, S.W., Chang, C.W., Ma, Y.C.: A new reality: exploring continuance intention to use mobile augmented reality for entertainment purposes. Technol. Soc. **67**, 101757 (2021)
20. Jen, C.L., Chen, Y.L., Lin, Y.J., Lee, C.H., Tsai, A., Li, M.T.: Vision based wearable eye-gaze tracking system. In: 2016 IEEE International Conference on Consumer Electronics (ICCE), pp. 202–203. IEEE (2016)
21. Kane, S.K., Linam-Church, B., Althoff, K., McCall, D.: What we talk about: Designing a context-aware communication tool for people with aphasia. In: Proceedings of the 14th International ACM SIGACCESS Conference on Computers and Accessibility, ASSETS 2012, pp. 49–56. Association for Computing Machinery, New York (2012). https://doi.org/10.1145/2384916.2384926
22. Kerdvibulvech, C., Wang, C.-C.: A new 3D augmented reality application for educational games to help children in communication interactively. In: Gervasi, O., et al. (eds.) ICCSA 2016. LNCS, vol. 9787, pp. 465–473. Springer, Cham (2016). https://doi.org/10.1007/978-3-319-42108-7_35
23. Klaib, A.F., Alsrehin, N.O., Melhem, W.Y., Bashtawi, H.O., Magableh, A.A.: Eye tracking algorithms, techniques, tools, and applications with an emphasis on machine learning and internet of things technologies. Expert Syst. Appl. **166**, 114037 (2021). https://doi.org/10.1016/j.eswa.2020.114037. https://www.sciencedirect.com/science/article/pii/S0957417420308071
24. Krishnamurthy, D., Jaswal, V., Nazari, A., Shahidi, A., Subbaraman, P., Wang, M.: Holotype: lived experience based communication training for nonspeaking autistic people. In: CHI Conference on Human Factors in Computing Systems Extended Abstracts, pp. 1–6 (2022)
25. Kristensson, P.O., Lilley, J., Black, R., Waller, A.: A design engineering approach for quantitatively exploring context-aware sentence retrieval for nonspeaking individuals with motor disabilities. In: Proceedings of the 2020 CHI Conference on Human Factors in Computing Systems, pp. 1–11 (2020)
26. Liu, R., Salisbury, J., Vahabzadeh, A., Sahin, N.: Feasibility of an autism-focused augmented reality smartglasses system for social communication and behavioral coaching. Front. Pediatr. **5** (2017). https://doi.org/10.3389/fped.2017.00145
27. Mcmahon, D., Cihak, D., Wright, R., Bell, S.: Augmented reality for teaching science vocabulary to postsecondary education students with intellectual disabilities and autism. J. Res. Technol. Educ. **48**, 1–19 (2015). https://doi.org/10.1080/15391523.2015.1103149
28. Mitchell, C., et al.: Ability-based keyboards for augmentative and alternative communication: Understanding how individuals' movement patterns translate to more efficient keyboards: Methods to generate keyboards tailored to user-specific motor abilities. In: Extended Abstracts of the 2022 CHI Conference on Human Factors in Computing Systems, CHI EA 2022. Association for Computing Machinery, New York (2022). https://doi.org/10.1145/3491101.3519845

29. Mystakidis, S., Christopoulos, A., Pellas, N.: A systematic mapping review of augmented reality applications to support stem learning in higher education. Educ. Inf. Technol. **27**(2), 1883–1927 (2022)
30. Obiorah, M.G., Piper, A.M.M., Horn, M.: Designing AACS for people with aphasia dining in restaurants. In: Proceedings of the 2021 CHI Conference on Human Factors in Computing Systems, pp. 1–14 (2021)
31. Panchanathan, S., Moore, M., Venkateswara, H., Chakraborty, S., McDaniel, T.: Computer vision for augmentative and alternative communication. In: Computer Vision for Assistive Healthcare, pp. 211–248. Elsevier (2018)
32. Plasson, C., Cunin, D., Laurillau, Y., Nigay, L.: 3d tabletop AR: a comparison of mid-air, touch and touch+ mid-air interaction. In: Proceedings of the International Conference on Advanced Visual Interfaces, pp. 1–5 (2020)
33. Porter, G., Kirkland, J., Spastic Society of Victoria: Integrating Augmentative and Alternative Communication Into Group Programs: Utilising the Principles of Conductive Education. Spastic Society of Victoria (1995). https://books.google.com/books?id=weYGPQAACAAJ
34. Ramires Fernandes, A., Almeida da Silva, C., Grohmann, A.: Assisting speech therapy for autism spectrum disorders with an augmented reality application, vol. 3, November 2014
35. Raudonis, V., Simutis, R., Narvydas, G.: Discrete eye tracking for medical applications. In: 2009 2nd International Symposium on Applied Sciences in Biomedical and Communication Technologies, pp. 1–6 (2009). https://doi.org/10.1109/ISABEL.2009.5373675
36. Rauschnabel, P.A., Felix, R., Hinsch, C.: Augmented reality marketing: how mobile AR-apps can improve brands through inspiration. J. Retail. Consum. Serv. **49**, 43–53 (2019)
37. Rocha, A.P., et aloward supporting communication for people with aphasia: the in-bed scenario. In: Adjunct Publication of the 24th International Conference on Human-Computer Interaction with Mobile Devices and Services, MobileHCI 2022. Association for Computing Machinery, New York (2022). https://doi.org/10.1145/3528575.3551431
38. Sezer, O.B., Dogdu, E., Ozbayoglu, A.M.: Context-aware computing, learning, and big data in internet of things: a survey. IEEE Internet Things J. **5**(1), 1–27 (2018). https://doi.org/10.1109/JIOT.2017.2773600
39. Shane, H.C., Blackstone, S., Vanderheiden, G., Williams, M., DeRuyter, F.: Using AAC technology to access the world. Assist. Technol. **24**(1), 3–13 (2012)
40. Shen, J., Yang, B., Dudley, J.J., Kristensson, P.O.: KWickChat: a multi-turn dialogue system for AAC using context-aware sentence generation by bag-of-keywords. In: 27th International Conference on Intelligent User Interfaces, pp. 853–867, IUI 2022. Association for Computing Machinery, New York (2022). https://doi.org/10.1145/3490099.3511145
41. Sobel, K., et al.: Exploring the design space of AAC awareness displays. In: Proceedings of the 2017 CHI Conference on Human Factors in Computing Systems, pp. 2890–2903 (2017)
42. Tzima, S., Styliaras, G., Bassounas, A.: Augmented reality applications in education: teachers point of view. Educ. Sci. **9**(2), 99 (2019)
43. Valencia, S., Cave, R., Kallarackal, K., Seaver, K., Terry, M., Kane, S.K.: "The less i type, the better": how AI language models can enhance or impede communication for AAC users. In: Proceedings of the 2023 CHI Conference on Human Factors in Computing Systems, pp. 1–14 (2023)

44. Wang, W., Lei, S., Liu, H., Li, T., Qu, J., Qiu, A.: Augmented reality in maintenance training for military equipment. In: Journal of Physics: Conference Series. vol. 1626, p. 012184. IOP Publishing (2020)
45. Zhang, X., Kulkarni, H., Morris, M.R.: Smartphone-based gaze gesture communication for people with motor disabilities. In: Proceedings of the 2017 CHI Conference on Human Factors in Computing Systems, pp. 2878–2889 (2017)
46. Zhao, H., Karlsson, P., Kavehei, O., McEwan, A.: Augmentative and alternative communication with eye-gaze technology and augmented reality: reflections from engineers, people with cerebral palsy and caregivers. In: 2021 IEEE Sensors, pp. 1–4 (2021). https://doi.org/10.1109/SENSORS47087.2021.9639819

Mixed-Integer Programming for Adaptive VR Workflow Training

Yongqi Zhang[1]([envelope]) [iD], Chuan Yan[1] [iD], Haikun Huang[1] [iD], Simon Su[2] [iD], and Lap-Fai Yu[1] [iD]

[1] George Mason University, Fairfax, VA 22030, USA
{yzhang59,cyan3,hhuang25,craigyu}@gmu.edu
[2] National Institute of Standards and Technology, Gaithersburg, MD 20899, USA
simon.su@nist.gov

Abstract. With advances in consumer-grade virtual reality (VR) devices, VR training gains unprecedented attention in research and industries. Although the nature of VR training encourages trainees to actively learn through exploring and gathering information in a simulated virtual environment, designing effective virtual training environments is non-trivial. We propose an adaptive approach that guides trainees to develop psychomotor skills in a simulated virtual environment. As a showcase, we demonstrate our novel approach for restaurant service using a game-based VR application. By incorporating the trainee's performance and learning progress into optimization objectives, our approach uses mixed integer programming (MIP) to generate VR training sessions iteratively. Through collecting the trainee's performance in VR training, our approach adapts the VR training sessions by considering the trainee's strengths and weaknesses, guiding the trainee to improve over training sessions. We validated our approach through two experimental studies. In the first study, we compared our approach with a random training task assignment approach and a performance-only MIP approach through performing simulated restaurant service training. In the second study, we compared our approach with the random assignment approach by evaluating trainees' skill developments in restaurant services. The results show that our skill-driven adaptive training approach outperforms the random assignment approach.

Keywords: game design · adaptive training · virtual reality · optimization

1 Introduction

With advances in consumer-grade virtual reality (VR) devices, many companies start to employ VR as a supplement to their workplace training. For example, Walmart uses VR to simulate common and uncommon scenarios that could happen during Black Friday and prepare their employees for all possible upcoming challenges [23]. Similarly, United Rentals, the world's largest equipment rental

J. Y. C. Chen and G. Fragomeni (Eds.): HCII 2024, LNCS 14708, pp. 325–344, 2024.
https://doi.org/10.1007/978-3-031-61047-9_21

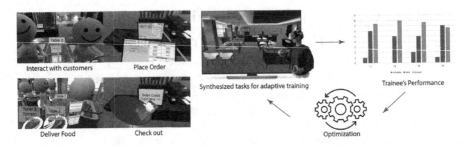

Fig. 1. Four tasks of restaurant service training are shown on the left. These tasks simulate common incidents a restaurant server faces at work. Given the trainee's performance, our approach adaptively generates training sessions. A trainee receives training in the interactive virtual restaurant as shown on the right. In this simulated training environment, the trainee can walk freely, interact with virtual customers, and take requests from tables like working in a real restaurant.

company, created virtual construction sites to engage their employees in learning customer service skills and raising safety and site awareness [34]. Both examples demonstrate that users can gain practical experience through interacting with and working in a simulated environment.

Compared to traditional training methods (e.g., lecture-based training), VR training appears to have many advantages. It is accessible from anywhere, configurable to anyone, and most importantly, provides an active learning environment for trainees to involve in gathering information, thinking, and problem solving [4,36]. However, designing VR training is not trivial because active learning does not simultaneously happen in the virtual environment, it requires a delicate design of teaching methods that are constantly adjusted based on the learning progress of a trainee. Such monitoring of trainee progress can help prevent the learning system from assigning a task too difficult too soon, which may discourage the trainee [22,26]. However, monitoring the progress of individual trainees and manually adjusting difficulty is not ideal as VR training is often applied to a large number of new employees with different skill levels in a company.

This highlights the necessity for adaptive learning, which employs computational techniques to customize learning materials and training based on individuals' needs and performance. [14]. Recent research in adaptive learning has focused on musical tasks [38], machine tasks [11], and academic skills [33] to improve individuals learning efficiency. However, there is a dearth of research to enable psychomotor learning developments. Psychomotor learning refers to the learning process of a person in learning component skills (e.g. how to interact with customers, how to place orders), then compiling these individual psychomotor skills together and automatizing them with higher-level executive functioning (e.g., to work in a restaurant) [7].

Acquiring psychomotor skills in some workplaces is challenging as trainees often have to learn in rapidly changing, intricate environments to gain proficiency, such as performing surgery or flying an aircraft. While VR can simulate these complex conditions, the training may not immediately enable active learning as individuals have unique learning curves. To this end, we propose an adaptive learning approach focused on psychomotor skill development using restaurant service training as a showcase. Our approach is driven by trainee performance on psychomotor skills (e.g., performance in interacting with customers), which are collectively measured and evaluated in an interactive and configurable simulated restaurant. Such an environment encourages trainees to actively gather knowledge about restaurant service responsibility and participate in restaurant service training. By adaptively adjusting training tasks and task difficulty, we provide a full psychomotor learning development experience in an efficient way.

There are four key attributes in constructing personalized adaptive learning: user profiles, competency-based progression, personal learning, and flexible learning environments [25]. Motivated by these design guidelines, we propose a skill-driven adaptive training approach. We build user profiles through pre-evaluation to understand the trainees' skill sets. We evaluate the trainees' progress at each training session by measuring their performances during training. Our approach uses an optimization-based algorithm to create the next training session, taking into consideration the trainee's performance records and their training experience (such as enjoyment). The algorithm balances conflicting training goals (such as being easy but boring vs. being challenging but exhausting) and adapts to each individual's needs, resulting in the creation of a personalized training path to develop their psychomotor skills. By using VR, we enable a flexible active learning environment that supports adaptive adjustment of learning materials. Furthermore, we chose a restaurant as our running example because its workflow is familiar to most people, with a dynamic nature which demands multi-tasking abilities, task priority assessment, and task management. Other workplace training programs and other VR game applications can be adapted into our approach similarly. The main contributions of our work include (Fig. 1):

- We present an optimization-based algorithm that considers a trainee's performance and eagerness to adaptively generate training sessions. This approach can be applied to workflow training in general.
- We created an interactive virtual restaurant to simulate restaurant service tasks. This simulated environment encodes many commmon scenarios a restaurant server faces. It also enables trainees to speak and interact with virtual customers. It is configurable and extensible for training staff to prepare for possible challenges in a real restaurant.
- We conducted a user study to compare our adaptive training approach with a baseline training approach. The results show that our adaptive training approach is more effective and efficient.

2 Related Work

2.1 Virtual Reality-Based Training

VR training is widely applied in different domains such as retail business [30], workplaces and factories [3,29], and vehicle control [17,20], because of its replicability and low cost. For high-risk occupations such as first responders and military and medical learners [27], VR training also provides a mistake-tolerant training environment. We refer our readers to a review on VR training applications for more details [36].

Many current VR training research focuses on knowledge acquisition through training. For example, Li et al. proposed an optimization-based approach for synthesizing construction safety training scenarios, allowing trainees to explore those training scenarios to identify potential hazards [19]. Similarly, Aati et al. developed work zone inspection scenarios for training engineers to inspect the quality of work zone sign placement. They believe this virtual simulator is a safer, cheaper, and more effective way to train inspectors than a field visit [1]. Shao et al. proposed an interactive-learning approach to teach American sign language. Their approach leveraged the third and first-person views for motion demonstration and practice [28]. Moreover, virtual patients have been widely used for testing clinical examination interview skills in the medical field [13,18]. For example, Tavassoli et al. presented a virtual training platform named JAYLA to teach medical students about symptoms and severity levels of Autism Spectrum Disorder in young children. Through encoding verbal and nonverbal behaviors associated with age-appropriate autism into virtual patients, JAYLA provided a new way to enhance professional training for early detection of autism in young children [31]. Another common use of virtual patients is for training clinicians to acquire social skills needed for clinician-patient interactions. Yao et al. trained a classifier to identify empathy levels of a clinician's responses from their interactions with virtual patients and to provide feedback based on evaluation results [37].

Since VR simulation can provide a blame-free environment, trial and error in VR training provides a powerful learning mechanism, especially for high-risk task training. For example, the Brazilian Navy developed a VR simulator for training landing signalman, who was responsible for visual signaling to the pilot and ensuring general safety conditions of the flight deck area [6]. Since this task is often performed under stressful conditions, VR simulation training can help relieve the burden of making mistakes. Crisis management training, another example that uses VR as a learning tool, has been shown to be efficient in VR. By training through a crisis in a subway station in VR, Conges et al. believed that they could prepare practitioners for real-life crises in cities [5]. Moreover, since VR training provides an accessible and scalable manner of training, it can help manufacturing industry to train inexperienced workers to fill workforce shortages. For example, Ipsita et al. present a VR-based welding training simulator that can be easily adapted and distributed at different scales [12]. Those works either focus on educating trainees through immersive simulation or on the interactions between virtual agents and trainees to improve interpersonal skills. In contrast, we propose an adaptive training approach integrated with virtual reality. Through tracking trainee performances during VR training, our approach adaptively modifies training tasks and adjusts the difficulty level of the next training session to enhance training efficiency.

2.2 Psychomotor Learning

Skill development generally involves complex muscular movement and cognitive control, which requires a substantial amount of practices. Psychomotor Learning refers to the relationship between cognitive functions and physical movement. Playing a sport, driving a car, or dancing are examples of psychomotor learning. Fitts and Posner proposed a three-stage model for psychomotor skills development, comprising the cognitive stage, the associative stage, and the autonomic stage. It describes the learning process of a person in accomplishing the task goals. The process starts from gaining theoretical information and attempting to take actions, then gradually becoming fluent in individual actions with slow transitions between these actions, and finally becoming capable of performing skills seamlessly. They also pointed out an important feature of the three-stage development model: a rapid progression usually happens in the cognitive stage and a slow progression usually takes place towards the autonomic stage [7,15]. It implied that trainees must take sufficient practice to achieve full psychomotor skill developments. Adaptive training appeals to fast-paced and high-demand work environments for training workforces to be proficient in multiple tasks in a short amount of time.

Merriënboer et al. defined complex learning as the achievement of multiple performance objectives and emphasized the importance of learning how to coordinate and integrate separate skills to achieve goals [32]. It suggests that when designing training for a complex learning environment (e.g., a workplace), one should not evaluate skills separately. They should also consider proficiency in completing tasks using skills in a coordinated and integrated fashion. In our approach we consider psychomotor skill development in our trainees; in particular, our trainees first obtain knowledge of each task (i.e. workflow of each task) and gradually progress through three stages of psychomotor learning. Since our approach uses mixed integer programming to synthesize training tasks targeted at addressing participants' weaknesses, our approach gradually increases the complexity of the multitasking level. To help trainees perform, we evaluate their performance from a complex learning perspective, that is, we evaluate not only the performance of completing each task, but also the ability to coordinate with other tasks through a multitasking lens.

2.3 Adaptive Training and Interfaces

Although research has shown that adding an extra layer of reality can bring effectiveness to training, it is not easy or intuitive for VR/AR creators to encode learning opportunities into AR/VR [2]. On one hand, many research focuses on

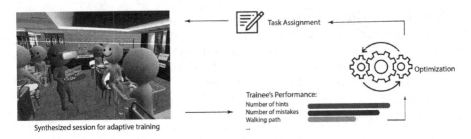

Fig. 2. An overview of our approach. Our approach obtains the trainee's performance metrics from a VR training session, including the number of hints asked, the number of mistakes made, the walking path, and the order of tasks performed. Then it leverages such performance metrics to adaptively generate the next training session through an optimization, aiming to help the trainee improve efficiently. In particular, it adjusts the difficulty levels and appearances of different tasks to keep the trainee engaged with the training.

creating personalized digital space and improving the usability of mixed reality interfaces. For instance, Lindlbauer et al. proposed a context-aware optimization-based approach to automatically control mixed reality interfaces [21]. In particular, this automated process leverages users' cognitive load and information about their tasks and environments to support MR interface adaptation. Inspired by this work, we track a trainee's performance during training and leverage this information to adaptively generate the next training session for the trainee to practice.

On the other hand, a few research investigates different training strategies to improve training performance. For instance, part-task training is often used for training sequential components of a complex task, and increasing training difficulty is effective as long as the increased difficulty is adaptive [7,35]. Yuksel et al. used an increasing-difficulty strategy to adaptively teach users to learn to play the piano with Bach's music pieces. They measured the learners' cognitive workload in real-time to increase the difficulty level of the music learning tasks [38]. Other research aims to combine multiple instructional strategies to achieve better training results. Huang et al. proposed a system that used a combination of macro and micros-approach for adaptation. They collected learner historical records and real-time input to adaptively teach users to master machine tasks [11]. The previous works focused on evaluating the effectiveness of different training strategies in music and machinery tasks. Inspired by these works, we devise an adaptive training approach to synthesize psychomotor skill training sessions for virtual reality-based training.

3   Overview

To illustrate our approach, we create a virtual restaurant to simulate training in a workplace. This virtual restaurant enables trainees to speak, walk and interact with virtual objects/agents in the environment. We describe the details of the virtual environment, object manipulation, and restaurant tasks involved in Sect. 4. By using this virtual restaurant as an illustrative example, we explain how our approach can generate tasks to train people adaptively with respect to skill development. Figure 2 shows an overview of our approach.

Since our approach focuses on psychomotor skill development and multitasking ability development, we formulate a trainee's learning experience and training record into design objectives (e.g., workflow of a task, number of hints used, mistakes made) as well as a set of constraints (e.g., multitasking difficulty level). We use mixed integer programming (MIP) to solve this multi-objectives optimization problem (Sect. 4.2) while satisfying the constraints. Given trainee performance from the previous training session, our approach assigns different tasks and adjusts their difficulty levels for the next training session, while gradually increasing the multitasking difficulty.

Lastly, we validate our approach through two experiments (see Sect. 5). In the first study, we compared our approach with a random assignment approach and a Performance-Only MIP approach through performing simulated training. The goal of this simulation experiment is to see whether our approach can train trainees to progress more efficiently than baseline approaches given the same trainee with a fixed learning ability. In the second study, we compare our approach with the random assignment approach by training trainees to work in a virtual restaurant. The goal of the second user study is to evaluate efficiency in restaurant skill development and multitask strategy skill development under two different training conditions.

4   Problem Formulation

4.1   Virtual Environment and Interaction

Restaurant Service Tasks. A good restaurant server must excel at communication, front-of-house tasks (e.g., cleaning up tables), time management, and also multitasking. Thus, a restaurant service training not only considers individual skill development but also the ability to combine and use skills in an optimal manner. For our virtual restaurant, we design eight tasks to represent major customer requests restaurant staffs need to handle in their daily work routine. We included regular tasks such as taking orders, delivering food and checkout; and two incident tasks that described some common accidents in a restaurant (e.g. drink dropped, food overcooked). Refer to Table 1 for description of four major tasks.

Fig. 3. A snapshot of the "check out" task. The trainee was about to return the credit card to the customer, who was angry as it was taking too long.

Each task has a difficulty level and a property that reveals the characteristic of this task. For example, the "check out" task is time sensitive because this task

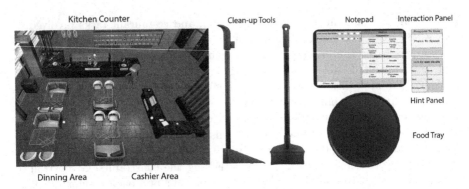

Fig. 4. Left: the virtual restaurant's layout. Right: the tools for performing tasks in virtual reality. Trainees used the left-hand controller to switch between tools for completing different tasks. They also used the interaction panel to interact with virtual customers and the hint panel to ask about the workflow of a task.

Table 1. The details of different tasks.

Task	Name	Description	Diff. level	Property (value)	Walking Path
1	Ready To Order	Interact with customers and ask what they want to order	3	Talk-centric(1)	Table->POS
2	Want Food	Grab food from kitchen and deliver food to each customers;Grab dirty plates	3	Service-centric(10)	Table->Kitchen ->Table
3	Reqeust Recipt	Print out receipt and deliver it to the table	3	Time-sensitive(100)	Table->POS ->Table
4	Checkout	Process payment for the customers	3	Time-sensitive(100)	Table->POS ->Table

requires trainees to return the customer's credit card within a time limit, otherwise the customer will be angry at him (see purple agent in Fig. 3). Each task also is associated with a property value, which is used to set up constraints for multitasking level difficulty training (see Sect. 4.3). Please refer to the supplementary material for more details of each task setting. With these constraints, trainees can practice their multitasking ability in training sessions generated by our optimizer.

Virtual Environment. As shown in Fig. 4 (left), our 6m X 6m simulated virtual restaurant contains four tables, one food counter, and one point-of-sale (POS) machine. A trainee can walk freely in this simulated environment. At the beginning of the simulation, the trainee will walk to a table first, interact with customers to get a request, then walk to the POS machine for placing an order, or go to the food counter to get items for the customers. After that, she will go back to the table to deliver the items for completion. During the simulation, each table will have at most one request.

User Interaction and Speech. The trainee uses the left-hand controller for switching tools between a food tray, a clean up tool, and an interaction panel. This interaction panel is used to interact with a customer. See Fig. 4 (right). By pressing the speak button, our program can record the trainee's speech. We use natural language processing from the Wit model[1] for speech recognition in our simulation. The model first extracts the trainee's intention from their speech, then it will check if this trainee's intention belongs to one of the three predefined categories: greeting response, ask for repeat response, and task-specific responses. If not, it will ask the trainee to speak again. Once the intention is recognized and matches with the current task's desired response, the customer will respond or react. See the supplementary material for responses of different categories. We also include a hint panel underneath the interaction panel. If the trainee is uncertain about the workflow of a task or a message to respond to, he can press this hint button to get the next step information.

4.2 Optimization Approach

Our approach aims to assign tasks with suitable difficulty for each training session while satisfying some training constraints (e.g., multitasking level constraint). We propose an objective with the following sub-objectives: repeated mistake avoidance (M), familiarity with the workflow (W), tolerance of repetition (R) and eagerness (E). M measures the number of mistakes made by a trainee. W measures the number of hints the trainee asked for, which reflects the trainee's familiarity with the current workflow. R measures the number of times a task is repeated in a row. E estimates the amount of eagerness with which the trainee is willing to play this task. Our approach seeks to maximize the overall objective function comprising the sub-objectives. For all tasks $t \in T = \{1, ...n\}$, our approach solves for the following:

$$\max \sum_t^n \sum_d^m X_{t,d} Y_{t,d} (\lambda_M M_{t,d} + \lambda_W W_{t,d} + \lambda_R R_{t,d} + \lambda_E E_{t,d}), \tag{1}$$

where $X_{t,d} \in \{0,1\}$ is a binary decision variable capturing whether task t with difficulty d will be used in a training session. $Y_{t,d}$ denotes whether task t has difficulty d. All sub-objective functions are calculated for the current task t with difficulty d, but for simplicity we drop the subscript later on. We empirically set the weight of each sub-objective function as 0.3. Table 2 summarizes the parameters and variables in our formulation.

Repeated Mistake Avoidance (M). Mistakes are a valuable indicator in designing a training session. This objective aims to let the trainee practice more if he exhibits repeated mistakes. It consists of two parts, persistent mistake and usability of task difficulty:

---

[1] https://wit.ai/.

Table 2. Descriptions of input parameters and variables in our formulation.

Parameter	Description	Variable	Description
m_t	number of mistakes made in a task t	$T = \{t_1, \ldots t_n\}$	all tasks
n_t	number of times task t has mistakes in the training sessions experienced so far	$X_{t,d}$	binary variable capturing whether task t with difficulty d showed up in training session
h_t	number of hints asked in task t	$Y_{t,d}$	binary variable indicating whether task t has difficulty d
p_t	number of times task t was played	λ_x	weight of a sub-objective function
R_t	number of times of repeating task t in a row		
P_t	task t's property value		
S	total number of training sessions		

$$E = \delta^{\text{MistPer}} U_{t,d}^{\text{MistPer}}. \tag{2}$$

First, we want to know on what percentage the trainee persistently made mistakes when doing this task, denoted by δ^{MistPer} and formulated as:

$$\delta^{\text{MistPer}} = \frac{1}{e^{\lambda_{\text{MistPer}}(K-n^t/p^t)}}, \tag{3}$$

where λ_{MistPer} is set as 2. Presumably, if a task has a large persistent mistake rate, then the trainee needs to work on this task more frequently. K is the largest persistent mistake rate of all tasks from the trainee's performance record. We use this term to evaluate the importance of this task in helping correct mistakes.

Secondly, we define the usability of this task difficulty, $U_{t,d}^{\text{MistPer}}$, in helping to correct persistent mistakes:

$$U_{t,d}^{\text{MistPer}} = \frac{(d_f - d_{\text{target}})^2}{0.5\sigma^2}, \tag{4}$$

where σ is empirically set as 0.8. d_f is the usability of a task with difficulty d which is defined in Table 1. d_{target} denotes the desired task usability a trainee should practice with respect to the persistent mistake rate of this task. In correcting mistake behaviors, it will be better if we start with an easy level task and then gradually increase the difficulty. Therefore, we set d_{target} as follows:

$$d^{\text{target}} = \begin{cases} 1 & \text{if } n^t/p^t \geq 0.8 \\ 0.6 & \text{if } 0.5 \leq n^t/p^t < 0.8 \\ 0.3 & \text{otherwise.} \end{cases} \tag{5}$$

Familiarity with Workflow (W). This objective evaluates whether the trainee understands and remembers the workflow of a particular task. As suggested by [26], we need to avoid fast progression to a difficult task when the trainee is still uncertain about the basic workflow. Thus, the usefulness of a particular task difficulty, U^{TaskDiff}, is defined as follows:

$$U^{\text{TaskDiff}} = \begin{cases} 1 & \text{if } d = 1 \\ 0.6 & \text{if } d = 2 \\ 0.3 & \text{if } d = 3. \end{cases} \tag{6}$$

In this way, we penalize the assignment of a difficult task to a trainee when he is not familiar with the task workflow.

Secondly, we want to know how much a trainee is familiar with the workflow of a task t, denoted as $\delta^{\text{Familiarity}}$, by measuring the number of hints asked in executing that task and normalizing into $[0, 1]$:

$$\delta^{\text{Familiarity}} = \frac{h_t}{h_{\max}}, \tag{7}$$

where $h_{\max}$ denotes the maximum number of hints the trainee asked in doing a task. We empirically set it to be 5. Overall, we have:

$$W = \delta^{\text{Familiarity}} U^{\text{TaskDiff}}. \tag{8}$$

Tolerance with Repetition (R). Repetition is a basic but powerful learning strategy used for training [24]. On one hand, it is desirable to let trainees practice a task repeatedly to strengthen their skills. On the other hand, trainees may lose interest in a certain task after it is repeated too many times. Thus, it is desirable to balance repetition and a trainee's interests during training. In game level design, it is common for game designers to vary game settings to avoid monotonous levels [8, 10]. Inspired by that, we consider the tolerance with repetition and the eagerness to learn to introduce variety to the training. We include the tolerance with repetition term to evaluate how much a trainee can tolerate training with the same task repeated in a row. It is defined as follows:

$$R = \gamma^{R_t} - \sigma^{\text{tolerance}} R_t, \tag{9}$$

where R_t is the number of times task t is repeated in a row. γ and $\sigma^{\text{tolerance}}$ determine the amount of decrease in tolerance; they are empirically set as 0.2.

Eagerness to Learn (E). Other than repetition, it is also important to review tasks to reinforce their learning. By introducing occasionally played tasks, we can let the trainee review the tasks while keeping their interests in training. Specifically, we define this term to evaluate how much a trainee is willing to play a task. This term is determined by the appearance rate of a task for the entire training. Our goal is to avoid assigning a frequently appearing task to training sessions. The term is formulated as follows:

$$E = \begin{cases} 0 & \text{if } \delta^{\text{appear}} < 0.4 \\ \Gamma^{\delta^{\text{appear}}} - 1 & \text{otherwise,} \end{cases} \tag{10}$$

where δ^{appear} is calculated by the number of times this task is played over the number of training sessions experienced so far. Γ controls the speed of decay and is empirically set as 0.2.

4.3   Constraints

We introduce a set of constraints to avoid duplicated tasks, limit training session length, and, most importantly, to perform multitask strategy training practice.

Task Duplicates. We avoid task duplicates by enforcing:

$$C_{\text{t}} = \sum_d X_{\text{t,d}} = 1, \forall t \in \{1,...n\}, \tag{11}$$

where C_{t} denotes the number of tasks appearing in a training session.

Training Session Length. This constraint ensures that each training session has a certain length:

$$1 \leq \sum_t \sum_d X_{\text{t,d}} \leq \delta^{\text{Length}}, \forall t \in \{1,...n\}, \forall d \in \{1...m\}. \tag{12}$$

For our running example, we set δ^{Length} to 4, meaning that at most four tasks appear in a training session.

Multitasking Level Constraint. In addition to skill level training, we define this constraint to help trainees improve their multitasking performance. When multitasking strategy training is enabled, our approach gradually increases the difficulty of multitasking training based on the trainee's current performance. The difficulty of multitasking level is set as easy, medium, or hard, corresponding to working on two, three, or four tasks at the same time. Presumably, since this constraint will affect the number of tasks assigned in a training session, we include this constraint only when the trainee is familiar with the workflow of all tasks. However, in our user study, we include this constraint in the first training session due to the time limit of our user study. Moreover, our optimizer increases the multitasking difficulty level if the multitasking strategy training score (defined in Dect. 6.1) obtained from the trainee reaches the maximum score.

To ensure that each multitasking difficulty level is meaningful, our optimizer selects tasks of different properties from the task list for combination. As shown in Table 1, we associate each task with a property and a property value (e.g., task 7's property is "walk-centric" with property value $Q_{\text{t}} = 1,000$). In this way, some judgments are needed for the trainee before deciding to serve a table:

$$\sum_t Q_{\text{t}} C_{\text{t}} = \delta^{\text{goal}}, \tag{13}$$

where δ^{goal} is from a set of all possible combinations of task property values of a certain difficulty level. For example, if the multitasking difficulty is specified as medium, then the set of all possible combinations of tasks of three, each with different task properties, is $\{111, 1011, 1110, 1101\}$. Then we create a constraint for each δ^{goal} in the set. Our optimizer will generate a solution that satisfies any one of these multitasking level constraints.

4.4   Implementation

We implemented our VR training scenarios using $C\#$ and the Unity game engine. We use the Gurobi solver to solve the mixed integer programming problem[2]. It took less than one second to generate a solution that satisfied the set of constraints with optimized objective values. This solution contains a set of tasks, each with a specific difficulty level. This set of tasks will be used for the current training session. Based on the trainee's performance tracked in the training, our approach uses the MIP optimizer to generate the set of tasks for the next training session. For delivering the synthesized VR training experiences, we used the Oculus Quest2 virtual reality headset.

Table 3. Descriptive statistics for the simulation experiment. We generated 20 hypothetical trainees to compare the training performance of three different conditions. A performance record is calculated as the sum of the number of hints asked and the number of mistakes made in all tasks. Then we obtain trainees' improvement records by subtracting trainees' final performance records from their initial performance records. The left table shows the average improvement record with the standard deviations in parentheses for the MIP approach, the Performance-Only approach (Performance), and the Random approach. The right table shows the p-values of t-tests for each pair of approaches.

	MIP	Performance	Random		MIP vs. Performance	MIP vs. Random	Performance. vs. Random
Mean (SD)	44.1 (6.6)	49.6 (7.8)	34.9 (5.9)	p-value	<0.001	<0.001	<0.001

5   Experiments

5.1   Simulation Experiment

We conducted a simulation experiment to determine whether our approach can train people more efficiently compared to other approaches given the same trainee as input. In this experiment, we focus on the development of individual psychomotor skill components. We compared our approach (MIP) with a random assignment approach (Random) and a performance-only MIP approach (Performance). In the random assignment approach, the optimizer randomly assigned

---

[2] https://www.gurobi.com.

two to four tasks for each training session. In the Performance-Only MIP approach, we only consider the repeated mistake and familiarity of workflow objectives. In general, trainees who received the Performance-Only MIP training had the highest improvement for all tasks in all three conditions; trainees taking the MIP approach has better improvement than those taking the random assignment training. The difference in improvement across the three approaches was significant with $p < 0.05$ for all pairs (see Table 3). Please refer to the supplementary material for more details about this simulation experiment.

5.2   Virtual Reality Training Experiment

We conducted user study experiments to measure the effectiveness of the personalized virtual training sessions synthesized by our approach. We compared trainees' performance under two conditions, adaptive training condition (AT) and random assignment condition (Random). In the adaptive training condition, we first updated trainee performance for each task, then used our optimizer to generate tasks for the next training. In the random assignment condition, we randomly assigned two to four tasks to participants.

Participants. We recruited 26 participants to simulate working in a restaurant. The participants were university students aged 19 to 37, with about 65% of males and 35% females. They were randomly and equally assigned to one of the two conditions. The user study was IRB-approved. We first gave a warm-up session for the participants to get familiar with the virtual environment and the controls. Then we give a pre-evaluation for the participants to evaluate their background knowledge of serving in a restaurant.

The goal of the second study is not only to evaluate mastery of individual restaurant tasks but also trainees' ability to apply multitasking strategies. Therefore, we teach the participants how to combine tasks in an optimal way at the beginning of the training.

Procedure. The participants practiced the multitasking skill for five training iterations. During training, they could request hints if they were uncertain about the workflow of the task either by pressing the hint buttons or talking to the instructor directly. We recorded the number of hints they asked and the number of mistakes they made during the training and also their multitasking performance. There was a two-minute break after each training. During this break, we told the participants about the mistakes they had made and reminded them about the workflow and multitasking strategies for those unfamiliar tasks.

In the end, we gave the participants a post-evaluation that had the exact same task as the pre-evaluation. Akin to the training, we asked them to combine all the tasks using the skills they learned. We recorded their performance. Upon training completion, we asked the participants to fill out a questionnaire. This questionnaire includes their training experience in the simulated restaurant and their enjoyment ratings.

6   Evaluation

6.1   User Evaluation

To help us evaluate the overall performance of our participants, we calculate a final performance score, f_{final}, for the pre-evaluation session and the post-evaluation session, as follows:

$$f_{final} = f_{strategy} - 0.1 \sum_{t} (h_t + m_t), \tag{14}$$

where h_t and m_t are the number of hints and the number of mistakes made by a participant, which we refer to as skill performance record. $f_{strategy}$ evaluates a participant's ability of multitasking, ranging from 0 to 3.

The goal of training multitasking skills is to minimize the average waiting time of customers as well as to improve restaurant server working efficiency. Therefore, a well-trained restaurant server should take multiple tasks from tables and combine workflow of some tasks (e.g., placing an order and printing a receipt at the POS machine) in order to complete tasks in a single run. Since each task has a different property, the order of taking these tasks is critical. A server may want to serve a ready-to-order table first before a check-out table, so that customers who want to check out do not need to wait for the server to help the ready-to-order table first. Similarly, the order of completing tasks is important. Since customers from a check-out table want to leave right after they receive their credit card, it is important for the server to deliver the credit card to them when he was back from the kitchen (or the POS station). Thus, we define these three metrics to evaluate the ability of participants in handling multiple tasks.

Based on the current virtual restaurant and task settings, we can define an optimal order of tasks a participant take at the beginning as follows: talk-centric task → service-centric task → walk-centric task → time-sensitive task. Similarly, the optimal order of tasks the participant completed is defined as: talk-centric task → time-sensitive task → walk-centric task → service task. Lastly, the participant's optimal walking path is Table → POS → Kitchen → Table. If the participant fails to follow the optimal order (or walking path), she will receive zero on that metric.

Table 4 shows the descriptive statistics and t-test results. As we can see, the average final performance score of the AT approach group is higher than that of the random assignment group. To investigate whether there is a statistically significant difference between the improvement made by the participants in the two groups, we performed two sample t-tests on each component of final performance score ($\alpha = 0.05$). As the results, there was no significant difference in the final performance ($F(24) = 0.68$, $p > 0.05$) or any components of final performance scores before training (skill performance record: $F(24) = -1.98$, $p = 0.06$; $f_{strategy}$: $F(24) = 0$, $p = 1$). However, there was a significant difference in the final performance ($F(24) = 3.83$, $p < 0.001$) and so for each component after training (skill performance: $F(24) = -3.26$, $p < 0.01$; $f_{strategy}$: $F(24) = 2.95$, $p < 0.01$). We also find significant differences in the overall training improvement

Table 4. Users' overall performance records in completing the pre-evaluation and post-evaluation sessions, and the overall training improvement for both conditions are shown. Specifically, we show skill performance record (the average total number of hints asked and the number of mistakes made), multitasking strategy training score, and final performance score. For each score category, the first and second rows show the means with the standard deviations in parentheses. The third row shows the p-values of t-tests comparing the results of the two approaches. Note that a lower number in the skill performance record indicates better performance while a higher number in the other terms indicates greater participant performance. Compared to the random approach, the AT approach leads to a significantly higher performance score and training improvement.

		Pre-evaluation	Post-evaluation	Training Improvement
Skill Performance record	AT	10.08(7.58)	1.23(0.86)	8.85(6.64)
	Random	11.85(2.81)	3.77(7.03)	8.08(9.58)
	p-value	0.06	**0.01**	0.50
Multitasking strategy training score $f_{strategy}$	AT	0.31(0.40)	2.85(0.31)	2.54(0.60)
	Random	0.31(0.23)	2.08(0.58)	1.37(0.53)
	p-value	1	**0.01**	**0.05**
Final performance scores f_{final}	AT	−0.70 (0.55)	2.72 (0.31)	3.42 (0.67)
	Random	−0.88 (0.33)	1.67 (0.68)	2.55 (0.57)
	p-value	0.50	**0.001**	**0.001**

Table 5. The PACES ratings.

	I enjoy it	I like it	I feel good physically	It's a lot of fun	I am not at all frustrated
AT	6.5(0.8)	6.4(1.0)	6.5(0.8)	5.8(1.1)	5.8(1.3)
Random	6.1(1.3)	6.2(1.1)	5.8(1.3)	5.7(1.2)	5.2(1.7)

(i.e. increase in final performance score) between the random assignment and AT groups $(F(24) = 2.84, p<0.01)$. Specifically, a significant difference was observed in the multitasking strategy training scores $(F(24) = 2.61, p<0.05)$ but not in skill performance record. $(F(24) = 0.69, p = 0.50)$. Refer to the supplementary material for additional analysis.

This result suggests that participants in both condition groups can master their restaurant skills in five training sessions. However, since there were only four restaurant tasks to learn in 90 min, the training might not have been challenging enough for participants in both groups. Moreover, a significant difference was observed in the multitasking strategy training score, indicating that our approach can be highly effective in helping trainees improve not only restaurant service skills but also their ability to apply multitasking strategies.

6.2 Participant Feedback

Physical Activity Enjoyment Rating. We asked our participants to fill out a physical activity enjoyment scale questionnaire (PACES) in both pre and post-evaluation sessions. PACES is a quantitative measurement of the perceived

Table 6. Selected participants from the AT approach and the random assignment approach. The multitasking training score has the most influence on the final training score in performance. The participant from the random approach had a difficult time in learning and applying multitasking skills because the multitasking difficulty assigned to him was not adjusted based on his performance. In contrast, the participant from the AT approach received gradually-increasing multitasking difficulty in training and she received a higher multitasking training score.

Participant (Condition)	# Hints + Mistakes for Task 1,4,7		Training Session	Multi-Tasking Training Score	
	Pre-evaluation	Post-evaluation		Pre-evaluation	Post-evaluation
P11(AT)	2,2,4	0,1,0	(T2,T7), (T1,T4), (T1,T2,T7), (T2,T4,T7), (T1,T2,T4)	0	3
P7(Random)	2,4,6	1,3,0	(T1,T2,T3,T4), (T1,T2,T7), (T1,T2,T7), (T1,T2), (T2,T4)	0	3

enjoyment level for a physical activity validated by Kendzierski and DeCarlo [16]. We used the short version [9] which consists of five 7-point Likert scale questions. Table 5 shows the results. Overall, the PACES percentage scores of the AT approach are slightly higher than those of the random assignment group. This suggests that the AT approach can lead to a similar level of enjoyment while training people more effectively.

Although all participants had improved after training, not all participants believed that the training sessions assigned to them were carefully selected based on their weakness. Participants from the AT group were more confident in believing that the tasks assigned to them were carefully picked ($M = 3.8$, $SD = 1.1$), compared to those from the random assignment group ($M = 2.7$, $SD = 1.1$). A two-sample t-test shows that there is a significant difference in this rating ($f(24) = 2.8$, $p < 0.01$).

Example Participants' Performance. To investigate further, we select one participant (P7) from the random assignment group and one participant (P11) from the AT group for comparison. Table 6 shows their pre-evaluation and post-evaluation performances. As we can see, the participant (P7) from the random assignment group got familiarized with task 1 and 7 and had made fewer mistakes (or asked fewer hints). However, he was not familiar with task 4 and performed poorly in multitasking. This is likely because tasks assigned by the random assignment approach did not target his weakness for training. Also, random multitask level difficulties were given to the participant. This participant started with a hard level of multitasking difficulty and practiced with an easy level of multitasking difficulty towards the end. This posed extra challenges for this participant to learn and master multitasking. He received 1 out of 3 for the multitasking training score.

In contrast, the AT approach would target all of the participants' weaknesss. The participant (P11) from the AT group was not good at doing task 7 at the beginning and repeatedly made mistakes for task 7. As a result, she was assigned by our adaptive approach to do task 7 three times in the five training iterations. On the other hand, our approach gradually increased the multitasking training difficulty after she showed proficiency at the current multitasking difficulty level. She got 3 out of 3 for the multitasking training score.

7   Discussion, Limitations and Future Work

Our work sheds light upon the novel research direction of adaptive game-based training via virtual reality. Using our approach, trainees can develop psychomotor skills in an efficient way. Driven by a trainee's performance, our approach can generate a suitable task list such that it targets the trainee's weaknesses while keeping the trainee engaged in game-based training. Moreover, other workplaces that require extensive hands-on training prior to work can benefit from game-based training. For instance, simulated medical skill training could be used in conjunction with our approach to provide a personalized training approach that meets individual needs and learning preferences [31, 37]. We demonstrate the hypothetical outcome of the Performance-Only approach if users want to have a results-oriented learning experience. Also, users can activate focus mode using our approach such that only specific types of tasks will be displayed for training.

Additionally, many workplace training programs focus on developing employees' social skills, such as effective communication, to help them establish and maintain positive social relationships with others. In this paper, we only focus on training verbal communication by identifying the intentions of each sentence. Other nonverbal aspects such as gestures, eye contact, volume, and so forth are also vital in delivering messages. Our approach can incorporate with other communication skill training models [39] to evaluate users' social skill development and adaptively generate training sessions.

Acknowledgements. The work is supported in part by NSF 1942531 and NSF 2128867. The user study was funded by NSF grants with the OSU IRB approval number 1690834-1. NIST's role was limited to activities not involved with the human subjects research. Any opinions, findings, and conclusions or recommendations expressed in this material are those of the author(s) and do not necessarily reflect the views of the National Institute of Standards and Technology. Certain commercial products are identified in this paper in order to specify the experimental procedure adequately. Such identification is not intended to imply recommendation or endorsement by the National Institute of Standards and Technology, nor is it intended to imply that the products identified are necessarily the best available for the purpose.

References

1. Aati, K., Chang, D., Edara, P., Sun, C.: Immersive work zone inspection training using virtual reality. Transp. Res. Rec. **2674**(12), 224–232 (2020)
2. Ashtari, N., Bunt, A., McGrenere, J., Nebeling, M., Chilana, P.K.: Creating augmented and virtual reality applications: current practices, challenges, and opportunities. In: Proceedings of the 2020 CHI Conference on Human Factors in Computing Systems, pp. 1–13 (2020)

3. Carlson, P., Peters, A., Gilbert, S.B., Vance, J.M., Luse, A.: Virtual training: learning transfer of assembly tasks. IEEE Trans. Visual Comput. Graphics **21**(6), 770–782 (2015)
4. Collins, J.W., O'Brien, N.P.: The Greenwood dictionary of education. ABC-CLIO (2003)
5. Conges, A., Evain, A., Benaben, F., Chabiron, O., Rebiere, S.: Crisis management exercises in virtual reality. In: 2020 IEEE Conference on Virtual Reality and 3D User Interfaces Abstracts and Workshops (VRW), pp. 87–92. IEEE (2020)
6. Doneda, A.L., de Oliveira, J.C.: Helicopter visual signaling simulation: integrating VR and ml into a low-cost solution to optimize brazilian navy training. In: 2020 22nd Symposium on Virtual and Augmented Reality (SVR), pp. 434–442. IEEE (2020)
7. Fitts, P.M.: Human performance (1967)
8. Franzwa, C., Tang, Y., Johnson, A.: Serious game design: motivating students through a balance of fun and learning. In: 2013 5th International conference on games and virtual worlds for serious applications (VS-GAMES), pp. 1–7. IEEE (2013)
9. Graves, L.E., Ridgers, N.D., Williams, K., Stratton, G., Atkinson, G.T.: The physiological cost and enjoyment of wii fit in adolescents, young adults, and older adults. J. Phys. Activity Health **7**(3), 393–401 (2010)
10. Heintz, S., Law, E.L.C.: Digital educational games: methodologies for evaluating the impact of game type. ACM Trans. Comput.-Hum. Int. (TOCHI) **25**(2), 1–47 (2018)
11. Huang, G., et al.: Adaptutar: an adaptive tutoring system for machine tasks in augmented reality. In: Proceedings of the 2021 CHI Conference on Human Factors in Computing Systems, pp. 1–15 (2021)
12. Ipsita, A., et al.: Towards modeling of virtual reality welding simulators to promote accessible and scalable training. In: CHI Conference on Human Factors in Computing Systems, pp. 1–21 (2022)
13. Johnsen, K., Raij, A., Stevens, A., Lind, D.S., Lok, B.: The validity of a virtual human experience for interpersonal skills education. In: Proceedings of the SIGCHI Conference on Human Factors in Computing Systems, pp. 1049–1058 (2007)
14. Kaplan, A.: Higher Education at the Crossroads of Disruption: The University of the 21st Century. Emerald Group Publishing, Bingley (2021)
15. Karahan, M., Kerkhoffs, G.M., Randelli, P., Tuijthof, G.J.: Effective Training of Arthroscopic Skills. Springer, Heidelberg (2015). https://doi.org/10.1007/978-3-662-44943-1
16. Kendzierski, D., DeCarlo, K.J.: Physical activity enjoyment scale: two validation studies. J. Sport Exerc. Psychol. **13**(1) (1991)
17. Lang, Y., Liang, W., Xu, F., Zhao, Y., Yu, L.F.: Synthesizing personalized training programs for improving driving habits via virtual reality. In: IEEE Virtual Reality (2018)
18. Lee, J., Kim, H., Kim, K.H., Jung, D., Jowsey, T., Webster, C.S.: Effective virtual patient simulators for medical communication training: a systematic review. Med. Educ. **54**(9), 786–795 (2020)
19. Li, W., Huang, H., Solomon, T., Esmaeili, B., Yu, L.F.: Synthesizing personalized construction safety training scenarios for VR training. IEEE Trans. Visual Comput. Graph. **28**(5), 1993–2002 (2022)
20. Li, W., Talavera, J., Samayoa, A.G., Lien, J.M., Yu, L.F.: Automatic synthesis of virtual wheelchair training scenarios. In: 2020 IEEE Conference on Virtual Reality and 3D User Interfaces (VR), pp. 539–547. IEEE (2020)

21. Lindlbauer, D., Feit, A.M., Hilliges, O.: Context-aware online adaptation of mixed reality interfaces. In: Proceedings of the 32nd Annual ACM Symposium on User Interface Software and Technology, pp. 147–160 (2019)
22. Michael, J.: Where's the evidence that active learning works? Adv. Physiol. Educ. (2006)
23. Mutual Mobile: Walmart (2022). https://mutualmobile.com/work/walmart
24. Nishiyama, Y., Sezaki, K.: Experience sampling tool for repetitive skills training in sports using voice user interface. In: Adjunct Proceedings of the 2021 ACM International Joint Conference on Pervasive and Ubiquitous Computing and Proceedings of the 2021 ACM International Symposium on Wearable Computers, pp. 54–55 (2021)
25. Peng, H., Ma, S., Spector, J.M.: Personalized adaptive learning: an emerging pedagogical approach enabled by a smart learning environment. Smart Learn. Environ. **6**(1), 1–14 (2019)
26. Romiszowski, A.: The development of physical skills: instruction in the psychomotor domain. Inst.-Des. Theories Models New Paradigm Inst. Theory **2**, 457–481 (1999)
27. Schott, D., et al.: A VR/AR environment for multi-user liver anatomy education. In: 2021 IEEE Virtual Reality and 3D User Interfaces (VR), pp. 296–305 (2021). https://doi.org/10.1109/VR50410.2021.00052
28. Shao, Q., et al.: Teaching American sign language in mixed reality. Proc. ACM Interac. Mobile Wearable Ubiq. Technol. **4**(4), 1–27 (2020)
29. Shen, S., et al.: Effects of level of immersion on virtual training transfer of bimanual assembly tasks. Front. Virtual Real. **2**, 58 (2021)
30. STRIVR: Protecting verizon's frontline workforce: Strivr testimonial (2021). https://www.strivr.com/resources/webinars/verizon-customer-experience/
31. Tavassoli, F., Howell, D.M., Black, E.W., Lok, B., Gilbert, J.E.: Jayla (junior agent to typify levels of autism): a virtual training platform to teach severity levels of autism. Front. Virtual Real. **2**, 96 (2021)
32. Van Merriënboer, J.J., Clark, R.E., De Croock, M.: Blueprints for complex learning: the 4c/id-model. Educ. Tech. Research Dev. **50**(2), 39–61 (2002)
33. Vanbecelaere, S., Van den Berghe, K., Cornillie, F., Sasanguie, D., Reynvoet, B., Depaepe, F.: The effectiveness of adaptive versus non-adaptive learning with digital educational games. J. Comput. Assist. Learn. **36**(4), 502–513 (2020)
34. VR, I.: Vr for workplace training (2021). https://immersionvr.co.uk/about-360vr/vr-for-workplace-training/
35. Wickens, C.D., Hutchins, S., Carolan, T., Cumming, J.: Effectiveness of part-task training and increasing-difficulty training strategies: a meta-analysis approach. Hum. Fact. **55**(2), 461–470 (2013)
36. Xie, B., et al.: A review on virtual reality skill training applications. Front. Virt. Real. **2**, 1–19 (2021)
37. Yao, H., de Siqueira, A.G., Foster, A., Galynker, I., Lok, B.: Toward automated evaluation of empathetic responses in virtual human interaction systems for mental health scenarios. In: Proceedings of the 20th ACM International Conference on Intelligent Virtual Agents, pp. 1–8 (2020)
38. Yuksel, B.F., et al.: Learn piano with bach: an adaptive learning interface that adjusts task difficulty based on brain state. In: Proceedings of the 2016 Chi Conference on Human Factors in Computing Systems, pp. 5372–5384 (2016)
39. Zhao, R., Li, V., Barbosa, H., Ghoshal, G., Hoque, M.E.: Semi-automated 8 collaborative online training module for improving communication skills. Proc. ACM Interact. Mobile Wearable Ubiq. Technol. **1**(2), 1–20 (2017)

Author Index